Technical and Business Communication

Technical and Business Communication

Bibliographic Essays
for Teachers and Corporate Trainers

Edited by
Charles H. Sides
Northeastern University

Copublished by
National Council of Teachers of English
1111 Kenyon Road, Urbana, Illinois 61801

Society for Technical Communication
815 15th Street, NW, Washington, DC 20005
(202) 737-0035

NCTE Editorial Board: Donald R. Gallo, Thomas Newkirk, Raymond Rodrigues, Dorothy Strickland, Brooke Workman; L. Jane Christensen, *ex officio;* John Lansingh Bennett, *ex officio*

Book Design: Interior, Tom Kovacs for TGK Design; cover, Michael J. Getz

Project Editor: Tim Bryant

Copyediting: Editorial Experts

NCTE Stock Number 53038-3020

© 1989 by the National Council of Teachers of English. All rights reserved. Printed in the United States of America.

It is the policy of NCTE in its journals and other publications to provide a forum for the open discussion of ideas concerning the content and the teaching of English and the language arts. Publicity accorded to any particular point of view does not imply endorsement by the Executive Committee, the Board of Directors, or the membership at large, except in announcements of policy, where such endorsement is clearly specified.

Library of Congress Cataloging-in-Publication Data
Technical and business communication : bibliographic essays for
   teachers and corporate trainers / edited by Charles H. Sides.
      p.   cm.
   Bibliography: p.
   ISBN 0-8141-5303-8 (National Council of Teachers of English). —
ISBN 0-914548-59-X (Society for Technical Communication)
   1. Communication of technical information.   2. Business
communication.   I. Sides, Charles H., 1952-
T10.5.T4   1989
808'.0666—dc20   89-34052
                                                                    CIP

Contents

Acknowledgments — vii

Introduction — 1

I Issues and Abilities in Technical Communication — 3

1. Technical Communication and Rhetoric — 5
   Roger E. Masse and Martha Delamater Benz
2. Reading and Technical Writing — 39
   Nina D. Ziv
3. Ethics and Technical Communication — 53
   Stephen Doheny-Farina
4. Technical Editing — 75
   Avon Jack Murphy
5. Trends in Visual Representation — 95
   Ben F. Barton and Marthalee S. Barton
6. Interpersonal Communication for the Technical Communicator — 137
   David M. Craig and Thomas M. Steinfatt
7. Communication Consulting — 169
   Raymond N. MacKenzie
8. Style and Technical Writing — 181
   James C. Addison, Jr.
9. Professional Presentations — 201
   James R. Weber

II Genres in Technical Communication — 221

10. Annual Reports, Brochures, and Newsletters — 223
    John W. Ferstel

11. Instructions, Procedures, and Style Manuals — 241
    Sherry G. Southard

12. Proposals: The Process and the Document — 265
    Alice E. Moorhead

13. Technical Advertising and Sales — 287
    Mary M. Lay

14. Letters and Memorandums — 303
    Nancy (Fitzgerald) Brown

15. Reports, Papers, and News Releases — 319
    Brenda Johns

16. Computer Documentation — 329
    Charles H. Sides

17. Medical Science and Technology — 341
    Barbara Gastel

Editor — 355

Contributors — 357

Acknowledgments

Several people and organizations are responsible for the success of bringing this book to press. Certainly the first are the contributors who worked on these essays for years, revising and updating as the publication process wound to its slow conclusion. Second are the National Council of Teachers of English and the Society for Technical Communication. Both organizations have provided moral support and the opportunity to have manuscripts read by knowledgeable reviewers who shared numerous helpful suggestions as to how this collection could be improved. Finally is my good friend and consulting colleague Professor David Carson of Rensselaer Polytechnic Institute. He saw the potential value of this collection from the very beginning in the fall of 1981 when I presented it to NCTE's Committee on Technical and Scientific Writing. He also advised me along the way as to how to make the collection succeed, and he fought for the collection's publication. The success of this book is in a large way due to his efforts.

Introduction

One of the hallmarks of a vibrant academic field is that it draws information and expertise from a variety of related fields. Technical communication is a perfect example. Fertile from the research from such endeavors as communication theory, reading theory, psycholinguistics, and human factors theory, technical communication provides challenges and rewards for instructors and researchers. However, the accompanying complexity of a field that draws from numerous related fields can pose problems as well.

This collection of essays addresses the challenges of technical communication. It provides detailed information for instructors and researchers who wish to further their knowledge of particular areas within technical communication. The essays in this collection also address the problems of a large, complex, and growing academic endeavor. Readers will find information to lead them to the solutions of their own particular teaching problems, from how one incorporates human factors research into a discussion about user manual design to reflective listening techniques and other interpersonal communication devices at work in small-group environments to reading models and reading theory as they apply to the design of technical reports.

Mark Twain once said that when one has a big idea, one writes a big sentence. This collection is large; it treats a large field—technical communication. No bibliographic collection is ever complete, and this one does not intend to be. Rather, it is an attempt to provide teachers of technical and business communication with source material to improve their craft. Some readers will find omissions of favorites; others will have difficulty relating particular essays to the courses they teach. That is the risk writers of bibliographic essays take. Nonetheless, all readers of this collection should find something worthwhile herein.

I Issues and Abilities in Technical Communication

1 Technical Communication and Rhetoric

Roger E. Masse
U. S. Sprint
Dallas, Texas

Martha Delamater Benz
NASA White Sands Test Facility
Las Cruces, New Mexico

Over the past decade and a half, technical communicators, teachers, and researchers have investigated the role of rhetoric in technical communication. A few of these experts in the field of technical communication believe that an emphasis on rhetoric in technical writing will ruin the field. Many others believe that rhetoric addresses major concerns of technical communication, develops a theoretical basis for technical communication, and provides practical approaches for technical communication. Because technical writing is mainly concerned with informing, some writers think that the persuasive element of rhetoric would harm the objective nature of such writing. Many others think that technical communicators and teachers need to acknowledge the persuasive nature of technical writing.

The investigation of the role of rhetoric in technical communication has appeared in professional articles, books, and conference proceedings. This bibliographical essay surveys these publications. It discusses ninety-six articles that address the role of rhetoric in technical communication and presents a three-section survey of the principal articles that deal with this role. The first section is on research related to teaching technical communication, the second section is on research related to writing technical communication, and the third section is on research related to editing technical communication.

The separation of the articles into these three categories allows an examination of the role that rhetoric plays in technical communication. Although some of the articles deal with all three categories, each article generally concentrates on one audience as it addresses teachers, writers, or editors. Thus, the articles are classified according to their main emphasis and their main audience. By far, the largest category of articles is the group on teaching technical communication.

Research on Teaching

Should simulated forms or rhetorical theory be the basis for preparing technical writers for future jobs? The question encapsulates the argument posed in the articles discussed in this section.

Simulated Forms as a Basis for Teaching Technical Communication

An article by Elizabeth Tebeaux (1980), in reaction to other articles discussed in this survey, and the accompanying responses to Tebeaux's article by Carolyn R. Miller (1980b) and Elizabeth Harris (1980) best clarify the central issue concerning the role of rhetoric in teaching technical communication. In "Let's Not Ruin Technical Writing, Too," Tebeaux (1980) charges that teaching rhetorical theory to technical writing students will ruin technical writing. She attacks Miller's suggestion that technical writing be taught against an ethical background to familiarize students with the community in which they will participate. Tebeaux writes that technical writing students should be taught pragmatically by indoctrinating them with experience in filling out forms that are similar to the writing that they will encounter in future jobs. She explains that to teach theory and ethics to technical writing students would be to ignore practical experience for the sake of theory.

In a response published with Tebeaux's article, Miller (1980b) writes that her teaching methods, which employ rhetorical theory, do not ignore pragmatic problems, but do teach ways to approach these problems and to solve them. Miller believes that the basic difference between her own teaching methods and those of Tebeaux is that rhetorical theory prepares technical writing students to become professionals equipped with critical thinking ability and treats their writing as an intellectual discipline, whereas Tebeaux's methods prepare students to be technicians and treat their writing as basic skills.

Tebeaux (1980) also attacks the methods advocated by Harris (1979). Harris, like Miller, advocates teaching technical communication by using rhetorical theory, in particular by using Kinneavy's classification modes discussed in *Theory of Discourse*. Tebeaux believes that people writing in the real world do not classify their writing and thus Harris is not addressing real concerns. In a response published with Tebeaux's article, Harris (1980) writes that by learning rhetorical theory, students can base practical aspects on the theoretical and, therefore, have the benefit of both theory and practice rather than practice only.

Two other authors, though, agree that teaching technical writing should not be based on rhetorical theory. In "It's a Craft Course: Indoctrinate, Don't Educate," John H. Mitchell (1976) reasons that because humanists are not in demand in today's job market, humanistic training will not prepare writers to perform well in that market. He advocates teaching technical writing as a skill. In "The Basic Technical Writing Course: Skills *and* Ethics?" William E. Evans (1981) also states that technical writing courses should be based on skills and not humanistic theory. He argues that ethics can and should be taught in separate courses.

In addition to Miller and Harris, many authors believe that rhetorical theory, not the use of simulated forms, is a good basis for teaching technical writing skills. Their articles explain that the link between technical writing and rhetoric lies in the fact that technical writing is persuasive and that rhetorical training teaches technical writing students to learn effective means of persuasion. Their argument illustrates why rhetorical theory prepares good technical writers and explains how invention techniques can help students in the process of technical writing. The authors also call for future research into the relationship of rhetorical theory to technical writing.

Rhetorical Theory as a Basis for Teaching Technical Writing

Generally, the authors discussed in this section agree that a technical writing curriculum based on rhetorical theory educates professionals to communicate, whereas the alternative forms-based curriculum merely trains nonprofessionals to write. The difference between having a profession, which is what students who have a rhetorically based education possess, and having a vocation, which is what students who have training filling out simulated forms possess, defines the advantages of what the authors here write about rhetorically based curriculum for technical writing classes.

Two of S. Michael Halloran's (1978a, 1978b) essays emphasize this point. In "Eloquence in a Technological Society," Halloran (1978a) decries the concept that people can be trained to speak and to write. He stresses the concept that people must be educated in these disciplines. Additionally, in "Technical Writing and the Rhetoric of Science," Halloran (1978b, p. 82) argues,

> To know anything at all is to entertain an arrangement of symbols, which is to command a system of symbols that can be arranged

and rearranged, which is to participate in the community that defines and is defined by that symbol system, or language.... Science, then necessarily involves rhetoric.

Only through a rhetorically based education will writers be able to command the system of symbols adequately. Halloran (1978b, p. 87) further states that "the study of technical writing could become a central element of liberal education for a technological society," strengthening the relationship between technical writing and liberal arts.

The education of future technical writers is also discussed by Merrill D. Whitburn (1976) in "Personality in Scientific and Technical Writing." Whitburn (1976, p. 305) writes,

> The problem of this inflexibility of using forms to teach technical writing is that it seems to be moving the field from a concern with the principles of rhetoric to a concern for the forms of writing. One is more concerned with drawing up a parts list than learning the principles of audience adaptation. Such an approach will ill prepare students for their concerns. For instance, the forms a student learns in school are not likely to be the exact forms used on a job.

This inflexibility in approach is thus used to explain the main inadequacy of a simulated forms-based curriculum.

Harris (1982) adds to this consensus on the inadequacy of forms-based curriculum in "In Defense of the Liberal-Arts Approach to Technical Writing." Harris writes that technical writing texts should present the relationship among meaning, structure, and function, as they apply to technical writing rather than simply teach students mindlessly to fill out forms. In "Applications of Kinneavy's *Theory of Discourse* to Technical Writing," Harris (1979) writes that Kinneavy's theories help provide more intellectual depth than other courses that teach technical writing by simulated forms.

Also referring to Kinneavy and others, Steven Lynn (1980) advocates a rhetorically based curriculum over a forms-based curriculum in "Kinneavy, Mathes, Mumford, and Lynn: Teaching the Classificatory Mode in Technical Writing." In this article, Lynn outlines his methods for teaching classificatory modes, contextual editing, and vertical thinking—all rhetorically based methods.

Patricia Y. Murray (1981) adds to the idea that a rhetorically based curriculum is advantageous to technical writing students. In "Rhetoric and the Business Administrator: Writing in the Professions," Murray (1981, p. 579) writes,

> Business Communications, Writing for the World of Work, Technical Writing, and similarly titled courses introduce students with

special interests to communication requirements in business, industry, and technology. But because some of these courses place emphasis on special forms, such as letters and reports, they often do little to introduce students to practical, career-oriented writing situations.

Murray goes on to describe the rhetorically based curriculum she uses in her class "Writing in the Professions."

Bruce T. Petersen (1984) echoes the idea of a broad curriculum in his article "Conceptual Patterns in Industrial and Academic Discourse." He says, "We should teach students in every discipline the whole universe of discourse" (Petersen 1984, p. 105) for students "to experience the whole range of rhetorical practice and to engage actively in the difficult conceptual tasks of generalizing and speculating from experimental data or reading" (Petersen 1984, p. 96). Petersen (1984, p. 95) bases his recommendations on a study that showed that "most good technical writing operates far beyond the mere reporting of information." He concludes that technical writers do more than simply report data; they also generalize, synthesize, and speculate. Thus, students need to be exposed to more than recorded data on forms; they need to be exposed to a variety of audiences, writing purposes, and conceptual levels.

In addition, in "The Essay and the Report: Expository Poles in Technical Writing," M. Jimmie Killingsworth (1985) provides a nice compromise between a total rhetorical approach and a total forms approach. He uses an essay and the report as two poles of expository writing, with rhetoric playing a key role in the essay for presenting ideas persuasively and with facts playing a key role in the report. He sees, however, that the essay needs facts to persuade and that the report needs rhetoric to select and to order facts to "create a compelling and persuasive structure for the author's ideas" (Killingsworth 1985, p. 228). He feels that authors like Miller (1979), in "A Humanistic Rationale for Technical Writing," and S. Michael Halloran (1978b), in "Technical Writing and the Rhetoric of Science," have "swung from one pole to the other, from naive positivism to rhetorical relativity" in suggesting "that courses in technical writing should be thoroughly humanistic in method and content" (Killingsworth 1985, p. 231). Killingsworth (1985, p. 231) believes that technical writing courses should be

> broad enough to encompass both poles as they are concretely represented in the report and the essay.... Only a report in its most simplistic form presents facts without ideas, and how many scientific or even engineering reports present facts without con-

clusions, recommendations, proposals, theory—without ideas that require rhetorical presentation?

He asks that academic biases not confuse students and that balances be sought between the forms that dominate technical fields and the rhetoric that is needed to present and organize ideas and data.

Aside from the authors who discuss the argument of simulated forms versus rhetorical theory as a basis for teaching technical communication, many authors examine aspects of rhetoric that apply well to teaching technical communication. The authors see persuasion as a strong link between rhetoric and technical communication, they provide various reasons and approaches for using rhetoric in technical communication, and they describe invention as the most useful rhetorical area for teaching technical communication.

Persuasion as a Link between Rhetoric and Technical Communication

Six essays show the strong link that persuasion provides between rhetoric and technical communication—a link that students need to be aware of. In "A Humanistic Rationale for Technical Writing," Miller (1979) discusses the idea that scientific writing should be clear, logical, and unemotional writing about reality, with the facts alone doing the persuading. Because rhetoric can appeal to emotions, it should not be used in scientific writing. Miller's (1979, p. 616) disagreement with thinking and its effect on teaching is expressed when she says,

> Science . . . is not concerned directly with material things, but with these human constructions, with symbols and arguments. Scientific verification relies on tacit conceptual theories, which may be said to "argue for" a way of seeing the world. Scientific verification requires the persuasion of an audience that what has been "observed" is replicable and relevant. Science is, through and through, a rhetorical endeavor.

As Miller (1979, p. 616) suggests, students must be taught that good technical writing is not "the revelation of absolute reality but a persuasive version of experience," one that involves a rhetorical endeavor.

Because technical writers must select the facts they present and organize them persuasively, James A. Grimshaw, Jr., and William E. McCarren (1981) agree with Miller's arguments. In "Hidden Persuasions in Technical Writing," they assert that reports usually have facts as a basis but that the report writer concentrates on personalizing an audience to argue with him or her. Because of this reality, Grimshaw and McCarren (1981, p. 19) write that, "we are arguing that all rhetorical sources of argument—*ethos* and *pathos* as well as *logos*—are essential to technical writing." To use all the rhetorical sources of argument, as the authors suggest, educators must teach rhetorical theory to technical writers. Grimshaw and McCarren (1981, p. 21) state,

> In the ETHICAL mode, the writers gain *good will* on the title page by identifying themselves by title . . . and by company. . . . They establish *good sense,* i.e. introduction through their statements of purpose, problem, and scope. And they reveal good moral character, i.e. sincerity and trustworthiness, through a style which is clear, straightforward, and logical. With their conclusions and recommendations they influence decision-makers *to act* the desired result of the PATHIC mode—not from anger, but from rational reasons.

The authors cite examples of persuasion in technical writing and in industry that support the links between rhetoric and technical writing.

In "Changing the Technical Writing Paradigm," McCarren (1985, p. 27) still argues that technical writing is persuasive and that students not be taught that "technical writing is primarily, and at times exclusively, objective referential discourse." As in the essay he coauthored with Grimshaw in 1981, McCarren (1985, p. 28) uses examples from industry to show the persuasive nature of technical writing, stating that

> in the business world, one works at Texas Instruments, or IBM, or EXXON; one writes about T.I., or IBM, or EXXON products—not about General Dynamics, or Wang, or Texaco. Consequently, one is prejudiced to begin with and is apt to select technical details that are most applicable to whatever product one is writing about. Rarely, very rarely, will the communication be purely objective.

McCarren says that teachers of technical writing need to be aware of shifts in the technical writing paradigm.

In "Ethos, Technical Writing, and the Liberal Arts," Arthur E. Walzer (1981) builds on the idea that the author's ethos is a deciding element that influences persuasion in technical writing. He cites Aristotle's idea that ethos is the most potent means of persuasion. When people write technical information that represents an industry, one purpose is to persuade the audience and one method is through the apparent trustworthiness of the author. Walzer says that correct rhetorical choices must be made before the author's trustworthiness can be established; thus, students need rhetorical training.

Another essay echoes this idea. Describing how studying ethos promotes increased authorial voice in technical writing, Ben F. Barton and Marthalee S. Barton (1981a) strongly advocate a rhetorical basis for technical writing pedagogy in "Ethos, Persona, and Role Confusion in Engineering: Toward a Pedagogy for Technical Discourse." The Bartons discuss how a formalist ideal disallows the authorial voice. They explain that the role of scientists and technical writers is changing because presently they need not only to formulate and to solve problems in a broad social context, but also to follow through by selling their solutions. The Bartons argue that students must be trained to use an authorial voice to sell their solutions.

In "Ethos in Technical Discourse," Dorothy Guinn (1983) also connects ethos to persuasion in technical communication. Guinn argues that ethos emerges in technical writing through the stylistic choices that a writer makes and that a positive ethos must emerge if the writer is to persuade. Guinn (1983, p. 37) argues that

> students need to know not only how their ethos emerges in what they write, but how to convey a positive ethos that will influence readers to accept their investigations and arguments.

These connections between rhetoric and technical communication suggest that exposure to rhetorical theory provides good preparation for technical writers. That exposure is emphasized in the articles in the next two sections.

Rhetorical Theory as Good Preparation for Technical Writers

Many authors argue that rhetorical theory prepares students well who intend to become technical writers. They offer various reasons for and approaches to the usefulness of rhetorical theory.

Even in 1972, Thomas M. Sawyer stressed that rhetorical preparation can help scientists and technicians to communicate accurately and precisely with one another. In "Rhetoric in an Age of Science and Technology," Sawyer (1972) cites statistics showing the growing number of students graduating in scientific and technological fields, and he forecasts the increasing demand for rhetorical training to help these graduates deal effectively with the information explosion.

In "Rhetoric—Warp and Woof of All Exposition," Ruth M. Walsh (1981) also asserts that rhetorical training is essential for technical writing students. Walsh (1981, p. 8) states,

> The discontinuation of rhetorical analysis seemed especially unfortunate because understanding rhetoric is germane to reading comprehension and writing ability. If students can learn to identify rhetorical techniques along with recognizing deductive or inductive structures, they have a bid up on understanding content. So

essential is a knowledge of the relationship of rhetoric to expository writing, that upper level business communication students are told that it is impossible to put together a piece of writing—including letters, memorandums, and reports—without using one, or a combination of rhetorical techniques.

Walsh supports this assertion by showing how certain teaching techniques that are based on rhetorical theory help students to write better.

In "A Rhetorician Looks at Technical Communication," Edward P. J. Corbett (1981) agrees and recommends that a rhetorical system be found that is congenial with the empirical spirit of modern technology. He bases his teaching of technical writing on rhetorical theory and strongly advocates his methods for preparing good writing.

In "Technical Communication: Meeting the Needs of Adult Writers," Steven Z. Rothmel (1981) reacts to an advertisement in the *Wall Street Journal* that offered a two-day seminar in technical writing and promised students improved writing abilities. Rothmel (1981, p. 470) writes, "Rhetorical training that oversimplifies the writing process for these adults does them a disservice." Rothmel (1981, p. 470) also states that students must use imagination rather than blind compliance to learn to communicate effectively and writes,

> Professionals in business and technology must know how to do more than merely use language correctly: they must learn to use it effectively. Correspondence, proposals, and reports are more than error-free forms of self-expression. Each must be designed for a specific purpose and audience.

To use language effectively for specific purposes and audiences, students require, Rothmel argues, rhetorical training to enable them to handle diverse writing situations.

In "Classical Rhetoric and Technical Writing," Andrea A. Lunsford (1976) builds on the use of rhetorical training to meet technical writing situations. She believes that a background in rhetoric will help students to see argumentative elements in what they thought were completely objective facts. According to Lunsford, this kind of training leads students to better writing and better oral techniques. Lunsford is grateful to her rhetorical training because it has helped her to become a better teacher of technical writing.

Kathryn L. Fialkowski (1986) feels that rhetorical training helped her to become a better technical writer. In her "Academia and Business: Preserving the Code of Honor," Fialkowski (1986, p. 248) says, "An education in technical writing has given me strong communication skills with a foundation in the rhetorical skills of invention, arrangement, and style." She finds that writers without that rhetorical background seem poorly qualified to communicate ideas. Fialkowski asserts that writers may have a scientific or technical background, but they also need a rhetorical one.

Teaching analytical skills to students is also the basis of A. Douglas Emerson's (1980) essay, "Apples Versus Oranges and Rhetorical Principles: Companies Pay the Bill." He discusses the needs of industry, teachers, and students and concludes that rhetorical training promotes good analytical skills and, therefore, makes students better functional writers.

Harris (1983) looks at the semantics, syntactics, and pragmatics of what she calls "how to" discourse in her essay, "A Theoretical Perspective on 'How to' Discourse." Harris (1983, p. 154) writes that with theoretical knowledge, writers and teachers will "take more rational and critical approaches to reading and writing 'how to' discourses and to constructing courses and curricula to teach them."

Mary G. La Roche, a teacher, shows that she has taken such an approach. In "Technical Writing as an Alternative Rhetoric for Composition Courses," La Roche (1981) explains her teaching methods for ninth and tenth grade students. Her curriculum assigns students to choose one technically based topic and to complete increasingly difficult written and oral assignments on that topic. The students present their final work to professionals. La Roche (1981, p. 73) states that her students improved in all areas of writing, including grammar, for the following reason:

> [T]echnical writing is essentially a rhetoric, a form for writing, rather than material or subject matter for writing.... Technical writing stresses efficient transmission of information rather than imaginative recreation of experience. The form can be applied to many kinds of subject matter.

Julia C. Dietrich (1979), who outlines her college course in "The Common Ground of Freshman Rhetoric and Technical Writing," agrees with La Roche. Dietrich (1979, p. 93) designed a course that she describes as a "technically oriented introductory rhetoric course." She stresses this description because she believes that freshmen are not far enough into their technical studies for her class to be labeled a technical writing class. She does believe, however, that her course prepares students to write technical data clearly, to organize that data effectively, and to provide reasoned conclusions.

Daniel R. Jones sees even more benefits of rhetoric for advanced students. In "The Challenge of Consensus Theory in Modern Rhetoric for Teaching Technical Writing," Jones (1986, p. 93) explains his belief that "rhetorical theory is central to teaching technical writing." In his course "Technical Vocabulary," Jones (1986, p. 97) uses "rhetorical theory to argue for more creativity in technical writing." Jones (1986, pp. 97–98) explains that creativity in technical writing means

> experimenting with and challenging conventions of technical writing to communicate more effectively, and often more informally, with the reader. Creativity includes all of those elements which are not readily associated with technical writing: literary devices such as metaphors, similes, point of view (our decision to be personal or impersonal in our writing), irony; persona or ethos (whether or not we convey a positive or negative image of ourselves in our writing); clever use of denotation and connotation of words; and humor. In short, creativity is employing all the fine points of style which intensify the power of the technical prose and which emphasize the presence of the writer.

In another course, "Survey of Scientific and Technical Literature," Jones uses consensus theory that science is rhetoric (or argument) and makes use of persuasive strategies. Jones describes this survey course at greater length in another essay, "A Rhetorical Approach for Teaching the Literature of Scientific and Technical Writing" (1985). In addition to dealing with persuasion in science in this second essay, Jones discusses rhetorical approaches to style analysis and the benefits of such approaches to students.

Rhetorical theory also prepares writers to examine audience and structure. David L. Carson (1979) compares modern technical writing to Aristotelian rhetoric in "Audience in Technical Writing: The Need for Greater Realism in Identifying the Fictive Reader." He writes that modern technical writing and Aristotelian rhetoric are alike because both inform and provide a basis for action and thus make audience analysis important. He states that audience analysis is more complex today than it was in the days of classical rhetoric because writers rarely meet their audiences and rarely receive feedback from them. He admonishes technical writing teachers to be more aware of the differences while preparing students to identify the real audience.

A teaching technique to provide such experiences is described by Michael Orth and Carl R. V. Brown (1984) in "Computer Generated Rhetorical Simulations for Business and Report Writing Courses." They show how computer "simulations" (or games) can provide workable rhetorical situations for technical writing assignments. They explain how simple and complex computer simulations provide realistic and complex rhetorical contexts for reports and other forms of technical writing.

In "Aristotle Inc.: Corporate Structure in the Technical Communication Course," Theresa Enos (1986) describes a course in which the traditional classroom is turned into a corporate structure. Enos (1986, p. 72) writes, "Encouraging students to form themselves into a corporate group that specializes in planning in-house technical writing programs for other companies would create sequential rhetorical contexts." And Enos (1986, p. 73) explains that the approach "helps students to create rhetorical stances firmly based in reality because it requires students to participate actively and cooperatively in real projects." The approach shows students how to work in groups, to depend on cooperation, and to understand the importance of audience in technical communication.

Looking at audiences from another aspect of rhetoric, Terri Paul and Mary Rosner (1983), in "Discovering and Teaching Syntactic Structures in Three Technical Disciplines," examine technical style for audiences in different disciplines. Wondering if different disciplines have different styles, Paul and Rosner analyzed style in engineering, agronomy, and home economics journals. They found that "different disciplines rely primarily on different types of subordinate clauses, sentence openers, and sentence types" and that paragraph length varies with audience level, as do the number of subject sentence openers and kinds of verb constructions (Paul and Rosner 1983, p. 109). Comparing their findings to recommendations on style in technical writing textbooks, Paul and Rosner (1983, p. 115) conclude that "textbook treatments of technical writing style would be more accurate, and consequently more helpful, if they gave more than a passing recognition to the fact that there are technical writing *styles*." By studying different styles, students can learn to adapt their writing to different readers.

Looking at another technical communication product—brochures—Jim Addison finds a definite pattern of rhetoric, a pattern that can form a teaching technique. In "Brochures: A Teaching Rhetoric," Addison (1982, p. 21) finds that the rhetoric of brochures "consists of an ordered manipulation of space on the page," an alternation of headings and visuals "to facilitate reading and rapid comprehension," and a use of headings in boldface and capitals "to segment the discourse" and aid understanding and recall. Addison then describes how to apply this rhetorical study of brochures to teaching.

Believing that technical writing students are more visually oriented than other students are, Patrick M. Kelley (1980) presents diagrams with explanations for presenting visually different kinds of paragraphs, in "Visual Rhetoric in Teaching Technical Writing." These diagrams help technical writing students to see structural relationships between sentences in paragraphs. Kelley (1980, p. R209) states that "visual rhetoric is a practice that enables technical writing teachers to teach verbal skills visually."

Using the rhetorical elements of invention, arrangement, and style and building on Kelley's visual rhetoric practice, three authors write about other ways to use diagrams to show technical writing students structural relationships. First, in "Visual Rhetoric in Technical Writing: Invention," Mary S. Hageman (1980, p. R217) discusses uses of visual rhetoric for invention:

> [T]he visual rhetoric diagrams enable the student to see structures and thus learn them quickly and efficiently. They make it possible for the beginning technical writer to select from a store of visual images the type of paragraph that best suits a particular writing situation.

Showing further uses for visual rhetoric, Adelaide (Johnnye) Burnham (1980) writes on arrangement in "Visual Rhetoric in Technical Writing: Arrangement." She indicates that structures should be studied first so that thought can be channeled in the right order, instead of in a free-flowing order. Her essay demonstrates the use of diagrams showing structure. A third author, Linda S. Chavarria (1980), builds further on Kelley's ideas about using visual rhetoric in "Visual Rhetoric in Technical Writing: Style." She asserts that when students can see style, they can revise by paying attention to stylistic devices.

Many authors advocate that rhetorical theory provides a good preparation for technical writers. It provides a basis for writing clearly and logically, handling diverse writing situations, developing analytical skills and critical approaches, examining audiences, studying different technical styles, and seeing structural relationships.

Another aspect of rhetoric that some authors see as important in teaching technical writing is invention.

Invention as a Strategy for Learning Technical Writing

One of the areas of rhetoric that many authors think provides good preparation for technical writing students is invention. Several authors view invention as a tool to accomplish diverse tasks. Some authors equate invention with heuristics (methods of discovery) and compare invention to algorithms (rule-governed procedures). Other authors believe that invention can be used in other steps of the writing process in addition to the prewriting phase. All the authors covered in this section feel that students of technical writing should be taught invention techniques.

In "The Role of Invention in Technical Writing," Dennis F. Hall (1976, p. 13) defines invention as

> the expository writer's artificial, systematic, and more or less exhaustive analysis of his or her knowledge and experience of the objects which have attracted or, much more commonly, demanded the writer's attention. It is conscious discovery of what one already knows and what one needs to find out, what can and should be said.

Hall explains that most technical writing texts avoid the subject of invention and that those that include it only tell readers that they should determine such obvious things as purpose before writing but do not suggest ways to determine these things. He feels adamantly that actual instruction in invention techniques needs to be strengthened.

Ardner Cheshire (1980) agrees with Hall in "Teaching Invention: Using Topical Categories in the Technical Writing Class" advocates teaching patterns of exposition with invention instruction to technical writing students. Cheshire (1980, p. 17) writes that even though technical writing students are usually more mature writers, "they, like all writers, must retrieve ideas about and discover an ordering principle for a topic," and adds that heuristics help a writer "go from nothing to a first draft, confident that he [or she] has probed his [or her] subject well and has something important to say about it." Cheshire also describes some of the procedures and assignments used in his technical writing classes.

In addition to the techniques described by Cheshire, David K. Farkas (1981), in "An Invention Heuristic for Business and Technical Communication," explains what he has labeled his "heuristic of professional communication goals." This heuristic consists of a checklist of six broad categories that "identify all the goals that pertain to a particular communication situation and generate subject matter that will achieve those goals" (Farkas 1981, p. 16). This article includes the checklist and the accompanying teaching techniques.

Another teaching technique that deals with invention is presented by J. W. Allen, Jr. (1978) in "Introducing Invention to Technical Students." He states that numerous heuristics are available to help students stimulate thought. He cites the use of the five W's as one example of a heuristic method that would test writing for completeness. The heuristic strategy that he discusses in detail is the "particle/wave/field" heuristic.

In "Heuristics for Invention in a Technical Writing Class," Nancy Roundy (1983) explains a study that she conducted of the invention processes of forty technicians. She says that "technicians employ two types of invention procedures: those for generating content and those for selecting content" (Roundy 1983, p. 200). Selection is the main invention procedure of technicians; they select according to audience, purpose, and use of the document; accepted technical structures; and ordering devices. Roundy used her study to teach her students to select "rhetorically appropriate information" that will fit audience, purpose, and use. She has her "students construct their rhetorical contexts" (Roundy 1983, p. 202). The students use classification, identification, and characterization to analyze an audience. They indicate their purposes and the audience's use of a document; state the reasons for including specific details according to audience, purpose, and use; and outline the major and minor divisions of the report. The students "simulate technicians' selection process and justify the content choices they make" (Roundy 1983, p. 202).

In his 1986 essay, "Aristotle and the Ways We Work Today: Part I, Classical Rhetoric in Technical Writing Textbooks," Terrance Skelton shows how current technical writing textbooks are returning to classical rhetoric by teaching invention heuristics. Skelton (1986, p. 239) explains how the textbooks "discuss invention as a means of discovering a document's purpose and content." He also discusses how the textbooks make use of classical strategies of arrangement and style.

Five important problem-solving strategies taught by Victoria M. Winkler (1980) in her technical writing classes are outlined in "Creative Design and Rhetorical Inquiry: Report Writing Strategies." She chooses to call the techniques "strategies" because she feels that heuristics are not prescriptive techniques that guarantee success, but instead are provisional strategies that increase the writer's possibility for success. She believes that her strategies help writers better to accept two different responsibilities: the role of investigator and the role of communicator.

In another essay, "The Role of Models in Technical and Scientific Writing," Winkler (1983) presents models that will help students to "invent" subject matter and to discover possible arrangements of the subjects.

Dealing with this dual role in writing assignments in "Some Applications of the New Rhetoric to the Teaching of Technical Writing: An Alternative to the Product Model," Margaret Shaw (1981, p. 462) indicates that most heuristics only solve the investigative role of the writer:

> When writers are through with their analysis, they have yet to work with the language they will use to write about that thing or problem. And the language students choose to use will finally transform the thing invention seeks to discover, whether they are

writing something as overtly persuasive as a proposal or as studiedly objective as a technical report.

She advocates extending the role of invention into the role of communication by helping writers to discover language appropriate to the writing situation.

In "Applying Selected New Rhetorical Strategies to Teaching Professional and Technical Writing," James M. DeGeorge (1981) agrees that most invention techniques cover only discovery. DeGeorge (1981, p. 479) writes,

> Many of them [heuristic schemes] propose to help the inexperienced writer find subject matter to write about. But the professional writer does not often need that kind of help. For the professional writer, the topic is well defined by the task in front of him/her. What the professional writer often needs is a guide to help him/her figure out a way to come to a written solution to a certain problem.

DeGeorge describes actual problem-solving heuristics that he believes will help technical writers.

In "Trends in Teaching Technical Writing," Jone R. Goldstein (1984) discusses all these techniques. She discusses the influence of modern rhetoric, composition pedagogy, and empirical research on technical writing. She also discusses the trend in teaching invention and ethos as part of the trend that has raised technical communication from being a handmaiden of technology to being a vehicle for creating substance and form. Goldstein (1984, p. 31) summarizes,

> These trends for teaching writing as process, for teaching invention and professional ethos, and for integrating the context and the reading process into the writer's procedures demonstrate the powerful combined influence of current rhetorical theory, composition pedagogy, and empirical research on the teaching of technical writing.

The preceding authors all agree that rhetorical theory (especially persuasion and invention) is essential for preparing students of technical writing for their future work. The next five essays discussed advocate extending present knowledge through research in specific areas of rhetoric to improve the teaching of technical writing.

Further Research in Rhetoric

Six authors call for research on rhetorical principles that can be used to teach technical writing.

In "Toward a Rhetoric of Scientific and Technical Discourse," Dwight W. Stevenson (1977) indicates that he has two purposes in writing the article: (1) to point out specific areas in which original work in the rhetoric of scientific and technical communication is needed and (2) to suggest ways this work might be conducted. He lists and explains three areas: (1) technology assessment, (2) visual communication, and (3) technical manuals.

Randall R. Freisinger and Bruce T. Petersen conducted a study that shows a need for additional research. The findings are discussed in "Toward Defining 'Good' Writing: A Rhetorical Analysis of the Words, Sentences, and Paragraphs in 16 Industrial Scripts" (Freisinger and Petersen 1981). Their study was conducted because they felt that technical writing teachers do not have a clear concept of what industries feel constitutes good writing. From writing samples collected from various industries, the authors made conclusions and recommendations that will give teachers of technical writing a better idea of what will be expected of their students in the workplace. They recommend that similar rhetorical studies be performed on writing in industry.

In "Syntax, Comprehension, and Believability: Implications for Technical Writers," Charles H. Sides (1981) relates surprising findings from a pilot study of the effects of syntax on reader comprehension. His findings show the need for further research in syntactical structure that technical writing teachers should teach their students. In another article, "Some Psychological Effects of Syntax," Sides (1983, p. 17) presents the same findings that "suggest that some college writing teachers value styles that did not list very well for comprehensibility." Sides's pilot study shows that some recommended styles inhibit comprehension and some "awkward" styles increase retention. He, again, recommends further research on style and teaching techniques.

In "Toward a Rhetoric of Visuals for the Computer Era," Barton and Barton (1985) examine graphics as a new area for study. They indicate that visual instruction has been neglected in teaching and in textbooks and that visual instruction has not kept up with current rhetorical theory. The Bartons (1985, pp. 141–42) suggest that teachers "adopt a rhetorical, rather than a formal, approach to visuals," that teachers adopt a "reader response orientation, including enhanced concern for the affective component of visual communication," and "adopt a process view of visuals to accord with the process view of rhetoric." They recommend that research be conducted on visual rhetoric to provide a rhetoric of visuals for the computer era.

Research on Writing

In addition to teachers instructing students in rhetorical principles for better technical communication, writers of technical and scientific information can use rhetorical principles in their work. The articles in this section show that rhetorical theory is important to technical writers because technical writing is persuasive and because style, arrangement, and ethos are important in technical writing. Although these essays also deal with the argument of forms versus rhetoric, their main focus is on writing rather than on teaching writing.

Persuasion in Technical Communication

Several essays stress the presence of persuasion in technical and scientific writing. They acknowledge how the term rhetoric is misunderstood and show why the persuasive nature of technical and scientific writing makes rhetorical theory the basis of good technical writing.

For instance, in "Are Scientists Rhetors in Disguise? An Analysis of Discursive Processes Within Scientific Communities," Herbert W. Simons (1980) explains the role that persuasion plays in scientific writing. Simons (1980, pp. 127–28) writes,

> Because "rhetoric" tends to be a "devil" term in our culture—often preceded by "mere," "only," "empty," or worse—scientists understandably recoil from it, insisting instead that their discourse is purely "objective." Yet in the classical, nonpejorative sense, "rhetorical" refers to reason-giving activity on judgmental matters about which there can be no formal proof.

He explains that scientific discourse depends on "extra-factual, extra-logical, arguments rather than purely factual, purely logical arguments; and it yields judgments, however credible, rather than certainties" (Simons 1980, p. 120).

In examining one of those scientific communities, Debra Journet (1984), in "Rhetoric and Sociobiology," also sees scientists as rhetors. In her essay, she uses a debate between sociobiologist E. O. Wilson and other scientists to call into question "many of the traditional assumptions about the objectivity of science" and to show "scientific communication that relies on traditional rhetorical techniques of persuasion" (Journet 1984, p. 339). To demonstrate the use of rhetoric in argument for and against sociobiology, Journet examines the pathos, ethos, and logos used by Wilson to support sociobiology and by other scientists to attack Wilson and sociobiology.

Philip C. Wander (1976) presents similar ideas in "The Rhetoric of Science." Wander states that rhetoric is used to present "scientific problems" convincingly. He also states that scientific writing is not just a giving of information, but depends on "the rhetorical significance of statistical reasoning, more specifically with its strategic value in light of the predispositions of a particular audience, those whose organizational role it is to distribute grants for scientific research" (Wander 1976, p. 231). Wander thus indicates part of the purpose of persuasion in scientific writing.

In "Some Thoughts on Rhetoric and Technical Communication," Daniel L. Plung, Jr. (1980) presents an incorrect definition of rhetoric (meaningless and empty verbiage) and supplies a correct one. He agrees with Aristotle, who felt that rhetoric was the faculty of discovering in the particular case what the available means of persuasion are by looking at each particular case to ascertain the best means of persuasion. Plung believes that this definition allows technical writers to use the art of rhetoric to improve the quality of technical communication.

James A. Kelso (1980), in "Science and the Rhetoric of Reality," explains another part that persuasion plays in scientific writing. He discusses the nature of scientific "laws" and reveals that these laws are actually determined by scientists who use persuasion techniques to convince others that their laws are true. The scientists do so by selecting "facts," emphasizing certain natural phenomena, and ignoring others. Kelso writes that the operant factor in scientific writing is not whether the image is true or not, but instead whether it is believed to be true.

In "Rhetoric: Its Functions and Its Scope," Donald C. Bryant (1972) presents similar ideas. Bryant discusses the value of rhetorical knowledge to effective communication. He identifies rhetoric as being primarily concerned with the "relations of ideas to the thoughts, feelings, motives, and behavior of men" (Bryant 1972, p. 25) and women. When contrasting rhetoric to science, which tries to take and find all facts before decisions can be made, Bryant explains how rhetoricians acknowledge that all facts cannot be found before a decision must be made. And, thus, the writer should use the known facts to make needed decisions based on informed opinion.

In "Science as a Rhetorical Transaction: Toward a Nonjustificational Conception of Rhetoric," Walter B. Weimer (1977) adds to the idea that the laws of science are simply those ideas accepted as laws. Weimer (1977, pp. 11-12) shows that justificationism is an inadequate methodology and explains,

> Traditional accounts portray the language of science as purely descriptive. Beginning from the truism that theories describe the nature of reality, they ignore the argumentative nature of explanatory discourse and assume that representation, the essential characteristics of science, is just descriptive. But not only is such an account deficient with regard to the argumentative force of theoretical explanation, it cannot account for communication in science.

Weimer (1977, p. 15) adds that "rhetoric produces only *belief* by argument and persuasion, and belief can at best be true opinion."

The idea that writers of scientific information select facts and, therefore, shape the laws of science by persuasion is reinforced by Daniel Marder (1978) in "Technical Reporting Is Technical Rhetoric." Marder decries the fact that some scientific writing is mere record-keeping, which leads to uninteresting "dead" technical reporting, and he explains how knowledge in technical rhetoric would change such technical reporting into effective presentations of information. Marder (1978, p. 11) writes,

> We fail to realize that in technical reporting, only the subject is technical. Despite all the razzle-dazzle in our most technical of technological times, the substance of technical reporting remains a formal discipline of the mind: a rhetorical discovery of the best ways and means to persuade an audience.

Thus, rhetoric enables technical writers to persuade more effectively.

What they are persuading readers to accept, Marilyn S. Samuels says, is a recreation of reality (in the sense of a "re-creation"). In "Technical Writing and the Recreation of Reality," Samuels (1985) argues that this recreation makes technical writing a creative act. She sees the technical writer as "a rhetorician who must design in the appropriate context" (with a knowledge of facts, audience, and situation) a persuasive view of reality (Samuels 1985, p. 7). Technical writing is seen as "a recreation of reality for special purposes" and as "an act of creation *without* becoming a departure from truth" (Samuels 1985, p. 11).

Barton and Barton also discuss the rhetorical nature of science and concur with other authors that scientific writing is not purely objective writing. In "What Is Technical Writing? Prolegomenon to a Contextual Definition," the Bartons (1981b) present many definitions of technical writing and show the inadequacies of each. For instance, they present the definition that "technical writing is expected to be objective, scientifically impartial, utterly clear and unemotional" and then dispute it by writing that "science is a rhetorical act" (Barton and Barton 1981b, pp. 4–5).

Similarly, Harley Sachs (1978) writes of the presence of persuasion in technical writing in "Rhetoric, Persuasion, and the Technical Communicator." He concentrates on the fact that a sender and a receiver are present in scientific communication and the sender's purpose is to persuade the receiver that his or her views are correct. He explains that when people write and read scientific communication, tools of persuasion are in operation.

Michael A. Overington also believes that science should be treated rhetorically because it is knowledge-producing and must be argued before an audience. In "The Scientific Community as Audience: Toward a Rhetorical Analysis of Science," Overington (1977) shows that the scientific method is persuasive in nature and presents what he considers to be rhetorical concepts in scientific writing.

Mary M. Lay (1984) sees ways of improving persuasion in technical writing through the enthymeme in "The Enthymeme: A Persuasive Strategy in Technical Writing." Lay (1984, p. 15) explains how the enthymeme can engage the audience in readily accepting the writer's assertions and thus "be seen as the basis for effective persuasion in all technical writing."

H. Lee Shimberg (1978), on the other hand, presents what he calls impediments to good scientific rhetoric in "Ethics and Rhetoric in Technical Writing." Shimberg explains that sophist practices, such as using ambiguity, understating or suppressing the negative, overstating the negative, and misusing semantics, undermine scientific writing and make writers reluctant to accept the presence of rhetoric in scientific writing. In addition to identifying the rhetorical element of persuasion in technical communication, authors have described other rhetorical devices in technical communication.

Style and Arrangement in Technical Communication

Several authors examine the role of style and arrangement in technical communication. They explain how rhetorical strategies can be used to influence the style and structure of technical writing.

In "Ciceronian Rhetoric and the Rise of Science: The Plain Style Reconsidered," Halloran and Whitburn (1982) explain how well Ciceronian rhetorical theory relates to scientific writing. They begin by explaining that plain style is used to instruct, middle style is used to delight, and grand style is used to move an audience to belief or action. They assert that technical writing has been excessively oriented around the plain style; they recommend that an ideal technical communicator command all three styles but place the heaviest emphasis on clarity, as Aristotle recommends. The authors believe that one of the problems with scientific writing is that it is not "audience friendly" because of the impersonality of technical writing. They call for a fuller, richer expression and experience of humanity in technical writing and argue that this goal can be accomplished by welding rhetorical style, which expresses personality, with technical discourse. They state, finally, that human judgment and imagination, enhanced by the understanding of rhetorical theory, are necessary to improve technical writing, rather than to have it depend strictly on scientific approaches.

In "Some Linguistic Components of Tone," Alan M. Perlman (1981) discusses similar stylistic choices when he explains how the right choices can lead to more effective persuasion through better expression of tone. In that article, he explains how rhetorical strategies can convey an author's attitude to an audience; how lexical, syntactic, and rhetorical choices affect the tone of a piece of writing; and, in turn, how these choices can affect a reader's acceptance of what a writer says. To demonstrate his point, he uses different versions of a company's directive on the need to fill out forms accurately.

Also dealing with audience reactions, Douglas R. Butler (1986) writes about the use of metaphors in technical communication, in "The Function of Metaphor in Technical Discourse." Butler classifies technical metaphors according to rhetorical function or effect on readers and defines metaphor in technical discourse as a verbal device to help readers to see some connections but to ignore others.

In "Redundancy in Aricola's *De Re Metallica*: Purpose and Execution," Jo Allen (1986) also talks about rhetorical comparisons. Jo Allen (1986, p. 184) deals with "redundancy as a means of clarifying and remembering information" by discussing a sixteenth-century Latin treatise on mining and metallurgy. She explains how rhetorical devices like comparisons, similes, analogies, and metaphors help to explain technical materials "because the writer intentionally structures the information to fit the reader's schema" (Allen 1986, p. 185). Her dated example shows how the rhetorical devices provide clear writing and how little they have changed over several centuries.

Taking another point of view about style in technical communication, in "Where Techne Meets Poesis: Some Semiotic Considerations in the Rhetoric of Technical Discourse," John S. Childs (1986) shows that technical and nontechnical expository prose have clear stylistic connections. In this article, Childs (1986, p. 63) maintains that technical writing "possesses a number of rhetorical features which further increase its likeness to literary writing. Both style and rhetoric of technical writing thus point toward non-referential functions in scientific discourse, including the operation of significant cultural codes."

In "The Concept of Consistency in Writing and Editing," Farkas (1985) claims that whatever stylistic choices are made must be consistent. Farkas (1985, p. 353) deals with consistency as "the orderly treatment of linked elements" that have "semantic, syntactic, stylistic, spatial, and mechanical consistency" and states that "consistency should be a component of any comprehensive rhetoric of technical communication."

The careful choice and arrangement of words and ideas forms the definition Frank R. Smith (1975) gives to rhetoric in "Use Rhetoric for Better Technical Proposals." He demonstrates how rhetorical awareness can help technical writers with good word arrangement, effective use of repetition, brevity, parallelism, and subordination. He advocates that writers spend time with important statements in proposals to find the best, most emphatic way to state the concept.

The same can be said for making choices about arrangement. In "Rhetoric and Technical Writing: Black Magic or Science?" Robert L. Corey (1978) explains that rhetorical forms can enhance meaning and convey it to an audience. Only by knowing rhetorical theory not by depending on black magic can authors improve their abilities to make good rhetorical choices that will get their messages across. To make those choices, technical writers need to be able to analyze form by separating it from content. In "The Persuasive Technical Proposal: Rhetorical Form and the Writer," Corey (1975) explains that technical writers should be aware of the meanings rhetorical forms carry in their proposals. To use the correct forms, the writer must be able to assess them.

Taking another approach to arrangement, Michael G. Moran (1984) looks at past scientific discourse for logical arrangement, in "Joseph Priestley, William Duncan, and Analytic Arrangement in 18th-Century Scientific Discourse." Using Priestley's and Duncan's writings as examples, Moran discusses synthesis and analysis as methods of arrangement for scientific discourse. Moran (1984, p. 208) says that synthesis and analysis

> assist the thinker in the exploration of a subject by providing predictable yet flexible structures. Second, they serve a communicative function because they organize a discourse so that an audience can comprehend it. This comprehension results when the ideas unfold in the reader's mind in the same order they were associated in the writer's.

Technical writers need to be aware of the role of ethos in addition to rhetorical considerations of style and arrangement.

Ethos in Technical Communication

With the growing acceptance of rhetorical devices in technical communication, authors are advocating that technical communicators take responsibility for their own words. Authors can do this by making certain rhetorical choices that allow more persona in technical communication and produce better ethos and ethics in technical writing.

The differences between ethos and ethics are explained by Jack Griffin (1980) in "When Do Rhetorical Choices Become Ethical Choices?" Griffin first states that ethics and ethos are not synonymous and then proceeds to outline the differences and explain their influence on writers, readers, and editors of technical communication.

In "Reinventing the Wheel? Ethics for Technical Communicators," Philip M. Rubens (1981) chastises Sachs and Shimberg for their failure to address important ethical aspects of technical communication. Rubens argues that Sachs (1980), in "Ethics and the Technical Communicator," and Shimberg (1980), in "Technical Communicators and Moral Ethics," use a "bandaid" approach to solving problems found in technical communication. For his approach, Rubens writes about three areas that he feels will improve technical communication. First, he writes that technical communicators hide behind the passive voice. Rubens believes that writers should take responsibility for their messages by making the agent visible to the readers. Second, he believes that writers should give fair treatment to facts and phenomena to make their writing as objective as possible. Third, Rubens recommends that writers manipulate the language but not abuse it.

W. Earl Britton also recommends that the agent's personality be present in technical communication. In "Personality in Scientific Writing," Britton (1973) advocates the use of the first person/active voice and even suggests the occasional use of humor in technical communication. He says that humor has the capacity to illuminate a subject and helps to relieve the tedium. He writes that the presence of personality in technical writing shows the "writer's lively and intelligent mind playing perceptibly upon his [or her] material.... It is primarily an intellectual quality" (Britton 1973, p. 10).

When the author's personality is present in technical communication, the ethos of the technical and scientific writer is more apparent. The authors covered in this section believe that this concept is important. The rhetorical goal of impersonality in technical communication was to force the attention of the reader to the logos, rendering the ethos of the writer as unobtrusive as possible. Many modern rhetorical authors advocate putting ethos back into technical communication.

For instance, in "Ethos in Technical Discourse: The Current State of the Question," Michael J. Marcuse (1980) discusses how the old theory regarded the reader as a "consumer of discourse," whereas the more modern theory regards the reader as a formative element in discourse. Writers are increasingly being asked to be aware of their readers' needs and their own ethos. Marcuse writes that authors should ask themselves, "What sort of person do you want your reader to feel you are?"

In two essays, "Technology as a Form of Consciousness: A Study of Contemporary Ethos" and "The Ethos of Science and the Ethos of Technology," Miller (1978 and 1980, respectively) discusses the nature of ethos and its effect on technical communication. She differentiates between science and technology in hopes of showing the differences in how the ethos of each will affect the rhetorical choices writers will have to make.

In "The Figures of Speech, *Ethos,* and Aristotle: Notes Toward a Rhetoric of Business Communication," Craig Kallendorf and Carol Kallendorf (1984) address the way that ethos is built through figures of speech. Through examples, the Kallendorfs show how writers use many classical figures of speech as tools for persuasion in modern business communication. Then, the authors (Kallendorf and Kallendorf 1984, p. 43) connect the figures of speech to ethos, writing that

> the figures of speech, as we have already seen, enable a writer to balance similar or contrasting ideas, to frame thoughts in epigrammatic expressions, to add a sense of drama or urgency to a message. The figures, in short, enable a writer to arrange, shape, and present ideas in a way that projects the image of a thoughtful and analytical person whose ideas deserve to be taken seriously. They provide the tools for communicating the intelligence, goodwill, and upright character which Aristotle said must be projected.

In "The New Role of Technical Communicators," David B. Bradford (1985) sees a new persona for technical writers. Bradford (1985, p. 15) feels that technical communicators are not only translators of programming for users but also teachers who reassure new users and says,

> We are not only responsible for disseminating information, but for structuring it as demanded by the audience, not the subjects. We are responsible for making the information not only accurate and readable, but even attractive and entertaining. The commitment to reaching the audience and engaging their interest is not easily satisfied via the traditional persona of the technical writer; it demands new rhetorical strategies that are foreign to our conservative "translator" approach.

The new rhetorical strategies involve "figures of speech and other products of personal style to enhance the information being conveyed." They also "include original style, metaphor, comic relief, incentive, and praise. All of these contribute to nonthreatening informality that reassures the new uses" (Bradford 1985, p. 15).

Stephen A. Bernhardt also sees the personality of the writer becoming more apparent in scientific texts. In "The Writer, the Reader, and the Scientific Text," Bernhardt (1985) explains his study of journals in the natural sciences and his finding that writers represent themselves at certain points in a piece of writing. They use personal references to acknowledge assistance, to refer to their own previous research, to state and justify chosen methods, to explain adjustments to methods, to compare findings to previous studies, and to discuss the implications of their work. Bernhardt (1985, p. 173) concludes,

> Personal intrusions are not scattered throughout a text, but tend to localize at certain junctures where the argumentative nature of the report heightens. It is when a writer feels the need to justify choices, decisions, interpretations, and suggestions that the writer intrudes.... All discourse, including scientific discourse, makes interpersonal meanings and employs interpersonal constructions.

Just as rhetorical theory can aid authors of technical communication, it can help editors of the same.

Research on Editing

In "Situational Editing: A Rhetorical Approach for the Technical Editor," Mary F. Buehler (1980) best sums up how rhetorical training helps editors. Buehler (1980, p. 22) states that "the editor functions in the center of a series of rhetorical situations, linking the author and the potential reader, and serving the needs of both." She recommends that the programmatic approach to editing be complemented by a rhetorical approach. She explains that the programmatic approach requires that the editor have knowledge of rules and the application of these rules, while the rhetorical approach requires that the editor see all elements in a rhetorical situation. The use of both approaches enables editors to serve the needs of both the writer and the reader.

In "Attitude Toward the Editing Process: Theory, Research, and Pedagogy," Jean A. Lutz (1986) also sees the editor serving the needs of both the writer and the reader. Lutz (1986, p. 161) says, "An editor sits between a writer and reader and has allegiances to both." She also uses her research to show "the influence of rhetorical context on the number and kinds of changes" that editors make (Lutz 1986, p. 158) and states that "the greater the context supplied to an editor, the more changes he/she can and will make" (Lutz 1986, p. 159). The editing function becomes even more complex when the editor and writer must work together. Lutz (1986, p. 163) explains,

Editors and writers who do negotiate changes must have expert interpersonal skills—for they must be able to understand and articulate reasons for changes they wish to make—or not make—in a manuscript. In this way only can they arrive at consensus about reality, based on their contextual understanding and rhetorical expertise. In this way only will the text be most likely to meet the readers' needs.

In "Understanding the Rhetoric of Scientific Writing," Sawyer (1983) explains that the overall plan of experiments in scientific writing is always the same. He describes the parts of the scientific method and sets up an outline of it so that anyone can understand the form. He advocates dealing with scientific jargon by asking scientists to define terms operationally, which is an important rhetorical device. By understanding what scientists actually did, editors can help writers to present their results clearly and persuasively.

Heuristics can be applied to all parts of the writing process, but heuristics can help with editing too, as explained by Charlotte Thralls (1980) in "Editing of Professional Reports: A Rhetorical Modes Approach." Thralls' editing process requires editors to break the report into segments and to analyze each segment according to its rhetorical mode or intent.

In "Redesigning Technical Reports: A Rhetorical Editing Method," Patrick Cheney and David Schleicher (1984, p. 336) provide a rhetorical method for editing "based on the postulate that every technical report should be usable to a specific audience for a specific purpose." Editing for correctness and style is not enough; often editors need to improve the scope and structure that authors have missed and that readers need. Cheney and Schleicher explain the five stages of their editing process: (1) identifying the audience and purpose of the report, (2) analyzing the ideas in the draft report, (3) synthesizing the ideas into a well-focused revision, (4) interviewing the author, and (5) finishing the report. Cheney and Schleicher (1984, p. 336) conclude, saying,

> Rhetorical editing calls on you to edit the report as a whole—specifically, to analyze the author's selection and arrangement of ideas throughout the report and to reselect the ideas that are necessary and sufficient for the audience and purpose of the report and rearrange those ideas so as to make the report most usable to the audience. . . . Only then are you ready for conventional editing for correctness and style.

Charles R. Fenno (1986) provides another editing technique in part 2 of "Aristotle and the Ways We Work Today," entitled "Classical Rhetoric and the Electronic Office." After defining rhetoric as "the analytical, structural, and stylistic processes which writers must control in order to gain reader understanding and assent" (Fenno 1986, p. 243) and explaining how the writer can use a word processor for invention and arrangement, Fenno shows how an editor can use a word processor to edit rhetorical style. He explains how the ability of the computer to "scroll" backward and forward allows the editor to check arrangement and coherence, how its ability to "search" allows the editor to check for inappropriate diction or for repetition of key terms, how its "spell-check" allows the editor to check for spelling or typing errors, and how software programs allow the editor to check the lengths of clauses and sentences and the frequency of types of sentences. Rhetorical strategies are thus adapted to the electronic technology that is changing the ways we write and edit.

Conclusion

The authors, teachers, editors, and researchers in technical communication who contributed to this essay examine the role of rhetoric in technical communication from various perspectives. Although a few believe that simulated forms provide a better approach to teaching and practicing technical communication than rhetoric does, most believe that rhetoric is related to the major concerns of technical communication and provides theoretical bases and practical approaches to technical communication. From their varying perspectives, all of the writers closely examine the role of rhetoric in teaching, writing, and editing technical communication.

Bibliography

Addison, Jim. "Brochures: A Teaching Rhetoric." *The Technical Writing Teacher* 10, no. 1 (1982): 21–24.

Allen, J. W., Jr. "Introducing Invention to Technical Students." *The Technical Writing Teacher* 5, no. 2 (1978): 45–49.

Allen, Jo. "Redundancy in Aricola's *De Re Metallica*: Purpose and Execution." In *Proceedings of the 33rd International Technical Communication Conference.* Washington, D.C.: Society for Technical Communication, 1986, pp. 184–86.

Barton, Ben F., and Marthalee S. Barton. "Ethos, Persona, and Role Confusion in Engineering: Toward a Pedagogy for Technical Discourse." In *Technical Communication: Perspectives for the Eighties,* edited by J. C. Mathes and Thomas E. Pinelli. Hampton, Va.: National Aeronautics and Space Administration, 1981a, pp. 447–53.

———. "What Is Technical Writing? Prolegomenon to a Contextual Definition." In *Technical Communcation: Perspectives for the Eighties,* edited by

J. C. Mathes and Thomas E. Pinelli. Hampton, Va.: National Aeronautics and Space Administration, 1981b, pp. 3–13.

———. "Toward a Rhetoric of Visuals for the Computer Era." *The Technical Writing Teacher* 12, no. 2 (1985): 126–45. (Also published as "Visual Rhetoric in Technical Communication," Part 1, "Theoretical, Empirical, and Intuitive Bases" and Part 2, "The Impact of the Computer." In *Proceedings 1985: The Council for Programs in Technical and Scientific Communcation,* edited by Marilyn Samuels. Cleveland, Ohio: Council for Programs in Technical and Scientific Communication, 1986, pp. 138–66.)

Bernhardt, Stephen A. "The Writer, the Reader, and the Scientific Text." *Journal of Technical Writing and Communication* 15, no. 2 (1985): 163–74.

Bradford, David B. "The New Role of Technical Communicators." *Technical Communication* 32, no. 1 (1985): 13–15.

Britton, W. Earl. "Personality in Scientific Writing." *Technical Communication* 23, no. 3 (1973): 8–13.

Bryant, Donald C. "Rhetoric: Its Function and Its Scope." In *Contemporary Rhetoric,* edited by Douglas Ehninger. Glenview, Ill.: Scott, Foresman, 1972, pp. 15–39.

Buehler, Mary F. "Situational Editing: A Rhetorical Approach for the Technical Editor." *Technical Communication* 29, no. 3 (1980): 18–22.

Burnham, Adelaide (Johnnye). "Visual Rhetoric in Technical Writing: Arrangement." In *Proceedings of the 27th International Technical Communication Conference.* Washington, D.C.: Society for Technical Communication, 1980, pp. R219–R221.

Butler, Douglas R. "The Function of Metaphor in Technical Discourse." *Journal of Technical Writing and Communication* 16, no. 1/2 (1986): 141–46.

Carson, David L. "Audience in Technical Writing: The Need for Greater Realism in Identifying the Fictive Reader." *The Technical Writing Teacher* 7, no. 1 (1979): 8–11.

Chavarria, Linda S. "Visual Rhetoric in Technical Writing: Style." In *Proceedings of the 27th International Technical Communication Conference.* Washington, D.C.: Society for Technical Communication, 1980, pp. R223–R227.

Cheney, Patrick, and David Schleicher. "Redesigning Technical Reports: A Rhetorical Editing Method." *Journal of Technical Writing and Communication* 14, no. 4 (1984): 317–37.

Cheshire, Ardner. "Teaching Invention: Using Topical Categories in the Technical Writing Class." *The Technical Writing Teacher* 8, no. 1 (1980): 17–21.

Childs, John S. "Where Techne Meets Poesis: Some Semiotic Considerations in the Rhetoric of Technical Discourse." *Journal of Technical Writing and Communication* 16, no. 1/2 (1986): 63–71.

Corbett, Edward P. J. "A Rhetorician Looks at Technical Communication." In *Technical Communication: Perspectives for the Eighties,* edited by J. C. Mathes and Thomas E. Pinelli. Hampton, Va.: National Aeronautics and Space Administration, 1981, pp. 213–18.

Corey, Robert L. "The Persuasive Technical Proposal: Rhetorical Form and the Writer." *Technical Communication* 22, no. 4 (1975): 2–5.

———. "Rhetoric and Technical Writing: Black Magic or Science?" *Technical Communication* 25, no. 4 (1978): 2–6.

DeGeorge, James M. "Applying Selected New Rhetorical Strategies to Teaching Professional and Technical Writing." In *Technical Communication: Perspectives for the Eighties,* edited by J. C. Mathes and Thomas E. Pinelli. Hampton, Va.: National Aeronautics and Space Administration, 1981, pp. 473–83.

Dietrich, Julia C. "The Common Ground of Freshman Rhetoric and Technical Writing." *The Technical Writing Teacher* 6, no. 3 (1979): 92–94.

Emerson, A. Douglas. "Apples Versus Oranges and Rhetorical Principles: Companies Pay the Bill." In *Proceedings of the 27th International Technical Communication Conference.* Washington, D.C.: Society for Technical Communication, 1980, pp. R183–R205.

Enos, Theresa. "Aristotle Inc.: Corporate Structure in the Technical Communication Course." *The Technical Writing Teacher* 13, no. 1 (1986): 71–77.

Evans, William E. "The Basic Technical Writing Course: Skills *and* Ethics?" In *Technical Communication: Perspectives for the Eighties,* edited by J. C. Mathes and Thomas E. Pinelli. Hampton, Va.: National Aeronautics and Space Administration, 1981, pp. 441–46.

Farkas, David K. "An Invention Heuristic for Business and Technical Communication." *The ABCA Bulletin* 44, no. 4 (1981): 16–19.

———. "The Concept of Consistency in Writing and Editing." *Journal of Technical Writing and Communication* 15, no. 4 (1985): 353–63.

Fenno, Charles R. "Aristotle and the Ways We Work Today." Part 2, "Classical Rhetoric and the Electronic Office." In *Proceedings of the 33rd International Technical Communication Conference.* Washington, D.C.: Society for Technical Communication, 1986, pp. 243–47.

Fialkowski, Kathryn L. "Academia and Business: Preserving the Code of Honor." In *Proceedings of the 33rd International Technical Communication Conference.* Washington, D.C.: Society for Technical Communication, 1986, pp. 248–50.

Freisinger, Randall R., and Bruce T. Petersen. "Toward Defining 'Good' Writing: A Rhetorical Analysis of the Words, Sentences, and Paragraphs in 16 Industrial Scripts." In *Technical Communication: Perspectives for the Eighties,* edited by J. C. Mathes and Thomas E. Pinelli. Hampton, Va.: National Aeronautics and Space Administration, 1981, pp. 291–304.

Goldstein, Jone R. "Trends in Teaching Technical Writing." *Technical Communication* 31, no. 4 (1984): 25–34.

Griffin, Jack. "When Do Rhetorical Choices Become Ethical Choices?" In *Proceedings of the 27th International Technical Communication Conference.* Washington, D.C.: Society for Technical Communication, 1980, pp. W77–W84.

Grimshaw, James A., Jr., and William E. McCarren. "Hidden Persuasions in Technical Writing." *The Technical Writing Teacher* 9, no. 1 (1981): 19–22.

Guinn, Dorothy M. "Ethos in Technical Discourse." *The Technical Writing Teacher* 11, no. 1 (1983): 31–37.

Hageman, Mary S. "Visual Rhetoric in Technical Writing: Invention." In *Proceedings of the 27th International Technical Communication Conference*. Washington, D.C.: Society for Technical Communication, 1980, pp. R215–R218.

Hall, Dennis F. "The Role of Invention in Technical Writing." *The Technical Writing Teacher* 4, no. 1 (1976): 13–24.

Halloran, S. Michael. "Eloquence in a Technological Society." *Central States Speech Journal* 29 (1978a): 221–27.

———. "Technical Writing and the Rhetoric of Science." *Journal of Technical Writing and Communication* 8, no. 2 (1978b): 77–88. (Reprinted in *Technical Communication* 25, no. 4 [1978]: 7–10.)

Halloran, S. Michael, and Merrill D. Whitburn. "Ciceronian Rhetoric and the Rise of Science: The Plain Style Reconsidered." In *The Rhetorical Tradition and Modern Writing*, edited by James J. Murphy, et al. New York: Modern Language Association, 1982, pp. 58–72.

Harris, Elizabeth. "Applications of Kinneavy's *Theory of Discourse* to Technical Writing." *College English* 40, no. 6 (1979): 625–31.

———. "Comment and Response: Elizabeth Harris Responds." *College English* 41, no. 7 (1980): 827–29.

———. "In Defense of the Liberal-Arts Approach to Technical Writing." *College English* 44, no. 6 (1982): 628–36.

———. "A Theoretical Perspective on 'How To' Discourse." In *New Essays in Technical and Scientific Communication: Research, Theory, Practice*, edited by Paul V. Anderson, R. John Brockmann, and Carolyn R. Miller. Farmingdale, N.Y.: Baywood Publishing Co., 1983, pp. 139–55.

Jones, Daniel R. "A Rhetorical Approach for Teaching the Literature of Scientific and Technical Writing." *The Technical Writing Teacher* 13, no. 2 (1985): 115–25.

———. "The Challenge of Consensus Theory in Modern Rhetoric for Teaching Technical Writing." In *Proceedings 1985: The Council for Programs in Technical and Scientific Communication*, edited by Marilyn S. Samuels. Cleveland, Ohio: Council for Programs in Technical and Scientific Communication, 1986, pp. 93–103.

Journet, Debra. "Rhetoric and Sociobiology." *Journal of Technical Writing and Communication* 14, no. 4 (1984): 339–50.

Kallendorf, Craig, and Carol Kallendorf. "The Figures of Speech, *Ethos*, and Aristotle: Notes Toward a Rhetoric of Business Communication." *Journal of Business Communication* 22, no. 1 (1984): 35–50.

Kelley, Patrick M. "Visual Rhetoric in Teaching Technical Writing." In *Proceedings of the 27th International Technical Communication Conference*. Washington, D.C.: Society for Technical Communication, 1980, pp. R209–R213.

Kelso, James A. "Science and the Rhetoric of Reality." *Central States Speech Journal* 31 (1980): 17–29.

Killingsworth, M. Jimmie. "The Essay and the Report: Expository Poles in Technical Writing." *Journal of Technical Writing and Communication* 15, no. 3 (1985): 227–33.

Kinneavy, James L. *Theory of Discourse*. New York: Norton, 1980.

La Roche, Mary G. "Technical Writing as an Alternative Rhetoric for Composition Courses." *The Technical Writing Teacher* 8, no. 3 (1981): 73–76.

Lay, Mary M. "The Enthymeme: A Persuasive Strategy in Technical Writing." *Technical Communication* 31, no. 2 (1984): 12–15.

Lunsford, Andrea A. "Classical Rhetoric and Technical Writing." *College Composition and Communication* 27, no. 3 (1976): 289–91.

Lutz, Jean A. "Attitude Toward the Editing Process: Theory, Research, and Pedagogy." *Journal of Technical Writing and Communication* 16, no. 1/2 (1986): 157–65.

Lynn, Steven W. "Kinneavy, Mathes, Mumford, and Lynn: Teaching the Classificatory Mode in Technical Writing." *Journal of Technical Writing and Communication* 10, no. 2 (1980): 115–24.

Marcuse, Michael J. "Ethos in Technical Discourse: The Current State of the Question." Paper presented at the Annual Meeting of the Conference on College Composition and Communication, 1980. ERIC Document 188 221.

Marder, Daniel. "Technical Reporting Is Technical Rhetoric." *Technical Communication* 25, no. 4 (1978): 11–12.

McCarren, William E. "Changing the Technical Writing Paradigm." *Journal of Technical Writing and Communication* 15, no. 1 (1985): 27–33.

Miller, Carolyn R. "Technology as a Form of Consciousness: A Study of Contemporary Ethos." *Central States Speech Journal* 29 (1978): 228–36.

———. "A Humanistic Rationale for Technical Writing." *College English* 40, no. 6 (1979): 610–17.

———. "The Ethos of Science and the Ethos of Technology." In *Proceedings of the 31st Conference on College Composition and Communication*, edited by John A. Muller. 1980a, pp. 184–91.

———. "Comment and Response: Carolyn Miller Responds." *College English* 41, no. 7 (1980b): 825–27.

Mitchell, John H. "It's a Craft Course: Indoctrinate, Don't Educate." *The Technical Writing Teacher* 4, no. 1 (1976): 2–6.

Moran, Michael G. "Joseph Priestley, William Duncan and Analytic Arrangement in 18th-Century Scientific Discourse." *Journal of Technical Writing and Communication* 14, no. 3 (1984): 207–15.

Murray, Patricia Y. "Rhetoric and the Business Administrator: Writing in the Professions." In *Technical Communication: Perspectives for the Eighties*, edited by J. C. Mathes and Thomas E. Pinelli. Hampton, Va.: National Aeronautics and Space Administration, 1981, pp. 579–87.

Orth, Michael, and Carl R. V. Brown. "Computer Generated Rhetorical Simulations for Business and Report Writing Courses." *Journal of Technical Writing and Communication* 14, no. 1 (1984): 29–34.

Overington, Michael A. "The Scientific Community as Audience: Toward a Rhetorical Analysis of Science." *Philosophy and Rhetoric* 10, no. 3 (1977): 143–64.

Paul, Terri, and Mary Rosner. "Discovering and Teaching Syntactic Structures in Three Technical Disciplines." *Journal of Technical Writing and Communication* 13, no. 2 (1983): 109–22.

Perlman, Alan M. "Some Linguistic Components of Tone." *Technical Communication* 32, no. 2 (1981): 12–15.

Petersen, Bruce T. "Conceptual Patterns in Industrial and Academic Discourse." *Journal of Technical Writing and Communication* 14, no. 2 (1984): 95–107.

Plung, Daniel L., Jr. "Some Thoughts on Rhetoric and Technical Communication." In *Proceedings of the 27th International Technical Communication Conference.* Washington, D.C.: Society for Technical Communication, 1980, pp. W69–W71.

Rothmel, Steven Z. "Technical Communication: Meeting the Needs of Adult Writers." In *Technical Communication: Perspectives for the Eighties,* edited by J. C. Mathes and Thomas E. Pinelli. Hampton, Va.: National Aeronautics and Space Administration, 1981, pp. 467–72.

Roundy, Nancy. "Heuristics for Invention in a Technical Writing Class." *The Technical Writing Teacher* 10, no. 3 (1983): 200–209.

Rubens, Philip M. "Reinventing the Wheel? Ethics for Technical Communicators." *Journal of Technical Writing and Communication* 11, no. 4 (1981): 329–39.

Sachs, Harley. "Rhetoric, Persuasion, and the Technical Communicator." *Technical Communication* 25, no. 4 (1978): 14–15.

———. "Ethics and the Technical Communicator." *Technical Communication* 27, no. 3 (1980): 7–10.

Samuels, Marilyn S. "Technical Writing and the Recreation of Reality." *Journal of Technical Writing and Communication* 15, no. 1 (1985): 3–13.

Sawyer, Thomas M. "Rhetoric in an Age of Science and Technology." *College Composition and Communication* 23, no. 5 (1972): 390–98.

———. "Understanding the Rhetoric of Scientific Writing." In *Technical and Business Communication in Two-Year Programs,* edited by W. Keats Sparrow and Nell Ann Pickett. Urbana, Ill.: National Council of Teachers of English, 1983, pp. 22–32.

Shaw, Margaret. "Some Applications of the New Rhetoric to the Teaching of Technical Writing: An Alternative to the Product Model." In *Technical Communication: Perspectives for the Eighties,* edited by J. C. Mathes and Thomas E. Pinelli. Hampton, Va.: National Aeronautics and Space Administration, 1981, pp. 461–66.

Shimberg, H. Lee. "Ethics and Rhetoric in Technical Writing." *Technical Communication* 25, no. 4 (1978): 16–18.

———. "Technical Communicators and Moral Ethics." *Technical Communication* 27, no. 3 (1980): 10–12.

Sides, Charles H. "Syntax, Comprehension, and Believability: Implications for Technical Writers." In *Technical Communication: Perspectives for the*

Eighties, edited by J. C. Mathes and Thomas E. Pinelli. Hampton, Va.: National Aeronautics and Space Administration, 1981, pp. 219–26.

———. "Some Psychological Effects of Syntax." *Technical Communication* 30, no. 1 (1983): 14–17.

Simons, Herbert W. "Are Scientists Rhetors in Disguise?: An Analysis of Discursive Processes Within Scientific Communities." In *Rhetoric in Transition: Studies in the Nature and Uses of Rhetoric,* edited by Eugene E. White. University Park, Pa.: Pennsylvania State University Press, 1980, pp. 115–30.

Skelton, Terrance. "Aristotle and the Ways We Work Today." Part 1, "Classical Rhetoric in Technical Writing Textbooks." In *Proceedings of the 33rd International Technical Communication Conference.* Washington, D.C.: Society for Technical Communication, 1986, pp. 238–42.

Smith, Frank R. "Use Rhetoric for Better Technical Proposals." *Technical Communication* 22, no. 3 (1975): 12–14.

Stevenson, Dwight W. "Toward a Rhetoric of Scientific and Technical Discourse." *The Technical Writing Teacher* 5, no. 1 (1977): 4–10.

Tebeaux, Elizabeth. "Let's Not Ruin Technical Writing, Too: A Comment on the Essays of Carolyn Miller and Elizabeth Harris." *College English* 41, no. 7 (1980): 822–29.

Thralls, Charlotte. "Editing of Professional Reports: A Rhetorical Modes Approach." In *Proceedings of the 27th International Technical Communication Conference.* Washington, D.C.: Society for Technical Communication, 1980, pp. W199–W203.

Walsh, Ruth M. "Rhetoric—Warp and Woof of All Exposition." *The ABCA Bulletin* 44, no. 2 (1981): 8–13.

Walzer, Arthur E. "Ethos, Technical Writing, and the Liberal Arts." *The Technical Writing Teacher* 8, no. 3 (1981): 50–53.

Wander, Philip C. "The Rhetoric of Science." *Western Speech Communication* 40, no. 1 (1976): 226–35.

Weimer, Walter B. "Science as a Rhetorical Transaction: Toward a Nonjustificational Conception of Rhetoric." *Philosophy and Rhetoric* 10, no. 1 (1977): 1–29.

Whitburn, Merrill D. "Personality in Scientific and Technical Writing." *Journal of Technical Writing and Communication* 6, no. 4 (1976): 299–306.

Winkler, Victoria M. "Creative Design and Rhetorical Inquiry: Report Writing Strategies." In *Proceedings of the 27th International Technical Communication Conference.* Washington, D.C.: Society for Technical Communication, 1980, pp. W89–W97.

———. "The Role of Models in Technical and Scientific Writing." In *New Essays in Technical and Scientific Communication: Research, Theory, Practice,* edited by Paul V. Anderson, R. John Brockmann, and Carolyn R. Miller. Farmingdale, N.Y.: Baywood Publishing Co., 1983, pp. 111–22.

2 Reading and Technical Writing

Nina Dansky Ziv
Merrill Lynch
New York, New York

In an article on designing a college-level professional writing course, Flower (1981) distinguishes between professional writing and "school" writing. The strategy of writing in college is to "state and elaborate" (Flower 1981, p. 37). On the other hand, writing as a professional entails developing a "communicative strategy." She defines a communicative strategy as a "self-conscious attempt on the part of the writer to get through to the reader—to communicate, not merely to express" (Flower 1981, p. 36). To make this strategy work, writers must transform, reorganize, and maybe even reconceptualize information and ideas to communicate them to the reader. Flower's idea on the need for the technical writer to communicate clearly with an audience is a theme that is echoed by many other practitioners. McCaskey (1973) writes that stimulating the reader's interest is the key to writing technical articles. Dulek (1980) argues that since many technical writers do not know their audiences, they should avoid making faulty assumptions about the reader and implement adaptive strategies such as motivating the reader by implying the benefits of reading a particular document. Whittaker (1980) and Van Duyn (1982) also urge the technical writer to consider the reader. Thus Van Duyn tells writers, as soon as they have a general idea of their subject to "begin your project by studying the prospective readers. Once you define your audience and zero in on their basic needs and preferences, take a closer look at your product and find out how its readers will use it" (Van Duyn 1982, p. 27). Roundy (1985) suggests that writers structure their documents according to the readers' needs. The writer must identify the requirements of the primary audience for a text and then set up the overall text to meet those requirements. A report can be structured deductively with conclusions and recommendations placed in the introduction or inductively with conclusions and recommendations at the end. Writers should also structure their paragraphs, sentences, and words for maximum efficiency.

The literature indicated that the relationship between the reader and writer of technical documents is a crucial one. Yet how is this relationship achieved? How does the writer tailor a text to a reader? The suggestions made by technical writers and technical writing teachers may be valid in particular situations; however, if these suggestions are to be applied universally, they must be based on theory and research. This essay will present an overview of the literature on reading as it relates to technical writing. Three major areas will be discussed: (1) theoretical models of reading and communication, (2) readability theory and research, and (3) research on reader response to technical writing.

Theoretical Models of Reading

Reading specialists have proposed various models of reading and communication. Some of these models have relevance to technical writing. The literature discussed in this section will concern reading and communication models that are applicable to technical writing.

Huckin (1983) describes three models of reading and then applies them to the reading of technical documents. He first discusses schema theory. Cognitive psychologists have postulated that on the basis of patterns of experience, the human mind constructs abstract concepts or schemata. These schemata are stored in long-term memory and guide the way a person perceives and remembers things. These schemata also influence the way a reader infers ideas from a text. When a writer and reader share a schema, the writer does not have to refer explicitly to all details of the schema; the reader will supply these missing details by inference. Thus, a single word or phrase can conjure up an entire set of images in the reader's mind. The process of schema-based inference helps readers to recall concepts better and gives them a means of filling in the missing links. This theory can apply to the communication between specialists with nonspecialists. For example, if engineers want to communicate a new concept to lay people, they can base their communication on analogies and metaphors that they share with lay people. Thus, common schemata can help communicate an idea to a reader.

The second theory is that of activated semantic contexts. Huckin states that generally a reader who is familiar with a subject can draw on many highly detailed schemata and thus make more sense of and comprehend a text better than a reader without such familiarity.

However, these schemata must be continuously in the mind of the reader during the ongoing process of comprehension. Studies suggest that semantic contexts are activated when the reader perceives them to be important. For example, explicitly stated material is better recalled when it is centrally important to a passage than when it is only marginally important.

The third theory that Huckin discusses is the "levels effect." This theory postulates that readers tend to process a text hierarchically. Thus, they pay more attention to information higher in the hierarchy and less attention to information lower in it.

Huckin suggests that these three theories have implications for technical writing. For example, the levels effect may have implications for how a text is structured; the important points of a text should be placed in headings, subheadings, and topic sentences. This placement will activate high-level schemata and thus make it easier for the reader to process the important information in a text. Based on the theories he describes, Huckin defines some guidelines for writers. These guidelines include stating the purpose of a document explicitly, making the topic of each section and paragraph visually prominent, and structuring the text according to the nature of the information to which the writer wants the reader to pay attention.

Other theories of reading also have implications for technical writing. One such theory is called the given-new contract. This theory, which has been described by Chafe (1970) and further developed and tested by Clark and Haviland (1977), states that there is an implicit agreement between writers and readers in which writers present "new" information to their readers by attaching it to "given," or previously presented, information. Thompson (1985, p. 207) writes that within the framework of the given-new contract, writers can require their readers to infer the connections between given and new information under the following conditions:

1. Appropriateness—The given information should be known and the new should be unknown.
2. Uniqueness—The given information should allow the reader to infer a unique antecedent. It cannot refer to more than one potential antecedent.
3. Computability—The reader should have the knowledge and skill to infer the correct antecedent.

De Beaugrande (1978) has applied the given-new contract to technical writing. He suggests that while both literary/artistic writing and technical writing contain a high concentration of information, technical writing is designed to be more efficient in terms of the flow of information from writer to reader. For this information to be rapidly comprehended, high priorities must be given to what the reader did not know before reading a particular text. Thus, De Beaugrande (1978, p. 9) writes, "The best text is not one in which the concentration of this 'new' information is the highest, but rather one which allows the most effective integration of the new information into the set of information already known to the reader, that is, the 'old' information."

Along with the models of the reading process already described, other communications models exist that specifically focus on accommodating the text to the reader's needs. For example, A. D. Van Nostrand and his colleagues developed the functional model of writing. This model is based on the "assumption that the product must be viewed in terms of the reader's need to understand and use that product" (Brostoff 1981, p. 66). Among the important aspects of the functional writing model is the need for writers to have an organizing idea and to understand the reader's frame of reference. Writers must also use the notion of forecasting, in which they indicate to the reader how the subject will be developed, and the notion of continuous forecasting, in which the writers reveal the direction or line of reasoning in an argument.

Wilkins (1977) posits a two-tiered communications model. The first tier (or level) is called the nuts-and-bolts level and concerns the form of the report. The second level is the communication level and concerns "factors relevant to the communication process in terms of receiver response" (Wilkins 1977, p. 36). These factors include the writer as the source of the message, the message itself, the channel for conveying the message, and the audience. The writer, states Wilkins, must not only have good communicative skills but also be knowledgeable about the subject and tailor the text to the needs of the audience. The message consists of two parts—the content or subject matter and the message treatment. The treatment involves how the content is to be arranged and ordered. Technical writing involves a more formalized treatment than do other forms of communication. Finally, the receiver of the message (or the reader) goes through three stages. The first stage is the attention stage, in which the reader decides whether to read the whole document or just to glance through it. The second stage is comprehension, in which the reader tries to understand what the writer has written. The final stage is the acceptance stage, in which the reader may have a cognitive response, an affective response, or an action response. The cognitive response indicates the degree to which the reader accepts the information in the message. The affective response indicates whether the reader considers the information desirable. If the reader accepts the information and considers it desirable, the reader may put the ideas in the message into practice and thus take overt action provoked by the message. Wilkins suggests that the technical writer be aware of this communication process to prepare an effective document.

The models of reading and communication described here provide a theoretical base for technical writers. Using these theories as guides, writers can practice their craft in a meaningful and effective way.

Readability and Technical Writing

Though reading and communication models provide a theoretical base, research is needed to prove that the theories are correct. One tool that reading specialists have used in their research is the readability formula. To understand the use of such formulas, it is necessary first to define readability. For Klare (1963, p. 1), readability encompasses three different aspects:

1. The legibility of either handwriting or typography.
2. The ease of reading due to either the interest-value or the pleasantness of writing.
3. The ease of understanding or comprehension due to the style of writing.

Selzer (1983) suggests that most researchers and readability advocates follow Klare's third definition. These researchers and advocates equate readability with comprehensibility. Selzer expands on Klare's definition and writes that "readability is simply the efficiency with which a text can be comprehended by a reader, as measured by reading time, amount recalled, questions answered, or some other quantifiable measure of a reader's ability to process a text" (Selzer 1983, p. 73).

Under the premise that it is possible to quantify comprehension and thereby to predict how easily a document will be read, researchers have used readability formulas. Such pioneers of readability research as Rudolf Flesch and Robert Gunning had enormous influence on educational textbooks, business texts, and technical texts. Flesch's (1948) formula was based on the average sentence length in words, the number of affixes, and the number of references to people. The basic formula for Flesch's Reading Ease Scale was the following:

$$\text{Reading ease} = 206.835 - 0.846 wl - 1.015 sl$$

Where wl = number of syllables per 100 words, and
sl = average number of words per sentence

Flesch proclaimed that this new "yardstick" would measure reading ease and human interest in a piece of writing. Gunning's (1952) popular FOG Index was based on word length and sentence length. In her review of literature on readability research, Van Rooy (1973) lists six different types of readability formulas. Along with the Flesch Reading Ease Scale, there is the Lorge Readability Index, the Dale-Chall Formula, the Spache Readability Formula, the Fry Readability Graph, and the McLaughlin SMOG Grading Scale. Clark (1975) discusses the Dale-Chall Formula and the Fry Readability Graph and writes that although as many as 289 factors have been proposed to affect the readability of prose, the two factors which have the greatest influence on comprehension are vocabulary load and sentence load.

The technical writing community widely uses readability formulas. Indeed, many writers have praised them and looked on these formulas as a panacea for the ills of technical writing. Barry (1980) computerized such formulas as the Dale-Chall Formula, FOG Index, and the Spache Readability Formula. By doing so, Barry claimed that he had made "a simple, automatic, scientific method to evaluate reading levels of text" (Barry 1980, p. 90). Vervalin (1980) describes the FOG Index in detail and states that using the formula will definitely help the writer to adapt the text to the reading level of a particular audience. MacDonald et al.'s (1982) Writer's Workbench Program for text analysis, which has been used widely in industry for analyzing technical documents, includes readability as one of the text analysis options. Carson (1979) points out that many technical writing educators have also accepted the premise of readability, that is, that better reading comprehension is achieved by short sentences and short words.

While readability formulas are regarded as a solution to the problem of accommodating texts to readers, there is a body of literature that calls these formulas into question. Indeed, some early readability advocates warned against using them as rules for writing texts. Such researchers as Lorge (1949), Dale and Chall (1948), and Fry (1969), agreed that writers should only use readability formulas after a passage has been written. Jeanne Chall (1958), a readability expert, wrote that more research was needed on the quantitative aspects of readability, which have so far been elusive to objective measurement (Chall 1958, p. 158). These elusive factors include "organization, logic, abstractness, and conceptual difficulty" (Chall 1958, p. 158).

Goodman and Bird (1984) studied intratext word frequency as a measure of readability in nontechnical texts. Most readability researchers who use word frequency as a criterion, assume that words are of equal difficulty regardless of where they occur, how they are related to cohesion, and what kind of contextual support is provided. Goodman and Bird found that there are powerful constraints on the wording of a text, and because of these constraints, the use of word frequency lists as a measure of readability and for the purpose of recreating texts "tampers with the very factors that may contribute both to the word frequency and text difficulty. There are good reasons why particular words occur in particular places in particular texts. . . . Tampering with the working of texts without understanding why words occur in texts may make texts less readable rather than more so" (Goodman and Bird 1984, p. 144). Thus, Goodman and Bird concluded that authors and editors should concentrate on relating the context of the text to an audience instead of on the readability score of a text.

Klare, who enthusiastically supported the use of readability as a measure of comprehension, reexamined his assumptions in a 1976 article on the subject (Klare 1976). He looked at thirty-six experimental studies on the effects of readability variables on reader comprehension and/or retention. He concluded that other factors can influence the reader's comprehension of a text. He cited motivation as one of these factors, stating that "motivation can sometimes override the effect of readability upon comprehension" (Klare 1976, p. 140). The time available for reading a text and reader preferences and interests also affect readability. Klare further remarked that many of the studies he examined had confounding variables or had attributed a higher readability score to a passage that had an entirely different content. Finally, reader competence was cited as a possible factor. Such aspects of reader competence as knowledge of the subject matter, reading skill level, and intellectual level of the reader could all influence readability scores.

Curran (1976) agreed with Klare that a reader's knowledge of the content of a text must be known when assessing readability. Summarizing the research presented at a conference on readability conducted by the Armed Forces, Curran reported that one problem discussed at the conference was "the tendency to talk about written materials as though they were all similar in structure or purpose" (Curran 1976, p. 283). Thus, Curran suggests a distinction between "operational" manuals, which tell people how to perform particular jobs, and training manuals, which help people to learn general information about jobs. Although a readability formula may be used on both types of documents, the readability of an operational manual would be best judged by task performance, while the readability of a training manual might be evaluated by such criteria as recall, recognition, or other appropriate learning measures. Curran, like many others in the field of readability, calls for more research on how writers can produce more effective texts for their readers.

Selzer (1983) echoes Curran's concern with the technical writer's audience. Thus, he writes that we must conduct research on readability as it relates to the real world. In particular, he feels that "we need to observe the effects of readability factors when the subject matter is technical and when the audiences are technically oriented" (Selzer 1983, p. 84).

The literature on readability indicates that although readability formulas are useful tools, they do not take into account several important factors that may influence how a reader comprehends a text. Such aspects of reading as reader interest, motivation, and the content of a text, may affect a readability score. Even the strongest proponents of readability formulas concede that more research must be done in this area. Indeed, as Selzer (1983) and Curran (1976) point out, the needs of the audience must become a paramount consideration in any future research on reading comprehension. Furthermore, it is important to note that readability formulas are only research tools and that researchers should not base their studies only on these tools but also on how various theories of reading can be applied to technical writing.

Reader Response to Technical Writing

Although the theories of reading described above and the readability formulas have been applied to technical writing, there has been little research on reader response to technical writing. Pinelli et al. (1984) conducted a reader preference survey of engineers and scientists at NASA's Langley Research Center and in three professional (technical) societies to determine the opinions of readers concerning the organization of technical reports. The results indicated that readers looked at certain parts of a report when deciding whether to read it. Thus, most of the respondents indicated that the components that they normally read when deciding whether to read a report were, in this order, the title page, abstract, summary, introduction, and conclusion. Although these results must be used with caution, this type of survey is useful because it indicates the reading habits of a typical technical writing audience.

Flower et al. (1983) also focus on structure in their research. They contend that most people read documents such as regulations, contracts, or manuals not just to learn information but also to do something. Thus, from a reader's point of view, good writing is writing that keeps the reader's goals and strategies in mind. The writer's job, therefore, is to structure information in a way that enables the reader to know how to act. Flower et al. designed a project to uncover some of the things readers need to process a functional document. They had readers give protocols on federal regulations. The readers were asked to paraphrase the meaning of these regulations as they read. Flower et al. found that readers were not breaking up sentences or substituting simpler words to understand the text, rather they were restructuring the information. They restructured the information by forming a story around the regulation or creating agents and actions that would explain the regulation. Based on their research, Flower et al. formulated the scenario principle that states that functional prose should be structured around a human agent performing actions in a particularized situation. If readers will be using a document for a particular purpose, for example, to perform a task, the writer should structure the document so that the reader's scenario is as efficient as possible. The researchers suggest that writers use revision strategies such as organizing a text around actions and not terms, organizing a text around a reader's questions, giving examples and cases, using headings with a human focus, and writing sentences with agents and actions in the subject and verb positions, respectively.

Along with structuring a text in a particular way, writers make certain rhetorical choices within a text that may influence a reader's comprehension. In an attempt to find the particular aspects of a text that affect comprehension, many researchers have studied how readers respond to texts in which there is a variation in the rhetorical choices made by the writer. Thus, Marshall and Glock (1978) manipulated clauses in sentences and the main ideas of paragraphs to see whether recall would be affected. They placed the main idea of a text either at the beginning or at the end of a passage and changed the position of a main clause in a sentence. They found that manipulation of the main clause and the main idea did affect the recall of the passages by community college students. Faigley and Witte (1983) conducted research along the same lines as Marshall and Glock did. They wanted to know whether the consistent assignment of a particular topic to the grammatical subject position of a sentence would affect what readers considered to be the topic of the passage. The participants in the study read passages and then gave protocols about the passages. The results of the study indicated that when the topic was consistently used as the subject of the sentence, readers were more easily able to pick out the topic of the passage. Faigley and Witte suggest that writers of texts keep the dominant subject matter as the grammatical subject of the sentence or in the main clause of the sentence. They also suggest that more research be done on how readers understand the topic of a given passage and how writers can signal readers about what information is important.

Selzer (1982) studied how certain cohesive elements such as the given/new contract, pronouns, synonyms, and topic sentences affect the readability of technical passages. He composed six alternative versions of technical paragraphs. Subjects were given cloze tests and a recall exercise on the paragraphs. The results indicated that violating the given-new contract, using pronouns instead of repeating nouns, and deleting topic sentences impeded the reader's comprehension.

Davis (1975) also manipulated texts, but for his subjects, he varied the materials in a different manner. Instead of varying the rhetorical aspects of the texts, he presented three different types of reading passages based on the description of a machine. One type of passage contained only drawings of the machine, a second type contained drawings plus a verbal description of the machine, and a third type contained only a verbal description. The subjects were given a version of the reading passage and then a comprehension test. The results of Davis's study indicated that "comprehension was higher when drawings were present than when they were absent. When drawings were present, the presence or absence of the verbal description of the machine and its parts made no difference in comprehension" (Davis 1975, p. 120).

Though the studies on reader response described here are an excellent beginning, more research clearly needs to be conducted that specifically focuses on reader response to technical writing. However, such research must not be conducted only in the classroom or laboratory; it must be conducted in the workplace, where technical writing is undertaken on a day-to-day basis and where many demands are made on the technical writer. McLean (1975) describes the demands made on writers in an industrial setting. These include the contractual and technical requirements and the particular pressures that writers may be under when producing a text.

To understand these demands, it is important to talk to writers in technical fields about the types of writing that they do and the problems that they encounter. Odell and Goswami (1982), for example, interviewed writers at their work sites and found that the writers at all levels are concerned with their audiences and try to tailor their writing to these audiences. Research in the workplace along with the continuation of what Marshall and Glock (1978) call "basic research," will help reading specialists to gain a better understanding of how technical writers can best convey their ideas to their readers.

Bibliography

Barry, A. G. "Computerized Readability Levels." *IEEE Transactions on Professional Communication* 23 (June 1980): 19-20.

Brostoff, A. "The Functional Writing Model in Technical Writing Courses." In *Courses, Components, and Exercises in Technical Communication,* edited by D. W. Stevenson. Urbana, Ill.: National Council of Teachers of English, 1981.

Carson, D. L. "Audience in Technical Writing: The Need for Greater Realism in Identifying the Fictive Reader." *The Technical Writing Teacher* 7 (1979): 8-11.

Chafe, W. L. *Meaning and the Structure of Language.* Chicago: University of Chicago Press, 1970.

Chall, J. S. *Readability: An Appraisal of Research and Application.* Columbus, Ohio: Ohio State University, 1958.

Clark, A. K. "Readability in Technical Writing—Principles and Procedures." *IEEE Transactions on Professional Communication* PC-18, no. 2 (1975): 6-70.

Clark, H. H., and S. E. Haviland. "Comprehension and the Given-New Contract." In *Discourse Production and Comprehension,* edited by R. O. Freedle. Norwood, N.J.: Ablex Publishing Co., 1977.

Curran, T. E. *Readability Research in the Navy.* Alexandria, Va.: Human Resources Research Organization Report, 1976.

Dale, E., and J. S. Chall. "A Formula for Predicting Readability." *Educational Research Bulletin* 27 (1948): 11-20, 37-54.

Davis, R. M. "Experimental Research in the Effectiveness of Technical Writing." In *The Teaching of Technical Writing,* edited by D. H. Cunningham and H. A. Estrin. Urbana, Ill.: National Council of Teachers of English, 1975.

De Beaugrande, R. A. "Communication in Technical Writing." *Journal of Technical Writing and Communication* 8 (1978): 5-15.

Dulek, R. "Writing to Unidentified Readers." *IEEE Transactions on Professional Communication* PC-23, no. 3 (1980): 125-27.

Faigley, L., and S. P. Witte. "Topical Focus in Technical Writing." In *New Essays in Technical and Scientific Communication: Research, Theory, Practice,* Baywood's Technical Communication Series: Vol. 2, edited by Paul V. Anderson, R. John Brockmann, and Carolyn R. Miller. Farmingdale, N.Y.: Baywood Publishing Co., 1983.

Flesch, R. A. "A New Readability Yardstick." *Journal of Applied Psychology* 32 (1948): 221-33.

Flower, L. "Communication Strategy in Professional Writing: Teaching a Rhetorical Case." In *Courses, Components, and Exercises in Technical*

Communication, edited by D. W. Stevenson. Urbana, Ill.: National Council of Teachers of English, 1981.

Flower, L., J. R. Hayes, and H. Swartz. "Revising Functional Documents: The Scenario Principle." In *New Essays in Technical and Scientific Communication: Research, Theory, Practice,* Baywood's Technical Communications Series: Vol. 2, edited by Paul V. Anderson, R. John Brockmann, and Carolyn R. Miller. Farmingdale, N.Y.: Baywood Publishing Co., 1983.

Fry, E. B. "The Readability Graph Validated at Primary Levels." *The Readability Teacher* 22 (1969): 534–38, 750.

Goodman, K. S., and L. B. Bird. "On the Wording of Texts: A Study of Intratext Word Frequency." *Research in the Teaching of English* 18 (May 1984): 119–45.

Gunning, R. *The Technique of Clear Writing.* New York: McGraw-Hill, 1952.

Huckin, T. N. "A Cognitive Approach to Readability." In *New Essays in Technical and Scientific Communication: Research, Theory, Practice,* Baywood's Technical Communications Series: Vol. 2, edited by Paul V. Anderson, R. John Brockmann, and Carolyn R. Miller. Farmingdale, N.Y.: Baywood Publishing Co., 1983.

Klare, G. R. *The Measurement of Readability.* Ames, Iowa: Iowa State University Press, 1963.

———. "A Second Look at the Validity of Readability Formulas." *Journal of Reading Behavior* 8 (1976): 129–52.

Lorge, I. D. "Readability Formulae—An Evaluation." *Elementary English* 6 (1949): 86–95.

MacDonald, N. H., L. T. Frase, P. S. Gingrich, and S. A. Keenan. "The Writer's Workbench: Computer Aids for Text Analysis." *IEEE Transactions on Communications* COM-30, no. 1 (1982): 105–10.

Marshall, N., and M. D. Glock. "Comprehension of Connected Discourse: A Study into the Relationship Between the Structure of Text and Information Recalled." *Reading Research Quarterly* 14 (1978): 10–56.

McCaskey, D. S. "Technical Writing: The Importance of Reader Interest." *Journal of Technical Writing and Communication* 3 (1973): 217–20.

McLean, D. M. "The Demands of Industry on the Technical Writer." In *The Teaching of Technical Writing,* edited by D. H. Cunningham and H. A. Estrin. Urbana, Ill.: National Council of Teachers of English, 1975.

Odell, L., and D. Goswami. "Writing in a Non-Academic Setting." *Research in the Teaching of English* 16 (October 1982): 201–23.

Pinelli, T. E., V. M. Cordle, and R. F. Vondran. "The Function of Report Components in the Screening and Reading of Technical Reports." *Journal of Technical Writing and Communication* 14 (1984): 87–93.

Roundy, Nancy. "Structuring Effective Technical Reports." *Technical Communication* 32 (1985): 26–29.

Selzer, J. "Another Look at Paragraphs in Technical Writing." *Journal of Technical Writing and Communication* 10 (1980): 293–301.

———. "Certain Cohesion Elements and the Readability of Technical Writing." *Journal of Technical Writing and Communication* 12 (1982): 285–98.

———. "What Constitutes a 'Readable' Technical Style?" In *New Essays in Technical and Scientific Communication: Research, Theory, Practice*, Baywood's Technical Communications Series: Vol. 2, edited by Paul V. Anderson, R. John Brockmann, and Carolyn R. Miller. Farmingdale, N.Y.: Baywood Publishing Co., 1983.

Thompson, I. "The Given/New Contract and Cohesion: Some Suggestions for Classroom Practice." *Journal of Technical Writing and Communication* 15 (1985): 205–14.

Van Duyn, J. *The DP Professional's Guide to Writing Effective Technical Communications*. New York: John Wiley, 1982.

Van Rooy, L. *Readability Studies and the Writer of Instructional Materials*. Carbondale, Ill.: Career Development for Children Project, 1973.

Vervalin, C. H. "Checked Your FOG Index Lately?" *IEEE Transactions on Professional Communication* 2 (June 1980): 87–89.

Whittaker, D. A. "Write for Your Reader." *IEEE Transactions on Professional Communication* PC-23, no. 4 (1980): 170–73.

Wilkins, K. A. "Technical Writing: Effective Communication." *Journal of Technical Writing and Communication* 7 (1977): 35–43.

3 Ethics and Technical Communication

Stephen Doheny-Farina
Clarkson University

Technical communication ethics concerns the relationship between the values held by technical communicators and their perceptions of the demands imposed on them from without—from the environments within which they work. An ethical dilemma may arise from this relationship when the perceived demands of work require communicators to act in ways that conflict with their values. A review of the relevant literature of the past 25 years shows that technical communicators do indeed face such conflicts on the job. In addition, this review reveals that some technical communicators hold divergent views on just what these conflicts mean and how they should be handled. Thus, this chapter (1) describes the major ethical issues that face practicing technical communicators, (2) offers some theoretical explanations of ethical problems in scientific and technical discourse, (3) discusses varying perspectives on the ethics of communicating scientific and technical information through the mass media, and (4) examines the teaching of ethics in technical writing courses.

Technical Communication Ethics in Practice

In "Responsibilities of Writers and Editors to Readers," J. C. Young (1961) described his view of the proper environment for ethical technical writers and editors. This environment provides the necessary "freedoms" from undue restrictions. The only constraints writers and editors should feel are those imposed by their responsibilities to their readers (Young 1961, p. 15):

> Those responsibilities are easily definable. They involve the communication of a message, of whatever type, to the reader—correctly, clearly, and concisely, and with a certain grace of style, if that is possible.

In a free environment, the job of the writer and editor is simple: provide your readers with appropriate, readable, and "correct" information.

If we compare Young's view to the actual practices of working technical writers and editors, we are faced with a number of significant questions. Do technical writers and editors typically work in such free environments? Do they ever feel pressure to express information that is not correct? For that matter, do they always know what the "correct" information is? Do they ever deceive their readers? If so, is this deception a serious problem for the writer?

In a surprisingly frank article, "Truth and Honesty in Science," William Winslade (1983) argues that expressing the truth is not always the right thing for a communicator to do. To illustrate his point, he (Winslade 1983, p. 62) suggests that fully accurate and truthful scientific case studies (which are meant to describe and explain significant scientific problems through the analysis of particular instances of those problems) may be less informative than ones that are deceptive:

> Case studies, like all scientific presentations, involve selection of material for purposes of clarity and simplicity at the expense of completeness. If the whole truth and nothing but the truth is our goal, then all science—not just case studies—necessarily falls short of that standard. But if we recognize that clarity and coherence require selectivity—e.g. to illustrate a particular theoretical point—then the goal is to illuminate that point, not to switch on a blinding floodlight. If we are willing to accept fragmentary truths, then the distorted, disguised, and even fictional case study can cast beams of light into the darkened shadows of our knowledge.

For Winslade, then, the ends of communication can justify the means. Deceptive writing for a good purpose is ethical behavior.

Regardless of the ends, communicating deceptive information is clearly an issue that faces many scientific and technical communicators. Lee Shimberg (1977), in "President's Plans—1977–78," a presidential address to the Society for Technical Communication (STC), emphasizes that technical communicators can be deceptive in ways that are sometimes difficult to perceive. Shimberg (1977, p. 31) suggests that many are unaware of this problem:

> Most of us do not, in fact, have any demands placed on us to tell outright lies, but shading the truth or reporting mostly favorable results or attributes happens often enough to be of concern to all of us who are aware of it.

In a later article, "Ethics and Rhetoric in Technical Writing," Shimberg (1978) provides examples of typical deceptive practices in technical communication. He categorizes four types of deception: (1) imprecision and ambiguity, (2) understating the negative, (3) overstating the positive, and (4) semanticism. Unfortunately, Shimberg does not see a clear course of action for communicators who face ethical conflicts with their employers. For example, when faced with writing something that one judges to be unethical, the writer may try to go through the proper channels to resolve the conflict (Shimberg 1978, p. 18):

> You donate your problem to your manager. The problem remains partly yours, however, because your manager will either act or not act. If he does act, his action may or may not satisfy your ethical needs; if he does not act, the ethical problem has just been compounded.

Shimberg concludes by suggesting that most employers wish to foster honest communication.

Nonetheless, in response to growing realizations that serious ethical issues are facing technical communicators, a 1980 issue of *Technical Communication* focused on professional ethics. These articles distinguish three differing ethical perspectives: (1) professional, (2) moral, and (3) legal. The following reviews these and other ethical perspectives.

The Professional Perspective

In the first of the *Technical Communication* articles, "STC and the Professional Ethic," Frank Radez (1980) deemphasizes moral and legal concerns and says that the STC should develop a code that will help guide professional behavior. He argues that STC should not concern itself with the laws of God nor with the laws of man. The code that Radez (1980, p. 5) calls for should answer the question, "What is the code by which a technical communicator must act to earn the respect of his peers as a professional?"

Radez (1980) believes that such a document should help technical communicators "judge the correctness or propriety of their own actions when faced with pressures on the job." Written especially for neophytes, the code (Radez 1980, pp. 6–7) would determine:

   a) When they deserve credits.
   b) How to handle documents written by committee.
   c) How to handle publishing outside the corporation.
   d) How to conduct themselves with media editors, publishers, and sales persons.
   e) How to conduct themselves with corporation writers, engineers, managers, and lawyers.
   f) The limits of their responsibility.

In an earlier article, "For the Technical Communicator: Pursuing Professional Identity and Maturity," Eugene Cogan (1974) attempts to define the concept of "professional." Cogan (1974, p. 2) defines a profession as an occupation in which certain types of services are provided:

- These services are useful.
- They are provided within a set of ethical bounds and rules that are defined by the group.
- Only a particular set of specifically defined services are provided.

Cogan (1974, p. 2) lists the attributes of the individual. A professional

- Is well paid.
- Is highly skilled in a rare capability.
- Has credentials of some sort.
- Has special title (such as Professor).
- Is regulated and/or licensed by government bodies.
- Has high status.

Finally, Cogan (1974, p. 2) states that the professional group

- Provides a specialized, standardized definition of the occupation.
- Establishes a formal body, invariably called an Association or Society.
- Sponsors technical journals and other technical literature.
- Foments and monitors training and educational programs.
- Develops mechanisms for sharing experiences, finding employment, setting fees or salaries, and so on.

In 1978, the STC adopted a brief one-page code of behavior that emphasized general principles of professionalism. The heart of this "Code for Communicators" was a list of commitments:

My commitment to professional excellence and ethical behavior means that I will

- Use language and visuals with precision.
- Prefer simple, direct expression of ideas.
- Satisfy the audience's need for information, not my own need for self-expression.
- Hold myself responsible for how well my audience understands my message.
- Respect the work of colleagues, knowing that seldom is only one communications solution right and all others wrong.
- Strive continually to improve my professional competence.
- Promote a climate that encourages the exercise of professional judgment and that attracts talented individuals to careers in technical communication.

In the introduction to the 1980 *Technical Communication* issue on ethics, Mary M. Schaefer (1980, p. 4) summarized widespread dissatisfaction with this code:

> The code deals largely with steps, somewhat limited, toward achieving professional competence. It offers little in the way of guidance or standards of conduct for technical communicators faced with ethical problems in the exercise of their profession. This lack has caused concern among members of the Society who feel that there is a definite need to have a code that will provide such guidance.

By 1985, members of the STC Ethics Committee proposed a more detailed code to replace this brief list of professional commitments. The model for this proposal was a 1958 code ("Code of Ethics") that had been adopted by the Society of Technical Writers and Editors (STWE), a forerunner of the STC. The STWE code listed twenty-seven statements that defined the communicators' "professional life," "relations with the public," and "relations with clients and employers." This detailed code not only committed communicators to professional behavior but also defined some of the legal parameters within which they should work. For example, the communicator

> will promptly disclose to his client or employer any interest in a business which may compete with or affect the business of his client or employer. He will not allow an interest in any business to affect his decision regarding work for which he is employed, or which he may be called upon to perform.*

The Moral Perspective

In the second of three 1980 *Technical Communication* articles, "Ethics and the Technical Communicator," Harley Sachs (1980) argues that technical communicators cannot separate moral judgment from a consideration of professional (or legal) ethics. However, he does not attempt to define a set of moral standards that all must follow. Instead, Sachs (1980, p. 7) emphasizes the seeming relativity of ethical behavior:

> What is ethical for one may seem unethical for another. Owners, managers, employees, colleagues, and the public each view products from a different point of view, and technical communications play a different role for each.

This relativity makes it difficult to define unethical behavior or to pinpoint the source of unethical behavior: "The victims of commu-

---

* As of the time of the printing of this book, the code proposed in 1985 had not been adopted by STC.

nication failures are easy to find. Those responsible are not, for each denies responsibility" (Sachs 1980, p. 7).

Although he does not explore the issue in any depth, Sachs clearly equates ethics with a morality that conflicts with some modern business practices. He implies that these practices deceive the consumer. "Ethics and profit may be in direct conflict. Ethics and self-interest also clash. Whom are you responsible to, the employer or the public? To both?" (Sachs 1980, p. 7).

Finally, Sachs provides nine cases that describe differing ethical dilemmas. These cases may be useful for teachers who wish to incorporate the study of ethics into their technical communication classes.

In "Honesty in Technical Communication," Louis Perica (1972) argues that the morality of the technical communicator is very important. Perica (1972, p. 6) calls for technical communicators that respect the truth:

> If the sense of values does not include a respect for truth and the respect for the rights of others, it will be easy for the individual to do whatever is propitious.

Perica describes a number of real-life cases that illustrate the ways that technical communicators can deceive audiences by suppressing information through the manipulation of language, graphics, and statistics.

The key issue that Perica (1972, p. 6) raises is the potential conflicts between a writer's morality and the demands put on the writer by the organization for which the writer works:

> A person with the sense of values that does respect truth may be hindered by the goals of the organization for which he works.... Can a technical communicator afford a conscience? Can he reconcile his ethics with the profit motive that frequently ignores moral imperatives?... Sooner or later the conscientious technical communicator will come up against a wall of corporate indifference to private moral values.

What can technical communicators do when their perspectives on truth conflict with their organizations' perspectives on effective communication? Perica proposes three alternative courses of action that paint a bleak picture for the communicator caught in such a conflict. According to Perica (1972, p. 6), the communicator can

1) Discipline himself to be indifferent (the easy way out).
2) Argue for change. If this adversely affects corporate earnings it could label him unrealistic or idealistic. This in turn could hamper his career or compel him to quit if he is too insistent.
3) Remain silent. This would cause loss of enjoyment of work and might cause loss of self-respect.

4) Move to another company with his industry. Very likely he would be exchanging one set of moral misgivings for another.

In conclusion, Perica tries to balance this bleak outlook by asserting that most corporations must be honest to achieve long-term prosperity.

The Legal Perspective

In "Technical Communicators and Moral Ethics," the third and final piece in the 1980 *Technical Communication* issue on ethics, Shimberg (1980) illustrates the three ethical perspectives (professional, legal, and moral) with real-life cases of each. Ultimately, Shimberg (1980, p. 11) suggests that the legal perspective is the most useful for technical communicators:

> I therefore feel that legal constraints imposed on technical communicators are infinitely simpler to deal with than are moral constraints. Legal restraints are rather clearly defined, whereas moral constraints result from (the degrees of) fine tuning of one's own judgment and conscience.

Not only are the legal restraints clearly defined, but the consequences of violating those restraints may be far more dramatic than violations to moral or professional constraints. For this reason, technical communicators should have a clear understanding of the ways that liability laws can affect the way they do their jobs.

A comprehensive overview of the legal issues that face technical communicators is provided by L. P. Driskill (1981) in "Trends in Liability Affecting Technical Writers." Driskill alerts technical writers to the dangers of product liability litigation.

Driskill describes two ways that a technical writer can become involved in such a lawsuit. First, the documentation for a product can serve as evidence in a trial. Any document written during the life cycle of a product can be used to show that a product was or was not defectively designed. Therefore, technical writers who work on any "pre-sale or post-sale documents ... can be drawn into the arena of product liability litigation" (Driskill 1981, pp. 597–98).

Secondly, technical writers are liable for the accuracy and clarity of the written statements that warn against the misuse of a product. The number of lawsuits based on a "failure to warn" has risen dramatically in recent years. Some of these cases have been brought against technical writers, or as in one case, against " 'the one who chose the words used' " (Driskill 1981, p. 599).

After citing numerous chilling examples of technical writers' potential liabilities, Driskill describes some useful liability prevention programs, listing the key elements of such programs. Finally, Driskill urges writers and publication managers to learn the legal regulations concerning product liability because the legal system is clearly holding writers liable for the words they write.

Such is also the advice of T. R. Girill (1985) in "Technical Communication and Law," Part 2. Girill reasons that technical writers have become involved in liability suits because technical documentation has increasingly become a major part of the products themselves: "Defects in the prose then become defects in the product, and hence they support liability claims just as would any manufacturing fault." Girill concludes by describing the other audience, the jury. When a fault in the documentation is examined in court, it will most likely be judged by "a jury of 'ordinary' readers—not engineers or editors" (Girill 1985, p. 37).

Since technical writers are open to such scrutiny, there is a need to develop ways for a jury to judge the adequacy of documentation. David Lenfest (1984) proposes general criteria for judging software documentation in "On Language, Liability, and Documentation." Lenfest describes (1) strategic errors (e.g., a reader has to skip sections to hunt for information), (2) structural errors (e.g., a reader has trouble following difficult preliminaries), (3) tactical errors (e.g., a reader has difficulty relating a figure to the appropriate text), and (4) errors in linearity (e.g., a reader has to change directions while reading). He points out that these errors usually occur because manufacturers pay little attention to documentation after their products are sold. In conclusion, Lenfest echoes Driskill by urging writers to become aware of how their words may be judged in a court of law.

Others see the need for expert communicators to influence the ways that warnings are written and judged. In "Warnings in the Workplace: The Need for a Synthesis of Law and Communication Theory," Victor E. Schwartz and Russell W. Driver (1983, p. 40) point out that professional communicators have had little effect on liability issues:

> The legal rules regarding warnings presently are being formulated and applied on a case-by-case basis in the emotional context of personal injury litigation. The complex and difficult issues relating to the adequacy of warnings generally have been decided by lay juries without either the benefit of testimony of those expert in the communication and dissemination of information or of reasonable judicial guidelines.

Schwartz and Driver explain that there is an urgent need to define better the limits of warning liability. They argue that communication theory offers the principles that can define and limit warning liability, providing more informed guidelines to the courts.

Because technical writers cannot always predict how their work will be judged in court, Dennis Hollow's (1979) article, "Responsibility— A Keynote for Ethics in Technical Communications," suggests that writers be included in a manufacturers' liability insurance coverage. So that this insurance need not be used, Hollow urges technical writers carefully to check all the facts in their documentation, taking special care to verify the (so-called) facts that cover up negative information. In the event that erroneous data slip through and are included in published documentation, however, Hollow proposes that writers have ready a "crisis response mechanism" designed to undo the error. Quick response to such incidents may lessen their impacts and keep writers (and other colleagues) out of court.

Finally, a collection of articles edited by Stephen Doheny-Farina (1987) that focuses in part on warnings, product liability, and other legal and ethical issues in technical communication has appeared in the *IEEE Transactions on Professional Communication.*

Other Perspectives

Rejecting the notion that technical communication ethics involves professional, legal, and moral concerns, Wicclair and Farkas (1980) choose to define ethics from a narrower perspective. In the article, "Ethical Reasoning in Technical Communication: A Practical Framework," the authors distinguish an ethical perspective from (1) self-interest, (2) legal, and (3) religious perspectives. A technical writer who acts on the basis of any of these three perspectives can still commit unethical acts (e.g., unethical actions are not necessarily illegal; likewise, not all legal acts are necessarily ethical).

Questions of ethics, then, must be decided by employing ethical principles, not self-interest, moral, or legal principles. The authors posit three types of ethical principles: (1) goal based, (2) duty based, and (3) rights based. Goal-based principles are utilitarian; that is, they support actions that offer the greatest good for the greatest number of people. Duty-based principles stipulate that some actions are wrong, regardless of their consequences, just for what they are. Rights-based principles stipulate that some actions are ethical because circumstances obligate those actions.

When faced with a potential ethical dilemma, the technical writer must answer two questions: (1) Does the situation involve any goals, duties, or rights? (2) Am I confusing self-interest, legal, or religious perspectives with the ethical perspectives? If an action does not violate the goals, duties, and rights principles, then it is an ethical action (even if that action violates other principles). The authors contend that most problematic situations involving technical writers are not purely ethical. To illustrate this point, the authors provide several real-life cases, one of which describes a writer who has to decide between an ethical decision and a self-interest decision.

Although this clarification of perspectives is theoretically useful, it does little to help the writer facing a dilemma that involves a complex mixture of legal, moral, and/or ethical issues. Robert Hays (1984) offers writers some practical suggestions for avoiding such problematic situations in "Political Realities in Reader/Situation Analysis."

Hays does not claim "to preach morals, propose ethical codes, or give legal advice." Instead, he describes a number of different types of "political situations" and explains ways to approach "political problems" (Hays 1984, p. 16). His list of political situations describes relationships between writers and others, such as "political stresses between writer and higher management" and "conflicts with readers diagonally above the writer."

So that a writer can anticipate political problems, Hays (1984, pp. 18–19) explains the following practical guidelines:

- Study the reporting situation from its political angles;
- Stay alert to people-pressure;
- Study the likely results, both desired and undesired;
- Decide where loyalty really lies;
- Consider some specific techniques.

Hays also suggests that teachers should incorporate guidelines such as these in technical communication classes. He notes, however, one major obstacle: technical writing texts ignore the need for writers to consider the "political" realities of their messages.

In summary, most of the works cited thus far depict a variety of ethical issues that technical communicators can encounter on the job. Some of the authors describe the dangerous consequences of unethical behavior. Some authors suggest certain responses to these difficult situations—responses such as negotiating with colleagues and supervisors, "blowing the whistle" on colleagues and superiors, quitting, or avoiding potentially difficult situations before they arise. Such advice was attacked, however, in an article by Philip Rubens (1981), "Reinventing the Wheel?: Ethics for Technical Communicators."

Specifically responding to the 1980 *Technical Communication* issue that focused on ethics, Rubens (1981, p. 330) contends that

It is certainly a simplistic solution to say that one can resign rather than engage in an unethical communication activity; it is equally simplistic to think that writers can use whistle-blowing as a tool to force management into ethical behaviors.

Rubens argues that we need to develop a more complex understanding of the sources of unethical communication, and he calls for research into these sources.

Technical Communication Ethics in Theory

One of the most significant issues that Rubens (1981) discusses is the relationship of ethics to the tradition of objectivity in scientific and technical discourse. Traditionally, technical and scientific communicators have valued objectivity as highly as they value clarity of expression. Communication that is not objective, in fact, cannot be clear and effective. Barbara G. Cox and Charles G. Roland (1973) provide a fitting example of this point of view in "How Rhetoric Confuses Scientific Issues."

Cox and Roland (1973, p. 140) find "rhetoric"—their term for nonobjective expression—rampant in medical articles, and they do not like it:

> Anyone who is convinced that only facts should persuade must, logically, condemn such rhetoric in the scientific literature. Realistically, of course, rhetoric cannot be eliminated entirely. But its use can be constricted significantly, and both readers and writers should be on guard against this violation of scientific principles.

Cox and Roland (1973, p. 142) call for authors and journal editors to be alert to emotive, rhetorical language that "can obscure or distort meaning. And these effects are antithetical to the journal editor's ethos to enhance objective communication." Objectivity in reporting, conclude the authors, is the "very foundation" of science.

Rubens (1981, p. 334) agrees that scientific and technical writers have attempted to "ignore the author's identity, voice, or stance" and "devalue the individual as both writer and reader." That is, the traditional point of view rejects the fact that writers and readers "bring their own perceptions to bear on a text." Rubens (1981, p. 335) argues that a devaluation of the individual writer's voice devalues "the presence of a strong personal element in referential prose (technical writing) which allows a sense of individual valuation and responsibility." When the individual writer must deny his or her own identity, voice, and stance, that writer loses a sense of responsibility for what is written.

This loss of responsibility enables a writer to do whatever is propitious regardless of ethical concerns.

In an earlier article, "Technology as a Form of Consciousness: A Study of Contemporary Ethos," Carolyn R. Miller (1978, p. 235) traces the source of this loss of responsibility to the nature of our technological society:

> What features of discourse come to seem "ethical" or persuasive because of the particular cast of mind we acquire from living in a highly technological culture?... impersonality, nonresponsibility, turgidity, narrow-mindedness.

In a technological culture, according to Miller, objective, nonresponsible discourse becomes ethical discourse. (See Cox and Roland [1973]).

Some theorists call for a very different definition of ethical discourse in a technological culture. In "Eloquence in a Technological Society," Stephen M. Halloran (1978, p. 227) argues that the ideal of eloquent discourse

> implies that a person is in a fundamental way what he says and writes. It would oblige people to take responsibility for their words and restore the connection between ethos and ethics.

An ideal approach to ethical communication is constructed by George Yoos (1979) in "A Revision of the Concept of Ethical Appeal." The ideal ethical appeal is one in which a writer or speaker makes his or her agenda and methods clear to the audience—even if that agenda is to persuade the audience to accept beliefs that the audience heretofore has not accepted. The ideal ethical appeal "does not lend itself to masking and dissembling. It is its nature to expose itself to critical appraisal" (Yoos 1979, p. 56). Such communication allows the audience to understand not only what is being communicated but also the author's true intentions in making that communication. "In short, a genuinely ethical appeal in rhetoric is an appeal to an audience to determine for itself whether or not the appeal should be accepted or rejected" (Yoos 1979, p. 58).

For a survey of conceptions of ethos and ethics from classical to modern rhetorical theorists, see Nan Johnson's (1984) "Ethos and the Aims of Rhetoric."

In recent years, there has been a steady stream of theorists, teachers, and practitioners who have argued for the recognition and cultivation of the technical communicator's persona. For theoretical and historical perspectives on objectivity in scientific and technical writing, see "The Personae of Scientific Discourse" by Paul N. Campbell (1975), "What's Technical About Technical Writing?" by David Dobrin (1983), "The

Ethos of Science and the Ethos of Technology" by Carolyn R. Miller (1980), and "Toward an Ethos for Technical Communication" by Gregory Clark and Jeffrey Denham (1985).

A brief but useful summary of the shifting theoretical perspective on authorial voice in scientific and technical discourse is provided by Ben Barton and Marthalee Barton (1981) in "Ethos, Persona, and Role Confusion in Engineering: Toward a Pedagogy for Technical Discourse." Barton and Barton (1981, p. 130) summarize the "paradigmatic shift" in technical communication "away from a Formalist model with its emphasis on the text and its attendant de-emphasis of the roles of the emitter and receiver in communication" and toward a theory of communication in which

> knowledge is created, and not found in an objective reality. Concomitantly, there has been a discrediting of the notion of the absence of an authorial voice in technical discourse.

The authors describe two views of technical communication ethos that have evolved with this paradigmatic shift. One view proposes that "the long-suppressed authorial personality should now be encouraged to emerge." A second view claims that the supposed absence of authorial voice is actually a persona—"a persona conveying notions of objectivity, impersonality, and detachment—in other words, a persona denying persona" (Barton and Barton 1981, p. 130).

Arguments specifically devoted to encouraging authorial persona in technical discourse have been made by Lee B. Woods (1972) in "Proposals Are People, Too," W. Earl Britton (1973) in "Personality in Scientific Writing," Merrill Whitburn (1976) in "Personality in Scientific and Technical Writing," Michael J. Marcuse (1980) in "Ethos in Technical Discourse: The Current State of the Question," Jacques G. Richardson (1980) in "Science and Technology as Integral Parts of Our Culture: Interdisciplinary Responsibilities of the Scientific Communicator," Jack Griffin (1980) in "When Do Rhetorical Choices Become Ethical Choices?", Arthur Walzer (1981) in "Ethos, Technical Writing and the Liberal Arts," Dorothy M. Guinn (1983) in "Ethos in Technical Discourse," Eve W. Stoddard (1984) in "The Role of Ethos in the Theory of Technical Writing," and David Bradford (1984) in "The Persona in Microcomputer Documentation."

The call for an infusion of authorial identity and responsibility in technical communication is not limited to the work of communicators writing in corporate settings. Others in recent years have emphasized the need for responsible, ethical scientific and technical communication through the mass media.

Mass Media and Technical Communication Ethics

Most considerations of ethics in scientific and technical communication concern writers in corporate settings writing for managers, engineers, scientists, technicians, and product users. Although most writers work in this arena, some will play a role outside of specific corporate settings. Some technical communicators will write for the general public, explaining scientific discoveries, new technologies, and new technological programs. The significance of this role lies in the fact that members of the general citizenry need to make informed decisions on which technologies and technological programs to support and which to vote down. "To be able to express a valid opinion about such issues, the layman must rely upon competent and unbiased people for information," says Richard W. Schmelzer (1981, p. 217) in "New Responsibilities for the Technical Writer." Therein lies an ethical responsibility to communicate this information effectively. In "Responsible Science Reporting in a Technological Age," John P. Kowal (1980, p. 307) states

> The future growth, direction, and concerns of science and technology will, more and more, become areas of public policy decided by nontechnological specialists. . . . [W]e will need complete, accurate, and unbiased information.

To view a specific application of this national need, see Nancy Condit's (1984) article, "Ethical Responsibilities of Medical Writers to the Lay Press: Editorial Comment in News Reporting." Condit (1984, p. 79) contends that it is the technical writer's responsibility to present accurate, complete, balanced, and nonemotional information "so that the lay reader has the same opportunity to make a decision based on the facts that the professional reader [has]."

A slight variation on this issue is proposed by Stephen M. Halloran (1971) in "Classical Rhetoric for the Engineering Student." Halloran emphasizes the ethical responsibility of engineers, not technical writers, to communicate the implications of new technologies clearly and accurately to the general public. Thus, Halloran proposes that college engineering curricula include rhetorical studies so that engineers will be better able to communicate to nonexpert audiences.

Whether the communicator is a scientist, engineer, technical writer, or journalist, the ethical imperative is to report accurate information to the public. Unfortunately, accurate reporting is not always achieved. Sometimes the source of inaccuracies is the scientist or engineer involved; sometimes the source is the technical writer or journalist. For a look at both sides of this issue, see "Garbage Under Glass: What

Are Scientists Dishing Out?" by Robert C. Cowen (1980) and "How Public Is Scientific Knowledge?" by Charles G. Roland (1971). In addition, a valuable analysis of the types of faulty scientific and technological reporting is provided by Sharon Dunwoody (1982) in "A Question of Accuracy."

Teaching Ethics in Scientific and Technical Communication Courses

Regardless of the concerns about ethical communication practices that have been expressed over the last twenty-five years, very little attention has been given to methods of teaching ethics in technical communication classes. In fact, the major argument recently debated has not focused on the ways to teach ethics in technical communication courses, but instead on whether it should be taught at all.

Arguing against the inclusion of ethics in technical communication courses is Elizabeth Tebeaux (1980) in "Let's Not Ruin Technical Writing Too!" Tebeaux does not believe that teachers should attempt to develop students' ethical sensibilities. Instead, teachers should narrow their focus to the teaching of communication skills.

In "The Basic Technical Writing Course: Skills *and* Ethics?" William E. Evans (1981) agrees with Tebeaux. Evans argues that technical communication teachers should teach skills. He warns that teachers should not assume that they can teach, in a writing course, the ethics of technology. According to Evans (1981, p. 445), that type of ethical instruction should be left to faculty in other disciplines:

> English teachers, well-intentioned though they are, may not have sufficient information to make ethical judgments on questions of ethics in technical areas.

Evans does add that writing teachers should urge students to be honest in all aspects of their writing.

Others suggest that courses focusing on writing in the working world should include considerations of ethics. For a theoretical examination of the relationship between writing and ethics instruction, see "Teaching Writing and Teaching Virtue" by Eugene Garver (1985). Garver (1985, p. 53) notes the exclusion of moral teaching in modern writing courses: "Any attempt to make morality the subject of discussion is seen as the imposition of a set of values on someone else." Teachers that avoid moral or ethical concerns in such courses assume that the courses become value free and morally neutral. Assumptions such as these, argues Garver (1985, p. 53), are just "modern, favorable sounding ways of saying amoral." Garver (1985, p. 68) urges writing instructors to teach prudent reasoning:

> ... the ability required to take general values, desires, and ideas and combine them with the facts and demands of some particular situation to arrive at a practical conclusion, a policy, an advocated action.

For a detailed course outline that includes instruction in ethics, see "How to Teach Ethics in a Basic Business Communication Class—Committee Report of the 1983 Teaching Methodology and Concepts Committee, Subcommittee 1" by Golen et al. (1985). The authors (1) provide an introduction to some fundamental ethical principles, (2) provide a course plan, and (3) suggest several class activities and films that illustrate ethical issues. In addition, the authors provide a brief annotated bibliography of related sources concerning business communication ethics.

A business communication course, say the authors, should develop each student's awareness of communication ethics "and provide the student with effective means to make decisions which reflect high ethical standards" (Golen et al. 1985, p. 78).

Several teachers and technical communicators have pointed out specific practices that can be taught that will enforce certain sometimes overlooked ethical standards. Katherine Brogan and James Brogan (1981) alert teachers to the rise in plagiarism in technical writing in "Yet Another Ethical Problem in Technical Writing." The authors note that most scientific and engineering reports are published without copyright protection, and as a result, the use of these reports without acknowledging the source is on the rise not only in student papers but also in dissertations and professional reports. The authors call on technical writing teachers to emphasize the seriousness of this problem and to help students by teaching them to summarize, paraphrase, and document sources.

Two articles emphasize the need for scientific and technical writers to include complete and accurate "materials and methods" sections when writing research reports. Anne H. Jones (1980) in "A Question of Ethics: Materials and Methods," and Lucinda Pitcairn (1982) in "Some Ethical Considerations in Medical Writing." These authors point out that the usefulness of the research report for other researchers may depend on their ability to replicate the tests described. Thus, incomplete materials and methods sections can mask faulty procedures and insignificant results. Jones urges teachers to stress the importance of this type of information.

Finally, a practice that indirectly incorporates the consideration of ethical concerns in the teaching of scientific and technical communication is the use of the case method of teaching communication. One of the best sources of cases for technical communication courses is Barbara Couture and Jone R. Goldstein's (1985) text, *Cases for Technical and Professional Writing*. Other valuable sources of cases are *Courses, Components, and Exercises in Technical Communication*, edited by Dwight Stevenson et al. (1981), and *The Case Method in Technical Communication: Theory and Models*, edited by R. John Brockmann et al. (1984).

Teachers who use the case method attempt to teach communication skills by simulating real-life communication situations and requiring students to respond to these situations. Often, when students find themselves communicating within these simulated cases, they must take into consideration the ethical consequences of their actions. For example, one case in Couture and Goldstein's (1985, p. 146) text requires a student to assume the role of an environmental engineer who must argue for a landfill that may or may not be harmful to the environment. Class discussions about this case may focus on ethical practices.

Conclusion

Perhaps the most practical notion of teaching ethics in technical communication courses is put forth by Dennis Minor (1981) in "Chair's Comments: Ethos in Technical Discourse." Minor (1981, p. 440) states,

> It was agreed (during a conference panel discussion) that one could not teach a person to be ethical; rather, one could teach a student how ethics have been formulated, defined, and applied in earlier times and at the present time.

A technical writing course is unlikely to change a student's ethical sensibility. Such a course can, however, change what a student knows about ethical communication. That knowledge may help the student make more informed decisions when faced with ethical dilemmas on the job. Therefore, after reviewing the relevant literature of the past 25 years, it seems clear that we should at least warn our students that such dilemmas can occur. "A failure to warn" may indeed be unethical behavior on our part.

Bibliography

Barton, Ben, and Marthalee Barton. "Ethos, Persona, and Role Confusion in Engineering: Toward a Pedagogy for Technical Discourse." In *Proceedings of the Conference on College Composition and Communication.* ERIC Document 229 782, 1981.

Bradford, David. "The Persona in Microcomputer Documentation." *IEEE Transactions on Professional Communication* 27 (1984): 65–68.

Britton, W. Earl. "Personality in Scientific Writing." *Technical Communication* 16, no. 17 (1973): 17–22.

Brockmann, R. John, et al., eds. *The Case Method in Technical Communication: Theory and Models.* The Association of Teachers of Technical Writing, 1984.

Brogan, Katherine, and James Brogan. "Yet Another Ethical Problem in Technical Writing." In *Proceedings of the Conference on College Composition and Communication.* ERIC Document 229 782, 1981.

Campbell, Paul N. "The Personae of Scientific Discourse." *Quarterly Journal of Speech* 61 (1975): 391–405.

Clark, Gregory, and Jeffrey Denham. "Toward an Ethos for Technical Communication." Unpublished paper. Brigham Young University, Provo, Utah, 1985.

"Code for Communicators." Society for Technical Communication, Washington, D.C., 1978.

"Code of Ethics." Society of Technical Writers and Editors, 1958.

Cogan, Eugene. "For the Technical Communicator: Pursuing Professional Identity and Maturity." ERIC Document 095 537, 1974.

Condit, Nancy. "Ethical Responsibilities of Medical Writers to the Lay Press: Editorial Comment in News Reporting." *Medical Communications* 12 (1984): 78–80.

Couture, Barbara, and Jone R. Goldstein. *Cases for Technical and Professional Writing.* Boston: Little, Brown and Co., 1985.

Cowan, Robert C. "Garbage Under Glass: What Are Scientists Dishing Out?" *IEEE Transactions on Professional Communication* 23 (1980): 116–17.

Cox, Barbara G., and Charles G. Roland. "How Rhetoric Confuses Scientific Issues." *IEEE Transactions on Professional Communication* 16 (1973): 140–42.

Dobrin, David. "What's Technical About Technical Writing?" In *New Essays in Technical and Scientific Communication: Research, Theory, Practice,* edited by Paul V. Anderson, R. John Brockmann, and Carolyn R. Miller. Farmingdale, N.Y.: Baywood Publishing Co., 1983, pp. 227–50.

Doheny-Farina, Stephen, ed. "Special Issue: Legal and Ethical Issues in Technical Communication." *IEEE Transactions on Professional Communication* 30 (1987): entire issue.

Driskill, L. P. "Trends in Liability Affecting Technical Writers." In *Proceedings of the Conference on College Composition and Communication.* ERIC Document 229 782, 1981.

Dunwoody, Sharon. "A Question of Accuracy." *IEEE Transactions on Professional Communication* 25 (1982): 196-99.

Evans, William E. "The Basic Technical Writing Course: Skills *and* Ethics? Prochnical Writing Too!" *Proceedings of the Conference on College Composition and Communication.* ERIC Document 229 782, 1981.

Garver, Eugene. "Teaching Writing and Teaching Virtue." *Journal of Business Communication* 22 (1985): 51-73.

Girill, T. R. "Technical Communication and Law," Part 2. *Technical Communication* 32 (1985): 37.

Golen, Steven, Celeste Powers, and M. Agnes Titkemeyer. "How to Teach Ethics in a Basic Business Communication Class—Committee Report of the 1983 Teaching Methodology and Concepts Committee, Subcommittee 1." *Journal of Business Communication* 22 (1985): 75-83.

Griffin, Jack. "When Do Rhetorical Choices Become Ethical Choices?" In *Proceedings of the 27th International Technical Communication Conference.* Washington, D.C.: Society for Technical Communication, 1980, pp. W/77-W/84.

Guinn, Dorothy M. "Ethos in Technical Discourse." *The Technical Writing Teacher* 11 (1983): 31-37.

Halloran, Stephen M. "Classical Rhetoric for the Engineering Student." *Journal of Technical Writing and Communication* 1 (1971): 17-24.

———. "Eloquence in a Technological Society." *Central States Speech Journal* 29 (1978): 221-27.

Hays, Robert. "Political Realities in Reader/Situation Analysis." *Technical Communication* 31, no. 1 (1984): 16-20.

Hollow, Dennis. "Responsibility—A Keynote for Ethics in Technical Communications." In *Proceedings of the 26th International Technical Communication Conference.* Washington, D.C.: Society for Technical Communication, 1979, pp. W/65-W/67.

Johnson, Nan. "Ethos and the Aims of Rhetoric." In *Essays on Classical Rhetoric and Modern Discourse,* edited by Robert J. Connors, Lisa S. Ede, and Andrea A. Lunsford. Carbondale, Ill.: Southern Illinois University Press, 1984, pp. 98-114.

Jones, Anne H. "A Question of Ethics: Materials and Methods." In *Proceedings of the 27th International Technical Communication Conference.* Washington, D.C.: Society for Technical Communication, 1980, pp. W/85-W/87.

Kowal, John P. "Responsible Science Reporting in a Technological Age." *Journal of Technical Writing and Communication* 10 (1980): 307-14.

Lenfest, David. "On Language, Liability, and Documentation." In *Proceedings of the 31st International Technical Communication Conference.* Washington, D.C.: Society for Technical Communication, 1984, pp. WE/180-WE/183.

Marcuse, Michael J. "Ethos in Technical Discourse: The Current State of the Question." Paper presented at the Annual Meeting of the Conference on College Composition and Communication, 1980. ERIC Document 188 221.

Miller, Carolyn R. "Technology as a Form of Consciousness: A Study of Contemporary Ethos." *Central States Speech Journal* 29 (1978): 228-36.

———. "The Ethos of Science and the Ethos of Technology." In *Proceedings of the 31st Conference on College Composition and Communication,* edited by J. Muller. Lubbock, Tex.: Association of Teachers of Technical Writing, 1980.

Minor, Dennis. "Chair's Comments: Ethos in Technical Discourse." In *Proceedings of the Conference on College Composition and Communication.* ERIC Document 229 782, 1981.

Perica, Louis. "Honesty in Technical Communication." *Technical Communication* 15 (1972): 2–6.

Pitcairn, Lucinda. "Some Ethical Considerations in Medical Writing." *Medical Communications* 10 (1982): 89–94.

Radez, Frank. "STC and the Professional Ethic." *Technical Communication* 27 (1980): 5–7.

Richardson, Jacques G. "Science and Technology as Integral Parts of Our Culture: Interdisciplinary Responsibilities of the Scientific Communicator." *Journal of Technical Writing and Communication* 10 (1980): 141–47.

Roland, Charles G. "How Public Is Scientific Knowledge?" *Journal of Technical Writing and Communication* 1 (1971): 289–97.

Rubens, Philip. "Reinventing the Wheel?: Ethics for Technical Communicators." *Journal of Technical Writing and Communication* 11 (1981): 329–39.

Sachs, Harley. "Ethics and the Technical Communicator." *Technical Communication* 27 (1980): 7–10.

Schaefer, Mary M. "Special Section on Ethics: Introduction." *Technical Communication* 27, no. 3 (1980): 4.

Schmelzer, Richard W. "New Responsibilities for the Technical Writer." *Journal of Technical Writing and Communication* 11 (1981): 217–21.

Schwartz, Victor E., and Russell W. Driver. "Warnings in the Workplace: The Need for a Synthesis of Law and Communication Theory." *University of Cincinnati Law Review* 52 (1983): 38–83.

Shimberg, Lee. "President's Plans—1977–78." *Technical Communication* 24, no. 3 (1977): 30–31.

———. "Ethics and Rhetoric in Technical Writing." *Technical Communication* 25, no. 4 (1978): 16–18.

———. "Technical Communicators and Moral Ethics." *Technical Communication* 27, no. 3 (1980): 10–12.

Stevenson, Dwight, et al., eds. *Courses, Components, and Exercises in Technical Communication.* Urbana, Ill.: National Council of Teachers of English, 1981.

Stoddard, Eve W. "The Role of Ethos in the Theory of Technical Writing." *The Technical Writing Teacher* 11 (1984): 229–41.

Tebeaux, Elizabeth. "Let's Not Ruin Technical Writing Too!" In *Proceedings of the Conference on College Composition and Communication,* edited by J. Muller. Lubbock, Tex.: Association of Teachers of Technical Writing, 1980.

Walzer, Arthur. "Ethos, Technical Writing and the Liberal Arts." *The Technical Writing Teacher* 8 (1981): 50–53.

Whitburn, Merrill. "Personality in Scientific and Technical Writing." *Journal of Technical Writing and Communication* 6 (1976): 299–306.

Wicclair, Mark, and David Farkas. "Ethical Reasoning in Technical Communication: A Practical Framework." *Technical Communication* 27 (1980): 15–19.

Winslade, William. "Truth and Honesty in Science." *Medical Communications* 11 (1983): 59–63.

Woods, Lee B. "Proposals Are People, Too." *Technical Communication* 15 (1972): 9–11.

Yoos, George. "A Revision of the Concept of Ethical Appeal." *Philosophy and Rhetoric* 12 (1979): 41–58.

Young, J. C. "Responsibilities of Writers and Editors to Readers." *STWP Review* (1961): 14–16.

4 Technical Editing

Avon Jack Murphy
Oregon Institute of Technology

The past twenty years have seen extraordinary developments in what technical editors do and how they do it and in the quantity and quality of their professional literature. The definition of "technical editor" has changed dramatically, and even as some voices bemoan editors' often lowly status and rugged schedule, many more proclaim the positive changes that made the work ever more intriguing and challenging.

Over three decades ago, Florence E. Wall (1953) lamented in "Requirements and Responsibilities of a Technical Editor," "A search of the literature has revealed pitifully little on technical editorial work." Such clearly is no longer the case. Led by such editors as Mary F. Buehler and Lola M. Zook, scores of writers have developed a massive critical literature. This essay selectively discusses the material within eight categories:

1. Books and bibliographical aids devoted to technical editing
2. Overall outlooks on technical editing and editors
3. The technical editor as a person
4. Getting the job done: macroview
5. Getting the job done: microview
6. Editing nonprose elements
7. Editing particular kinds of material
8. Technical editing pedagogy

One initial clarification seems necessary. "Technical editing" refers here to the reshaping, refocusing, and polishing that a professional communicator does on someone else's work. This discussion does not touch on "editing" in the sense of editing one's own writing.

Materials described in this essay have been selected because they are original, significant contributions to thinking about technical editing or provide eminently useful details that technical editors and their teachers will want to apply. Items that merely repeat earlier publications are excluded.

Books and Bibliographical Aids

Before 1985, technical editors did not have an adequate bibliography of writings about their discipline. But that problem is rapidly disappearing. Roger E. Masse's (1985b) "Theory and Practice of Editing Processes in Technical Communication" contains an "Appendix: Selected Resources on Editing Processes." This nonannotated listing gathers 143 heretofore scattered references. More useful for some purposes is the same writer's "Solutions to a Technical Editor's Problems: A Selected Bibliography on Technical Editing" (Masse 1985a). Concentrating on writings published since the mid-1970s, Masse provides annotations for sixty-five journal and conference papers grouped in three sections: technical editors' roles, effective editing techniques, and effective techniques for working with authors. Finally, readers will find invaluable the annotated bibliography of 313 items (with subject index) compiled by Carolyn D. Rude and Rex W. Castle (1985) in Rude's (1985) *Teaching Technical Editing.*

Several books cover numerous aspects of technical editing. Wallace Clements and Robert G. Waite's (1983) indispensable *Guide for Beginning Technical Editors* is the finest concise guide to the discipline. The *Guide* discusses technical editors' duties and skills, technical editing in perspective, a systematic seven-part breakdown of the editing process, proofreader's marks, and editing nontext elements such as mathematics and tables. New editors will appreciate the excellent examples of edited pages and seasoned advice. The authors discuss how they developed the *Guide* as an efficient training tool in "A Guide for Beginning Technical Editors" (Clements and Waite 1979). Arthur Plotnik (1982), addressing editors of all types, succinctly offers sensible hints about editor-author relations, legal problems, editorial graphics, and other relevant topics in *Elements of Editing: A Modern Guide for Editors and Journalists.* And Editorial Experts, Inc., publishes a handful of books, including Peggy Smith's *Directory of Editorial Resources* (1987a) and *Mark My Words: Instruction and Practice in Proofreading* (1987b), as well as *The Editorial Eye,* a newsletter treating such specialized topics as proofreading, computerized editing, style manuals, and indexing.

Very useful are three anthologies on technical editing (many anthologized papers are discussed in appropriate sections of this essay).

A longtime favorite, *Technical Editing: Principles and Practices,* edited by Lola M. Zook (1975), collects eighteen papers originally published between 1965 and 1974. Despite the material's age, almost every piece still has relevance, for Zook (1975, p. iii) consciously chooses "articles that present a broad and flexible view of the editorial job." H. Lee Shimberg (1981b) accomplishes much the same effect in a special issue of *Technical Communication* on technical editing. All authors in this collection are also found in Zook's anthology. Carolyn D. Rude's (1985) fine anthology, *Teaching Technical Editing,* consists of eighteen essays plus bibliography; while focusing on pedagogy, this book offers stores of information about content and production editing, statistics, graphics, management, and much else.

Overall Outlooks on Technical Editing and Editors

Little extensive research beyond the bibliographical studies noted above has focused on trends within technical editing. The most insightful article to date is Zook's (1983) "Technical Editors Look at Technical Editing." Analyzing six editors' and managers' responses to a lengthy questionnaire, Zook says much on how technical editors define and view their work. She concludes that technical editing has been changing as technical publication has grown more sophisticated, that more editors are realistically doing "the best work possible under the constraints that exist" (Zook 1983, p. 25), and that the advent of computerized editing will let editors do more substantive editing. If Zook is right, much has changed since James W. McCafferty (1971) in his enlightened "Constructive Editing" assumed that all editors work in engineering firms, and he advised editors to maintain large supplies of red pencils.

The many writers who attempt to define technical editing do best when they specify editors' functions. E. F. Boomhower (1975) classifies such functions in "Producing Good Technical Communications Requires Two Types of Editing." While the literary (or copy) editor, says Boomhower, concentrates on correct grammar, linguistic structure, and format, the technical editor plays the reader's role, taking pains to ensure that the outline, text and art coordination, emphases and transitions, indexing, and other elements are handled to facilitate reading. Alberta L. Cox (1975), in "The Editor as Generalist as well as Specialist," counsels editors to communicate with fellow workers along the whole production process; she particularly recommends editors' knowing enough about composition, illustration, layout, and printing that they can suggest improvement at each step. The most helpful overall outline of functions remains the *Guide for Beginning Technical Editors* (pp. 10–18), wherein Clements and Waite (1983) describe "A Systematic Approach to Editing Technical Manuscripts." These pages put into sequential order the tasks editors receiving finished manuscripts perform: (1) appraising the job, (3) editing the draft, (3) reviewing the editing with the author, (4) preparing the reviewed draft for composition and artwork, (5) conducting the author review of finished galleys and artwork, (6) preparing the reviewed galleys and artwork for corrections and layout, and (7) verifying that corrections and layout are done satisfactorily.

Numerous writers offer general guidelines for editors. In "Patterns for Making Editorial Changes," Buehler (1975) recommends keeping in mind three kinds of changes, each of which has its own patterns: structural, language, and mechanical. Patricia N. Smith (1981), offering another type of structured approach, suggests in "Here, Edit This!" that new editors can quickly gain respect if they deliver a good job (by initially understanding the task, pinpointing problems, and resolving difficulties) and deliver on time. New editors might prefer reading the witty "Strategies of a Technical Editor," in which Don Bush (1979) outlines thirteen strategies to make authors accept one as an editor. Suggestions include finding a technical mistake, flattery, humor, chicanery, enlisting the boss, and common courtesy.

Lola M. Zook has written two articles that, like Bush's, offer advice humanely. "Editing and the Editor: Views and Values" (Zook 1981) affirms that editors can make their editing an art if they feel committed to striving for an ideal; set standards for themselves; have a command of the medium; have an instinctive feeling for order, logic, and priorities; and work easily with people, keeping a light touch. Equally sensitive but wittier is "Lessons Learned—Not Always by Choice" (Zook 1980). Here Zook draws from her own experience four sorts of lessons all editors might take to heart. She describes "Lessons I Wish I Hadn't Had to Learn" (including the need to compromise), "Lessons I Wish I Had Learned Sooner," "Lessons I Never Did Learn" (such as an abhorrence of the passive voice), and "Lessons I Am Still Trying to Learn" (including the need to set realizable goals).

One special type of overall advice is that technical editors emphasize more substantive editing. David L. McGough (1975), in "Production Editor: Key to New Effectiveness," persuasively argues for the production editor's significance. McGough points out that the production editor concept is a production control system in miniature, this one person coordinating various people's contributions, elements of the production effort, and end results. A decade later Bush (1981) takes much the same point in a new direction, in "Content Editing, an Opportunity for Growth." He urges technical editors to earn equality with their authors by going beyond error-finding and stylebook editing. Seeking technical accuracy, clarity, English correctness, and consistency, this new breed, Bush believes, attacks underlying writing problems, teaches effective writing, and persuades employers to value significant language skills. How the production editor solves varied publication production problems is explored in Jean Hasch and Val Chepeleff's (1982) detailed "Wearing the Production Editor's Hat." They analyze strategies useful in formulating the basic idea, budgeting time and money, reviewing the draft, finalizing the document, and getting it printed and bound. David K. Farkas (1985) combines an imaginative case study, thoughtful student responses, and his own recommendations in "Teaching the Administrative and Policy Aspects of Editing"; he shows how he teaches budgeting, scheduling, and establishing of policies.

The Technical Editor as a Person

The effective technical editor's personality has received considerable attention. At one extreme, we have John L. Simons (1980), who in "The Technical Editor as a Decision-Maker" insists that a technical editor, like a baseball umpire, be "a self-confident, decisive individual, one who considers all his decisions as correct." At the other extreme of complexity, we find Lola M. Zook (1975), who in "Training the Editor: Skills Are Not Enough" counsels new editors to learn seven attitudes, including the readiness to work at varying levels, the ability to view their own work in perspective, humility, and a distrust of oversimplification.

Not surprisingly, most writers discuss the editorial personality in the context of the author-editor relationship. Only rarely do editors analyze their authors, as does Eva Dukes (1981) in her entertaining "Some Authors I Have Known." She describes working with hostile/distrustful, know-it-all, cooperative, vicious, perfectionist, and ideal authors. Far more often, writers examine what editors must do to make the relationship run smoothly. Dukes (1975) again, for example, describes the human art of avoiding rudeness, conveying suggestions about alterations, asking questions, and apologizing when wrong, in "The Art of Editing." In a similar vein, Michael S. Genin (1979), in "Turning Adversaries into Allies—Avoiding Tension in an Author-Editor Relationship," recommends defusing potentially explosive confrontations by establishing rapport before editing, assuring authors that marks are not intended as criticism, avoiding hostile language, reminding authors that changes can be unmade, and convincing authors that both the author and the editor want to communicate with the audience. Susan K. Batchelder's (1983) "Friends or Foes? The Relationship Between Writer and Editor" more rigorously argues that authors must view technical editors as a resource that saves time, guarantees cleaner manuals, and facilitates brainstorming; authors can especially use editors at the stages of research, rough draft preparation, and assembling of official review copies. Gerry Brenner (1988), in "Editing 101: All about Authors," describes three classroom strategies to teach how to handle on-the-job relationships: interviews with professional editors, impersonations of authors, and structured simulations. Brenner concludes that editing internships would be far more preferable. For editors unable to grasp their authors' intent, Judith Ramey (1985) recommends in "Educating the Editorial Guess" systematically tackling problems of language, logic, rhetoric, and technical accuracy.

Clarkson University professors show in two papers how a technical editing workshop can help students develop vital interpersonal skills. In "Interpersonal Skills: An Essential Component in the Editing Class," Patricia R. Barkman et al. (1985) present activities teaching students to work collaboratively, listen, eliminate one-sided dominance, ask open-ended questions, and plan conferences early in a project's life. They reprint a script that can be used in classes and a lengthy annotated bibliography on "Improving Editing Through Collaboration." Herb Smith (1985), assessing the course rationale and structure in "Methods for Training the Technical Editor in Interpersonal Skills," provides a detailed table analyzing the course into segments and indicating for each what Smith teaches, what the students do, and what they learn.

One special approach to author-editor relations is that fully presented in Nelson A. Briggs's (1975) "Editing by Dialogue." Briggs applies Martin Buber's subtle distinction between "I-it" and "I-thou" relations. The latter can produce a dialogic author-editor relation emphasizing their mutuality, their "tribalization." Editors can enhance the relationship by taking a genuine interest in authors' works, avoiding subjective changes and red pencils, and remaining humble about their own knowledge. Briggs especially greatly influenced writers at New Mexico State University, as best seen in Mary S. Hageman et al.'s (1981) "Editorial Dialogue: An Alternative Writer-Editor Relationship." These writers add to Briggs's insights Richard L. Johannesen's components of dialogue; genuineness, accurate emphatic understanding, unconditional positive regard, presentness, a spirit of mutual equality, and a supportive psychological climate. Although their fervor for "a caring, supportive human relationship" borders on the sentimental, they nurture a potentially useful approach to editing.

A more immediately useful approach is to consider how editors might teach authors. The fullest earlier treatment of this concept is Sylvia Fourdrinier's (1975) "The Editor as a Teacher." Fourdrinier sensibly observes that good editors do not do all the correcting of a manuscript but teach their authors how to make improvements; a good teacher herself, she recommends telling authors why particular revisions might improve a document. Judith W. Radford (1985) notes in "Instruction Through Edits" how editors can help authors by providing instruction, giving authors the responsibility for making changes, and motivating them to make changes. Editors, says Radford, must establish rapport and editing limits; in presenting comments, they must explain marking methods and select both positive points and passages needing improvements.

Getting the Job Done: Macroview

Strong management is necessary to make editing efficient. New editing managers will profit from "Stranger in a Strange Land: My First Year as an Editing Manager," wherein Lynn Behnke (1982) discusses scheduling, analyzing editing costs, job satisfaction, job demands, and the future of technical editing. Terry M. Dalla Santa (1983) cites the need for formalized procedures in "Managing the Editing Function on Large Publication Tasks with Short Flow Times." She finds that such solutions as established editing standards, realistic schedules, concise written instructions, manageable work packages, and esprit de corps can solve problems of poor writing, little time, and no one editor's seeing the whole project.

David K. Farkas (1984) addresses a vexing managerial question in "Professional and Informal Editing in Complex Organizations." The writer argues that organizations hiring professional editors will preserve human resources, reduce friction, and realize better writing and lower costs. B. Michael Kantrowitz (1985) provides statistical support for hiring editors in "What Price Technical Editing? Phase I: Reaching a Lay Audience." His research indicates greater comprehension, shorter completion time, and higher message acceptability among a lay audience if technical documents have been edited. One point arises if company officials agree with these writers: how do editing managers hire able, experienced editors? Kathryn S. Macal (1984) constructs a specific answer in "Hiring a Technical Editor." Her process contains seven steps: explicitly define job qualifications, seek a large applicant pool, rigorously screen resumes and letters, request work samples, use varied interviewers, focus interviews, and rank interviewed candidates.

Since technical editors work under various constraints, they never have unlimited time and money. David E. Vaughn (1975) suggests ways of achieving the optimum balance between (1) speed and (2) accuracy and quality in "A Logical Approach to Editing Proposals, Reports, and Manuals." The most interesting feature in this paper is a graph and a table that, says Vaughn, one can use to determine accuracy/quality ratings for manuscripts, given certain numbers of pages and hours. Editors facing short deadlines can apply "Coping with Crash Editing," in which Brian Jarman (1980) offers extremely practical advice on psyching up, attacking the manuscript, and compromising on editing quality (this final section provides fine tables). Another approach is that of Gerald A. Mann (1980, p. W5), who in "Minimal Editing: How Much Is Too Much?" notes several things editors should and should not do in "performing the least editing needed to make a document communicate effectively."

The most important development in thinking about how best to estimate the kinds and amounts of effort needed on a project is the levels-of-edit concept. Robert Van Buren and Mary F. Buehler (1980) describe the concept in their detailed booklet *The Levels of Edit*. Buehler (1981) provides further explanations and examples in "Defining Terms in Technical Editing: The Levels of Edit as a Model." These writers analyze editorial work into nine types of edits (for each of which they supply a lengthy list of specific duties): coordination, policy, integrity, screening, copy clarification, format, mechanical style, language, and substantive. These nine types are cumulatively combined into five levels of edit, 1 through 5. A Level 1 edit, that performed on highest-class Jet Propulsion Laboratory documents, involves all nine types, while a Level 5 edit demands only coordination and policy editing. When editing managers anywhere must decide what work can be devoted to particular documents, their major planning tool is now *The Levels of Edit*.

Getting the Job Done: Microview

Recent pleas that technical editors assume wider responsibilities than line-by-line improvement do not mean that editors no longer do such work. Rhetorical and stylistic concerns, indeed, remain critically important within the editing process. However, few writers have discussed rhetoric itself in connection with what this essay defines to be editing. One notable exception is Buehler (1980), in "Situational Editing: A Rhetorical Approach for the Technical Editor." She believes that the editor can serve both the writer and the reader by using both a programmatic approach (which involves applying rules) and a rhetorical one (which demands seeing all elements in a document's rhetorical context as one edits its sentences). Patrick Cheney and David Schleicher (1984) expand Buehler's method in "Redesigning Technical Reports: A Rhetorical Editing Method." Working on the scale of the whole report, these writers construct a five-step process: identify the audience and purpose, analyze the draft report's ideas, synthesize those ideas into a focused revision, interview the author, and finish the report. David K. Farkas's (1985) "The Concept of Consistency in Writing and Editing" applies rhetorical theory to show editors how to establish semantic, syntactic, stylistic, spatial, and mechanical patterns "that are logical, evident, functional, resource efficient, and stable."

Technical editors seeking help when doing strictly stylistic editing have many resources. Numerous journals in technical communication and in English regularly publish articles on writing style that editors can easily apply to their work. And they can refer as needed to the *Harbrace College Handbook* (Hodges et al. 1986) and other like grammar texts, and to such style manuals as *The Chicago Manual of Style* (University of Chicago Press 1982), the *U.S. Government Printing Office Style Manual* (GPO 1984), and the *Council of Biology Editors Style Manual* (Council of Biology Editors 1983); William Strunk, Jr., and E. B. White's (1979) *The Elements of Style;* Joseph M. Williams's (1981) *Ten Lessons in Clarity and Grace;* and Wilson Follett's (1979) *Modern American Usage: A Guide.*

Several more tightly focused publications on stylistic editing may also prove helpful. In "Editing Authors' Style—A Few Guidelines," Shimberg (1981a) offers four suggestions: editors enjoy only a limited right to alter authors' style; editors must be able to recognize extreme styles; editors must help authors resolve such problems as poor organization and verbosity; and editors must remain unobtrusive when editing nonusers of standard English. A common problem is investigated in Charles R. Stratton's (1975) "Ambiguity: An Exercise in Practical Semantics." Stratton uses closely analyzed examples to show how editors can help authors identify lexical or structural ambiguities and then either help the authors resolve the ambiguities or do it themselves. And Wayne A. Losano (1985) tackles a thorny difficulty in "Editing for Style and Consistency: The Multiple Author Manuscript." Losano gives expert advice on how not to offend authors when suggesting simple physical changes (in headings, figures, references, lists, and tables) and stylistic changes (such as sentence length and formality).

The much-maligned specialty of copyediting has become a respectable endeavor. As Cox (1981) explains in "Copy Editing—The Final Word," copyediting can be a demanding, invaluable step in which editors review already edited documents to remove all errors in the grammatical and mechanical presentation. Such a view receives full development in *How to Copyedit Scientific Books and Journals,* wherein Maeve O'Connor (1986, p. 5) states that scientific copyeditors cope, "if required, with substantive editing, administration, and proofreading." O'Connor provides especially strong details about handling and marking up manuscripts. Karen Judd's (1982) *Copyediting: A Practical Guide* likewise provides bountiful explanations of how to execute these tasks.

The computer has both frightened and excited technical editors. Deborah E. Swain (1985) takes a sensible approach in "Automated Editing: Computer Tools and Human Communication." She writes that editors communicate more fully with their writers, illustrators, and production specialists when the team uses computers within a process featuring mutually approved rules for changing text, trains on the same system, and uses electronic mail and common storage for a publication's files and when writers and editors train together on editing tools. Since relevant computer software and hardware change constantly, editors must follow current articles in such periodicals as *(The SIGDOC Newsletter)* and *folio* (Pakin and Associates).

Editing Nonprose Elements

The very nature of their documents requires that technical editors master strategies of nonprose material, especially graphics and mathematics. Good reference handbooks include Jack Klasnic's (1981) *Inplant Printing Handbook* and the handy little *Pocket Pal: A Graphic Arts Production Handbook* (Bruno 1983). For explicit suggestions on using graphics expertise in editing, two excellent starting places are Dorothy C. Amsden's "Get in the Habit of Editing Illustrations" (1980) and "Exercise Your Visual Thinking" (1982). In her first paper, she enthusiastically encourages verbally oriented editors to enjoy working with graphics. She provides guidelines for editing black-and-white illustrations, covering general considerations, graphs, diagrams and drawings, and reductions. The second paper succinctly advises how to recognize when graphics might make dense prose more readable and how to suggest appropriate choices. Editors who must often reduce document length will profit from Muriel Zimmerman's (1983) "Reducing by Design: A Checklist for Editors." Instead of cutting text, Zimmerman explains, editors can manipulate such features as type size, white space, and column arrangement. Finally, the best-organized exposition on teaching graphics editing is Robert S. Kellner's (1985) "The Editor as Artist."

Editors working with mathematics should have access to reference guides such as the *Mathematics Dictionary,* edited by Robert C. James and Edwin F. Beckenbach (1976). Edwin J. Podell (1984) presents ten rules that editors can apply to clarify mathematics in "Mathematics Must Be Effective in Technical Communication." Podell shows how to eliminate problems of indiscriminate use, mathematical inaccuracies, typographic errors, and ambiguities. Procedures observed at the Lawrence Livermore National Laboratory underlie two succinct treatments: Peter W. Murphy's (1983) "Typography for Mathematics" and the chapter "Editing Mathematical Material" in Clements and Waite's (1983) *Guide.* Teachers of technical editing will appreciate Alice I. Philbin's (1985) "Editing Statistics." This writer defines kinds of statistics and discusses numbers as facts, as symbols, and as a classification system; the article provides a fine glossary for editing students. Also helpful is Gail W. Pieper's (1985) concise, insightful advice on teaching students to edit mathematical text in "Editing Equations for Form, Grammar, and Style."

Editing Particular Kinds of Material

Relatively little has been written about editing specific genres and subgenres encountered in technical communication. One of the better treatments of proposal editing is "Editing the Small Study Proposal" (Rohne 1975). Here Carl F. Rohne offers still relevant advice on how editors can help develop winning proposals through such means as storyboarding projects, assuring quality in artwork and technical details, and keeping everyone on schedule. An authoritative paper within its niche is "How Does a Presentation Editor Help Clients Communicate?" by Marilyn B. Kamelgarn (1984). She explains how editors can create interactions between clients, artists, and editors by overseeing early conferences, storyboarding, artist-editor collaboration, client's practice of oral delivery, and production of photocopied visuals.

A newer specialty is editing computer documentation. Two fine discussions constitute chapters in professional "how-to" books. In "Editing, Review, and Evaluation Procedures" within *Creating Com-*

puter Software User Guides, Doann Houghton-Alico (1985) explains how to improve documentation through proofreading, editing, technical review, beta tests, and user surveys—all activities in which editors can participate. Jonathan Price's (1984) *How to Write a Computer Manual: A Handbook of Software Documentation* includes "Reviewing Someone Else's Manual." This lively chapter treats how editors can spot authors' irritating habits, help develop active style and sensible structure, ensure consistency, and write comments to authors. Finally, in *Writing Better Computer User Documentation,* R. John Brockmann (1986) explains how editors can apply the levels-of-edit concept within a documentation project.

Technical Editing Pedagogy

Discussions of how best to teach technical editing have certainly become more numerous and better informed with the publication of Rude's (1985) *Teaching Technical Editing.* Several essays from Rude's anthology have already been discussed in this bibliography, and others will be described in this section.

All technical editing teachers should immerse themselves in Farkas's (1986) *How to Teach Technical Editing.* This book seeks "to provide a pedagogy of editing" and "help demonstrate . . . how complex and intellectually challenging editing really is." After defining technical editing, Farkas develops twelve chapters, one on each of the following topics: language skills, computer skills, introducing students to work settings, substantive and rhetorical editing, marking copy, preserving the author's meaning, sweep strategies, levels of edit, house style, consistency, deciding editing time and payment systems, and handling editing assignments. The author knows editing research and trends and suggests many usable techniques.

Excellent articles have recently become available. Zook (1985) has written an article on pedagogical theory that should become a classic, "We Start with Questions: Defining the Editing Curriculum." Zook discusses not how to teach units but what should be learned: the editing process, the nature of "technical editing," students' varied objectives, qualities of good technical editors, and working as a professional. Several other teachers report on their technical editing courses. Described in "A Necessary and Natural Sequel: Technical Editing," Kellner's (1982) course stresses rigorous work in language editing, formats, graphics, layout and design, and publications production.

Four of the articles in Rude's anthology not yet alluded to are William O. Coggin's (1985) "A Workshop Approach to the Editing

Class," Sherry G. Southard's (1985) "Teaching Editing: Copy and Production," Donald E. Zimmerman's (1985) "Teaching Content Editing," and JoAnn T. Hackos's (1985) "A Graduate Course with a Research Component." Coggin's efficiently run pass/fail class teaches management of the entire publication process as well as interpersonal and mechanical skills; interesting features include the use of secondary reviewers, guest professionals, and agreement forms. Southard offers sensible advice on accommodating limited budgets and student inexperience. She thoughtfully describes her assignments, including proofreading, graphics editing, typesetting, and producing a newsletter. Zimmerman teaches students how to learn technical fields, develop a questioning attitude, and detect errors in technical and scientific thinking. Hackos describes coursework emphasizing editing, career awareness, professional issues, and research. She helpfully reflects on three problems: the limited classroom environment, students' fears of technology, and students' discourtesy toward authors.

Internships offer students the best way to gain editing experience. Gerry Brenner's (1988) "Does Your Curriculum Need Editing?" urges English departments to offer technical or freelance editing courses and to arrange internships. The same author, in "Editing Internships: An Exhortation for Launching" (Brenner 1985), outlines program requirements and goals, ways to find and keep sponsors, and benefits to the teacher. Three arrangements at NASA are detailed by Freda F. Stohrer and Thomas Pinelli (1980) in "Traditional and Nontraditional Internships in Companies": traditional cooperative education plans, nontraditional use of student teams to edit single documents, and short-term training ventures. Still more information will be available in *Establishing and Supervising Internships,* edited by Coggin (in press).

Good in-house training work is being done. Course developers will find valuable Susan M. Briles's (1982) "Designing a Training Program for a Technical Editing Department." Briles shows specifically how to assess job needs and employees' skills and then how to devise appropriate lessons for almost all new employees, new employees without practical experience, those with special jobs, and newly hired experienced editors. Finally, in "Training the Technical Editor," Margaret E. Cathcart (1983) outlines two modular in-house courses for inexperienced editors.

Conclusion

The professional literature on technical editing has definitely come of age. Writers surveyed in this essay say much about what technical editors do, author-editor relations, how to edit, and how to teach editing. Two especially active current research areas are bibliographical analysis of the literature and pedagogy. Areas in which editors can expect to see much more work in the future include editors' increasing involvement in project development and editing within high-technology environments, especially as more writing and editing are done with increasingly sophisticated computer equipment. Technical editing has long been a dynamic field, and its literature continues to reflect its vitality.

Bibliography

Amsden, Dorothy C. "Get in the Habit of Editing Illustrations." In *Proceedings of the 27th International Technical Communication Conference.* Washington, D.C.: Society for Technical Communication, 1980, pp. W147–W54.

———. "Exercise Your Visual Thinking." In *Proceedings of the 29th International Technical Communication Conference.* Washington, D.C.: Society for Technical Communication, 1982, pp. W12–W15.

Barkman, Patricia R., et al. "Interpersonal Skills: An Essential Component in the Editing Class." In *Teaching Technical Editing,* edited by Carolyn D. Rude. Lubbock, Tex.: Association of Teachers of Technical Writing, 1985, pp. 109–28.

Batchelder, Susan K. "Friends or Foes? The Relationship Between Writer and Editor." In *Proceedings of the 30th International Technical Communication Conference.* Washington, D.C.: Society for Technical Communication, 1983, pp. WE73–WE74.

Behnke, Lynn. "Stranger in a Strange Land: My First Year as an Editing Manager." In *Proceedings of the 29th International Technical Communication Conference.* Washington, D.C.: Society for Technical Communication, 1982, pp. C11–C14.

Bishop, Claude T. *How to Edit a Scientific Journal.* Philadelphia: ISI Press, 1984.

Boomhower, E. F. "Producing Good Technical Communications Requires Two Types of Editing." *Journal of Technical Writing and Communication* 5 (1975): 277–81. (Reprinted in *Directions in Technical Writing and Communication,* edited by Jay R. Gould. Farmingdale, N.Y.: Baywood, 1978, pp. 71–75.)

Brenner, Gerry. "Does Your Curriculum Need Editing?" *College Composition and Communication.* 39 (1988): 220–23.

———. "Editing Internships: An Exhortation for Launching." In *Teaching Technical Editing,* edited by Carolyn D. Rude. Lubbock, Tex.: Association of Teachers of Technical Writing, 1985, pp. 51–56.

———. "Editing 101: All about Authors." *Righting Words* 2, no. 6 (1988): 11–17.

Briggs, Nelson A. "Editing by Dialogue." In *Technical Editing: Principles and Practices,* edited by Lola M. Zook. Washington, D.C.: Society for Technical Communication, 1975, pp. 56–61.

Briles, Susan M. "Designing a Training Program for a Technical Editing Department." In *Proceedings of the 29th International Technical Communication Conference.* Washington, D.C.: Society for Technical Communication, 1982, pp. C15–C18.

Brockmann, R. John. *Writing Better Computer User Documentation.* New York: Wiley, 1986.

Buehler, Mary F. "Situational Editing: A Rhetorical Approach for the Technical Editor." *Technical Communication* 27, no. 3 (1980): 18–20.

———. "Defining Terms in Technical Editing: The Levels of Edit as a Model." *Technical Communication* 28, no. 4 (1981): 10–15.

———. "Patterns for Making Editorial Changes." In *Technical Editing: Principles and Practices,* edited by Lola M. Zook. Washington, D.C.: Society for Technical Communication, 1975, pp. 1–6.

Bush, Don. "Strategies of a Technical Editor." *The Technical Writing Teacher* 7 (1979): 19–23.

———. "Content Editing, an Opportunity for Growth." *Technical Communication* 28, no. 4 (1981): 15–18.

Cathcart, Margaret E. "Training the Technical Editor." In *Proceedings of the 30th International Technical Communication Conference.* Washington, D.C.: Society for Technical Communication, 1983, pp. RET13–RET15.

Cheney, Patrick, and David Schleicher. "Redesigning Technical Reports: A Rhetorical Editing Method." *Journal of Technical Writing and Communication* 14 (1984): 317–37.

Clements, Wallace, and Robert G. Waite. "A Guide for Beginning Technical Editors." In *Proceedings of the 26th International Technical Communication Conference.* Washington, D.C.: Society for Technical Communication, 1979, pp. W32–W36.

———. *Guide for Beginning Technical Editors.* Washington, D.C.: Society for Technical Communication, 1983.

Coggin, William O., ed. *Establishing and Supervising Internships.* Lubbock, Tex.: Association of Teachers of Technical Writing, in press.

———. "A Workshop Approach to the Editing Class." In *Teaching Technical Editing,* edited by Carolyn D. Rude. Lubbock, Tex.: Association of Teachers of Technical Writing, 1985, pp. 43–50.

Council of Biology Editors. *Council of Biology Editors Style Manual.* Bethesda, Md.: Council of Biology Editors, 1983.

Cox, Alberta L. "Copy Editing—The Final Word." *Technical Communication* 28, no. 4 (1981): 18–20.

———. "The Editor as Generalist as Well as Specialist." *Technical Editing: Principles and Practices,* edited by Lola M. Zook. Washington, D.C.: Society for Technical Communication, 1975, pp. 7–11.

Dalla Santa, Terry M. "Managing the Editing Function on Large Publication Tasks with Short Flow Times." In *Proceedings of the 30th International*

Technical Communication Conference. Washington, D.C.: Society for Technical Communication, 1983, pp. WE21–WE24.

Dukes, Eva. "The Art of Editing." In *Technical Editing: Principles and Practices,* edited by Lola M. Zook. Washington, D.C.: Society for Technical Communication, 1975. pp. 62–66.

———. "Some Authors I Have Known." *Technical Communication* 28, no. 4 (1981): 27–31.

Farkas, David K. "Professional and Informal Editing in Complex Organizations." In *Communications: A Means of Exchange: Record of the Proceedings of the 1984 Canadian Regional Business and Technical Communication Conference.* New Westminster, British Columbia: Douglas College, 1984, pp. 3–10.

———. "The Concept of Consistency in Writing and Editing." *Journal of Technical Writing and Communication* 15 (1985): 353–64.

———. *How to Teach Technical Editing.* Washington, D.C.: Society for Technical Communication, 1986.

———. "Teaching the Administrative and Policy Aspects of Editing." In *Teaching Technical Editing,* edited by Carolyn D. Rude. Lubbock, Tex.: Association of Teachers of Technical Writing, 1985, pp. 165–69.

Follett, Wilson. *Modern American Usage: A Guide,* edited by Jacques Barzun. New York: Hill and Wang, 1979.

Fourdrinier, Sylvia. "The Editor as a Teacher." In *Teaching Technical Editing: Principles and Practices,* edited by Lola M. Zook. Washington, D.C.: Society for Technical Communication. 1975, pp. 67–70.

Genin, Michael S. "Turning Adversaries into Allies—Avoiding Tension in an Author-Editor Relationship." In *Proceedings of the 26th International Technical Communication Conference.* Washington, D.C.: Society for Technical Communication, 1979, pp. W59–W60.

Hackos, JoAnn T. "A Graduate Editing Course with a Research Component." In *Teaching Technical Editing,* edited by Carolyn D. Rude. Lubbock, Tex.: Association of Teachers of Technical Writing, 1985, pp. 36–42.

Hageman, Mary S., Louise M. Vest, and Patrick M. Kelley. "Editorial Dialogue: An Alternative Writer-Editor Relationship." In *Proceedings of the 28th International Technical Communication Conference.* Washington, D.C.: Society for Technical Communication. 1981, pp. W38–W40.

Hasch, Jean, and Val Chepeleff. "Wearing the Production Editor's Hat." In *Proceedings of the 29th International Technical Communication Conference.* Washington, D.C.: Society for Technical Communication, 1982, pp. G23–G26.

Hodges, John C., Mary E. Whitten, and Suzanne S. Webb, eds. *Harbrace College Handbook.* 10th edition. San Diego: Harcourt, 1986.

Houghton-Alico, Doann. *Creating Computer Software User Guides.* New York: McGraw-Hill, 1985.

James, Robert C., and Edwin F. Beckenbach, eds. *Mathematics Dictionary.* 4th edition. New York: Van Nostrand, 1976.

Jarman, Brian. "Coping with Crash Editing." In *Proceedings of the 27th International Technical Communication Conference.* Washington, D.C.: Society for Technical Communication, 1980, pp. W9–W12.

Judd, Karen. *Copyediting: A Practical Guide.* Los Altos, Calif.: Kaufmann, 1982.
Kamelgarn, Marilyn B. "How Does a Presentation Editor Help Clients Communicate?" In *Proceedings of the 31st International Technical Communication Conference.* Washington, D.C.: Society for Technical Communication, 1984, pp. VC50–VC52.
Kantrowitz, B. Michael. "What Price Technical Editing? Phase I: Reaching a Lay Audience." *IEEE Transactions on Professional Communication* PC-28, no. 1 (1985): 13–19.
Kellner, Robert S. "The Editor as Artist." In *Teaching Technical Editing,* edited by Carolyn D. Rude. Lubbock, Tex.: Association of Teachers of Technical Writing, 1985, pp. 89–108.
———. "A Necessary and Natural Sequel: Technical Editing." *Journal of Technical Writing and Communication* 12 (1982): 25–33.
Klasnic, Jack. *Inplant Printing Handbook.* Salem, N.H.: Gama, 1981.
Losano, Wayne A. "Editing for Style and Consistency: The Multiple-Author Manuscript." In *Teaching Technical Editing,* edited by Carolyn D. Rude. Lubbock, Tex.: Association of Teachers of Technical Writing, 1985, pp. 63–71.
Macal, Kathryn S. "Hiring a Technical Editor." In *Proceedings of the 31st International Technical Communication Conference.* Washington, D.C.: Society for Technical Communication, 1984, pp. MPD55–MPD58.
McCafferty, James W. "Constructive Editing." In *Handbook of Technical Writing Practices.* 2 vols. Edited by Stello Jordan. New York: John Wiley & Sons, 1971, pp. 909–24.
McGough, David L. "Production Editor: Key to New Effectiveness." In *Technical Editing: Principles and Practices,* edited by Lola M. Zook. Washington, D.C.: Society for Technical Communication, 1975, pp. 71–76.
Mann, Gerald A. "Minimal Editing: How Much Is Too Much?" In *Proceedings of the 27th International Technical Communication Conference.* Washington, D.C.: Society for Technical Communication, 1980, pp. W5–W7.
Masse, Roger E. "Solutions to a Technical Editor's Problems: A Selected Bibliography on Technical Editing." In *Proceedings of the 32nd International Technical Communication Conference.* Washington, D.C.: Society for Technical Communication, 1985a, pp. WE29–WE32.
———. "Theory and Practice of Editing Processes in Technical Communication." *IEEE Transactions on Professional Communication* PC-28, no. 1 (1985b): 34–42.
Murphy, Peter W. "Typography for Mathematics." Paper presented at 7th annual Practical Conference on Communication, 1983.
O'Connor, Maeve. *How to Copyedit Scientific Books and Journals.* Philadelphia: ISI Press, 1986.
Philbin, Alice I. "Editing Statistics." In *Teaching Technical Editing,* edited by Carolyn D. Rude. Lubbock, Tex.: Association of Teachers of Technical Writing, 1985, pp. 72–88.
Pieper, Gail W. "Editing Equations for Form, Grammar, and Style." In *Teaching Technical Editing,* edited by Carolyn D. Rude. Lubbock, Tex.: Association of Teachers of Technical Writing, 1985, pp. 161–64.

Plotnik, Arthur. *Elements of Editing: A Modern Guide for Editors and Journalists.* New York: Macmillan, 1982.

Pocket Pal: A Graphic Arts Production Handbook. 13th edition. New York: International Paper, 1983.

Podell, Edwin J. "Mathematics Must Be Effective in Technical Communication." *IEEE Transactions on Professional Communication* PC-27, no. 2 (1984): 97–100.

Price, Jonathan. *How to Write a Computer Manual: A Handbook of Software Documentation.* Menlo Park, Calif.: Benjamin/Cummings, 1984.

Radford, Judith W. "Instruction Through Edits." In *Proceedings of the 32nd International Technical Communication Conference.* Washington, D.C.: Society for Technical Communication, 1985, pp. WE65–WE66.

Ramey, Judith. "Educating the Editorial Guess." In *Teaching Technical Editing,* edited by Carolyn D. Rude. Lubbock, Tex.: Association of Teachers of Technical Writing, 1985, pp. 59–62.

Rohne, Carl F. "Editing the Small Study Proposal." In *Technical Editing: Principles and Practices,* edited by Lola M. Zook. Washington, D.C.: Society for Technical Communication, 1975, pp. 77–81.

Rude, Carolyn D., ed. *Teaching Technical Editing.* Anthology 6. Lubbock, Tex.: Association of Teachers of Technical Writing, 1985.

Rude, Carolyn D., and Rex W. Castle. "Technical Editing: A Selected, Annotated Bibliography." In *Teaching Technical Editing,* edited by Carolyn D. Rude. Lubbock, Tex.: Association of Teachers of Technical Writing, 1985, pp. 173–204.

Shimberg, H. Lee. "Editing Authors' Style—A Few Guidelines." *Technical Communication* 28, no. 4 (1981a): 31–35.

———. Special Issue on Technical Editing. *Technical Communication* 28, no. 4 (1981b).

Simons, John L. "The Technical Editor as a Decision-Maker." In *Proceedings of the 27th International Technical Communication Conference.* Washington, D.C.: Society for Technical Communication, 1980, pp. W27–W30.

Smith, Herb. "Methods for Training the Technical Editor in Interpersonal Skills." *IEEE Transactions on Professional Communication* PC-28, no. 1 (1985): 46–50.

Smith, Patricia N. "Here, Edit This!" In *Proceedings of the 28th International Technical Communication Conference.* Washington, D.C.: Society for Technical Communication, 1981, pp. W92–W94.

Smith, Peggy, ed. *Directory of Editorial Resources.* 1987–88 edition. Alexandria, Va.: Editorial Experts, 1987a.

———. *Mark My Words: Instruction and Practice in Proofreading.* Alexandria, Va.: Editorial Experts, 1987b.

Southard, Sherry G. "Teaching Editing: Copy and Production." In *Teaching Technical Editing,* edited by Carolyn D. Rude. Lubbock, Tex.: Association of Teachers of Technical Writing, 1985, pp. 27–35.

Stohrer, Freda F., and Thomas Pinelli. "Traditional and Nontraditional Internships in Companies." *The Technical Writing Teacher* 7 (1980): 133–38.

Stratton, Charles R. "Ambiguity: An Exercise in Practical Semantics." In *Technical Editing: Principles and Practices,* edited by Lola M. Zook. Washington, D.C.: Society for Technical Communication, 1975, pp. 47–52.

Strunk, William, Jr., and E. B. White. *The Elements of Style.* 3rd edition. New York: Macmillan, 1979.

Swain, Deborah E. "Automated Editing: Computer Tools and Human Communication." In *Proceedings of the 32nd International Technical Communication Conference.* Washington, D.C.: Society for Technical Communication, 1985, pp. ATA3–ATA6.

U. S. Government Printing Office (GPO). *U. S. Government Printing Office Style Manual.* Washington, D.C.: U. S. Government Printing Office, 1984.

University of Chicago Press. *The Chicago Manual of Style.* 13th edition. Chicago: University of Chicago Press, 1982.

Van Buren, Robert, and Mary F. Buehler. *The Levels of Edit.* 2nd edition. Pasadena, Calif.: Jet Propulsion Laboratory, 1980.

Vaughn, David E. "A Logical Approach to Editing Proposals, Reports, and Manuals." *Technical Editing: Principles and Practices,* edited by Lola M. Zook. Washington, D.C.: Society for Technical Communicaton, 1975, pp. 20–27.

Wall, Florence E. "Requirements and Responsibilities of a Technical Editor." *Journal of Chemical Education* 30 (1953): 516–21.

Williams, Joseph M. *Ten Lessons in Clarity and Grace.* Glenview, Ill.: Scott, Foresman, 1981.

Zimmerman, Donald E. "Teaching Content Editing." In *Teaching Technical Editing,* edited by Carolyn D. Rude. Lubbock, Tex.: Association of Teachers of Technical Writing, 1985, pp. 21–26.

Zimmerman, Muriel. "Reducing by Design: A Checklist for Editors." In *Proceedings of the 30th International Technical Communication Conference.* Washington, D.C.: Society for Technical Communication, 1983, pp. WE18–WE20.

Zook, Lola M. "Training the Editor: Skills Are Not Enough." In *Technical Editing: Principles and Practices,* edited by Lola M. Zook. Washington, D.C.: Society for Technical Communication, 1975, pp. 12–16.

———. "Lessons Learned—Not Always by Choice." In *Proceedings of the 27th International Technical Communication Conference.* Washington, D.C.: Society for Technical Communication, 1980, pp. W31–W36.

———. "Editing and the Editor: Views and Values." *Technical Communication* 28, no. 4 (1981): 5–9.

———. "Technical Editors Look at Technical Editing." *Technical Communication* 30, no. 3 (1983): 20–26.

———. "We Start with Questions: Defining the Editing Curriculum." In *Teaching Technical Editing,* edited by Carolyn D. Rude. Lubbock, Tex.: Association of Teachers of Technical Writing, 1985, pp. 3–9.

———, ed. *Technical Editing: Principles and Practices.* Anthology Series 4. Washington, D.C.: Society for Technical Communication, 1975.

5 Trends in Visual Representation

Ben F. Barton and Marthalee S. Barton
University of Michigan

In a recent article, "Toward a Rhetoric of Visuals for the Computer Era," Ben F. Barton and Marthalee S. Barton (1985b) appraised the course materials and literature related to visual instruction in technical communication, finding evidence of a de facto devaluation of visuals. Furthermore, their pedagogical materials on visuals were seen as strongly ad hoc and behaviorist, as according meaningfully with neither theory nor experimental evidence, and as reflecting product and static views at odds with current rhetorical theory and increasingly anachronistic in the computer era. There, they focused on visual pedagogy in technical communication, with visual studies in other fields as a backdrop; here, they reverse the figure-ground relation and look to other fields for help in overcoming the limitations of their outdated pedagogical materials on visuals. For outside of technical communication, they find a rich, albeit fragmented, multidisciplinary body of knowledge on visual representation. They are thus led to a broad, if brief, survey of contributions to visual research theory and practice in such diverse disciplines as perceptual and cognitive psychology, instructional science, rhetoric, communication, art history, graphic design, typography, cartography, statistics, computer graphics, and human factors. Since the visual field is interdisciplinary, they have chosen not to organize their discussion of these contributions along disciplinary lines. Rather, they portray contributions to knowledge about visuals in terms of major trends—trends that cumulatively are so profound as to suggest a paradigmatic shift. First, however, they review the considerable body of literature pertaining to a central problem, namely, the importance of visual representation, on the one hand, and the prevalence of visual illiteracy, on the other.

The Importance of Visual Representation

Many claims have been made for the importance of the visual mode. The power of visuals to convey information quickly and succinctly was recognized in 1801 by William Playfair, the father of modern graphics: "As much information may be obtained in five minutes [from a graph] as would require whole days to imprint on the memory, in a lasting manner, by a table of figures" (*The Commercial and Political Atlas,* Playfair 1801, p. xii). More recently, a 1982 study at the Wharton School of Business confirmed the power of visual aids to enhance productivity. As reported by Maxine D. Brown (1984) in "Mainframe Business Graphics," business meetings conducted with graphics averaged 28 percent shorter than meetings without graphics. Moreover, the use of graphics also correlated favorably with the credibility of presentations: proposal presentations with graphics enjoyed a two-thirds rate of success, compared to a one-third rate for presentations without graphics. W. J. Seiler's (1971) "The Effects of Visual Materials" offers corroborating results for oral presentations. The use of visuals has also been shown to improve both short-term and long-term remembrance of information. Allan Paivio's (*Imagery and Verbal Processes,* 1971; "The Mind's Eye," 1983) reviews of studies comparing memory for pictures and memory for words clearly indicate superior short-term recall for pictures. The "pictorial superiority effect" is confirmed, in the case of long-term memory, by M. H. Erdelyi and T. G. Becker ("Hypermnesia for Pictures," 1974), whose experiments suggest that pictures fade less rapidly from memory over time than do words.

Perhaps the most sweeping claims for the visual mode in communicating information are those of Gyorgy Kepes (1951, p. 13): "Visual communication is universal and international: it knows no limits of tongue, vocabulary, or grammar, and it can be perceived by the illiterate as well as by the literate. Visual language can convey facts and ideas in a wider and deeper range than almost any other means of communication" (*Language of Vision*). Such claims for the primacy of visual communication are ambitious, too ambitious for many to endorse without reservation, as the technical communication specialist confronted with a complex electronic circuit diagram intuitively knows. More convincing—to judge from the frequency of citations in the technical communication literature—is Rudolf Arnheim's claim for the primacy of vision in cognition. Arnheim's (1969) landmark work, *Visual Thinking,* challenges the classic philosophical position that separates seeing from thinking, treating them as discrete processes— one purely sensory, the other purely mental—and privileging the mental. For Arnheim (1969) "the cognitive operations called thinking are not the privilege of mental processes above and beyond perception, but the essential ingredients of perception itself" (p. 13); in short, "sensory responsiveness as such [is] intelligent" (p. 17). Thus, according to

Arnheim (1969), "vision is the primary medium of thought" (p. 18) because "visual perception is visual thinking" (p. 14). Eugene S. Ferguson (1977) sees visual thinking as "an essential strand in the intellectual history of technological development" ("The Mind's Eye," p. 827). He extols the strong symbiotic relationship between technology and the visual arts in Renaissance engineering, particularly in design; laments the subsequent devaluation of the visualizing faculty in favor of the analytical faculty in engineering education, and calls for a reinstitution of visual education.

Arthur I. Miller (1978), too, is concerned with the efficacy of visual thinking, the domain of thinking where "distinctions between conception in art and science become meaningless" ("Visualization Lost and Regained," p. 73). Unlike Ferguson, who surveys engineering from the Renaissance to the present, Miller adopts a case study approach to the genesis of quantum theory in the years 1913–27. He traces the path of quantum theory from Bohr's highly visual atomic model, with its discrete planetary electrons, through Heisenberg's mathematical, matrix-mechanical representation that removed the pictorial effect to the great dismay of Bohr and Schroedinger, to Schroedinger's subsequent restoration of visualization based on wave mechanics. Toward this end, Bohr's complementarity principle assigns dual, mutually exclusive particle and wave properties to atomic constituents; thus "the pictures of light and matter as waves and particles are not contradictory, as had been thought previously, but are 'complementary pictures' because they are both necessary for a complete description of atomic phenomena" (Miller 1978, p. 95). In another case study, "Darwin's 'Tree of Nature' and Other Images of Wide Scope," Howard E. Gruber (1978) argues that a recurrent image—that of an "irregularly branching tree"—antedated, foreshadowed, and guided Charles Darwin's development of the theory of evolution through natural selection. The image's importance lies in its sharp contrast with the symmetric images of nature favored by his contemporaries in its departure from prior scientific images reflecting platonic perfection and celestial harmony. For Darwin, the accidental aspects of his "tree of nature" captured the potential for explosive growth or extinction, as well as the fortuitous and the irregular, in the natural panorama. In a study of the importance of visualization in the career of Albert Einstein, Gerald Holton (1973) attributes Einstein's early academic "failure" to the uncongeniality of traditional schools for a student with a marked propensity for visual thinking. Holton speculates that the turning point in Einstein's career was enrollment in a school founded on the principles of Johann Pestalozzi, a Swiss educational reformer who viewed visual understanding as the foundation of conceptual understanding and visual instruction as "the basis on which the other means of instruction must be founded" (cited in *Thematic Origins of Scientific Thought,* Holton 1973, p. 371). Elsewhere, Steven Shapin ("Pump and Circumstance," 1984) presents a case study of the role of visualization in the rhetoric of Robert Boyle, while Jack Goody (*The Domestication of the Savage Mind,* 1977) examines the relation between lists and tables, on the one hand, and modes of reasoning, on the other.

More direct, testimonial evidence of the importance of visual thinking in science and technology is offered by practitioners themselves. The *locus classicus* is, of course, Albert Einstein's oft-quoted response to Jacques Hadamard's (1949, pp. 142–43) questionnaire on the nature of mental representations used by mathematicians:

> The words or the language, as they are written or spoken, do not seem to play any role in my mechanism of thought. The physical entities which seem to serve as elements in thought are certain signs and more or less clear images.... [These elements] are, in my case, of visual and some of muscular type. Conventional words or other signs have to be sought for laboriously only in a secondary stage.

Less well known, but more dramatic, testimony to the importance of the visual is Friedrich Kekulé's re-creation of his discovery of the closed "ring" rather than open structure of organic molecules such as benzene (cited in "August Kekulé" by Richard Anschutz [1961, p. 700]):

> Again the atoms gamboled before my eyes. Smaller groups this time kept modestly to the background. My mind's eyes, trained by repeated visions of a similar kind, now distinguished larger formations of various shapes.... everything in movement, winding and turning like snakes. And look, what was that? One snake grabbed its own tail, and mockingly the shape whirled before my eyes. As if struck by lightning I awoke.

More recently, the popularized account, in *The Double Helix* by James D. Watson (1980), of the discovery of the DNA structure portrays the discoverers' reliance on a highly visual modeling—indeed, a "tinkertoy"—approach to the problem.

The Problem of Visual Illiteracy

Despite the acknowledged importance of the visual mode, the literature provides considerable evidence of widespread visual "illiteracy" among students and professionals. Jenny Preece (1983) concludes from a study of 14- and 15-year-old students at the Open University in England that "many pupils cannot interpret cartesian graphs adequately, and that multiple curve graphs are particularly difficult" ("Graphs Are Not Straightforward," p. 54). Similarly, in the United States, Irvin Hashimoto (1983) observes that "many incoming freshmen [at Whitman College] neither understand simple graphing procedures nor recognize the kind of information that graphics can provide" ("Helping Students to Sort and Display Their Information," p. 281).

Among professionals, Michael Macdonald-Ross finds widespread visual illiteracy in a highly unexpected group, namely, graphic designers. Thus, in his review of research on the way quantitative data are presented to the general public, he finds that the advice of only the best graphic designers, the "master performers," is substantially vindicated. "[M]ost practitioners," concludes Macdonald-Ross (1977), "are more or less incompetent!" ("How Numbers Are Shown," p. 403). Howard Wainer (1980) comes to a similar conclusion in his examination of visuals in the popular media ("Making Newspaper Graphs Fit to Print"). Documenting various kinds of data distortion and visual excesses rife in newspaper graphs, he, like Macdonald-Ross, finds evidence of widespread incompetence among graphic designers; for Wainer, however, the bleak media scene is not relieved by the presence of "master performers." Less surprising, perhaps, is the finding of visual illiteracy by graphic designers looking outside their field: Calvin F. Schmid notes the "extraordinary prevalence of graphic illiteracy among practitioners in [the social sciences and statistics]" (*Statistical Graphics,* 1983, p. 2) and "the clumsy and amateurish charts produced by or under the direction of statisticians" ("The Role of Standards in Graphic Presentation," 1978, p. 79). Such criticism does not come solely from graphic designers: statistician Stephen E. Fienberg (1979) concurs, observing that "actual practice in statistical graphics is highly varied, good graphics being overwhelmed by distorted data presentation, cumbersome charts, and perplexing pictures" ("Graphical Methods in Statistics," p. 165). Management specialist Blake Ives (1982) is concerned about the quality of computer-generated visuals in business and concludes that information presentations likely will suffer rather than improve as graphics are increasingly generated with computers in the hands of broad classes of users unskilled in graphic design ("Graphical User Interfaces for Business Information Systems"). Cartographer George F. Jenks (1976) offers an indictment of computer-generated graphics in his field, though he lays the blame on the programmer's ignorance, not only of graphic design but also of the user's reference discipline—in this case, cartography ("Contemporary Statistical Maps—Evidence of

Spatial and Graphic Ignorance," p. 11). Jack Bishop is concerned less about the poor design of graphics than about the frequent meaninglessness of graphics generated with statistically sophisticated software. According to Bishop (1983), the fault is less with the programmer's ignorance of graphic design or of the user's reference discipline than with the user's ignorance of statistics ("Three Generations of Charts for the IBM PC," p. 358).

The charge of widespread incompetence among producers of graphics need not rest solely on opinions, however expert and numerous. Readers who desire ocular proof of visual illiteracy in published graphics can find parades of visual horrors set out in Gerald A. Mann's (1984) "How to Present Tabular Information Badly," Gene Zelazny's (1975) "Grappling with Graphics," Howard Wainer's (1980) "Making Newspaper Graphs Fit to Print," Darrell Huff's (1954) *How to Lie with Statistics,* and Jacques Bertin's (1983) "A New Look at Cartography," as well as in Edward R. Tufte's (1983) chapter on "chartjunk." For that matter, many will find excesses of attention getting and distortion well represented in the "private showing" by Nigel Holmes (1984), graphics editor of *Time,* in *Designer's Guide to Creating Charts and Diagrams.*

Explanations of visual illiteracy generally emphasize the paucity of visual education. Arnheim (1969) argues that the lamentable cultural divide between scientists and artists originates in "the widespread neglect of art at all levels of our educational system" (*Visual Thinking,* p. 295). In a corroborating indictment of visual education, James L. Adams (1976) notes that "a great deal of effort has been put into [Stanford students'] verbal (and mathematical) abilities during their formal education, but little into their visual ability" (*Conceptual Blockbusting,* p. 104). Similarly, Robert H. McKim (1972) observes that "one-sided education in the 3 R's, with few exceptions, results in massive visual atrophy" (*Experiences in Visual Thinking* p. 24). From J. Carter Brown (1983), Director of the National Gallery of Art, we hear: "For all its other deficiencies, the American educational system has one in particular that gets continuingly overlooked. We persist in turning out students who remain visual illiterates" ("Excellence and the Problem of Visual Literacy," p. 11).

It hardly needs to be said that schools are also blamed for visual illiteracy among professionals, who are, after all, products of our educational system; it is, however, notable that professional establishments have not picked up the slack. Examining the field of statistics, for example, Schmid (1978) faults the programs of professional societies and the policies of journals, which consign visual representation to marginal niches ("The Role of Standards in Graphic Presentation," p. 79). And, indeed, Stephen E. Fienberg (1979) documents a "prolonged decline in the relative use of graphs in statistical journals"—based on studies of *Biometrika* and *JASA* from 1920 to 1975--and this despite "an almost astonishing increase over the last 20 years in innovative graphic ideas for data display and analysis" ("Graphical Methods in Statistics," p. 169). Albert D. Biderman offers, in effect, one plausible explanation for the decline noted by Fienberg: according to Biderman (1980), the editorial policies of professional journals generally foster underuse of visuals, e.g., by enjoining authors to keep visuals to a minimum, to those "essential for the correct interpretation of the article" ("The Graph as a Victim of Adverse Discrimination and Segregation," p. 232).

Findings of widespread visual illiteracy have led to several proposed solutions. For dealing with incompetence among professionals, both Marie Neurath ("Isotype," 1974) and Macdonald-Ross ("Graphics in Texts," 1978) call for a graphic specialist termed a "transformer," similar in role to the graph editor advocated by Wainer (1980) in "Making Newspaper Graphs Fit to Print." To resort to such graphics specialists, however, does not seem a viable solution in this era of widely dispersed computer graphics. Wainer sees an interim solution through software operation under default conditions, and an ultimate solution in graphics expert systems. Like Ives ("Graphical User Interfaces for Business Information Systems," 1982), A. Paller et al. (1980) are less optimistic, particularly on the basis that default operations have typically been devised by programmers without graphic design experience (*Choosing the Right Graph*). Moreover, Barton and Barton (1985b) find that the trend from hand- to computer-executed graphics in student reports merely exchanges one set of pedagogical problems for another. Thus, they find that in the computer era, underuse of visuals gives way to overuse; similarly, primitive visuals give way to overblown visuals ("Toward a Rhetoric of Visuals for the Computer Era," Barton and Barton 1985b, pp. 136–37).

These observations suggest that there is no easy way of circumventing the need for increased visual education. Admittedly, there are some (e.g., Beck and Wallisch [1981], in "Technical Illustration") who argue that wide exposure to visual images, for example, on television and computer displays, promotes visual literacy. But most commentators believe that exposure alone, whether to visuals or to texts, does not produce literacy and that overexposure to visuals in an image-saturated environment such as ours may, in fact, be counterproductive to the goal of visual literacy. In "Semiotics and the Graphic Sign," Luc

Vanmalderen (1969, p. 89) inveighs against an "escalating visual cacophony" in a culture "choked with redundant signs" and without coherent visual education. He calls for a rational, international dictionary of graphic semiotics so that the meaning of signs can be coherently taught. Tom Porter and Byron Mikellides (1978) focus on the contribution to the modern visual cacophony of one of the visual elements, namely, color. In the present climate of "color chaos," according to these authors, "we have lost both the knowledge and ability to manipulate either the biological or symbolic colour languages." Porter and Mikellides (1978) recall the suggestion that the former is eroded the moment we give a string of multicolored beads to a baby, who is thereby unwittingly being taught to ignore color as a signal operating within a system of codes ("The Language of Colour," p. 9). Communication educators B. F. Hammet and Peter M. Illick (1971) call for the teaching of visual literacy as a discipline based on the systematic learning of operant visual codes ("Visual Literacy: A Perceptual Discipline").

For some educators, establishing a canon of exemplary graphics would be a useful preliminary step in combating visual illiteracy. And, indeed, such a canon is slowly emerging in the literature. Certainly, the innovative work of Playfair gains entry by acclamation. According to Fienberg (1979), "his work provides excellent examples of good graphics" ("Graphical Methods in Statistics," p. 165). Tufte's (1983) *The Visual Display of Quantitative Information* is suffused with praise for Playfair's work. H. G. Funkhouser (1937) concurs, singling out for special praise the "Chart of the National Debt of Britain from the Revolution to the End of the War with America" and the "Chart Shewing at One View the Price of the Quarter of Wheat & Wages of Labour by the Week from the Year 1565 to 1821" ("Historical Development," p. 287). A canon of good graphics surely also includes the work of the prominent nineteenth-century engineer Charles Joseph Minard, deemed the "Playfair of France" by Funkhouser (1937, p. 305). He finds especially praiseworthy Minard's map portraying the devastating losses suffered by Napoleon's armies in the Russian campaign of 1812. For Tufte (1983, p. 40), "it may well be the best statistical graphic ever drawn." Another sure canon entrant is the work of Otto Neurath, whose staunchest supporter, Macdonald-Ross, endorses Neurath's isotype system of pictorial representation as "one of the great graphic inventions of the century" (*Graphics in Text: A Bibliography*, Macdonald-Ross and Smith 1977, p. 26). Among individual visuals, a prominent candidate for the canon is the London Underground Diagram (LUD) which, according to Arnheim (1974), "gives the needed information with utmost clarity, and at the same time delights the eye with the harmony of its design" (*Art and Visual Perception,* p. 159). John A. Walker (1979) dubs the LUD "a masterpiece of twentieth century graphic art" in an endorsement laudable for its analytical basis ("The London Underground Diagram," p. 2). Walker's analysis is of particular interest to scholars of technical and business communication for its recognition of the LUD as a prototype diagram affording an exemplary visual solution to a wide class of problems common in engineering and business management, namely network routing problems. More typically, however, prospective canon members garner mixed reviews. For example, Arnheim (1969) comments that "the visual information on the pages of the *Scientific American* is consistently excellent" (*Visual Thinking,* p. 306); however, the quality of that publication's graphics is more uneven than this unqualified praise suggests. Similarly, Leonard P. Ayres's (1919) heavily illustrated report, *The War with Germany,* is unequivocally deemed by both Funkhouser (1937, p. 375) and Paul J. FitzPatrick ("The Development of Graphic Presentation," 1962, p. 211) some of the best graphic work done in the United States; according to Schmid, however, "several bar charts without scale lines and scale figures would be classified as deficient" ("The Role of Standards in Graphic Presentation," 1978, p. 81) and "none are 'distinguished' or 'outstanding' " (*Statistical Graphics,* 1983, p. 128). Divergent opinions may occur even in examining purported collections of good graphics, such as Walter Herdeg's (1974) *Diagrams,* particularly when little analytical basis is provided for the inclusion of individual works.

Most educators, however, feel that good models alone are not an adequate antidote to widespread visual illiteracy, that only a broad program of visual education will suffice. Thus, W. G. V. Balchin and Alice M. Coleman (1966) advocate that "graphicacy" be taught as a fourth necessary intellectual skill along with reading, 'riting, and 'rithmetic ("Graphicacy Should Be the Fourth Ace in the Pack"). The linchpin for such a broad program of visual education has long been the so-called "visual literacy" movement. The status of research related to this movement was assessed recently by David Sless (1984) in "Visual Literacy: A Failed Opportunity?" While defending the importance of research in visual literacy in principle, he concludes nevertheless that most research has been too narrowly conceived. For him the root problem has been a broad failure among researchers to recognize and to exploit the rich visual tradition in such fields as art, cartography, engineering, architecture, and typography. Ultimately, Sless makes the imparting of disciplinary visual skills to the public at large the basis for revitalizing the visual literacy movement. In the following sections, such disciplinary visual skills are portrayed from an interdisciplinary perspective in terms of six major trends.

Trend from the Verbal to the Visual Mode

The literature reveals a trend toward greater recognition and exploitation of the "visualness" of text. In part, this means a tendency to seek visual rather than verbal representations, to explore visual alternatives to linear texts. This quest constitutes a mounting challenge to the hegemony of text, to the view of visuals as handmaidens of text. Donald F. Ford (1984), for example, counsels tabular rather than narrative formatting of information to communicate more clearly complex policies, concepts, or procedures ("Packaging Problem Prose"). At times, the verbal is even subordinated to the visual. Richard Braby et al. (1982), for example, extol highly graphic presentations with supporting text in manuals for training personnel in military procedures. Based on tests, they conclude that these "learning aids" are most effective when procedures taught must be performed frequently from memory or correctly for safety ("Illustrated Formats to Teach Procedures"). In "Visual Rhetoric in Teaching Technical Writing," Patrick M. Kelley (1980) suggests the use of visual representations to teach verbal skills. Thus, a student is taught first to visualize a well-constructed paragraph. In the limit, under this trend, the verbal disappears. In "Developing Wordless Instructions," for example, Richard Hodgkinson and John Hughes (1982) advocate exclusive use of the pictorial mode to circumvent the barriers posed by both technical and natural languages. Their field testing established the effectiveness of the pictorial mode for teaching Europeans to unpack and set up IBM Selectric II typewriters.

The interest in visual alternatives to linear text is generally validated by other experimental evidence. In "Written Information," Patricia Wright and Fraser Reid (1973) evaluate alternatives to prose for expressing outcomes under complex contingencies. They compare times and accuracies for the lay solution, under fixed criteria, of reasoning and information-encoding problems represented in either bureaucratic prose or short-sentence, flow chart, or tabular form. Performances were slowest and least accurate with prose, most rapid with tables for easy problems, and most accurate with flow charts for harder problems.

Admittedly, performance improved over trials from memory of both prose forms, and deteriorated over trials from memory of flow charts and tables. A. S. Blaiwes ("Formats for Presenting Procedural Instructions," 1974) also found that flow charts produced fewer errors for difficult problems, in comparison with short sentences. Richard Kammann ("The Comprehensibility of Printed Instructions and the Flowchart Alternative," 1975) compares the effectiveness of the prose instructions in a Bell Laboratories telephone directory with two flow charts representing only that half of the directory information directly relevant to the solution of a specific set of dialing problems. Subjects included corporate engineers and scientists familiar with the directory and housewives presumably unfamiliar with it. Both groups made significantly fewer errors with the flow charts, though time savings were significant only for the housewives. A later field test conducted one to two months after distributing flow charts to a sample of all listed laboratory employees revealed that only a minority used the flow charts when confronted with a dialing problem. Compared to the prose instructions, the two flow charts were both effective in reducing errors, although only the more visually directive of them produced a time savings. In "An Evaluation of Alphanumeric, Graphic, and Color Information Displays," Thomas S. Tullis (1981) evaluates speed and accuracy in interpreting results displayed in four different formats by a computer-based, telephone-line-testing system, namely, prose, tables, black-and-white graphics, and color graphics. Response times, for both graphic formats, consistently shorter than those for prose, were matched for tabular format only after practice. Users expressed a clear preference for color graphics.

The trend toward fuller exploitation of the visual mode in text includes efforts to enhance the visualness of visuals. The impulse for these efforts was pioneering work dating from the 1960s to expose and overcome the limitations of traditional graphic methods, for example, Roberto Bachi's (1968) "Applications, Limitations and Shortcomings of Usual Graphic Methods," Jacques Bertin's *Graphics and Graphic Information-Processing* (1981) and *Semiology of Graphics* (1983b), and John W. Tukey's (1977) *Exploratory Data Analysis.* One result has been the rediscovery of some relatively neglected genres such as pictographs, which are discussed from a historical perspective by Marie Neurath (1974) in "Isotype." Pictographs—enthusiastically endorsed by Macdonald-Ross ("How Numbers are Shown," 1977), especially for innumerate or lay viewers—are enjoying a revival in the representation of queueing problems. Macdonald-Ross attributes their heretofore restricted use to difficulty of hand execution, a restriction inapt for the computer era.

Other research has focused on methods for increasing the visualness of traditional genres, such as demographic maps. Bertin (1981) for example, distinguishes between "reading maps" and "seeing maps" (*Graphics and Graphic Information-Processing,* p. 147). The traditional reading maps use abstract symbols, frequently of the same size, interpreted with legends; in contrast, seeing maps employ symbols differing only in size to facilitate the concrete representation of values. Readers with literary backgrounds will recognize a parallel between Bertin's "seeing" and "reading," on the one hand, and Percy Lubbock's (1921) "showing" and "telling," on the other. Bertin employs graded symbols of less than perhaps ten different sizes on various "seeing" maps that have extraordinary visual impact. For a recent summary of his ideas, see Bertin's (1983a) "A New Look at Cartography." Jon Bentley ("Programming Pearls: Graphic Output," 1984a) illustrates methods for enhancing the visual qualities of traditional genres; in an interesting follow-on article (Bentley's [1984b] "Programming Pearls: Updates," p. 634), John Tukey shows how to heighten the visualness of one of Bentley's revisions.

Efforts to enhance the visualness of visuals has also led, in the words of Fienberg (1979), to "an almost astonishing increase over the last 20 years in innovative graphic ideas for data display and analysis" ("Graphical Methods in Statistics," p. 169). New graphic genres include the cartoonlike faces of Herman Chernoff ("Using Faces to Represent Points in k-Dimensional Space Graphically," 1973c); the "star charts" or "circle graphs" described by A. P. Friedman et al. ("A Graphic Way of Describing Changing Multivariate Patterns," 1984); the "box plots" of Tukey (*Exploratory Data Analysis,* 1977); and "fuzzy graphs." Some of these new graphic genres were born of the need for highly integrated visual displays to facilitate the analysis and control of large-scale systems such as nuclear power plants, chemical process units, and airliners. The cartoon faces of Chernoff can represent up to nineteen independent, continuously variable parameters. A viewer can quickly gain an overall impression of system status by interpreting facial "expression." Alternatively, star charts are formed by plotting variable values at equal angles on a polar plot and connecting the points to form a polygon. Again, a viewer can quickly gain an overall impression, in this case by interpreting polygon shape. Timothy E. Goldsmith and Roger W. Schvaneveldt ("Facilitating Multiple-Cue Judgments with Integral Information Displays," 1984) report empirical studies showing the superiority of star charts over multiple bar graphs for users processing complex information. William B. Rouse (*Advances in Man-Machine Systems Research,* 1984) summarizes recent research dealing with system applications of new visual genres.

Trend from Presentational to Analytical Graphics

A trend from a product to a process view of visuals, can be seen in the recent tendency to deemphasize presentational, as opposed to analytical, graphics. In mundane definitions, for example, in trade journals, presentational graphics are distinguished by high quality or formal purpose, whereas analytical graphics are associated with "working," or informal "peer," situations. More aptly, presentational graphics serve for communicating given ideas to others whereas analytical graphics aim at generating hypotheses from, or analyzing, data. Presentational graphics have had a long heyday; see, for example, the historical treatment by FitzPatrick ("The Development of Graphic Presentation," 1962) of presentational graphics in the United States. More recently, Macdonald-Ross ("How Numbers Are Shown," 1977) reviews research on ways of presenting quantitative data to the general public; elsewhere, he reviews treatments of presentational graphics in textbooks and other instructional materials ("Graphics in Texts," 1978). Concern in the pedagogical literature and textbooks of technical communication has also focused on presentational graphics, as pointed out and critiqued by Barton and Barton ("Toward a Rhetoric of Visuals for the Computer Era," 1985b, pp. 134–35). Similarly, presentational graphics are the dominant concern of technical drawing textbooks like Frederick E. Giesecke's (1981) *Engineering Graphics* and Thomas E. French et al.'s (1984) *Graphic Science and Design* and of engineering handbooks like George E. Rowbotham's (1982) *Engineering and Industrial Graphics Handbook.* At the level of professional communication, the focus on presentational graphics is shown in the 1982 special issue of the *IEEE Transactions on Professional Communications* (1982) and in standards such as *Time-Series Charts* (American National Standards Institute 1979), as well as in the articles by Andrew S. C. Ehrenberg ("Rudiments of Numeracy," 1977) and Mary F. Buehler ("Report Construction: Tables," 1977) on tables, by Alan G. Gross ("A Primer on Tables and Figures," 1983) on tables and figures, and by A. Jean MacGregor ("Selecting the Appropriate Chart," 1982) on charts. In business communication, a similar focus is shown by A. Paller et al. (*Choosing the Right Graph,* 1980), Robert Lefferts (*Elements of*

Graphics, 1981) and Raymond K. Gust ("Designing Effective Business Graphics," 1983). The literature of graphic design is concerned almost exclusively with presentational graphics, as exemplified in Matthew P. Murgio's (1969) *Communications Graphics,* Calvin F. Schmid and Stanton E. Schmid's (1979) *Handbook of Graphic Presentation,* Calvin F. Schmid's (1983) *Statistical Graphics,* Jan V. White's (1984) *1000 Ideas for Visual Persuasion,* and Russell W. Blanchard's (1984) *Graphic Design.*

Not uncommonly, the emphasis on presentational graphics leads to systematic procedures for subordinating the visual components of texts. Kathryn Szoka (1982), for example, makes the creation of a "focus sentence summarizing what you want the chart to say" the key step in effective chart design ("A Guide to Choosing the Right Chart Type," p. 101). William A. Simcox ("A Design Method for Graphic Communication," 1984) goes further and outlines a seven-step procedure for the systematic generation of a presentational graphic: formulating a focus statement summarizing the point of the visual, analyzing this statement for informational attributes, selecting and organizing the visual format, and evaluating and redesigning the resulting graph.

The emergent widespread interest in analytical graphics has been interpreted differently in various quarters. Laura Tilling ("Early Experimental Graphs," 1975) sees a progressive development in the use of geological graphs as a means of first collection, then presentation, and finally analysis of data. On the other hand, James R. Beniger and Dorothy L. Robyn ("Quantitative Graphics in Statistics," 1978) show that the idea of analytical graphics is not new by tracing its historical antecedents back through several centuries and longer. Thus, they see analytical graphics as a historically important tool that has reemerged in the computer era. Focusing on the work of Charles S. Peirce, Macdonald-Ross ("Scientific Diagrams," 1979) explores the philosophical underpinnings of the notion that diagrams play important roles in the generation of scientific hypotheses. Susan Marcus ("Diagramming Complex Systems," 1980) presents a case study of the use of diagrams as tools for research into long-term planning and analysis on global problems. "From Data to Image to Action," a survey by Stanley Aronoff and Glyn F. Jones (1985) of image processing as an analytical tool in natural resource management is informative and handsomely illustrated.

Much of the initial impetus toward modern analytical graphics came from Tukey (*Exploratory Data Analysis,* 1977); the work of Tukey and colleagues is most fully presented by John M. Chambers et al. (1983) in *Graphical Methods for Data Analysis.* Wainer (1981) provides an excellent review of recent developments in analytical graphics in "Graphical Data Analysis." Tukey's (1983) "Another Look at the Future" identifies as particularly promising the burgeoning field of decision support. This field offers compelling evidence of the heuristic value of visual representations for generating ideas. A variety of highly visual representations are used in recent software packages that go beyond traditional integrated software in support of decision making. Charles Spezzano (1985) discusses several such new packages in "Decision Support Software," addressed to computer novices.

Budding attempts to develop a pedagogy for analytical graphics should be noted. In *Understanding Data,* Bonnie H. Erickson and T. A. Nosanchuk (1977) reduce Tukey's approach to a pedagogy suitable for an undergraduate statistics course for social science students. Eschewing the classical "number-crunching" approach in statistics courses oriented toward "math-bent" technical students, they emphasize the qualitative finding rather than the quantitative testing of hypotheses. In technical communication, Elizabeth Tebeaux ("Using Computer Printouts to Teach Analysis and Graphics," 1981) discusses a series of exercises in visual communication based on a computer printout of tabular data. Some of the exercises introduce visuals as tools for analysis; students are expected to "massage" the data to generate hypotheses. In composition, Hashimoto ("Helping Students to Sort and Display Their Information," 1983) discusses visual aids beyond the traditional linear outline as tools for invention. He illustrates, in an interesting series of problems involving complex or qualitative information, how various kinds of imaging can facilitate the discovery of interrelations among complex data.

We would note a tendency in the work reported above to take data as given and thus to mask built-in preconceptions and data collection pitfalls that are also issues in hypothesis generation. A welcome contribution to the field of analytical graphics is, then, the recent spate of books designed to foster visual thinking at the data generation stage, including Ralph E. Wileman's (1980) *Exercises in Visual Thinking,* Robert McKim's *Experiences in Visual Thinking* (1972) and *Thinking Visually* (1980), and Omar Faruque's (1984) *Graphic Communication as a Design Tool.* Technical communication specialists Dawn Rodrigues and Raymond J. Rodrigues (1984) offer a computer-based program designed to foster inventive skills in students by means of visual synectics—a technique that encourages a participant to compare his or her topic with normally unassociated items identified from a randomly selected picture, for example to compare nuclear waste disposal to a beach ball, a bathing suit, sand, an ocean, and suntan lotion ("Computer-Based Creative Problem Solving," pp. 36–39).

Trend from a Positivistic to a Constitutive View of Visuals

Although the view of visuals in the literature and textbooks of technical communication remains largely positivistic in underlying epistemology, elsewhere visual representation is undergoing a paradigmatic shift. Above all, the shift is impelled by the rejection of logical positivism in favor of theories that make visual representations constitutive of knowledge and knowledge itself consensual. What, then, is the positivistic view of visuals currently under attack? To pose the question more specifically, in terms that reflect the orientation of a literature dominated by a "worst-case analysis," what is the positivistic view of photographs or pictures, that is, of visuals that seem to offer the most faithful renditions of reality?

In the positivistic view, reality resides in the external world and a picture is an accurate, unmediated transposition of that reality. Not only does the picture represent reality itself—faithfully and without distortion, in the ideal—but the picture also is perceived by a viewer with equal fidelity and without distortion. The picture is, then, a transparent medium of transmission between reality and viewer. In the positivistic view, pictures are fundamentally arhetorical as no persuasion is necessary: seeing is believing. For the positivist par excellence, here is the early James J. Gibson (1954): "A faithful picture is a delimited physical surface processed in such a way that it reflects (or transmits) a sheaf of lightrays to a given point which is the same as would be the sheaf of rays from the original to that point" ("A Theory of Pictorial Perception," p. 14). Since the eye is a passive registrant of incoming sensory information, the children do not need to "read" a picture; they perceive the object in a picture as soon as they perceive it directly. John M. Kennedy (*A Psychology of Picture Perception,* 1974) reviews the experimental evidence on the question, "Is the Perception of Pictures Learnt?" and answers "No." The crucial evidence is an experiment by Julian Hochberg and Virginia Brooks ("Pictorial Recognition as an Unlearnt Ability," 1962) in which the Hochberg child, deprived of pictorial imagery until 19–months-old, had no trouble naming familiar objects represented in line drawings and photographs. Also contributory is the subsequent experiment by T.G.R. Bower ("The Object in the World of the Infant," 1971) in which infants presented with stereoscopic pictures took the depicted objects as real. As implied by this research and as Michael F. Cassidy and James Q. Knowlton (1983) explicitly point out, one consequence of the positivistic viewpoint is that visual literacy need not be taught: "Given any of a wide range of reasonably normal environments (at least in Western technical societies), and given an infant or young child with reasonably normal perceptual apparatus, we know that the child's perceptual skills will develop normally and without teaching of any sort" ("Visual Literacy: A Failed Metaphor?" p. 80).

But challenges to the concept of a self-evident realism in visual representation have arisen in the fields of psychology, photography, semiotics, art history, and cartography. For the post-positivists, the relation between the picture and the depicted object is no longer direct and unmediated: believing is seeing. The most radical challenge to the positivistic view is the position of total relativism represented by psychologist Nelson Goodman (1968, pp. 37–39) in *Languages of Art*:

> Realism is relative.... [It] is a matter not of any constant or absolute relationship between a picture and its object but of a relationship between the system of representation employed in the picture and the standard system.... That a picture looks like nature often means only that it looks the way nature is usually painted.

Goodman finds support from an unexpected quarter. By 1978, James J. Gibson (1978), in effect, renounces his earlier positivistic position: "It is impossible to copy a piece of the environment. What may be copied is another drawing. We have been misled for too long by the fallacy that a picture is *similar* to what it depicts, a *likeness,* or an *imitation* of it" ("The Ecological Approach to the Visual Perception of Pictures," p. 231). Thus, Gibson not only denies the directness of the link between picture and underlying reality but also denies the paramountcy of the link. The important link now is that between the picture and other pictures. In "Looking at Photographs," photography theorist Victor Burgin (1982, p. 144) agrees that the focal problem is now "intertextuality":

> The intelligibility of the photograph is no simple thing; photographs are *texts* inscribed in terms of what we call 'photographic discourse', but this discourse, like any other, engages discourses beyond itself; the 'photographic text', like any other, is the site of a complex 'intertextuality', an overlapping series of previous texts 'taken for granted' at a particular cultural and historical conjunc-

ture. These prior texts, those *presupposed* by the photograph, are autonomous; they serve a role in the actual text but do not appear in it, they are latent to the manifest text and may only be read across it 'symptomatically'.... Treating the photograph as an object-text, 'classic' semiotics showed that the notion of the 'purely visual' *image* is nothing but an Edenic fiction.

The relation between text and viewer is equally problematical for the post-positivist. Attacking the "bucket theory" of passive registration of stimuli, Ernst H. Gombrich (1984) claims that there is more to seeing than meets the eye; there is the "beholder's share" (*The Sense of Order,* p. 107). Gombrich draws approvingly on the work of cognitive psychologist Ulric Neisser (1976), whose oft-referenced *Cognition and Reality* is based on the assumption that perception is a constructive rather than a receptive act. What determines our constructions are preconceptions, and these are largely based on culturally determined rules for interpreting visual artifacts, that is, conventions. In the words of cartographer Marc Treib (1980): "All communication depends upon accepted conventions. If there is no agreement, there is no mutual understanding. Because it is a conventionalized form, the map imposes a structure on the world, rather than merely describing it" ("Mapping Experience," p. 6). Stan Pinkwas ("Three Mapmakers," 1984) documents the view that the conventions of maps are not neutral, that maps are persuasive views of reality. He contrasts several well-known mapping systems in terms of their constitutive conventions and underlying ideologies. Thus, Mercator's mapping system, long a standard, placed the designer's homeland, Germany, at the center of the map—a scheme quickly adopted in other European countries. The eurocentric mercatorial map manifests clear distortions, for example, Russia, with 8.7 million square miles of area, looks twice the size of Africa, with 11.6 million square miles. Peter's "Third World Map" avoids this bias but, not surprisingly, introduces others. If Pinkwas focuses on broad cultural and political conventions, Michael Lynch ("Discipline and the Material Form of Images," 1985) emphasizes the importance of disciplinary conventions in his study of selected scientific illustrations.

The literatures on both broad cultural and discipline-specific conventions are large. Illustrative studies of broad cultural conventions in pictorial representation include James Mangan's (1978) "Cultural Conventions of Pictorial Representation" and Rune Pettersson's (1982) "Cultural Differences in the Perception of Image and Color in Pictures." Visual conventions are traced in the history of art by Gombrich (1959) in *Art and Illusion* and David Summers (1981) in "Conventions in the History of Art" and in the social sciences by Funkhouser (1937) in "Historical Development of the Graphical Representation of Statistical Data," Beniger and Robyn (1978) in "Quantitative Graphics in Statistics," and FitzPatrick (1962) in "The Development of Graphic Presentation of Statistical Data in the United States." Developments of visual conventions in scientific research are examined by Martin J. S. Rudwick (1976) in "The Emergence of a Visual Language for Geological Science 1760–1840," William M. Ivins, Jr. (1969), in *Prints and Visual Communication,* Laura Tilling (1975) in "Early Experimental Graphs," and Samuel Edgerton (1976) in *The Renaissance Discovery of Linear Perspective.* Philip B. Meggs (1983) traces trends in the conventions of graphic design in *A History of Graphic Design.* Codified graphic conventions, that is, graphic standards, are examined by Calvin F. Schmid ("The Role of Standards in Graphic Presentation," 1978) and delineated by H. P. Van Cott and R. G. Kinkade (*Human Engineering Guide to Equipment Design,* 1972). Sources of information on technical-drawing conventions include the standard treatises listed by Calvin F. Schmid (1983) in *Statistical Graphics* and the historical treatment by Ken Baynes and Francis Pugh (1981) in *The Art of the Engineer.*

While the view of visual representations as conventional is an important corrective to naive positivistic views, it is increasingly seen as problematical—especially in its extreme expressions. Thus, recent theorists are uneasy over Goodman's (1968) assertion that "almost any picture may represent almost anything" (*Languages of Art,* p. 38). In such a view, there is no essential difference between, say, a schematic diagram and a photograph of an electronic circuit. Admittedly, the interpretation of either depends on a knowledge of conventions, but the conventions of the photograph are surely easier to master than those of engineering schematics. In other words, the ease of interpretation of visual representations is a matter of degree. Thus, to insist on a dichotomy of nature versus convention—or of equivalent expressions in the literature, for example, *physis* versus *nomos,* or reception versus construction—is simplistic. Attacking such traditional oppositions, Gombrich (1982) sensibly observes "a continuum between skills which come naturally to us and skills which may be next to impossible for anyone to acquire" (*The Image and the Eye,* p. 283). Reviewing empirical studies of pictorial representations, D. N. Perkins ("Pictures and the Real Thing," 1980) also finds a middle ground in the nature-versus-convention debate. He recommends taking the resemblance view of picturing as a first-order approximation that ultimately must accommodate custom, invention, and learning to determine how people make and make sense of pictures (Perkins, 1980, pp. 274–75).

Trend toward Integration of the Verbal and the Visual

Review of the literature also reveals a trend toward a more integrated view of the verbal and visual components of representations, toward a holistic view of "text." In the traditional atomistic view of text, the verbal and the visual are segregated, with the latter subordinated. Thus, one speaks of verbal texts and visual aids. The interrelation of the two occurs primarily in the verbal component, under the classic dictum that the visual be introduced and interpreted. The new view is concerned with visual aspects of the text as a whole, including those of the verbal component, for example, through typography. The trend towards textual holism is captured in such new disciplinary names as "document design" and "information display," as well as in such terms as "visual writing" and "visible language." The choice of these terms is not casual: as Daniel B. Felker (1980, p. 2) affirms in the introduction to *Document Design: A Review of the Relevant Research,* "the words 'document design' are a deliberate choice because they convey the complexity of the field. . . . The organization and format of a document may be just as important as its language." A corollary trend is the growing appreciation of the visual aspects of verbal materials. In "Text as Diagram," Robert H. W. Waller (1982, p. 141) argues that written texts, like diagrams, are visual in nature, in other words, that writing "has a physical and spatial presence as well as abstract meaning." Fernand Baudin (1984) would agree: "Any piece of writing is an image as well as a message" ("The Visual Editing of Texts," p. 81), and writers should be aware of the form as well as the content of text. His call for the development of skill in "visual editing," as a matter of general literacy, is designed to heal the form/content split. For communication specialist Stephen A. Bernhardt ("Seeing the Text," 1986), the development of such visual editing skills in students will require a major reorientation of composition instruction. He attributes the traditional insensitivity to the visual aspects of text to the unfortunate hegemony of the relatively visually impoverished essay in the classroom. Josh Ard's (1983) "The Semiotics of Mathematical Symbolism" extends appreciation of the visual to the formulary components of text. He observes that, while the shape of symbols is not of significance in mathematical theory, symbols differ enormously in their effects on readers in practice.

Noting the mnemonic value of symbols with high iconicity, Ard argues that suggestive shape is explicitly valued in standardizing symbols.

Research in cognitive psychology and instructional science indicates that documents are more usable when visual aspects of the document reflect the hierarchy of information in the text *The Psychology of Written Communication,* Hartley (1980b); *The Technology of Text,* Jonassen (1982); "Usability," Wright (1980); "Graphic Aspects of Complex Texts," Waller (1980). Researchers of visual aspects of text generally distinguish spatial cues (white space) and typographic cues (italic, boldface, or capital letters and the like), both purposing to clarify the structure and contents of complex materials, Hartley's (1980b) review of the research literature on cueing finds spatial cueing generally more influential on viewers than typographic cueing (*The Psychology of Written Communication*). Indeed, James Hartley et al. ("The Role of Spatial and Typographic Cues," 1980) find both American and British subjects prefer spatial to typographic cues in the layout of journal references. L. T. Frase and B. J. Schwartz ("Typographical Cues that Facilitate Comprehension," 1979) of Bell Laboratories investigate the use of spatial cueing at the level of clauses. They find that readers can answer questions more quickly from technical text "chunked" into "meaningful elements," for materials extracted mainly from laboratory instruction manuals; see also Hartley's (1980a) "Spatial Cues in Text." R. E. Horn (*How to Write Information Mapping,* 1976) exploits spatial cues at the paragraph level to map information in technical and reference manuals. Donald L. Jewett ("Self-Instruction and Multi-Level Textbooks," 1972) would divide textbook materials into three levels—main arguments, explanations/examples, and incidentals—and distinguish them by increasing degrees of indention. Jeremy J. Foster ("The Use of Visual Cues in Text," 1979) summarizes the findings of research on typographic cueing; see also Waller ("Graphic Aspects of Complex Texts," 1980). Frances J. Laner ("Readability Techniques," 1978) applies the findings of early research by Miles A. Tinker (1963) (*Legibility of Print*) to the technical research report. Specifically, she looks at margins, page layout, relation of illustrations to text, location of captions, and choice of type. Attempting a synthesis of writing and design in "Writing Visually," Philippa J. Benson (1985) applies research findings to printed document, or page, design. Such a synthesis is called for, she argues, as computers increasingly give writers control over typography and page format. In a companion article, "Application of Research on Document Design to Online Displays," Philip M. Rubens and Robert Krull (1985) apply research findings to on-line display, or screen, design. In "Unbounded Text," Philippe C. Duchastel (1982) even challenges the page as the basic unit of text. Of course, the "multiple-window" methods of computer displays represent a parallel challenge.

While a relatively new idea in technical communication, the suggestive power of the visual aspects of words has, of course, long been appreciated in the arts, for example, in concrete poetry or Letterism. John Milner ("On the Fusion of Verbal and Visual Media," 1976) discusses attempts by various artists and poets of the late nineteenth and twentieth centuries to synthesize the verbal and visual media. Stephen C. Foster ("Letterism," 1983) places the Letterist movement, with its respect for the visual nature of language, in a historical perspective along with Dadaism and Surrealism. Bill Bonnell and Stephan Geissbühler (1984) describe a recent movement in graphic design that has mounted diverse visual challenges to the premise of the prevailing modern "Swiss design," that is, to "objective, uncluttered rationality," in search of greater expressiveness ("New Wave in Graphic Design USA," p. 39). Moreover, these trends cannot be dismissed as confined to art publications and advertisements. To see radical departures from traditional approaches in published academic materials, consult the special double issue of *Visible Language* published in 1981, Duchastel's (1984) "Marginalia," and Richard Showstack's (1980) "Discourse Punctuation." More significantly, Bonnell and Geissbühler (1984, p. 40) note that these new designs are slowly finding their way into the hardcore corporate world of annual reports and previously untouchable financial documents.

Trends in Visual Theory and Research Methodology

An examination of theory and research methodology reveals several trends in approaches to visual representation. A widespread dependence on intuition or "common sense," noted by many commentators, is abating under the mounting weight of discrediting evidence. For statistician William H. Kruskal (1975), the intuitional approach was an expedient: "In choosing, constructing, comparing, and criticizing graphical methods we have little to go on but intuition, rule of thumb, and a kind of master-to-apprentice passing along of information" ("Visions of Maps and Graphs," p. 27). J. Lincoln DeVillier's (1972, p. 15) experimental study, "Communication Effects of Variations in Organization and Format," speculates that "perhaps some of the recommendations in business communication textbooks are based more on authors' preferences than on scientific experimentation" and, more importantly, proceeds to show that such preferences clash with experimental evidence. Perkins (1980) offers a broader indictment: his review of research on pictures concludes with the warning that "the intuitions of textbook designers and illustrators should not be relied on too heavily" ("Pictures and the Real Thing," p. 272). In light of Perkins' findings, one is scarcely surprised by Francis M. Dwyer's discovery of a disparity between the intuitive choices of laymen and experimental evidence. Reviewing over 100 studies of learning facilitation with visual aids conducted by him and his associates and involving more than 40,000 subjects of at least high school age, Dwyer found that the subjects' intuitive choices of the most informative depictions often ran counter to experimental findings (*Strategies for Improving Visual Learning,* 1978; "The Program of Systematic Evaluation," 1982–83). A classic case of the failure of intuition, or "common sense," involves the so-called "inside-out" and "outside-in" approaches to aircraft "attitude," or roll, display. The traditional inside-out display, rooted in an intuitive visual approach, presents the view one would see through a small, circular forward port in a following aircraft maneuvering in synchronism with its target. Thus, during a right turn, the displayed "artificial horizon" appears to rotate counterclockwise, while the displayed aircraft image remains parallel to the cockpit floor. But human factors research over decades has established the superiority of the counterintuitional, outside-in display on which the aircraft image rotates clockwise, while the artificial horizon remains parallel to the cockpit floor, during the same right turn ("An Experimental Evaluation of the Interpretability of Various Types of Aircraft Attitude Indicators," Loucks 1947; "Airborne Displays for Flight and Navigation," Roscoe 1968). Today, the felt merit of this display is that corrective action involves control movement in a direction counter to that of the moving display element, that is, the aircraft image.

But the results of empirical studies have not been immune to criticism. Many commentators have called attention to procedural flaws in visual research. Macdonald-Ross (1977) makes the telling observation that substandard stimulus material is the rule rather than the exception in graphics research ("How Numbers Are Shown," p. 402). Hartley (1978) notes that most evaluation methods used in visual research have questionable built-in assumptions. His illustration is the common assumption that readers begin at the beginning of a text and read it through steadily to the end (*Designing Instructional Text,* p. 105). Elsewhere, Kathryn L. Alesandrini and Anees A. Sheikh (1983) observe that "the verbal comprehension tests typically used in research studies may not test the kind of knowledge resulting from a pictorial representation" ("Research on Imagery," p. 539). A lack of isomorphism between stimulus and test mode may explain, for example, the observation by J. R. Levin ("Inducing Comprehension in Poor Readers," 1973) that verbally tested comprehension is not facilitated when information is presented only in pictorial form.

Moreover, criticism of experimental studies is not confined to procedural flaws; the theoretical bases of empirical research have also been subject to attack. Attempts to provide a theoretical basis for studies of visual representation have long been dominated by Gestalt principles of perceptual psychology, an area reviewed by Ralph N. Haber ("Visual Perception," 1978), D. Brandes ("The Present State of Perceptual Research in Cartography," 1976) and Gerald M. Murch ("Physiological Principles for the Effective Use of Color," 1984). Apart from its valuable contributions, one side effect of Gestalt psychology has been to focus attention on the visual artifact at the expense of context, for Gestalt psychology emphasizes the intrinsically expressive power of visual elements as perceived by a universalistically conceived viewer. As such, it remains concerned largely with the syntactic and semantic aspects of visual communication. Thus, due to a concern with universal principles of perception, approaches based on Gestalt psychology and its derivatives do not accommodate the communication needs of diverse audiences ("Toward a Rhetoric of Visuals for the Computer Era," Barton and Barton, 1985b, pp. 135–36). The attendant emphasis on universalistic models of viewers in both theoretical and empirical visual research has been roundly criticized in various treatments, for example, Frances C. Butler's (1984) "Eating the Image," Lida M. Cochran et al.'s (1980) "Exploring Approaches to Researching Visual Literacy," Philippe C. Duchastel's (1980), "Research on Illustrations in Text," David Sless's (1981) *Learning and Visual Communication,* and Ben F. Barton and Marthalee S. Barton's (1985a) "On Approaches to User-Friendliness for Computer Systems."

The limitations of behaviorist approaches to visual research and practice have also been noted in technical communication by Barton and Barton ("Toward a Rhetoric of Visuals for the Computer Era," 1985b) and in instructional science by Sless (*Learning and Visual Communication,* 1981). Sless contends that behaviorism cannot account for selective attention, based as it is on the supposed primacy of the stimulus. Stimulus primacy is also a cornerstone of the aesthetic, or formalist, approach to visual design, which is equally under attack. For Waller ("Functional Information Design," 1979), so-called functional design in graphics has been dominated by aesthetics since the heyday of the international style in design and architecture. There is, for him, a sense of bankruptcy in continuing to judge graphics largely for their visual impact or technical excellence. Hanno H.J. Ehses (1978) attacks graphic designers for "regarding design elements as *autonomous structures* seen in isolation, without considering the ways in which they are linked within the entire social context" ("Design and Semiotics," p. 30). In "Simplicity in Visual Representation," Barton and Barton (1987) develop a semiotic approach to design that considers the semantic and the pragmatic as well as the syntactic aspect of visual communication. In a similar vein, Sless (*Learning and Visual Communication,* 1981) proposes that the activities culminating in the production and reading of texts be regarded as social practices, as a pattern of actions governed by cultural conventions. Moreover, in his most recent work, "Reading Semiotics," Sless (1986) proposes going beyond the study of visuals as embodiments of cultural conventions to the study of the ideologies that, in turn, inevitably underlie those conventions.

One influence of the formalist approach has been the fostering treatments of visuals based on genre. Here, Duchastel ("Research on Illustrations in Text," 1980) makes a telling distinction: he contrasts taxonomies based on morphology—on what pictures look like—with those based on function—on what pictures do in particular contexts. Duchastel views as impoverished visual research rooted in morphology, that is, genre, and advocates functional approaches as revitalizing alternatives. His proposed taxonomy of pictures serving in learning processes distinguishes attentional, explicative, and retentional functions. Levin ("Inducing Comprehension in Poor Readers," 1973) identifies eight hierarchically ordered functions for instructional pictures, ranging from decorative through motivational to interpretive. Roger Smith's (1986) recent contribution, "Terminological Inexactitudes," offers a fourfold classification of graphic images according to their typical function: pictures depict or describe, diagrams explain, signs designate or nominate, and symbols mediate or interpret.

Several proposed solutions to the fragmentation of knowledge about visual representations are attuned to modern psychological theory that closely links perception with cognitive processes. In Neisser's (1976) excellent introductory treatment, *Cognition and Reality,* perception is linked to hypothesized mental constructs, termed *schemata,* with Piagetian roots. Schemata enable us to use stored information about visual experiences in later perceptual undertakings; they may be more or less shared and can account for the phenomenon of selective attention. As characterized by Neisser, perception both depends on and fosters cognitive development, subject to physiological limitations. Several recent publications consider the influences of visual representations on schemata, that is, cognitive functions. Film specialist Gavriel Salomon

(1979) seeks to identify differential cognitive effects among media in *Interactions of Media, Cognition, and Learning*. Employing Goodman's concept of symbol systems, he associates multiple symbol systems—a symbol scheme—with each medium (Goodman, *Languages of Art*, 1968). The filmic symbol scheme, for example, is articulated at one level in film, sequence, and shot. It is also articulated in zoom, fade, and closeup at a lower level. The differential cognitive effects on viewers of various media due to differences in their symbol schemes are discussed in terms of the activation or elaboration of schemata and of the reinforcement or supplantation of associated mental skills. Salomon ("The Use of Visual Media," 1980) reports an attestation by a student of changes in his modes of understanding directly related to and prompted by visual techniques closely associated with film. Goals similar to Salomon's are sought by Carmen Luke (1985) in "Television Discourse Processing." Cochran et al. ("Exploring Approaches to Researching Visual Literacy," 1980) argue that purpose and intention must be made central issues in studies of visual processes; more specifically, they advocate an approach recognizing a wide variety of cognitive functions that representations perform and an ethnography of situations in which individuals interact with them.

Generally speaking, then, recent proposals would replace perceptual/behaviorist with cognitive/mentalist learning models; formalist with audience-centered approaches; and universalistic with classes of user models. Recent proposals would also replace the classic experiment—the quantitative measurement of selected variables with subjects performing contrived tasks in laboratory settings—with methodologies entailing the qualitative in-depth observation of subjects performing "real-life" tasks in "natural" settings. Thus, Barton and Barton ("On Approaches to User-Friendliness for Computer Systems," 1985a) have recently advocated a shift from etic to emic methodologies in computer display research. In this spirit, too, Waller ("Functional Information Design," 1979) calls for "ecological" rather than "statistical" validity, and Patricia Wright ("Usability," 1980) calls for "usability" rather than "readability," as evaluation criteria in visual research. T. H. Penniall ("Trends in Graphics," 1980) advocates a case study approach to display design, especially in the context of industrial power plants, where the use of graphics in process control is projected to have imminent major impact. JoAnne Yates ("Graphs as a Managerial Tool," 1985), seeing graphic management tools as a modern phenomenon, does a case study. She traces the rise, starting early in the twentieth century, of graphics as a management tool at DuPont. The trend culminated before 1920 in the "chart room," a dominant facility in DuPont's central administrative office complex—a facility whose felt importance apparently warranted masking its very existence from public knowledge until 1949.

Moreover, as computer displays come into widespread use, we face a new set of methodological issues. Lacking conventions unique to displays, designers have understandably turned to those well established in prior disciplines: examples are those discussed by Aaron Marcus ("Computer-Assisted Chart Making," 1980) and Ware Myers ("Computer Graphics," 1981a, 1981b) for graphic design as well as Susan S. Reilly and John W. Roach ("Improved Visual Design for Graphics Display," 1984) for advertising. But the wholesale importation of ideas from other technologies that characterized the nascent field of computer display design has recently been seen as inappropriate. The 1984 special issue of *Visible Language* on some effects of communication medium on visible language is dedicated to explorations of "the way visible language inevitably has to change as new display techniques are adopted" (p. 99). Focusing, therefore, on distinctive rather than shared features of display- and paper-based representations, contributor Pat Norrish (1984) "examines the ways in which tabular information can be structured and displayed in one of the new computer-based media and contrasts this with the way such information was previously presented in the medium of print" ("Moving Tables from Paper to CRT Screen," p. 154). Linda Reynolds' (1982) "Display Problems for Teletext" stresses that information cannot be transferred directly from a printed document to an electronic display without extensive editing.

Trend toward a Broad View of Rhetoric in Visual Representations

Jim W. Corder attacks the provincialism of the current rhetorical tradition and calls for an expanded purview of rhetorical study. Corder (1985) urges looking outside the field "to see that there is a rhetoric of painting, a rhetoric of biology, a rhetoric of any made form or expression, whatever the medium. Painters and composers surely have their schemes and tropes" ("On the Way, Perhaps, to a New Rhetoric," p. 164). Corder notes that rhetorical treatments of nonverbal discourse are generally done outside rhetoric. The highly visual rhetoric of advertising is, of course, a notable exception. In fact, among the resources available for instruction in visual rhetoric, advertisements are the *locus classicus*. D. G. Kehl (1975) describes the use of advertisements to foster appreciation of effective rhetorical strategies. As Kehl shows, advertisements can serve to illustrate the notion of a controlling idea or theme, modes of development, invention, critical thinking—including inductive and deductive reasoning—and use of diction. Whether fraudulent or not, Kehl (1975) notes that advertising exemplifies some of the most effective rhetoric at hand ("The Electric Carrot," p. 134). Additional references on the rhetoric of advertisements include "Adverteasement" by Richard D. Zakia (1986), "La Lecture de l'Image Publicitaire" by Geneviève Cornu (1985), "Subliminal Seduction" by Frank J. D'Angelo (1986), *Visual Persuasion* by Stephen Baker (1961), *Decoding Advertisements* by Judith Williamson (1978), the chapter entitled "Sweet Talk: The Rhetoric of Advertising" in *Tough, Sweet and Stuffy* by Walker Gibson (1966), and the special issue of *Word and Image* published in 1985. Those interested in the rhetoricity of related popular genres should consult Martin J. Medhurst and Michael A. Desousa ("Political Cartoons as Rhetorical Form," 1981) on political cartoons and Alan Gowans ("Posters as Persuasive Arts in Society," 1984) and Hanno Ehses ("Representing Macbeth," 1984) on poster art. Sonja K. Foss (1982) describes a teaching unit "designed primarily to teach theories of contemporary rhetorical theory through visual elements..., to help students approach their visual environment from a rhetorical perspective" ("Rhetoric and the Visual Image," p. 56). Specifically, she offers sample analyses of three visual images—a painting by Miró, a Burger King restaurant, and the Virginia Beach resort strip—based on selected concepts from the rhetorics of I. A. Richards, Kenneth Burke, and Richard Weaver, respectively. Though devised for a course in rhetorical theory, such a teaching unit may be appropriate for less specialized courses. Technical communication instructors interested in pursuing Kehl's strategy, but who prefer advertisements dealing with technology, should consult *The Un/Necessary Image* by Peter D'Agostino and Antonio Muntadas (1982); they offer brief rhetorical analyses of selected technical advertisements.

Advertisements are not unique as vehicles of visual rhetoric. As designer Gui Bonsiepe (1965) rightfully observes: " 'Pure' information exists for the designer only in arid abstraction. As soon as he begins to give it concrete shape, to bring it within the range of experience, the process of rhetorical infiltration begins" ("Visual/Verbal Rhetoric," p. 30). Unfortunately, Bonsiepe (1965, p. 30) later claims that a table of logarithms, or a train timetable, are "examples of information innocent of all taint of rhetoric." Robin Kinross's (1985) "The Rhetoric of Neutrality" counters Bonsiepe's exception by exposing the rhetoric underlying a series of railway timetables. Kinross (1985, p. 29) concludes that "nothing is free of rhetoric, that visual manifestations emerge from particular historical circumstances, that ideological vacuums do not exist." Among references dealing with rhetoricity in technical visuals, we should again mention the article by Pinkwas (1984), "Three Mapmakers," documenting the idea that maps are persuasive views of reality. Anders Vinberg and James E. George ("Computer Graphics and the Business Executive," 1981) offer an excellent, if somewhat contrived, hypothetical example of visual rhetoric involving the Johnson & O'Rourke Manufacturing Company, the object of a government antitrust suit related to its chief product, the Clasmatron. The authors present six graphs, highly rhetorical visuals based on a noncommunicative computerized tabulation of product sales for the industry, each devised to represent the viewpoint of a special interest: company president, sales unit, antitrust prosecutor, defense attorney, management consultant, and antiregulation lobby. As class handouts, the seven visuals (including the table of sales data) are not only convincing illustrations of rhetoricity in graphics, but are also highly entertaining.

To go beyond these beginnings, the trends described earlier can be reinterpreted as a broadening of the view of rhetoric in visual representations. Among the five sister arts of classical rhetoric—invention, arrangement, style, delivery, and memory—treatments of visuals in technical communication have traditionally emphasized arrangement and style. This emphasis can be seen in the longstanding focus on presentational graphics discussed earlier. It can also be seen in the work of Bonsiepe ("Persuasive Communication," 1962), who long ago sought a visual rhetoric based on verbal rhetoric. He looked for and found visual analogs to numerous rhetorical figures. Similarly, Bonsiepe ("Visual/Verbal Rhetoric," 1965) finds tropes and figures in the interplay of words and pictures. Peter Croy (*Signs and Their Message,* 1972) also emphasizes arrangement and style.

A broadened view of rhetoric in visuals is, then, most apparent in the growing interest in the art of invention, shown by the recent focus on analytical graphics. Furthermore, a broadening to include the art of delivery can be seen in efforts toward a fuller visual integration of texts. Walter Nash sees layout, or graphic presentation, as a "rhetorical apparatus," as a visual extension of the oral art of delivery, or *actio.* Thus, "the disjunctions, the insets, the parentheses, etc. are no more than the notations of the gestures and vocal inflections which rhetoric has always allowed as part of the armoury of effective pleading" ("Layout and Rhetorical Pattern," Nash 1980, p. 4). Robert J. Connors ("*Actio*: A Rhetoric of Manuscripts," 1983) would agree with Nash's designation of layout as rhetorical, specifically as *actio.* Looking at *actio* in manuscripts, Connors focuses on the contribution of layout, typography, and even choice of paper to ethos, the image of the author communicated in discourse. In general, efforts to enhance the informative, expressive, or suggestive qualities of texts through fuller visual integration of their components reflect a rhetorical stance.

The trend from a positivistic to a constitutive view of visual representations reflects a growing recognition of knowledge as consensual in nature and, therefore, more fundamentally rhetorical. Modern (Rogerian) rhetoric emphasizes negotiation as an alternative to argumentation, in a search for consensus; in this spirit, visuals can be used to invite participation. Thus, efforts to exploit more fully the visual mode often aim at "showing" rather than "telling," at eliciting the viewer's active participation and, therefore, commitment. In graphics, as noted earlier, such participation is invited through the use of concrete elements rather than abstract elements that overtly reflect the author's imported perspective. Moreover, the quest for visual alternatives to verbal representations has expanded the options available in rhetorical undertakings.

Conclusion

Outside technical communication, (while remaining a fragmented, multidisciplinary area of knowledge), visual representation is undergoing a paradigmatic shift. Above all, the shift is impelled by rejection of logical positivism in favor of theories that make representations constitutive of knowledge and knowledge itself consensual. A concomitant contributing shift in psychological theories of learning emphasizes the role of cognitive processes in perceiving, that is, in acquiring knowledge visually. Thus, there is more to seeing than meets the eye; there is the "beholder's share." The view that knowledge acquisition through vision is processual, for example, depends on the development of "schemata," has had important consequences. In particular, there is increasing awareness of the importance of the integrated, or cumulative, visual qualities of external representations. Hence, concern over visual qualities of representations has broadened to encompass all components of texts, for example, the "shapes" of words as well as the interrelations among them. The view of knowledge acquisition as process has led to a new emphasis on the roles of visual representations in discovery and learning rather than, as is traditional, on their role in presenting information. The view that knowledge is consensual entails the assumption that all visual representations are rhetorical in nature. None of these perspectives is adequately reflected in the visual research and pedagogy of technical communication. We seek ground for new visual research and pedagogy in a broadly stroked sketch of our surroundings.

If this representation of the visual world is not picture perfect, perhaps we have at least suggested a shape for things to come.

Acknowledgments

The authors gratefully acknowledge the careful and conscientious work of Izena Goulding in the preparation of the manuscript.

Bibliography

Adams, James L. *Conceptual Blockbusting: A Pleasurable Guide to Better Problem Solving.* San Francisco: San Francisco Book Co., Inc., 1976.

Alesandrini, Kathryn L., and Anees A. Sheikh. "Research on Imagery: Implications for Advertising." In *Imagery: Current Theory, Research, and Application,* edited by Anees A. Sheikh. New York: John Wiley, 1983, pp. 535–56.

Anschutz, Richard. "August Kekulé." In *Great Chemists,* edited by Eduard Farber. New York: Interscience Publishers, 1961, pp. 697–702.

American National Standards Institute (Committee Y15). *Time-Series Charts.* New York: American Society of Mechanical Engineers, 1979.

Ard, Josh. "The Semiotics of Mathematical Symbolism." *Ars Semeiotica* 6, no. 1–2 (1983): 3–14.

Arnheim, Rudolf. *Visual Thinking.* Berkeley and Los Angeles: University of California Press, 1969.

———. *Art and Visual Perception: A Psychology of the Creative Eye, the New Version.* Berkeley and Los Angeles: University of California Press, 1974.

Aronoff, Stanley, and Glyn F. Jones. "From Data to Image to Action." *IEEE Spectrum* 22, no. 12 (1985): 45–52.

Ayres, Leonard P. *The War with Germany: A Statistical Summary.* Washington, D.C.: U.S. Government Printing Office, 1919.

Bachi, Roberto. "Applications, Limitations and Shortcomings of Usual Graphical Methods." In *Graphical Rational Patterns: A New Approach to Graphical Presentation of Statistics.* Jerusalem: Israel Universities Press, 1968, pp. 7–32.

Baker, Stephen. *Visual Persuasion.* New York: McGraw-Hill, 1961.

Balchin, W. G. V. and Alice M. Coleman. "Graphicacy Should Be the Fourth Ace in the Pack." *The Cartographer* 3, no. 1 (1966): 23–28.

Barton, Ben F., and Marthalee S. Barton. "On Approaches to User-Friendliness for Computer Systems." In *Proceedings in Technical and Business Communication: The Conference on College Composition and Communication, Minneapolis—1985,* edited by Douglas M. Catron. Ames, Iowa: Iowa State University, 1985a, pp. 112–21.

———. "Toward a Rhetoric of Visuals for the Computer Era." *The Technical Writing Teacher* 12, no. 2 (1985b): 126–45.

———. "Simplicity in Visual Representation: A Semiotic Approach." *Iowa State Journal of Business and Technical Communication* 1, no. 1 (1987): 9–26.

Baudin, Fernand. "The Visual Editing of Texts." *Visible Language* 18, no. 1 (1984): 81–86.

Baynes, Ken, and Francis Pugh. *The Art of the Engineer.* Woodstock, N.Y.: Overlook Press, 1981.

Beck, Charles E., and William J. Wallisch, Jr. "Technical Illustration." In *Courses, Components, and Exercises in Technical Communication,* edited by Dwight W. Stevenson. Urbana, Ill.: National Council of Teachers of English, 1981, pp. 122–31.

Beniger, James R., and Dorothy L. Robyn. "Quantitative Graphics in Statistics: A Brief History." *The American Statistician* 32, no. 1 (1978): 1–11.

Benson, Philippa J. "Writing Visually: Design Considerations in Technical Publications." *Technical Communication* 32, no. 1 (1985): 35–39.

Bentley, Jon. "Programming Pearls: Graphic Output. *Communications of the ACM* 27, no. 6 (1984a): 529–36.

———. "Programming Pearls: Updates." *Communications of the ACM* 27, no. 7 (1984b): 630–36.

Bernhardt, Stephen A. "Seeing the Text." *College Composition and Communication* 37, no. 1 (1986): 66–78.

Bertin, Jacques. *Graphics and Graphic Information Processing.* Translated by William J. Berg and Paul Scott. Berlin: Walter de Gruyter and Co., 1981.

———. "A New Look at Cartography." In *Graphic Communication and Design in Contemporary Cartography,* edited by D. R. F. Taylor. London: John Wiley and Sons, 1983a, pp. 69–86.

———. *Semiology of Graphics: Diagrams, Networks, Maps.* Translated by William J. Berg. Madison, Wis.: University of Wisconsin Press, 1983b.

Biderman, Albert D. "The Graph as a Victim of Adverse Discrimination and Segregation: Comment Occasioned by the First Issue of *Information Design Journal." Information Design Journal* 1, no. 4 (1980): 232–41.

Bishop, Jack. "Three Generations of Charts for the IBM PC." *Byte* 8 (1983): 352–66.

Blaiwes, A. S. "Formats for Presenting Procedural Instructions." *Journal of Applied Psychology* 59 (1974): 683–86.

Blanchard, Russell W. *Graphic Design.* Englewood Cliffs, N.J.: Prentice-Hall, 1984.

Bonnell, Bill, and Stephan Geissbühler. "New Wave in Graphic Design USA." *Graphis* 40, no. 229 (1984): 38–40.

Bonsiepe, Gui. "Persuasive Communication: Towards a Visual Rhetoric." *Upper Case* 5 (1962): 19–34.

———. "Visual/Verbal Rhetoric." *Ulm* 8 (1965): 23–40.

Bower, T. G. R. "The Object in the World of the Infant." *Scientific American* 225, no. 4 (1971): 30–38.

Braby, Richard, et al. "Illustrated Formats to Teach Procedures." *IEEE Transactions on Professional Communication* PC-25, no. 2 (1982): 61–66.

Brandes, D. "The Present State of Perceptual Research in Cartography." *The Cartographic Journal* 13 (1976): 172–76.

Brown, J. Carter. "Excellence and the Problem of Visual Literacy." *Design* 85, no. 2 (1983): 11–13.

Brown, Maxine D. "Mainframe Business Graphics." *Datamation* 30, no. 6 (1984): 89–95.

Buehler, Mary F. "Report Construction: Tables." *IEEE Transactions on Professional Communication* PC-20, no. 1 (1977): 29–32.

Burgin, Victor. "Looking at Photographs." *Thinking Photography*, edited by Victor Burgin. London: Macmillan Press, 1982, pp. 142–53.

Butler, Frances C. "Eating the Image: The Graphic Designer and the Starving Audience." *Design Issues* 1, no. 1 (1984): 27–40.

Cassidy, Michael F., and James Q. Knowlton. "Visual Literacy: A Failed Metaphor?" *Educational Communication and Technology Journal* 31, no. 2 (1983): 67–90.

Chambers, John M. *Graphical Methods for Data Analysis.* Boston: Duxbury Press, 1983.

Chernoff, Herman. "Using Faces to Represent Points in k-Dimensional Space Graphically." *Journal of the American Statistical Association* 68 (1973): 361–68.

Cochran, Lida M., et al. "Exploring Approaches to Researching Visual Literacy." *Educational Communication and Technology Journal* 28, no. 4 (1980): 243–66.

Connors, Robert J. "*Actio*: A Rhetoric of Manuscripts." *Rhetoric Review* 2, no. 1 (1983): 64–73.

Corder, Jim W. "On the Way, Perhaps, to a New Rhetoric, but Not There Yet, and if We Do Get There, There Won't Be There Anymore." *College English* 47, no. 2 (1985): 162–70.

Cornu, Geneviève. "La Lecture de l'Image Publicitaire." *Semiotica* 54, no. 3–4 (1985): 405–28.

Croy, Peter. *Signs and Their Message.* Göttingen, Frankfurt, and Zurich: Musterschmidt, 1972.

D'Agostino, Peter, and Antonio Muntadas, eds. *The Un/Necessary Image.* New York: Tanam Press, 1982.

D'Angelo, Frank J. "Subliminal Seduction: An Essay on the Rhetoric of the Unconscious." *Rhetoric Review* 4, no. 2 (1986): 160–71.

DeVillier, J. Lincoln. "Communication Effects of Variations in Organization and Format." *Journal of Business Communication* 9, no. 3 (1972): 5–18.

Duchastel, Philippe C. "Research on Illustrations in Text: Issues and Perspectives." *Educational Communication and Technology Journal* 28, no. 4 (1980): 283–87.

———. "Unbounded Text." *Educational Technology* 22, no. 8 (1982): 19–21.

———. "Marginalia." In *The Technology of Text, Volume Two: Principles for Structuring, Designing and Displaying Text,* edited by David H. Jonassen. Englewood Cliffs, N.J.: Educational Testing Publications, 1984, pp. 210–36.

Dwyer, Francis M. *Strategies for Improving Visual Learning: A Handbook for the Effective Selection, Design, and Use of Visualized Materials.* State College, Pa.: Learning Services, 1978.

———. "The Program of Systematic Evaluation: A Brief Review." *International Journal of Instructional Media* 10 (1982-83): 23-38.

Edgerton, Samuel. *The Renaissance Discovery of Linear Perspective.* New York: Harper and Row, 1976.

Ehrenberg, Andrew S. C. "Rudiments of Numeracy." *Journal of the Royal Statistical Society,* Series A, 140, no. 3 (1977): 277-97.

Ehses, Hanno H. J. "Design and Semiotics: Some Aspects Concerning the Design Process." *Icographic* 1, no. 12 (1978): 30-31.

———. "Representing Macbeth: A Case Study in Visual Rhetoric." *Design Issues* 1, no. 1 (1984): 53-63.

Erdelyi, M. H., and T. G. Becker. "Hypermnesia for Pictures: Incremental Memory for Pictures But Not Words in Multiple Recall Trials." *Cognitive Psychology* 6 (1974): 158-71.

Erickson, Bonnie H., and T. A. Nosanchuk. *Understanding Data.* Toronto: McGraw-Hill Ryerson Limited, 1977.

Faruque, Omar. *Graphic Communication as a Design Tool.* New York: Van Nostrand Reinhold, 1984.

Felker, Daniel B., ed. *Document Design: A Review of the Relevant Research.* Washington, D.C.: American Institutes for Research, 1980.

Ferguson, Eugene S. "The Mind's Eye: Nonverbal Thought in Technology." *Science* 197 (1977): 827-36.

Fienberg, Stephen E. "Graphical Methods in Statistics." *The American Statistician* 33, no. 4 (1979): 165-78.

FitzPatrick, Paul J. "The Development of Graphic Presentation of Statistical Data in the United States." *Social Science* 37, no. 4 (1962): 203-14.

Ford, Donald F. "Packaging Problem Prose." In *Proceedings of the 31st International Technical Communication Conference.* Seattle, Wash.: Society for Technical Communication, 1984, pp. WE52-WE55.

Foss, Sonja K. "Rhetoric and the Visual Image: A Resource Unit." *Communication Education* 31 (1982): 55-65.

Foster, Jeremy J. "The Use of Visual Cues in Text." In *Processing of Visible Language.* Vol. 1. Edited by Paul A. Kolers et al. New York and London: Plenum Press, 1979, pp. 189-203.

Foster, Stephen C. "Letterism: A Point of Views." *Visible Language* 17, no. 3 (1983): 7-12.

Frase, Lawrence T., and Barry J. Schwartz. "Typographical Cues That Facilitate Comprehension." *Journal of Educational Psychology* 71 (1979): 197-206.

French, Thomas E., Charles J. Vierck, and Robert J. Foster. *Graphic Science and Design.* 4th ed. New York: McGraw-Hill, 1984.

Friedman, A. P., et al. "A Graphic Way of Describing Changing Multivariate Patterns." In *Proceedings of the 6th Annual Symposium on Computer Science Statistics.* Berkeley: University of California, 1972.

Funkhouser, H. G. "Historical Development of the Graphical Representation of Statistical Data." *Osiris* 3 (1937): 269-404.

Gibson, James J. "A Theory of Pictorial Perception." *Audio-Visual Communication Review* 1, no. 3 (1954): 3–23.

———. "The Ecological Approach to the Visual Perception of Pictures." *Leonardo* 11 (1978): 227–35.

Gibson, Walker. *Tough, Sweet and Stuffy: An Essay on Modern American Prose Styles.* Bloomington, Ind.: Indiana University Press, 1966.

Giesecke, Frederick E., Alva Mitchell, Henry C. Spencer, Ivan L. Hill, Robert O. Loving, and John T. Dygdon. *Engineering Graphics.* 3d ed. New York: Macmillan, 1981.

Goldsmith, Timothy E., and Roger W. Schvaneveldt. "Facilitating Multiple-Cue Judgments with Integral Information Displays." In *Human Factors in Computer Systems,* edited by John C. Thomas and Michael L. Schneider. Norwood, N.J.: Ablex Publishing Corp., 1984, pp. 243–70.

Gombrich, Ernst H. *Art and Illusion: A Study of the Psychology of Pictorial Representation.* New York: Pantheon Books, 1959.

———. *The Image and the Eye: Further Studies in the Psychology of Pictorial Representation.* Ithaca, N.Y.: Cornell University Press, 1982.

———. *The Sense of Order: A Study in the Psychology of Decorative Art.* 2d ed. Ithaca, N.Y.: Cornell University Press, 1984.

Goodman, Nelson. *Languages of Art: An Approach to a Theory of Symbols.* Indianapolis: Bobbs-Merrill, 1968.

Goody, Jack. *The Domestication of the Savage Mind.* Cambridge, England: Cambridge University Press, 1977.

Gowans, Alan. "Posters as Persuasive Arts in Society." *Art Journal* 44, no. 1 (1984): 9–10.

Gross, Alan G. "A Primer on Tables and Figures." *Journal of Technical Writing and Communication* 13, no. 1 (1983): 33–55.

Gruber, Howard E. "Darwin's 'Tree of Nature' and Other Images of Wide Scope." In Wechsler, pp. 121–40.

Gust, Raymond K. "Designing Effective Business Graphics." *IEEE Computer Graphics and Applications* 3, no. 4 (1983): 33–36.

Haber, Ralph N. "Visual Perception." *Annual Review of Psychology* 29 (1978): 31–59.

Hadamard, Jacques. *The Psychology of Invention in the Mathematical Field.* Princeton, N.J.: Princeton University Press, 1949.

Hammet, B. F., and Peter M. Illick. "Visual Literacy: A Perceptual Discipline." *Journal of Technical Writing and Communication* 1, no. 3 (1971): 255–66.

Hartley, James. *Designing Instructional Text.* London: Kogan Page, 1978.

———. "Spatial Cues in Text." *Visible Language* 14, no. 1 (1980a): 62–70.

———, ed. *The Psychology of Written Communication: Selected Readings.* New York: Nichols Publishing Co., 1980b.

Hartley, James, Mark Trueman, and Peter Burnhill. "The Role of Spatial and Typographic Cues in the Layout of Journal References." *IEEE Transactions on Professional Communication* PC-23, no. 3 (1980): 138–42.

Hashimoto, Irvin. "Helping Students to Sort and Display Their Information." *College English* 45, no. 3 (1983): 277–87.

Herdeg, Walter. *Diagrams: The Graphic Visualization of Abstract Data.* Zurich: Graphis Press, 1974.

Hochberg, Julian, and Virginia Brooks. "Pictorial Recognition as an Unlearnt Ability: A Study of One Child's Performance." *American Journal of Psychology* 75 (1962): 624–28.

Hodgkinson, Richard, and John Hughes. "Developing Wordless Instructions: A Case History." *IEEE Transactions on Professional Communication* PC-25, no. 2 (1982): 74–79.

Holmes, Nigel. *Designer's Guide to Creating Charts and Diagrams.* New York: Watson-Guptill Publications, 1984.

Holton, Gerald. *Thematic Origins of Scientific Thought: Kepler to Einstein.* Cambridge, Mass.: Harvard University Press, 1973.

Horn, R. E. *How to Write Information Mapping.* Lexington, Mass.: Information Resources, 1976.

Huff, Darrell. *How to Lie with Statistics.* New York: Norton, 1954.

IEEE Transactions on Professional Communication. Special Issue on Making Information More Usable through Graphics. 25, no. 2 (1982).

Ives, Blake. "Graphical User Interfaces for Business Information Systems." *Management Information Systems Quarterly* 6 (Dec. 1982): 15–47.

Ivins, William M., Jr. *Prints and Visual Communication.* Cambridge: Massachusetts Institute of Technology Press, 1969.

Jenks, George F. "Contemporary Statistical Maps—Evidence of Spatial and Graphic Ignorance." *The American Cartographer* 3, no. 1 (1976): 11–19.

Jewett, Donald L. "Self-Instruction and Multi-Level Textbooks." *Perspectives in Biology and Medicine* 15, no. 3 (1972): 450–72.

Jonassen, David H., ed. *The Technology of Text: Principles for Structuring, Designing and Displaying Text.* Englewood Cliffs, N.J.: Educational Technology Publications, 1982.

Kammann, Richard. "The Comprehensibility of Printed Instructions and the Flowchart Alternative." *Human Factors* 17 (1975): 183–91.

Kehl, D. G. "The Electric Carrot: The Rhetoric of Advertisement." *College Composition and Communication* 26, no. 2 (1975): 134–40.

Kelley, Patrick M. "Visual Rhetoric in Teaching Technical Writing." In *Proceedings of the 27th International Technical Communication Conference.* Minneapolis, Minn.: Society for Technical Communication, 1980, pp. R209–R213.

Kennedy, John M. *A Psychology of Picture Perception.* San Francisco: Jossey-Bass, 1974.

Kepes, Gyorgy. *Language of Vision.* Chicago: Paul Theobald, 1951.

Kinross, Robin. "The Rhetoric of Neutrality." *Design Issues* 2, no. 2 (1985): 18–30.

Kolers, Paul A., et al., eds. *Processing of Visible Language* 2. New York and London: Plenum Press, 1980.

Kruskal, William H. "Visions of Maps and Graphs." In *Auto-Cart II: Proceedings of the International Symposium on Computer-Assisted Cartography,* edited by John Kavaliunas. Washington, D.C.: Bureau of the Census, 1975, pp. 27–36.

Laner, Frances J. "Readability Techniques for Authors and Editors." In *Directions in Technical Writing and Communication,* edited by Jay R. Gould. Farmingdale, N.Y.: Baywood Publishing Co., 1978, pp. 136–47.

Lefferts, Robert. *Elements of Graphics: How to Prepare Charts and Graphs for Effective Reports.* New York: Harper and Row Publishers, 1981.

Levin, J. R. "Inducing Comprehension in Poor Readers: A Test of a Recent Model." *Journal of Educational Psychology* 65 (1973): 19–24.

Loucks, Roger B. "An Experimental Evaluation of the Interpretability of Various Types of Aircraft Attitude Indicators." In *Psychological Research on Equipment Design.* Report no. 19. Washington, D.C.: U. S. Government Printing Office, 1947, pp. 111–35.

Lubbock, Percy. *The Craft of Fiction.* London: Jonathan Cape, 1921.

Luke, Carmen. "Television Discourse Processing: A Schema Theoretic Approach." *Communication Education* 34, no. 2 (1985): 91–105.

Lynch, Michael. "Discipline and the Material Form of Images: An Analysis of Scientific Visibility." *Social Studies of Science* 15, no. 1 (1985): 37–66.

Macdonald-Ross, Michael. "How Numbers Are Shown: A Review of Research on the Presentation of Quantitative Data in Texts." *Audio-Visual Communication Review* 25, no. 4 (1977): 359–409.

———. "Graphics in Texts." In *Review of Research in Education,* Vol. 5, edited by Lee S. Shulman. Itasca, Ill.: F. E. Peacock, 1978, pp. 49–85.

———. "Scientific Diagrams and the Generation of Plausible Hypotheses: An Essay in the History of Ideas." *Instructional Science* 8 (1979): 223–34.

Macdonald-Ross, Michael, and Eleanor Smith. *Graphics in Text: A Bibliography.* Monograph no. 6. Milton Keynes, Great Britain: Open University Institute of Educational Technology, 1977.

MacGregor, A. Jean. "Selecting the Appropriate Chart." *IEEE Transactions on Professional Communication* PC-25, no. 2 (1982): 102–4.

Magnan, George A. "Technical Illustrations." In *Engineering and Industrial Graphics Handbook,* edited by George E. Rowbotham. New York: McGraw-Hill, 1982, pp. 1.1–1.107.

Mangan, James. "Cultural Conventions of Pictorial Representation: Iconic Literacy and Education." *Educational Communication and Technology Journal* 26, no. 3 (1978): 245–67.

Mann, Gerald A. "How to Present Tabular Information Badly." In *Proceedings of the 31st International Technical Communication Conference.* Seattle, Wash.: Society for Technical Communication, 1984, pp. WE48–WE51.

Marcus, Aaron. "Computer-Assisted Chart Making from the Graphic Designer's Perspective." In *Computer Graphics,* edited by James J. Thomas. SIGGRAPH '80 Conference Proceedings (July 1980): 247–53.

Marcus, Susan. "Diagramming Complex Systems." *Information Design Journal* 1 (1980): 167–73.

McKim, Robert H. *Experiences in Visual Thinking.* Monterey, Calif.: Brooks/Cole Publishing Co., 1972.

———. *Thinking Visually: A Strategy Manual for Problem Solving.* Belmont, Calif.: Lifetime Learning Publications, 1980.

Medhurst, Martin J., and Michael A. DeSousa. "Political Cartoons as Rhetorical Form: A Taxonomy of Graphic Discourse." *Communication Monographs* 48, no. 3 (1981): 197–236.

Meggs, Philip B. *A History of Graphic Design.* New York: Van Nostrand Reinhold, 1983.

Miller, Arthur I. "Visualization Lost and Regained: The Genesis of the Quantum Theory in the Period 1913–27." In Wechsler, pp. 73–102.

Milner, John. "On the Fusion of Verbal and Visual Media." *Leonardo* 9, (1976): 5–9.

Murch, Gerald M. "Physiological Principles for the Effective Use of Color." *IEEE Computer Graphics and Applications* 4, no. 11 (1984): 49–54.

Murgio, Matthew P. *Communications Graphics.* New York: Van Nostrand Reinhold, 1969.

Myers, Ware. "Computer Graphics: The Need for Graphics Design," Part 1. *Computer* 14, no. 6 (1981a): 86–92.

———. "Computer Graphics: The Need for Graphics Design," Part 2. *Computer* 14, no. 7 (1981b): 82–88.

Nash, Walter. "Layout and Rhetorical Pattern." In *Designs in Prose: A Study of Compositional Problems and Methods.* London and New York: Longman, 1980, pp. 1–20.

Neisser, Ulric. *Cognition and Reality: Principles and Implications of Cognitive Psychology.* San Francisco: W. H. Freeman and Company, 1976.

Neurath, Marie. "Isotype." *Instructional Science* 3 (1974): 127–50.

Norrish, Pat. "Moving Tables from Paper to CRT Screen." *Visible Language* 18, no. 2 (1984): 154–70.

Paivio, Allan. *Imagery and Verbal Processes.* New York: Holt, Rinehart and Winston, 1971. (Reprinted by Lawrence Erlbaum Associates, Hillsdale, N.J., 1979.)

———. "The Mind's Eye in Arts and Science." *Poetics* 12, no. 1 (1983): 1–18.

Paller, A., et al. *Choosing the Right Graph: A Comprehensive Guide for Computer Graphics Users.* San Diego and London: ISSCO Graphics, 1981.

Penniall, T. H. "Trends in Graphics." *Ergonomics* 23, no. 9 (1980): 921–33.

Perkins, D. N. "Pictures and the Real Thing." In Kolers, et al., pp. 259–78.

Pettersson, Rune. "Cultural Differences in the Perception of Image and Color in Pictures." *Educational Communication and Technology Journal* 30, no. 1 (1982): 43–53.

Pinkwas, Stan. "Three Mapmakers." *Industrial Design* 31, no. 6 (1984): 50–55, 86–87.

Playfair, William. *The Commercial and Political Atlas.* 3d ed. London: J. Wallis, 1801.

Porter, Tom, and Byron Mikellides. "The Language of Colour" *Icographic* 1, no. 12 (1978): 9–11.

Preece, Jenny. "Graphs Are Not Straightforward." In *The Psychology of Computer Use,* edited by Thomas R. G. Green, S. J. Payne, and G. C. Van Der Veer. New York: Academic Press, 1983, pp. 41–56.

Reilly, Susan S., and John W. Roach. "Improved Visual Design for Graphics Display." *IEEE Computer Graphics and Applications* 4, no. 2 (1984): 42–51.

Reynolds, Linda. "Display Problems for Teletext." In Jonassen, pp. 415–37.

Rodrigues, Dawn, and Raymond J. Rodrigues. "Computer-Based Creative Problem Solving." In *The Computer in Composition Instruction: A Writer's Tool,* edited by William Wresch. Urbana, Ill.: National Council of Teachers of English, 1984, pp. 34–46.

Roscoe, Stanley N. "Airborne Displays for Flight and Navigation." *Human Factors* 10, no. 4 (1968): 321–32.

Rouse, William B., ed. *Advances in Man-Machine Systems Research: A Research Annual.* Vol. 1. Greenwich, Conn.: JAI Press, 1984.

Rubens, Philip M., and Robert Krull. "Application of Research on Document Design to Online Displays." *Technical Communication* 32, no. 4 (1985): 29–34.

Rudwick, Martin J. S. "The Emergence of a Visual Language for Geological Science 1760–1840." *History of Science* 14 (1976): 149–95.

Salomon, Gavriel. *Interactions of Media, Cognition, and Learning: An Exploration of How Symbolic Forms Cultivate Mental Skills and Affect Knowledge Acquisition.* San Francisco: Jossey-Bass Publishers, 1979.

———. "The Use of Visual Media in the Service of Enriching Mental Thought Processes." *Instructional Science* 9 (1980): 327–39.

Schmid, Calvin F. "The Role of Standards in Graphic Presentation." In *American Statistical Association, Proceedings of the Social Statistics Section, 1976.* Washington, D.C.: American Statistical Association, 1976, pp. 74–81. (Reprinted in *Graphical Presentation of Statistical Information,* Technical Report 43. Washington, D.C.: U.S. Bureau of the Census, 1978, pp. 69–78.)

———. *Statistical Graphics: Design Principles and Practices.* New York: John Wiley and Sons (Wiley-Interscience), 1983.

Schmid, Calvin F., and Stanton E. Schmid. *Handbook of Graphic Presentation.* 2d ed. New York: John Wiley and Sons (Ronald Press), 1979.

Seiler, W. J. "The Effects of Visual Materials on Attitudes, Credibility, and Retention." *Speech Monographs* 38 (1971): 331–34.

Shapin, Steven. "Pump and Circumstance: Robert Boyle's Literary Technology." *Social Studies of Science* 14 (1984): 481–519.

Showstack, Richard. "Discourse Punctuation: The Next Stage of Printing." *IEEE Transactions on Professional Communication* PC-23, no. 3 (1980): 143–47.

Simcox, William A. "A Design Method for Graphic Communication." *ABCA Bulletin* 47, no. 1 (1984): 3–7.

Sless, David. *Learning and Visual Communication.* New York: John Wiley and Sons, 1981.

———. "Visual Literacy: A Failed Opportunity?" *Educational Communication and Technology Journal* 32, no. 4 (1984): 224–28.

———. "Reading Semiotics." *Information Design Journal* 4, no. 3 (1986): 179–89.

Smith, Roger. "Terminological Inexactitudes: Image Functions in Graphic Communication." *Information Design Journal* 4, no. 3 (1986): 199–205.

Spezzano, Charles. "Decision Support Software." *Popular Computing* Oct. (1985): 56–61+.

Summers, David. "Conventions in the History of Art." *New Literary History* 13, no. 1 (1981): 103-25.

Szoka, Kathryn. "A Guide to Choosing the Right Chart Type." *IEEE Transactions on Professional Communication* PC-25, no. 2 (1982): 98-101.

Tebeaux, Elizabeth. "Using Computer Printouts to Teach Analysis and Graphics." *Journal of Technical Writing and Communication* 11, no. 1 (1981): 13-22.

Tilling, Laura. "Early Experimental Graphs." *The British Journal for the History of Science* 8, no. 30 (1975): 193-213.

Tinker, Miles A. *Legibility of Print.* Ames, Iowa: Iowa State University Press, 1963.

Trieb, Marc. "Mapping Experience." *Design Quarterly* no. 115 (1980): 5-32.

Tufte, Edward R. *The Visual Display of Quantitative Information.* Cheshire, Conn.: Graphics Press, 1983.

Tukey, John W. *Exploratory Data Analysis.* Reading, Mass.: Addison Wesley, 1977.

———. "Another Look at the Future." *Computer Science and Statistics: Proceedings of the 14th Symposium on the Interface,* edited by Karl W. Heiner, Richard S. Sacher, and John W. Wilkinson. New York: Springer-Verlag, 1983, pp. 2-8.

Tullis, Thomas S. "An Evaluation of Alphanumeric, Graphic, and Color Information Displays." *Human Factors* 23 (1981): 541-50.

Van Cott, H. P., and R. G. Kinkade, eds. *Human Engineering Guide to Equipment Design.* New York: McGraw-Hill, 1972. (Also published by U. S. Government Printing Office, Washington, D.C.)

Vanmalderen, Luc. "Semiotics and the Graphic Sign." *Print* 23, no. 6 (1969): 56-58, 89.

Vinberg, Anders, and James E. George. "Computer Graphics and the Business Executive—The New Management Team." *IEEE Computer Graphics and Applications* 1, no. 1 (1981): 57-71.

Visible Language: 15, no. 2-3 (1981).

Visible Language: Special Issue on Some Effects of Communication Medium on Visible Language. 18, no. 2 (1984).

Wainer, Howard. "Graphical Data Analysis." *Annual Review of Psychology* 32 (1981): 191-241.

———. "Making Newspaper Graphs Fit to Print." In Kolers, et al., pp. 125-42.

Walker, John A. "The London Underground Diagram." *Icographic* 1, no. 14/15 (1979): 2-4.

Waller, Ronald H. W. "Functional Information Design: Research and Practice." *Information Design Journal* 1, no. 1 (1979): 43-50.

———. "Graphic Aspects of Complex Texts: Typography as Macro Punctuation." In Kolers, et al., pp. 241-53.

———. "Text as Diagram: Using Typography to Improve Access and Understanding." In Jonassen, pp. 137-66.

Watson, James D. *The Double Helix: A Personal Account of the Structure of DNA.* Edited by Gunther S. Stent. New York: W. W. Norton, 1980.

Wechsler, Judith, ed. *On Aesthetics in Science.* Cambridge, Mass.: The MIT Press, 1978.

White, Jan V. *1000 Ideas for Visual Persuasion.* New York: R. R. Bowker Company, 1984.

Wileman, Ralph E. *Exercises in Visual Thinking.* New York: Hastings House Publishers (Visual Communication Books), 1980.

Williamson, Judith. *Decoding Advertisements: Ideology and Meaning in Advertising.* London and Boston: Marion Boyars, 1978.

Word and Image: Special Issue on Advertising. 1, no. 4 (1985).

Wright, Patricia. "Usability: The Criterion for Designing Written Information." In Kolers, et al., pp. 183–205.

Wright, Patricia, and Fraser Reid. "Written Information: Some Alternatives to Prose for Expressing the Outcomes of Complex Contingencies." *Journal of Applied Psychology* 57, no. 2 (1973): 160–66.

Yates, JoAnne. "Graphs as a Managerial Tool: A Case Study of DuPont's Use of Graphs in the Early Twentieth Century." *The Journal of Business Communication* 22, no. 1 (1985): 5–33.

Zakia, Richard D. "Adverteasement." *Semiotica* 59, no. 1/2 (1986): 1–11.

Zelazny, Gene. "Grappling with Graphics." *Management Review* 64, no. 10 (1975): 4–16.

6 Interpersonal Communication for the Technical Communicator

David M. Craig
Clarkson University

Thomas M. Steinfatt
University of Miami

A cursory glance through virtually any technical communications bibliography will reveal the scanty attention that interpersonal communication receives. The extensive reference work, *An Annotated Bibliography on Technical Writing, Editing, Graphics, and Publishing* (Carlson et al. 1983), lists, for example, just four items on interpersonal communication in its over 4,700 entries.[1] There are obvious reasons for this lack of attention, for there are notable differences between the two disciplines. Technical communications grew out of writing practice, and it continues to focus on writing issues. Only recently has technical communications become interested in exploring its history or in becoming more theoretically oriented. By contrast, interpersonal communication has its roots in the social sciences, especially in psychology, and has always had a theoretical focus. It comes into practice, for example, in dealing with stage fright, through the lenses of description and theory. But these disciplinary differences need not prevent technical communicators from taking advantage of interpersonal communication literature, and the relative inattention that interpersonal communication has received in technical communications literature should not continue.

In presenting this literature review, we believe that background in interpersonal communication can enrich the work of the technical communications teacher and scholar. (The converse is also true, of course, but that is an issue for another article.) We have noted differences between the two disciplines, and we also want to call attention to a core similarity that defines the connections between the two disciplines and that suggests directions for future mutual learning. As communication fields, both draw on the same base. Both cite the communication models of Shannon and Weaver (1949), Schramm (1954), David K. Berlo (1960), and Miller (1966), among others, to formulate, present, and analyze research data. This theoretical base is crucial to effective technical communication. In fact, George A. Barnett and Carol Hughes (1985) argue that the future development of technical communication depends in part on its application of communication theory and its testing theory with empirical research. We believe that technical communicators can develop further this theoretical grounding by learning from the interpersonal communications literature. Certainly, Barnett and Hughes have, for in referring to the work of Berlo and Miller, they cite prominent interpersonal communication scholars.

If technical communications bibliographies do not yet show much concern with interpersonal communications, technical communications literature and practice do. Of the many examples that could be given, we cite the work of Herb J. Smith (1985), "Methods for Training the Technical Editor in Interpersonal Skills," and Smith et al. (1985), "Interpersonal Skills: An Essential Component in the Editing Class." In emphasizing the role interpersonal skills play in the editorial relationship, Smith demonstrates what experienced technical communicators already know—that is, that people are the critical dimension of any technical communication. Or more simply, as Berlo first formulated almost thirty years ago, "meaning resides in people." In dealing with the people within whom meaning resides, technical communicators can learn much from the interpersonal communications literature.

Although a relatively new field, not firmly established as a distinct teaching and research discipline until the 1960s, interpersonal communication has developed a rich and varied literature. The development of a nonverbal communication literature is typical of what is happening in interpersonal communication. Nonverbal communication was virtually unknown until the 1950s, but it has undergone exponential growth so that a complete bibliography would have some 3,000 items. A hallmark of interpersonal communication literature is the high-quality texts available, particularly on the introductory level, and many of these texts review the most recent discoveries and research. Given the wealth of material available, the technical communications teacher or researcher who taps these sources has extensive opportunities for enriching the study of technical communications.

Broadly defined, interpersonal communication is the process of exchanging mutually understood symbols between two people. It involves five subprocesses: (1) the formation of meaning, (2) the phenomenological construction of a message, (3) the physical delivery of a message to another person, (4) the interactions between the two as perceived by each, and (5) the internal reactions of the participants to what is taking place.² Thus, interpersonal communication studies such things as dyadic communication, conflict, messages, meanings, and self-disclosure to list a few representative topics. But the common ground of all study of interpersonal communication is its focus on the simultaneous exchange of symbols between people, and this ground establishes it as an area of concern for technical communication.

Although complete agreement does not exist for classifying the subdisciplines of interpersonal communication, the areas that we have chosen for our literature review are (1) self and self-disclosure, (2) relationships and interpersonal bonding, (3) interpersonal conflict, (4) message variables and message exchange, (5) communication apprehension and rhetorical sensitivity, and (6) nonverbal communication.³ When we discuss such closely related topics as group and organizational communication, we consider them as aspects of the areas that we have chosen to review. Our focus is interpersonal communication per se rather than on its applications.

Interpersonal communication can be approached from several different theoretical positions, and the one that we have chosen and the one that underpins our choice of interpersonal communication topics is Levels of Meaning theory.⁴ This theory is grounded in the position of general semanticists that "meaning resides in people." This formulation holds that meanings are *only* in people and that meaning is phenomenological, not physical or lexical. Meaning exists then in the cognitive processing systems of individuals. The starting point for Levels of Meaning theory is the reception of a message. It is concerned with the formation of individual meaning through the person's knowledge, beliefs, and experiences taken together with what the person is experiencing at the moment. Language and experience provide multiple possible meanings for any symbol. This emphasis on the individual interpretation of meaning is in accord with technical communications practice and its emphasis on audience and audience analysis. Interpersonal communication can enrich this aspect of technical communications as well as have many practical applications.

One place to begin the study of interpersonal communication is with three classic texts that have influenced many interpersonal scholars. Jurgen Ruesch and Gregory Bateson's (1951) *Communication: The Social Matrix of Psychiatry* began the relationship approach to the study of interpersonal communication. Distinguishing between "report" (the information or content as a message) and "command" (the constraints on the receiver inherent as message), Ruesch and Bateson build their study of relationships on the command aspect. From Ruesch and Bateson, then, interpersonal communication gets its concern with the extra-verbal elements of communication. In the second classic text, *The Process of Communication,* David K. Berlo (1960) draws on the findings of other disciplines: perception and learning theory from psychology and the languages findings of semanticist Alfred Korzybski. With Berlo, the interpersonal communications axiom—meanings are not in words, but in people—gets formalized. The third classic text, *Pragmatics of Human Communication,* extends the relationship approach that Ruesch and Bateson initiated and formulates a number of axioms of communication (Watzlawick et al. 1967). Perhaps the most famous and influential of these is the notion that one "cannot not communicate."

A second place to begin is with some of the introductory textbooks now on the market, most of which give overviews of the field. Although there are literally dozens from which to select, four that might be particularly useful to the technical communications teacher are Gerald R. Miller and Mark Steinberg's (1975) *Between People,* Thomas M. Steinfatt's (1977) *Human Communication,* Michael E. Roloff's (1981) *Interpersonal Communication,* and Kathleen K. Reardon's (1987) *Where Minds Meet.* Miller and Steinberg suggest that prediction of another's behavior is a central concern in communication exchanges, and they organize their text around this theme. Steinfatt's (1977) *Human Communication* is organized around the notion of levels of reality: physical, phenomenological, and transactional. It is the most inclusive of these introductory texts. Roloff's (1981) *Interpersonal Communication,* the briefest and most focused of the four, uses the social exchange theory as a model—the notion that people form and continue their relationships on the basis of self-interest. Reardon includes a history of interpersonal communication and presents a relational approach to interpersonal communications. Each of these texts suggest directions for further study.

Self and Self-Disclosure

The concepts of self and self-disclosure are treated in virtually every interpersonal communication text, yet they have come to prominence in different ways. The concept of self has developed simultaneously with developments in psychology and sociology, particularly as they have emerged as experimental disciplines. As a behavioral science concept, the idea of the self has its roots in the work of William James (1890), for with James begins the famous distinction between the I and the me—the self as subject and knower posed against the self as object and known. George H. Mead's (1934) immensely influential *Mind, Self and Society* lays the foundation for virtually all contemporary thought and research on the self, with his exploration of the way in which one's self-consciousness emerges in commerce with others. To trace the development of the self as a concept would be to take a course in the history of the social sciences, for one would need to look at the work of Harry Stack Sullivan, Charles Horton Cooley, Alfred Adler, Karen Horney, Carl Rogers, Eric Erickson, Abraham Maslow, and Erich Fromm to isolate a few of the more prominent contributors. By contrast, the concept of self-disclosure began in the 1950s with the work of a single individual, Sidney Jourard. Since then it has undergone exponential growth with over 1,000 articles, dissertations, and books published on the subject between 1970 and 1980 alone. Each area, self and self-disclosure, provides a wealth of sources from which the teacher can draw, and we can only highlight a few of those most likely to enrich the teacher's background or to acquaint the teacher with the central issues of self and self-disclosure.

Given the rich history of the self as a behavioral science concept, teachers would do well to examine its evolution. Chad Gordon and Kenneth Gergen's (1968) anthology, *The Self in Social Interaction,* can provide this history in miniature, for it reproduces many of the classic texts beginning with James's work. Gordon and Gergen also provide a useful orientation to the issues of the self: the self as fact versus construct, as subject versus object, as structure versus process, and as single versus multiple. Teachers might want to explore other work by Gergen as well, for he is a proponent of the idea that people have multiple rather than single selves. Gergen's (1972) article, "Multiple Identity: The Healthy, Happy Human Being Wears Many Masks," has been reprinted several times and is often referred to; the article argues for the existence of multiple selves in a manner easily accessible to students.

The teacher might want to extend this history of the self as a concept by examining the work of Carl Rogers, R. D. Laing, Erving Goffman, and William Schutz, as representing important ideological positions that are influencing the work that is being done today. Of Rogers's numerous publications, his *Client-Centered Therapy: Its Current Practices, Implications, and Theory* (1951) and *On Becoming a Person* (1961), are the most useful for the interpersonal communications teacher. From the definition, "the self-structure is an organized configuration of perceptions of the self which are admissible to awareness," Rogers develops his theory that the healthy self seeks first awareness and then acceptance of what it is. More simply, "the self is a continuing way of life." Rogers's work is also important for the interpersonal communications teacher because it is with him that the concept of empathetic, or reflective, listening gains prominence. Although Rogers's ideas have influenced many textbooks, one, *Interpersonal Behavior* (Athos and Gabarro 1978), might be singled out for the technical communications teacher because it focuses on interpersonal relationships within the world of business and the professions. Taking their key from Rogers, Athos and Gabarro explore the self concept as it relates to one's professional career.

R. D. Laing, Erving Goffman, and William Schutz represent the modern view that moves away from seeing the self as a single, fixed entity. In *The Divided Self* (1960) and *Self and Others* (1961) Laing attempts what he calls an existential and phenomenological account of the functioning self. The root of his study is what he calls man's existential existence, "his being-in-the-world"—an idea that in effect, turns James's I and me selves from a state into a process. With their phenomenological base, Laing's ideas become highly influential, perhaps most notably on Sidney Jourard and his ideas about self-disclosure. In his popular *The Presentation of Self in Everyday Life* (1959) and in *Interaction Ritual* (1967), Goffman examines the self as it is presented to others. Goffman argues that the presentation of the self proceeds by wearing a series of masks and in rituals that both the presenter and the audience know and agree on. Like Goffman, William Schutz explores self presentation. In *FIRO: A Three Dimensional Theory of Interpersonal Behavior* (1958), *The Interpersonal Underworld* (1966), and *Elements of Encounter* (1975), Schutz advances his FIRO theory that the presentation of self is shaped by a person's attempt to fulfull his needs. Specifically, self presentation grows out of the need for inclusion with others, for affection from others, and for control over others. The work of Rogers, Laing, Goffman, and Schutz will offer departure points for the many theorists whom we have not discussed.

The idea of the self is much bound up with the notion of the self concept, and for exploration of the self-concept, the teacher can learn much from the work of a single scholar, Ruth Wylie. *The Self Concept* (Wylie 1961)—with its subsequent revisions, one volume in 1974 on methodology and one in 1978 on theory and research—provides a comprehensive account of what has been done on the self-concept. Wylie's books are most valuable as critical surveys, especially in her efforts to disentangle scientific approaches and instruments for studying the self from the approaches of the more humanistically based theorists. More recently, Morris Rosenberg's (1979) *Conceiving the Self* confronts many of the issues with which Wylie deals, except from an argumentative perspective. Revising what he calls the passive object self of James to his own "self as active coper," Rosenberg asserts that two primary forces shape the self: self-esteem and self-consistency. Through Rosenberg, teachers can also find entrance to the vast literature on self-esteem.

Three other books provide useful introductions to self-awareness and self-concept—as well as to self-disclosure. The most useful of the three is Joseph Luft's (1969) *Of Human Interaction,* because Luft explains most fully the Johari Window that he and Harrington Ingram developed. Luft stresses the transactional relationships among self-knowledge, self-esteem, feedback, and self-disclosure. In *Encounters with the Self,* Don Hamachek (1978) provides accounts of self-awareness and the self-concept on levels readily accessible to students. Finally, John Powell's (1969) *Why Am I Afraid to Tell You Who I Am?* explores the risks that self-disclosure raises for one's self-esteem and self-awareness.

To explore the work done in the 1980s on the self concept would be an enormous task. For example, 500 articles, dissertations, and studies were done from 1980 to 1983, with ninety dissertations listed in *Dissertation Abstracts* for the years 1982 and 1983 alone. The easiest way to become oriented, given the mass of material, is to use a guide like Ruth Wylie to the research issues. As the wealth of research indicates, perhaps no other issue is so central to the issues of interpersonal communication.

Because self-disclosure had its genesis and essential lines of development in the work of Sidney Jourard, any review of the literature must start with him. Beginning with *Personal Adjustment,* Jourard (1958) announces his central approach: to study the workings of the self by examining the healthy personality. But Jourard's (1964) ideas gain their fullest treatment in *The Transparent Self,* in which he states that "no man can know himself except as an outcome of disclosing himself to another person." Following from this premise, Jourard concludes that personal health depends on disclosing oneself to others. An important counterbalance to his idea of the necessity of self-disclosure is his belief that social and familial structures often retard or restrict self-disclosure, thus producing an unhealthy tension. Jourard continues to provide verification for his ideas in *Disclosing Man to Himself* (1968) and *Self-Disclosure: An Experimental Investigation of the Transparent Self* (1971). With intellectual roots in existentialism and phenomenology, Jourard becomes a voice for a humanistic approach to interpersonal communication. Drawing particularly on Martin Buber's notion of the I and the thou as well as on Jean Paul Sartre's famous idea that "existence precedes essence," Jourard comes to argue that humans have no predetermined existence, but instead create themselves through their choices and actions—self awareness coming as they become aware of their own choice—and action-making processes.

For teachers interested in self-disclosure, especially research on self disclosure after Jourard, Gordon Chelune's (1979) *Self-Disclosure* is particularly useful because it traces the development of self-disclosure as a concept and describes key subsets of self-disclosure research. Chelune's anthology, a collection of nine essays, sorts out the tangled issues of self-disclosure into topical categories, for instance, family patterns of self-disclosure or the appropriateness of self-disclosure. Especially valuable is Chelune's closing essay, "Summary, Implications, and Future Directions," for, as the title indicates, it provides an orientation to past research and future goals. *Self-Disclosure* also includes Lawrence B. Rosenfeld's 800-item bibliography of self-disclosure literature published between 1970 and 1978. Three other works which survey self-disclosure research are P. C. Cozby's (1973) "Self-Disclosure: A Literature Review;" V. J. Derlega and A. L. Chaikin's (1975) *Sharing Intimacy: What We Reveal to Others and Why;* and Shirley J. Gilbert's (1976) "Empirical and Theoretical Extensions of Self-Disclosure."

Teachers who want to explore research done in the past ten years might examine Shirley J. Gilbert as a representative figure because Gilbert has worked in many of the present research areas: on sex differences (Gilbert and Whiteneck 1976), "Toward a Multidimensional Approach to the Study of Self-Disclosure"); on self-esteem (Gilbert and Whiteneck 1977, "Effects of Unanticipated Self-Disclosure on Recipients of Varying Levels of Self-Esteem: A Research Note"); on valence (Gilbert and Hornstein 1975). Among the numerous others working presently on self-disclosure, Lawrence R. Wheeless and Lawrence B. Rosenfeld have both published important articles; Rosenfeld's (1979) "Self-Disclosure Avoidance: Why I Am Afraid to Tell You Who I Am?" is among the most referred to of recent articles. In the article, Rosenfeld contrasts the reasons that males and females are reticent to disclose themselves.

In the 1980s, the number of studies done on self-disclosure continues to grow, now clustered around core issues, most notably: reciprocity, intimacy, self-esteem, familial patterns of disclosure, gender differences in disclosure, and factors influencing disclosure. To explore this work, teachers might want to focus on a single issue. Reciprocity might be a good choice because the large number of dissertations written on reciprocity have provided a wealth of new data. For a sample in miniature of recent studies on reciprocity in self-disclosure, the teacher could see Charles T. Hill and Donald E. Still's (1982, pp. 238–44) "Disclosure Reciprocity: Conceptual and Measurement Issues" and David R. Shaffer's (1982) "Self-Monitoring as a Determinant of Self-Disclosure Reciprocity During the Acquaintance Process." To look at these articles or most other work done during the 1980s is to become aware immediately of the increasing reliance on statistical data and on carefully controlled empirical experimentation.

Relationships

The study of human relationships is an essential area of interpersonal communication but not a unique or clearly demarcated one. Relationship research overlaps with the concerns of many other interpersonal areas, most notably with those of self-disclosure, nonverbal communication, and meaning formation and exchange. A section on relationships, however, is a vital component of virtually every interpersonal textbook, and some textbooks like Gerald M. Phillips and Julia T. Woods's (1983) *Communication and Human Relationships* and Mark L. Knapp's (1984) *Interpersonal Communication and Human Relationships* use relationships to provide a controlling focus to the study of interpersonal communication. Recently, texts like Athos and Gabarro's (1978) *Interpersonal Behavior* have applied the study of human relationships to the workplace. Examining such topics of popular and professional interest as marital and friendship bonds, the nature of intimacy, and mentor relationships, the study of relationships will remain ever important and ever new.

Probably the single most comprehensive introduction to the issues of human relationships is Ben W. Morse and Lynn A. Phelps's (1980) *Interpersonal Communication: A Relational Perspective*. This collection of forty-three essays contains introductory surveys, theoretical perspectives, and research findings organized by topic areas. Typical of the book's method is "Relational Termination and Redefinition," a section that includes important work by one of the major contributors to research on the termination of relationships (Knapp et al. 1973, "The Rhetoric of Goodbye") as well as previously unpublished material (Bradford, "The Death of a Dyad"). Knapp reports the results of research that asked two questions: What specific verbal and nonverbal behaviors are associated with taking leave of someone? And, what effects do status and acquaintanceship have on leave-taking behavior? By contrast, Larry Bradford investigates the disintegration of interpersonal relationships that precedes divorce. This variety of contributors and approaches distinguishes *Interpersonal Communication* (Morse and Phelps 1980) and makes it especially valuable to the technical communications teacher who wants to survey a new area. Because many of the articles have elaborate research reviews and bibliographies, the book also becomes a guide to further research.[5]

Much of the research on human relationships has had to do with the development or the stages of relationships. Although there are many schemata for the stages, four representative and commonly referred to frameworks are those of Mark L. Knapp, Steven W. Duck, Irwin Altman and Dalmas Taylor, and Charles Berger and Richard J. Calabrese. In *Interpersonal Communication and Human Relationships,* Knapp (1984) presents a ten-step process for how relationships are established, maintained, and ended. A subtheme of Knapp's book is how to maintain healthy relationships. Like Knapp, Duck approaches relationships developmentally and temporally; his books include *Personal Relationships and Personal Constructs: A Study in Friendship Formations* (1973) and *The Study of Acquaintance* (1977). He also coauthored the *Personal Relationships* series (Duck and Gilmour 1981–83). While Knapp and Duck present developmental models, Altman and Taylor use a descriptive model for characterizing the scope and magnitude of relationships. Their book, *Social Penetration: The Development of Interpersonal Communication* (Altman and Taylor 1973), uses a model based on the breadth and depth of shared information. In "Some Explorations in Initial Interaction and Beyond: Towards a Developmental Theory of Interpersonal Communication," Berger and Calabrese (1975) develop a research theory to examine the roles that uncertainty, communication reciprocity, intimacy, and the similarity of the interactants play in the opening stages of a relationship. Out of these variables, they devise twenty-one theorems to describe possible patterns for the beginning of relationships.

Within the work on the stages of relationships, some topics gain special prominence and are worth consideration just for themselves. Two such topics are attraction and intimacy. Research on attraction inevitably revolves around the question of why—why do people enter into relationships? While a number of factors have been identified, five receive the most research attention: proximity, similarity, complementarity, possibility of personal reward, and physical attractiveness. In *Interpersonal Attraction,* Ellen Berscheid and Elaine Walster (1978) summarize many of the findings about attraction. For work with a greater research orientation, Berscheid and Walster's (1974) "Physical Attractiveness" is also valuable. Two other general sources on attraction are Ted L. Huston's (1974) *Foundations of Interpersonal Attraction* and Donald Byrne's (1974) essay collection, *The Attraction Paradigm.*

As one might expect, intimacy has long been a topic receiving much attention and one of particular interest to a general audience. Given the nature of audience interest and expectations, much of the work on intimacy has a self-help orientation—what one can do to participate in more satisfying relationships. Also, of course, popular literature is inundated with pseudoscientific solutions to the problems of intimate relationships. In the mountains of material available, five books come to mind as helpful introductions to the issues. George R. Bach and Ronald Deutsch's (1975) *Pairing* stresses the skills necessary for success at all stages of an intimate relationship. Gerald M. Phillips and Nancy Metzger's (1976) textbook, *Intimate Communication* also discusses relational skills but frames them within the larger context of interpersonal communication. Much referred to, Rubin Zick's (1973) *Living and Loving* distinguishes liking and loving and provides scales for identifying each state. In *Intimate Behavior,* sociologist Murray Davis (1977) examines the problems of creating and maintaining intimate relationships, while Desmond Morris (1971) investigates, as his title *Intimate Behavior* indicates, behavior itself, especially the role touching plays in relationships.

Rather than approaching relationships developmentally, some interpersonal scholars approach relationships through interaction rituals or through the rules governing interpersonal exchanges. In contrast to the developmental scholars, such researchers usually stress the way meaning is negotiated. Goffman's books, *Interaction Ritual* (1967) and *Relations in Public* (1971), are rich sources for investigating the ritualistic elements of public encounters and relationships. For interpersonal communications specialists, the names most associated with the rules approach to relationships are those of W. Barnett Pearce and Vernon E. Cronen. Their book, *Communication, Action, and Meaning* (Pearce and Cronen 1980), is the most comprehensive source on this approach; it summarizes the findings of other researchers while advancing their own ideas. Through the work of Pearce and Cronen, one can gain access to the whole rules approach to relationships.

A number of recent textbooks examine human relations in a business or professional context. Again, we note Athos and Gabarro's (1978) *Interpersonal Behavior: Communication and Understanding in Relationships* because it provides both a theoretical background on relationships and actual case histories to which the theoretical information can be applied. The rich and provocative case studies reveal human relationships and their problems to be the stuff of daily business life.

Two other texts with this applied approach to relationships are Robert A. Baron's (1985) *Understanding Human Relationships: A Practical Guide to People at Work* and Dalmar Fisher's (1981) *Communication in Organizations*. Examining such topics as motivation, prejudice, discrimination, and burn-out, Baron takes a problems approach to human relationships in the workplace. Relationships per se receive less attention in Fisher's book but are examined as part of the totality of professional communication. One final book, *Interpersonal Helping Skills* (Marshall and Kurtz 1982) extends Rogers' inquiry about the helping process into the workplace. The book's primary focus is the training process, and technical communications teachers might find this book a useful tool to explore how interpersonal research findings are given practical application.

These applied human relations texts are predictive of the way in which the concerns of technical communications and interpersonal communication will increasingly overlap and will become mutually enriching. Human relationships research can help the technical communications scholar investigate such relationships as those between a writer and editor or the writer and the audience. For the interpersonal scholar, the workplace has been a relatively underdeveloped research area. The study of human relationships reminds us that relationships are the touchstones of our daily lives.

Interpersonal Conflict

Spurred by the publication of Thomas C. Schelling's (1960) classic *The Strategy of Conflict,* Richard E. Walton's (1969) *Interpersonal Peacemaking,* Paul Swingle's (1970) *The Structure of Conflict,* and Morton Deutsch's (1973) *The Resolution of Conflict,* social conflict research became an important interpersonal communication topic in the 1970s. Schelling's work is the first major attempt to discuss the role of communication in conflict situations. He approaches conflict from the viewpoint of an economic game theorist, but one who is dissatisfied with purely rational formulations. *The Strategy of Conflict* (Schelling 1960) incorporates into the theory of games such nonrational features as threats and promises. It also includes strategies for employing communication and the strategic implications of destroying possibilities for communication. Walton's *Interpersonal Peacemaking* (1969) is based on the theory of organizational development. He analyzes three case studies, presenting them with the detail that makes them interesting and useful vehicles for learning. *Interpersonal Peacemaking* presents a diagnostic model of interpersonal conflict, integrating case studies into the model. An important Walton concern, third-party interventions, occupies the final third of the book. He presents a good and practical introduction to interpersonal conflict in organizational settings, but his discussion of the role of communication in such conflicts is more incidental than central.

Swingle's (1970) *The Structure of Conflict* and Deutsch's (1973) *The Resolution of Conflict* will be of most value to scholars doing research on communication and conflict. Swingle's book consists of a series of summaries of influential research. These articles show why conflict studies became so important in the 1970s. Deutsch's book is similar to Swingle's in its technical difficulty. Deutsch was one of the earliest researchers in the area of social conflict, and *The Resolution of Conflict* is a coherent summary of most of the social psychological research in conflict that was conducted in the 1960s. Much of this research either ignored the role of communication in the bargaining process or treated it as a side issue. Chapter 6, on threats and promises, and chapters 9 and 10, on threats and interpersonal bargaining, are the principal contributions to the literature on communication and conflict.

Perspectives on Communication in Social Conflict (Miller and Simons 1974) grew out of the 1972 Speech Communication Association special conference on conflict. As its title suggests, each chapter contains a research summary in a particular area of interpersonal conflict. Steinfatt and Miller summarize much of the social psychological literature, some of which is also discussed by Deutsch. Steinfatt and Miller emphasize communication in game theoretic models of conflict. Fred Jandt discusses simulations of social conflict, and C. David Mortensen presents a transactional view of verbal conflict. John Waite Bowers' chapter considers the strategies of individuals engaged in conflicts with large organizations, and a chapter by Phillip K. Thompkins, Jeanne Y. Fisher, Dominic A. Infante, and Elaine L. Thompkins discusses communication and conflict within the university. Herbert W. Simons discusses the role of persuasion in conflict, distinguishing between coercion and persuasion and arguing that persuasion is part of the coercive process. The prologue by Simons and the epilogue by Miller are helpful in understanding the thrust of the conference and the book as a whole. In addition to the reviews of Deutsch (1973), and Steinfatt and Miller (1974), persons interested in the gaming approach to communication and conflict might see Lawrence S. Wrightsman, Jr., et al.'s (1972) *Cooperation and Competition: Readings on Mixed-Motive Games;* Charlan Nemeth's (1972) "A Critical Analysis of Research Using the Prisoner's Dilemma Paradigm for the Study of Bargaining"; J. T.

Tedeschi et al.'s (1973) *Conflict, Power, and Games;* and Erika Apfelbaum's (1974) "On Conflicts and Bargaining."

Three other sources worth noting are H. Charles Pyron's (1972) *Communication and Negotiation,* Alan C. Filley's (1975) *Interpersonal Conflict Resolution,* and Joyce H. Frost and William W. Wilmot's (1978) *Interpersonal Conflict.* Pyron presents an applied approach to communication and negotiation for the right-of-way professional. Based on the work of Berlo and Bateson, as well as on his own observations and experience, Pyron develops a practical method of approaching problems of bargaining using right-of-way negotiations as a model. Alan C. Filley's (1975) *Interpersonal Conflict Resolution,* a handbook for group problem solving in organizational settings, discusses transactional analysis, Jay Hall's *Conflict Management Survey* (1969), and the steps of integrative decision making. Although a useful introduction, it has a number of loose ends, such as a classification of conflicts and solutions into paradigms where the examples provided contradict the classification scheme. Frost and Wilmot's (1978) *Interpersonal Conflict* provides a readable introduction to the general area of communication and conflict. Unfortunately, however, Frost and Wilmot's book also has a number of annoying flaws for the more advanced reader, such as the presentation of six Prisoner's Dilemma game matrices, two of which do not meet the technical criteria for a Prisoner's Dilemma game.

As a final source for those interested in a gaming approach to conflict, David R. Seibold and Thomas M. Steinfatt's (1979) "The Creative Alternative Game: Exploring Interpersonal Influence Processes" summarizes a decade of research into the Creative Alternative game. The Creative Alternative game was developed by Steinfatt as an alternative to the Prisoner's Dilemma game as a paradigm for studying the role of communication in interpersonal conflict.

Message Variables and Message Exchange

There are three areas of message variables research: studies in linguistics, studies of persuasion, and studies of content/control. The linguistic approach to interpersonal communication examines the rules and patterns of message exchange in everyday conversations and the functional associations between various message forms. It does not concentrate on the level of phonemes and morphemes. With the exception of several model-based lines of inquiry, much of the work in this area descriptively analyzes conversations in particular contexts. For example, Gary Philipsen has studied "Speaking 'Like a Man' in Teamsterville" (1975) and "Places for Speaking in Teamsterville" (1976); Robert Hopper (1977) reports on "Employment Interviewers' Reactions to Mexican American Speech" and Betty J. Haslett (1983) discusses "Communicative Functions and Strategies in Children's Conversations." Some theory-based papers, which may be of most interest to persons in technical communications, include a grammar of conversation proposed and tested by Ernest L. Stech (1979) in "A Grammar of Conversation with a Quantitative Empirical Test" and a model proposed by Joseph N. Capella (1979, 1980, 1981) in his three-part article, "Talk and Silence Sequences in Informal Conversation," which offers an interesting line of research on talk-silence sequences.

Research on persuasion, the second area of message variables, is based on the assumption that the speaker has a persuasive intent with respect to the receiver and selects a message based on that intent. Several good summaries of the research in this area exist. *Persuasion: New Directions in Theory and Research* by Michael E. Roloff and Gerald R. Miller (1980) provides a somewhat technical but generally quite readable and comprehensive overview of the area. In addition to introductory articles by Miller and Roloff on the process of persuasion and the role of self awareness in persuasion, Michael Burgoon and Erwin P. Bettinghaus's chapter "Persuasive Message Strategies," is especially valuable. Burgoon and Bettinghaus begin with a summary of the rational approach, leading into the research on syllogistic and other logical forms. They consider evidence and how it relates to general message structure and organization. They also discuss the use of emotional strategies such as fear appeals and intense language. The second portion of their chapter moves from message structure questions to the use of messages to induce compliance. Persuasive message strategies that facilitate the foot-in-the-door and the door-in-the-face techniques are considered. In "On Resistance to Persuasive Communications," Leon Festinger and Nathan Maccoby (1964) suggest that persons subvocalize counterarguments against the position advocated in a persuasive message. Distractions that occur in a persuasive message may help to reduce counterarguing and thereby reduce resistance to persuasive attempts. Burgoon and Bettinghaus summarize the extensive literature on distraction. Other good summaries of the persuasive message literature may be found in Gary Cronkhite's (1969) *Persuasion* and Kenneth E. Andersen's (1971) *Persuasion*. Although these summaries are older, they provide more extensive coverage of certain topics than Burgoon and Bettinghaus do.

Content/control study of messages, the third research area, was initiated by Bateson. Of these two message dimensions, content concerns what is said, and control concerns how it is said and what it implies for the relationship. Bateson was particularly interested in measuring and classifying the control dimension, and early message research followed in Bateson's footsteps. A summary of the major instruments for measuring control patterns is contained in Nicholas O'Donnell-Trujillo's (1981) "Relational Communication: A Comparison of Coding Systems." An exchange between Joseph P. Folger and Marshall S. Poole (1982), who question the validity of some of the systems, and L. Edna Rogers and Frank Millar (1982), who defend their system, in Michael Burgoon's (1982) *Communication Yearbook Vol. 5* is illustrative of the practical problems that may be encountered in such classification attempts.

Partially as a result of the difficulties of coding, the literature in the content/control areas has concentrated on individual utterances and brief statements and has generally failed to investigate the possibilities for research in longer conversational sequences. Given this limitation, several interesting areas of research exist. Rogers and Millar's (1979) "Domineeringness Versus Dominance" investigates peoples' attempts to control another. In a dominance situation the other accepts this definition of the current relationship, while in domineeringness the other rejects this definition attempt. Millar et al. in "Relational Control and Dyadic Understanding (1979) and Courtright et al. in "Domineeringness and Dominance: Replication and Expansion" (1979) and "Message Control Intensity as a Predictor of Transactional Redundancy" (1980a) have expanded this research and studied the variable of intensity of the control attempt in the message.

Several other important variables relating to the content and control dimensions of messages have been investigated. The nature of the relationship between the two dimensions is discussed by B. Aubrey Fisher et al. (1977) in "The Nature of Complex Communication Systems." In "A Cyclical Model of Developing Relationships," B. Aubrey Fisher and G. Lloyd Drecksel (1983) have investigated cycles in the control of relationships. Janet B. Bavelas and Beverly J. Smith's (1982) "A Model for Scaling Verbal Disqualifications" and Bavelas's (1983) "Situations that Lead to Disqualifications" discuss the use of the control dimension in attempts to disqualify the messages of another person. William A. Donohue's "Development of a Model of Rule Use in Negotiation Interaction" (1981) and "Analyzing Negotiation Tactics" (1981a) and Linda L. Putnam and Tricia S. Jones's (1982) "The Role of Communication in Bargaining" examine the uses of the control dimension in situations involving negotiations and bargaining. And an overview of the use of the content/control concept in family therapy is provided by Carol Wilder's (1979) "The Palo Alto Group."

Communication Apprehension

Communication apprehension is a major area of interpersonal communication research that has considerable practical relevance to technical communication. Communication apprehension is the fear of communicating with another person. In the 1950s, considerable research was conducted on the effects of stage fright and the general fear of speaking in public that is generally listed by Americans as the most dreaded anticipated experience. In "A Synthesis of Experimental Research in Stage Fright," Theodore Clevenger, Jr. (1959), pulls together much of this seminal research. Communication apprehension is not stage fright. It refers instead to the fear and anxiety associated with interpersonal interactions and everyday human communication encounters. Data from national studies of communication apprehension indicate that approximately one out of every five adults is severely apprehensive concerning everyday interpersonal communication encounters. About 15 percent of the college population is severely communication apprehensive. The problem is considerably more severe in technically oriented populations such as engineers, pharmacists, and students enrolled in technical subjects, as Bruce Berger et al. (1982) report in "Implementation of a Systematic Desensitization Program and Classroom Instruction to Reduce Communication Apprehension in Pharmacy Students."

Several different forms of the Personal Report of Communication Apprehension (PRCA) are available for the measurement of communication apprehension. The most common forms are the PRCA-25, which was used in most of the validity studies, and the PRCA-20 and PRCA-24. The forms vary in emphasis on interpersonal versus public speaking situations, and PRCA-24 is recommended for most interpersonal situations. The most available sources for the tests are James C. McCroskey and Virginia P. Richmond's (1980) *The Quiet Ones: Communication Apprehension and Shyness* and James C. McCroskey's *An Introduction to Rhetorical Communication* (1982a) and "Oral Communication Apprehension: A Reconceptualization" (1982b). Norms and scoring for the tests are available in these sources.

Several related concepts, such as shyness, social anxiety, reticence, and unwillingness to communicate, may be found in the literature (see John A. Daly and James C. McCroskey's [1984] *Avoiding Communication: Shyness, Reticence, and Communication Apprehension*). As defined by Phillip G. Zimbardo (1977) in *Shyness,* shyness is a general term for all anxiety and behavior related to a fear and avoidance of social interaction. It mixes internal states such as anxiety with external behaviors of avoidance and social inhibition in an affective-behavioral syndrome and may be too broad a concept to be especially useful in interpersonal communication. Reticence (see Gerald M. Phillips's [1981] *Help for Shy People*) and unwillingness to communicate (see Judee K. Burgoon's (1976) "The Unwillingness-to-Communicate Scale") refer to overt patterns of behavior, not to internal states. The psychological concepts of introversion and low sociability refer to similar behaviors. In contrast, communication apprehension refers to an internal state of fear and tension, a subjective psychological experience. As Mark R. Leary (1983) demonstrates in "Social Anxiousness: The Construct and Its Measurement," communication apprehension combines worry, cognitive tension, and physiological arousal.

It is possible to exhibit the avoidance behaviors of reticence and unwillingness to communicate while not experiencing communication apprehension. A person may lack the social skills of interpersonal interaction yet experience no anxiety. Conversely, it is possible to experience communication apprehension yet to exhibit no behaviors symptomatic of avoidance of communication. Some highly communication apprehensive persons have learned to control their outward behaviors while inwardly experiencing high levels of anxiety. Although many persons who score highly on communication apprehension experience both behavioral and anxiety problems, at least one study indicates that treatments directed toward the specific type of difficulty, emotional or behavioral, are significantly more effective than treatments that ignore the distinction and attempt to treat an affective-behavioral syndrome. Persons who exhibit reticence and unwillingness-to-communicate behaviors may be treated by providing an adequate and appropriate repertoire of social skills or through a program of rhetoritherapy, as Gerald M. Phillips and Kent A. Sokoloff (1979) demonstrate in "An End to Anxiety: Treating Speech Problems with Rhetoritherapy." Communication apprehension seems best treated as a form of conditioned anxiety through systematic desensitization as discussed by Berger et al. (1982) or through cognitive therapy (William J. Fremouw 1977, *Client Manual for Integrated Behavioral Treatment of Speech Anxiety;* D. Meichenbaum, "Applications of Cognitive Behavioral

Therapy"). Systematic desensitization pairs a communication apprehension hierarchy with successively more anxiety producing steps, with a program of deep muscular relaxation. Cognitive restructuring therapy makes people aware of their own negative statements, behaviors, and cognitions about themselves; changes these negative statements into positive ones; and changes peoples' awareness of what actually happens in the communication process.

Nonverbal Communication

As an area for scientific investigation, nonverbal communication had its origin in Charles Darwin's 1872 book *The Expression of the Emotions in Man and Animals* (Darwin 1955). Yet its development as an aspect of interpersonal communication has had a much different tenor because during the 1960s and 1970s a series of books on nonverbal communication gained large general audiences, with some books like Julian Fast's (1970) *Body Language* becoming best sellers. A journalist, Fast popularized fundamental notions of nonverbal communication: that space and time, body gesture, and facial expression communicate. But Fast also oversimplified nonverbal concepts, for instance, linking a certain gesture with a specific meaning, as folded arms with concern for self. In doing so, he disregarded the findings of communication theory: that meaning is not universal and that it does not reside in specific symbols but rather in the users of those symbols. The mainlines of the study of nonverbal communication were laid by a series of textbooks that appeared during the 1970s, and through these texts, both teacher and student gain their easiest access to the study of nonverbal communication. We have chosen to focus on the work of Paul Ekman, Mark L. Knapp, Randall Harrison, Albert E. Scheflen, and Albert Mehrabian as representative of the developments that are influencing the work being done in nonverbal communication today. Our choices are of necessity incomplete and in some senses idiosyncratic, and someone desiring a more complete survey might explore the work of Michael Argyle, Irmgard Bartinieff (whose work on dance is particularly evocative and insightful), and Eliot Chapple.

Two men stand as predecessors to Ekman and the others: Ray L. Birdwhistell, who originated the concept of kinesics, and Edward T. Hall, who introduced the concept of proxemics. In Birdwhistell's books, *An Introduction to Kinesics* (1952) and *Kinesics and Contexts* (1970), he develops a system for codifying and analyzing body motions and gestures. Influenced by the findings of structural linguistics and cultural anthropology, Birdwhistell tries to provide a rigor of methodology that supplies for nonverbal communication what linguistics supplies for language. In anthropologist Hall's books, *The Silent Language* (1959) and *The Hidden Dimension* (1966) he describes the way in which people's use of time and space communicates and announces his famous spatial classification system from intimate to public distance. Curiously, Hall comes to his interest in nonverbal communication as a byproduct of investigating quite a different question: Why Americans fail to communicate effectively when they are outside of the United States.

Paul Ekman and his research associates have focused on facial nonverbal communication. Paul Ekman and Wallace Friesen's (1975) textbook, *Unmasking the Face: A Guide to Recognizing Emotion from Facial Clues,* introduces his core ideas in a manner that is accessible to teachers and students alike. Ekman tries to construct a physiological lexicon of facial expressions so that observers can read and assign meaning to facial behavior. Underlying Ekman's research is his assumption that facial behavior represents emotional actions and reactions. Ekman has a distinguished list of research publications, including Ekman et al.'s (1972) *Emotion in the Human Face: Guidelines for Research and Integration of Findings* and Ekman and Wallace Friesen's *The Facial Action Coding System* (1978), and *The Face of Man: Expressions of Universal Emotion in a New Guinea Village* (1980), and *Telling Lies* (1985). As the titles indicate, Ekman brings a scientific rigor to the investigation of facial communication.

While Ekman supplies the rigor of the scientist, Knapp provides nonverbal communication with the clarity of the teacher. Best known for his textbooks, most notably *Nonverbal Communication in Human Interaction,* Knapp (1978) is particularly adept at describing and analyzing nonverbal communication research. Knapp's books correct many of the misconceptions that popular press treatments of nonverbal communication have produced. John M. Wiemann et al.'s (1978) "Nonverbal Communication: Issues and Appraisal" is often cited for its thoughtful analysis of nonverbal communication research issues.

Like Knapp, Randall Harrison uses his textbooks to explore his central concerns, his interest in signs and symbolic behavior. His influential text, *Beyond Words: An Introduction to Nonverbal Communication* (Harrison 1974), exemplifies its own message; its photographs and cartoons provide a series of nonverbal communication experiences. In his more recent book, *The Nonverbal Dimension of Human Communication,* Harrison (1981) announces an integrative theory of nonverbal communication—an attempt that is representative of present nonverbal communication researchers' efforts to shift from the impressionistic and to diffuse early studies to the more systematic and experimentally based research of the present.

Albert Scheflen, a practicing psychotherapist, comes to nonverbal communication out of his interest in the psychology of communication and his holistic sense of the communication process. His textbook, *Body Language and Social Order* (1972), looks at nonverbal communication as it is affected by the socialization process. Taking his cue from anthropologists and biologists, Scheflen focuses on the concept of territoriality, seeing it as an emblem of interpersonal bonding. In his later books, *Communicational Structure: Analysis of a Psychotherapy Transaction* (1973) and *How Behavior Means* (1974), Scheflen brings the findings of psychologists, especially Gestalt psychologists, to nonverbal communication. *How Behavior Means* is particularly interesting for the comparison that Scheflen develops between Einsteinian physics and nonverbal communication, with Scheflen arguing that nonverbal communication should adopt the systemic outlook of Einsteinian physics.

With his emphasis on the applications of nonverbal communication, Albert Mehrabian defines one of the lines that contemporary thought on nonverbal communication has taken. Unlike other researchers who look at stimulus features (e.g., facial expressions), Mehrabian investigates the functions performed by sets of features (e.g., a raised eyebrow together with a tilt of the head and a particular vocal intonation). These sets express what Mehrabian calls the three metaphorical dimensions of nonverbal communication: immediacy, status, and responsiveness. Each dimension works as a polarity, as, for example, in responsiveness active and passive. As coded into nonverbal gestures, these dimensions enable people to express and share nuances of feeling. Mehrabian's (1972) first textbook, *Silent Messages,* announces his ideas and takes an applications approach to nonverbal communication, examining nonverbal communication as a component in selling, political campaigning, and advertising. His second text, *Nonverbal Communication* (1977), has a greater emphasis on research than his first does, as Mehrabian raises such issues as the possibility for multidimensional referents and the implications of implicit nonverbal communication.

For teachers interested in gaining the kind of overview that anthologies can provide, two anthologies come to mind: Shirley Weitz's (1974) *Nonverbal Communication: Readings and Commentary* and Jonathan Benthall and Ted Polhemus's (1975) *The Body as Medium of Expression.* Weitz's anthology, a collection of classic studies (as in Scheflen's

"Quasi-Courtship Behavior in Psychotherapy" [1974] or Birdwhistell's "Toward Analyzing American Movement" [1974]), has become a classic of its own kind. Benthall and Polhemus's book is less research oriented but includes essays by Birdwhistell, Argyle, and other theorists.

Bibliographic research in nonverbal communication is particularly easy as a result of two annotated bibliographies: *Understanding Body Movement* (Davis 1971) and *Bodily Movement and Nonverbal Communication* (Davis and Skupien 1982). Together these books include over 2,300 entries representing work done from Darwin's seminal studies through 1980. The introductions to Davis's two books provide insightful thumbnail sketches of the history of nonverbal communication research; identify key figures in the development of nonverbal communication concepts; and describe present research trends and issues. Martha R. Key (1977) has also done a bibliography, *Nonverbal Communication: A Research Guide and Bibliography,* although it is not as comprehensive as Davis's. Key's bibliography provides easy access to nonverbal communication issues because entries are grouped by topic area. Another useful, topically arranged bibliography is Jerry Frye's (1980) *Index to Nonverbal Data.* Frye's index contains over 400 items classified by sixteen categories and fifty subcategories.

In the 1980s, nonverbal communication research continues to flourish, as more attention is directed to methodological problems and to using the findings of anthropology, linguistics, and psychology to enrich nonverbal research. Martha Davis and Janet Skupien (1982) perhaps best describe the promise of the 1980s:

> The signs of the times point to a synthesis of advanced statistical method and complex descriptions of the ongoing behavior stream. "Developmental kinesics" and the study of "kinesics acquisition"... should come of age. By 1990 there should be far more documentation of cultural differences in nonverbal communication and rich description of diverse cultural movement styles. (xviii–xix)

Notes

1. When work is done on interpersonal communication within technical communications, it almost always has a skills orientation on the applicability of interpersonal skills within a business or industrial context. Interpersonal communication receives more attention within business communications, although it remains a relatively underdeveloped area. Ruth M. Walsh and Stanley Birkin's (1980) *Business Communications: An Annotated Bibliography* is fairly representative when it lists thirteen entries in its section on interpersonal communication. Interpersonal communication receives much more

attention as an area of organizational communication, but organizational communication is often taught as part of a business or management curriculum, rather than as part of a communications curriculum.

2. For further explanation of this definition, see Thomas M. Steinfatt's (1977) *Human Communication: An Interpersonal Introduction.*

3. For a complete bibliographic survey, see Joe Ayre's "The Study of Interpersonal Communication by Speech Communication Scholars" (1983) and "Four Approaches to Interpersonal Communication" (1984).

4. See Thomas M. Steinfatt's (1981) "A Communication Theory of Humor."

5. For a briefer, yet comprehensive, review of the issues of relational communication than Ben W. Morse and Lynn A. Phelps provide, see Stephen W. Littlejohn's (1983) *Theories of Human Communication.*

Bibliography

Altman, Irwin, and Dalmas Taylor. *Social Penetration: The Development of Interpersonal Communication.* New York: Holt, 1973.

Andersen, Kenneth E. *Persuasion.* Boston: Allyn & Bacon, 1971.

Apfelbaum, Erika. "On Conflicts and Bargaining." In *Advances in Experimental Social Psychology.* Vol. 7. Edited by Leonard Berkowitz. New York: Academic Press, 1974.

Athos, Anthony G., and John J. Gabarro. *Interpersonal Behavior.* Englewood Cliffs, N.J.: Prentice-Hall, 1978.

Ayre, Joe. "The Study of Interpersonal Communication by Speech Communication Scholars." *Australia Communication Review* (1983).

———. "Four Approaches to Interpersonal Communication." *Western Journal of Speech Communication* (Fall 1984): 408–40.

Bach, George R., and Ronald Deutsch. *Pairing.* New York: Avon, 1975.

Barnett, George A., and Carol Hughes. "Communication Theory and Technical Communication." In *Research in Technical Communication,* edited by Michael G. Moran and Debra Journet. Westport, Conn.: Greenwood, 1985, 39–83.

Baron, Robert A. *Understanding Human Relationships: A Practical Guide to People at Work.* Boston: Allyn & Bacon, 1985.

Bavelas, Janet B. "Situations that Lead to Disqualifications." *Human Communication Research* 9 (1983): 130–45.

Bavelas, Janet B., and Beverly J. Smith. "A Model for Scaling Verbal Disqualifications." *Human Communication Research* 8 (1982): 214–27.

Benthall, Jonathan, and Ted Polhemus. *The Body as Medium of Expression.* New York: Dutton, 1975.

Berger, Bruce A., H. John Baldwin, James C. McCroskey, and Virginia P. Richmond. "Implementation of a Systematic Desensitization Program and Classroom Instruction to Reduce Communication Apprehension in Pharmacy Students." *American Journal of Pharmaceutical Education* 46 (1982): 227–34.

Berger, Charles, and Richard J. Calabrese. "Some Explorations in Initial Interaction and Beyond: Towards a Developmental Theory of Interpersonal Communication." *Human Communication Research* 2 (1975): 99–112.

Berger, Charles, and Michael E. Roloff. "Thinking about Friends and Lovers: Social Cognition and Communication and Relational Trajectories." In *Social Cognition,* edited by Michael E. Roloff and Charles Berger. Beverly Hills: Sage, 1982.

Berlo, David K. *The Process of Communication.* New York: Holt, 1960.

Berscheid, Ellen, and Elaine Walster. "Physical Attractiveness." In *Advances in Social Psychology.* Vol. 7. Edited by Leonard Berkowitz. New York: Academic Press, 1974.

———. *Interpersonal Attraction.* Reading, Mass.: Addison-Wesley, 1978.

Birdwhistell, Ray L. *An Introduction to Kinesics.* Louisville: University of Louisville Press, 1952.

———. *Kinesics and Contexts.* Philadelphia: University of Pennsylvania Press, 1970.

———. "Toward Analyzing American Movement." In *Nonverbal Communication,* edited by Shirley Weitz. New York: Oxford University Press, 1974.

Bradford, Larry. "The Death of a Dyad." In *Interpersonal Communication: A Relational Perspective,* edited by Ben W. Morse and Lynn A. Phelps. Minneapolis: Burgess Publishing, 1980.

Burgoon, Judee K. "The Unwillingness-to-Communicate Scale." *Communication Monographs* 43 (1976): 60–69.

Burgoon, Michael, ed. *Communication Yearbook, No. 5.* New Brunswick, N.J.: Transaction Books, 1982.

Burgoon, Michael, and Erwin P. Bettinghaus. "Persuasive Message Strategies." In *Persuasion: New Directions in Theory and Research,* edited by Michael E. Roloff and Gerald R. Miller. Beverly Hills: Sage, 1984.

Byrne, Donald, ed. *The Attraction Paradigm.* New York: Academic Press, 1974.

Cappella, Joseph N. "Talk-Silence Sequences in Informal Conversations I." *Human Communication Research* 6 (1979): 3–17.

———. "Talk and Silence Sequences in Informal Conversations II." *Human Communication Research* 6 (1980): 130–45.

Cappella, Joseph N., and Sally Planalp. "Talk and Silence Sequences in Informal Conversations III: Interspeaker Influence." *Human Communication Research* 7 (1981): 117–32.

Carlson, Helen V., et al. *An Annotated Bibliography of Technical Writing, Editing, Graphics, and Publishing.* Washington, D.C.: Society for Technical Communication, 1983.

Chelune, Gordon. *Self-Disclosure.* San Francisco: Jossey-Bass, 1979.

Clevenger, Theodore, Jr. "A Synthesis of Experimental Research in Stage Fright." *Quarterly Journal of Speech* 45 (1959): 134–45.

Courtright, John, Frank Millar, and L. Edna Rogers-Millar. "Domineeringness and Dominance: Replication and Expansion." *Communication Monographs* 46 (1979): 179–92.

———. "Message Control Intensity as a Predictor of Transactional Redundancy." *Communication Yearbook,* No. 4, edited by Dan Nimmo. New Brunswick, N.J.: Transaction Books, 1980a.

———. "Message Control Intensity: Rationale and Preliminary Findings." *Communication Monographs* 47 (1980b): 201-19.

Cozby, P. C. "Self-Disclosure: A Literature Review." *Psychology Bulletin* 79 (1973): 73-91.

Cronkhite, Gary. *Persuasion.* Indianapolis: Bobbs-Merrill, 1969.

Daly, John A., and James C. McCroskey, eds. *Avoiding Communication: Shyness, Reticence, and Communication Apprehension.* Beverly Hills: Sage, 1984.

Darwin, Charles. *The Expression of the Emotions in Man and Animals.* 1872. New York: Philosophical Library, 1955.

Davis, Martha. *Understanding Body Movement.* New York: Arno Press, 1971.

Davis, Martha, and Janet Skupien. *Bodily Movement and Nonverbal Communication.* Bloomington: Indiana University Press, 1982.

Davis, Murray. *Intimate Behavior.* New York: Free Press, 1977.

DeLaZerda, Nancy, and Robert Hopper. "Report on Language Attached in Employment Interviews." *Communication Monographs* 46 (1979): 126-34.

Derlaga, V. J., and A. L. Chaikin. *Sharing Intimacy: What We Reveal to Others and Why.* Englewood Cliffs, N.J.: Prentice-Hall, 1975.

Deutsch, Morton. *The Resolution of Conflict.* New Haven: Yale University Press, 1973.

Donohue, William A. "Analyzing Negotiation Tactics." *Human Communication Research* 7 (1981a): 273-87.

———. "Development of a Model of Rule Use in Negotiation Interaction." *Communication Monographs* 48 (1981): 106-20.

Duck, Steven W. *Personal Relationships and Personal Constructs: A Study of Friendship Formations.* London: Wiley, 1973.

———. *The Study of Acquaintance.* Westmead, England: Saxon House, 1977.

Duck, Steven W., and Robin Gilmour, eds. *Personal Relationships.* 4 vols. New York: Academic Press, 1981-83.

———. "Social and Personal Relationships." In *Handbook of Interpersonal Communication,* edited by Mark L. Knapp and Gerald R. Miller. Beverly Hills: Sage, 1985, pp. 655-86.

Ekman, Paul, and Wallace Friesen. *Unmasking the Face: A Guide to Recognizing Emotion from Facial Clues.* Englewood Cliffs, N.J.: Prentice-Hall, 1975.

———. *The Facial Action Coding System.* Palo Alto, Calif.: Consulting Psychologists Press, 1978.

———. *The Face of Man: Expressions of Universal Emotion in a New Guinea Village.* New York: Garland Press, 1980.

———. *Telling Lies.* New York: Norton, 1985.

Ekman, Paul, Wallace Friesen, and Phoebe Ellsworth. *Emotion in the Human Face: Guidelines for Research and Integration of Findings.* New York: Pergamon Press, 1972.

Fast, Julian. *Body Language.* New York: Evans, 1970.

Festinger, Leon, and Nathan Macoby. "On Resistance to Persuasive Communications." *Journal of Abnormal and Social Psychology* 68 (1964): 359–66.

Filley, Alan C. *Interpersonal Conflict Resolution.* Glenview, Ill.: Scott, Foresman, 1975.

Fisher, B. Aubrey, Thomas Glover, and Donald G. Ellis. "The Nature of Complex Communication Systems." *Communication Monographs* 44 (1977): 231–40.

Fisher, B. Aubrey, and G. Lloyd Drecksel. "A Cyclical Model of Developing Relationships." *Communication Monographs* 50 (1983): 66–78.

Fisher, Dalmar. *Communication in Organizations.* St. Paul, Minn.: West, 1981.

Folger, Joseph P., and Michael S. Poole. "Relational Coding Schemes: The Question of Validity." In *Communication Yearbook 5,* edited by Michael Burgoon. New Brunswick, N.J.: Transaction Books, 1982.

Fremouw, William J. *Client Manual for Integrated Behavioral Treatment of Speech Anxiety.* Morgantown, W.Va.: West Virginia University, 1977. (In *Catalogue of Selected Documents in Psychology,* Feb. 1977.)

Frost, Joyce H., and William W. Wilmot. *Interpersonal Conflict.* Dubuque, Iowa: Brown, 1978.

Frye, Jerry. *Index to Nonverbal Data.* Duluth, Minn.: University of Minnesota Press, 1980.

Gergen, Kenneth. "Multiple Identity: The Healthy, Happy Human Being Wears Many Masks." *Psychology Today,* May 1972, 31–35, 64–66.

Gilbert, Shirley J. "Empirical and Theoretical Extensions of Self-Disclosure." In *Explorations in Interpersonal Communication,* edited by Gerald R. Miller. Beverly Hills: Sage, 1976.

Gilbert, Shirley J., and David Hornstein. "The Communication of Self-Disclosure: Level Versus Variance." *Human Communication Research* 1 (Summer 1975): 316–22.

Gilbert, Shirley J., and Gale Whiteneck. "Toward a Multidimensional Approach to the Study of Self-Disclosure." *Human Communication Research* 2 (Summer 1976): 347–55.

———. "Effects of Unanticipated Self-Disclosure on Recipients of Varying Levels of Self-Esteem: A Research Note." *Human Communication Research* 3 (1977): 368–71.

Goffman, Erving. *The Presentation of Self in Everyday Life.* Garden City, N.Y.: Doubleday, 1959.

———. *Interaction Ritual.* Garden City, N.Y.: Doubleday, 1967.

———. *Relations in Public.* New York: Basic Books, 1971.

Gordon, Chad, and Kenneth Gergen. *The Self in Social Interaction.* New York: Wiley, 1968.

Hall, Edward T. *The Silent Language.* Greenwich, Conn.: Fawcett, 1959.

———. *The Hidden Dimension.* Garden City, N.Y.: Doubleday, 1966.

Hall, Jay. *Conflict Management Survey.* Austin, Tex.: Teleometrics, Inc., 1969.

Hamachek, Don. *Encounters with the Self.* New York: Holt, 1978.

Harrison, Randall. *Beyond Words: An Introduction to Nonverbal Communication.* Englewood Cliffs, N.J.: Prentice-Hall, 1974.

———. *The Nonverbal Dimension of Human Communication.* Englewood Cliffs, N.J.: Prentice-Hall, 1981.

Haslett, Betty J. "Communicative Functions and Strategies in Children's Conversations." *Human Communication Research* 9 (1983): 114–29.

Hill, Charles T., and Donald E. Still. "Disclosure Reciprocity: Conceptual and Measurement Issues." *Social Psychology Quarterly* 45 (Dec. 1982): 238–44.

Hopper, Robert. "Employment Interviewers' Reactions to Mexican American Speech." *Communication Monographs* 44 (1977): 346–51.

Huston, Ted L. *Foundations of Personal Attraction.* New York: Academic Press, 1974.

James, William. *Principles of Psychology.* New York: Henry Holt, 1890.

Jandt, Fred E. *Conflict Resolutions Through Communication.* New York: Harper and Row, 1973.

Jourard, Sidney. *Personal Adjustment.* New York: Macmillan, 1958.

———. *The Transparent Self.* New York: Van Nostrand, 1964.

———. *Disclosing Man to Himself.* New York: Van Nostrand, 1968.

———. *Self-Disclosure: An Experimental Investigation of the Transparent Self.* New York: Wiley, 1971.

Kelley, H. H. "Love and Commitment." In *Close Relationships,* edited by H. H. Kelley, et al. New York: Freeman, 1983.

Key, Martha R. *Nonverbal Communication: A Research Guide and Bibliography.* Metuchen, N.J.: Scarecrow Press, 1977.

Knapp, Mark L. *Nonverbal Communication in Human Interaction.* New York: Holt, 1978.

———. *Interpersonal Communication and Human Relationships.* Boston: Allyn, 1984.

Knapp, Mark L., et al. "The Rhetoric of Goodbye: Verbal and Nonverbal Correlates of Human Leave-Taking." *Speech Monographs* 40 (1973): 182–98.

Laing, R. D. *The Divided Self.* London: Tavistock, 1960.

———. *Self and Others.* London: Tavistock, 1961.

Leary, Mark R. "Social Anxiousness: The Construct and Its Measurement." *Journal of Personality Assessment* 47 (1983): 65–75.

Littlejohn, Stephen W. *Theories of Human Communication.* Belmont, Calif.: Wadsworth, 1983, pp. 161–91.

Luft, Joseph. *Of Human Interaction.* Palo Alto, Calif.: National Press Books, 1969.

Marshall, Eldon K., and P. David Kurtz, eds. *Interpersonal Helping Skills.* San Francisco: Jossey-Bass, 1982.

McCroskey, James C. *An Introduction to Rhetorical Communication.* 4th ed. Englewood Cliffs, N.J.: Prentice-Hall, 1982a.

———. "Oral Communication Apprehension: A Reconceptualization." In *Communication Yearbook 6,* edited by Michael Burgoon. Beverly Hills: Sage, 1982b.

McCroskey, James C., and Virginia P. Richmond. *The Quiet Ones: Communication Apprehension and Shyness.* Dubuque: Gorsuch Scarisbrick, 1980.

Mead, George H. *Mind, Self, and Society.* Chicago: University of Chicago Press, 1934.

Meichenbaum, D. "Applications of Cognitive Behavioral Therapy." New York: BMA Audio Cassette Publications. Sound Cassette.

Mehrabian, Albert. *Silent Messages.* 2d ed. Belmont, Calif.: Wadsworth, 1972.

———. *Nonverbal Communication.* Chicago: Aldine Atherton, 1977.

Millar, Frank, L. Edna Rogers, and John Courtright. "Relational Control and Dyadic Understanding." *Communication Yearbook, No. 3,* edited by Dan Nimmo. New Brunswick, N.J.: Transaction Books, 1979.

Miller, Gerald R. *Speech Communication: A Behavioral Approach.* Indianapolis: Bobbs-Merrill, 1966.

Miller, Gerald R., and Herbert W. Simons. *Perspectives on Communication in Social Conflict.* Englewood Cliffs, N.J.: Prentice-Hall, 1974.

Miller, Gerald R., and Mark Steinberg. *Between People.* Chicago: SRA, 1975.

Moran, Michael G., and Debra Journet. *Research in Technical Communication.* Westport, Conn.: Greenwood, 1985.

Morris, Desmond. *Intimate Behavior.* New York: Random House, 1971.

Morse, Ben W., and Lynn A. Phelps. *Interpersonal Communication: A Relational Perspective.* Minneapolis: Burgess, 1980.

Mortensen, C. David. A Transactional Paradigm of Verbalized Social Conflict. In *Perspectives on Communication in Social Conflict,* edited by G. R. Miller and H. W. Simons. Englewood Cliffs, N.J.: Prentice-Hall, 1974.

Nemeth, Charlan. "A Critical Analysis of Research Using the Prisoner's Dilemma Paradigm for the Study of Bargaining." In *Advances in Experimental Social Psychology.* Vol. 6. Edited by Leonard Berkowitz. New York: Academic Press, 1972.

O'Donnell-Trujillo, Nicholas. "Relational Communication: A Comparison of Coding Systems." *Communication Monographs* 48 (1981): 91-105.

Pearce, W. Barnett, and Vernon E. Cronen. *Communication, Action, and Meaning.* New York: Praeger, 1980.

Philipsen, Gerry. "Speaking 'Like a Man' in Teamsterville." *Quarterly Journal of Speech* 61 (1975): 13-22.

———. "Places for Speaking in Teamsterville." *Quarterly Journal of Speech* 62 (1976): 15-25.

Phillips, Gerald M. *Help for Shy People.* Englewood Cliffs, N.J.: Prentice-Hall, 1981.

Phillips, Gerald M., and Nancy Metzger. *Intimate Communication.* Boston: Allyn & Bacon, 1976.

Phillips, Gerald M., and Kent A. Sokoloff. "An End to Anxiety: Treating Speech Problems with Rhetoritherapy." *Journal of Communication Disorders* 12 (1979): 385-97.

Phillips, Gerald M., and Julia T. Woods. *Communication and Human Relationships.* New York: Macmillan, 1983.

Powell, John. *Why Am I Afraid to Tell You Who I Am?* Chicago: Argus Communications, 1969.

Putnam, Linda L., and Tricia S. Jones. "The Role of Communication in Bargaining." *Communication Monographs* 49 (1982): 171–91.

Pyron, H. Charles. *Communication and Negotiation.* Los Angeles: American Right of Way Association, 1972.

Reardon, Kathleen K. *Where Minds Meet.* Belmont, Calif.: Wadsworth, 1987.

Rogers, Carl. *Client-Centered Therapy: Its Current Practices, Implications, and Theory.* Boston: Houghton, 1951.

———. *On Becoming a Person.* Boston: Houghton, 1961.

Rogers-Millar, L. Edna, and Frank E. Millar III. "Domineeringness Versus Dominance: A Transactional View." *Human Communication Research* 5 (1979): 238–46.

———. "A Question of Validity: A Pragmatic Response." *Communication Yearbook, No. 5,* edited by Michael Burgoon. New Brunswick, N.J.: Transaction Books, 1982.

Roloff, Michael E. *Interpersonal Communication.* London: Sage, 1981.

Roloff, Michael E., and Gerald R. Miller. *Persuasion: New Directions in Theory and Research.* Beverly Hills: Sage, 1980.

———. *Persuasion: New Directions in Theory and Research.* Beverly Hills: Sage, 1984.

Rosenberg, Morris. *Conceiving the Self.* New York: Basic, 1979.

Rosenfeld, Lawrence B. "Self-Disclosure Avoidance: Why Am I Afraid to Tell You Who I Am?" *Communication Monographs* 46 (March 1979): 63–74.

Ruesch, Jurgen, and Gregory Bateson. *Communication: The Social Matrix of Psychiatry.* New York: Norton, 1951.

Scheflan, Albert. *Body Language and Social Order.* Englewood Cliffs, N.J.: Prentice-Hall, 1972.

———. *Communicational Structure: Analysis of a Psychotherapy Transaction.* Bloomington, Ind.: Indiana University Press, 1973.

———. *How Behavior Means.* New York: Jason Aronson, 1974.

———. "Quasi-Courtship Behavior in Psychotherapy." In *Nonverbal Communication,* edited by Shirley Weitz. New York: Oxford University Press, 1974.

Schelling, Thomas C. *The Strategy of Conflict.* Cambridge, Mass.: Harvard University Press, 1960.

Schramm, Wilbur. "How Communication Works." In *The Process and Effects of Mass Communication,* edited by Wilbur Schramm. Urbana, Ill.: University of Illinois Press, 1954.

Schutz, William. *FIRO: A Three Dimensional Theory of Interpersonal Behavior.* New York: Holt, 1958.

———. *The Interpersonal Underworld.* Palo Alto, Calif.: Science and Behavior, 1966.

———. *Elements of Encounter.* New York: Bantam, 1975.

Seibold, David R., and Thomas M. Steinfatt. "The Creative Alternative Game: Exploring Interpersonal Influence Processes." *Simulation and Games* 10 (1979): 429–57.

Shaffer, David R., Jonathan E. Smith, and Michele Tomarelli. "Self-Monitoring as a Determinant of Self-Disclosure Reciprocity During the Acquaintance Process." *Journal of Personality and Social Psychology* 43 (July 1982): 163–75.

Shannon, Claude E., and Warren Weaver. *The Mathematical Theory of Communication.* Urbana, Ill.: University of Illinois Press, 1949.

Sillars, A. L., and M. D. Scott. "Interpersonal Perception Between Intimates: An Integrative Review." *Human Communication Research* 10 (1983): 153–76.

Sillars, A. L., et al. "Communication and Understanding in Marriage." *Human Communication Research* 10 (1984): 315–50.

Smith, Herb J. "Methods for Training the Technical Editor in Interpersonal Skills." *IEEE Transactions on Professional Communications* PC-28, no. 1 (1985): 46–50.

Smith, Herb J., et al. "Interpersonal Skills: An Essential Component in the Editing Class." In *Teaching Technical Editing,* 109–28. Lubbock, Tex.: Association of Teachers of Technical Writing, 1985.

Stech, Ernest L. "A Grammar of Conversation with a Quantitative Empirical Test." *Human Communication Research* 5 (1979): 158–70.

Steinfatt, Thomas M. *Human Communication: An Interpersonal Introduction.* Indianapolis: Bobbs-Merrill, 1977.

———. "A Communication Theory of Humor." In *Proceedings of the Western Humor Meeting.* Phoenix, Ariz.: Arizona State University Press, 1981.

Steinfatt, Thomas M., and Gerald R. Miller. "Communication in Some Theoretic Models of Conflict." In *Perspectives on Communication in Social Conflict,* edited by Gerald R. Miller and Herbert W. Simons. Englewood Cliffs, N.J.: Prentice-Hall, 1974.

Swingle, Paul. *The Structure of Conflict.* New York: Academic Press, 1970.

Tedeschi, J. T., Barry R. Schlenker, and Thomas V. Bonoma. *Conflict, Power, and Games.* Chicago: Aldine, 1973.

Walsh, Ruth M., and Stanley Birkin. *Business Communications: An Annotated Bibliography.* Westport, Conn.: Greenwood Press, 1980.

Walton, Richard E. *Interpersonal Peacemaking.* Reading, Mass.: Addison-Wesley, 1969.

Watzlawick, Paul, Janet H. Beavin, and Don D. Jackson. *Pragmatics of Human Communication.* New York: Norton, 1967.

Weaver, Warren. "The Mathematics of Communication." *Scientific American* 181 (1949): 11–15.

Weitz, Shirley. *Nonverbal Communication: Readings and Commentary.* New York: Oxford University Press, 1974.

Wheeless, Lawrence R. "A Follow-Up Study of the Relationships Among Trust, Disclosure, and Interpersonal Solidarity." *Human Communication Research* 4 (1978): 143–57.

Wiemann, John M., John A. Daly, and Mark L. Knapp. "Nonverbal Communication: Issues and Appraisal." *Human Communication Research* 4 (1978): 271–80.

Wilder, Carol. "The Palo Alto Group: Difficulties and Directions of the Interactional View for Human Communication Research." *Human Communication Research* 5 (1979): 171–86.

Wrightsman, Lawrence S., Jr., John O'Connor, and Norma J. Baker, eds. *Cooperation and Competition: Readings on Mixed-Motive Games.* Belmont, Calif.: Brooks/Cole, 1972.

Wylie, Ruth. *The Self Concept.* Lincoln, Neb.: University of Nebraska Press, 1961.

Zick, Rubin. *Living and Loving.* New York: Holt, 1973.

Zimbardo, Phillip G. *Shyness.* Reading, Mass.: Addison-Wesley, 1977.

7 Communication Consulting

Raymond N. MacKenzie
Cray Research, Inc.
Mendota Heights, Minnesota

Most technical writing teachers find, within their first few years of teaching the subject, that people in business and industry are interested in employing them as consultants. For most of us, coming from a background in teaching mostly freshman composition or literature, consulting at first seems to be one of the wonderful perquisites of teaching technical writing: we not only find ourselves with students who are more highly motivated and with papers that are easier and far more interesting to grade, but now we also find we can actually make extra money with this subject. For those of us who do make the leap and try one or two consulting tasks, we soon see that experience consulting in the field actually helps back in the classroom: providing more and better examples, a much clearer sense of what kind of writing actually goes on outside the university environment, and countless little perceptions that add up to a much rounder and broader perspective on the whole subject. And at that point, we realize that consulting is more than a perk: it is a tremendous asset to the teaching of technical writing and to our own professional development. The teacher who does not consult is missing out on a great deal.

Leaving the classroom and entering the corporate world can be a difficult process. Many of the classroom techniques that make for a good teacher can carry over and make for a good consultant—but not all of them. And, especially at first, it is hard to know exactly how to present oneself and the subject matter, how to deal with management, how to price one's services, and so on. There are no answers that are always right to such questions, but there is a small and gradually growing body of literature on the subject that can help the beginning consultant a great deal.

It is wise to start—as we often tell our students—by defining the subject. A somewhat old but still excellent definition of consultation is that given by R. Lippet in "Dimensions of the Consultant's Job" (*Journal of Social Issues* 15, no. 2 [1959]: 5–12):

> Consultation, like supervision, or love, is a general label for many variations of relationship. The general definition of consultation... assumes that
> 1. The consultation relationship is a voluntary relationship between
> 2. a professional helper (consultant) and help-needing system (client)
> 3. in which the consultant is attempting to give help to the client in the solving of some current or potential problem,
> 4. and the relationship is perceived as temporary by both parties.
> 5. Also, the consultant is an "outsider," i.e., is not part of any hierarchical power system in which the client is located.

This definition is a good one, partly because it is very broad: the types of consulting work a technical writing teacher might be called on to do vary widely, and Lippet's definition is one that should cover most of them. For the purpose of this essay, I will divide consultation into two main types: (1) *training,* in which one goes on-site to deliver a course in technical communication, and (2) *project consulting,* in which one is hired to help produce or edit a specific document.

These two types of consulting are not, in theory, necessarily separate, but in practice one will find them very different types of experience, with very different sets of challenges and rewards.

Training

The need for better communication skills in business, industry, and government is well known. We have been hearing for a long time that college graduates cannot write clearly and effectively; here is one statement of the problem:

> For many years, complaints have been heard from engineering managers, training directors, publishers and editors of technical periodicals, the evaluators of military proposals and reports, and even from engineers themselves, that the ability of engineers to communicate effectively in writing is not as good as it should be.

This statement will sound very familiar—but the surprising part is the date it was published: 1964. It is taken from Charles A. Meyer's "Seminar on Writing Improvement Programs for Engineers: A Report" (*IEEE Transactions on Engineering Writing and Speech* [Dec. 1964]:

18-22). The date helps demolish the idea that poor writing among college graduates originated sometime after the educational reforms of the late 1960s, and it also helps show that the problem is a perennial one; it is not likely to go away soon. Meyer's article summarizes presentations made by several of the seminar's participants and concludes that "some way must be found to prove to management that time and money spent improving [engineers' writing] pays off, not only in better communications, but in better engineering."

A recent essay by Jo Lundy Pevey, "Preparing for the First Consulting Assignment" (*Bulletin of the Association for Business Communication* 48, no. 2 [June 1985]: 42–44), is a good place for the beginning consultant to start, as it stresses the need to package and *adapt* the college course to business needs. Her article is a highly specific description of the physical materials she uses in her courses and should help warn the beginner away from using unprofessional-looking materials.

Adaptation is a key concept in communication consulting. It may be possible to get away with presenting the same canned course to every audience for a while, but this seems like a dubious proposition: every situation is different, and not all employees have the same communication needs. How does one find out, then, what the needs are? One answer is in William J. Buchholz's "Interviewing and Auditing Procedures for In-House Communication Seminars" (in *Communication Training and Consulting in Business, Industry, and Government*, edited by William J. Buchholz. University of Illinois at Urbana-Champaign, American Business Communication Association, 1983, pp. 105–13). Buchholz stresses the interview stage—when the client and consultant first meet—as being crucial to the success of the program. The consultant should be careful here not to promise a panacea, so the client knows what can realistically be expected, and at this stage the consultant should also size up the situation by determining who is the "critical power": Is it the manager who is doing the hiring, or perhaps that manager's superior? And, what exactly does the client mean by "bad writing?" A definition of the term as the client sees it is essential at this early stage. Finally, Buchholz presents a good, brief "Audit Questionnaire" to distribute to the employees before planning the course.

The questionnaire as a means of determining what the employees' needs are is widely used. Another example, with discussion, is presented in William J. Rothwell's "Assessing Attitudes about Organizational Communications (Buchholz, *Communication Training and Consulting*: 119–22). The emphasis in Rothwell's instrument is on attitudes. Part of the questionnaire lists thirty statements like "I prefer a phone call or a visit to writing," and "I enjoy communicating with superiors," all measured on a Strongly Agree to Strongly Disagree scale. Such attitudes can be highly significant, of course, although Rothwell's phrasing may be too general for some. A somewhat more pointed set of questions is in Steven Golem and Thomas Inman's "A Questionnaire to Determine Barriers to Effective Communication" (Buchholz, *Communication Training and Consulting,* 123-26).

A fuller discussion of the value of such research instruments is in John Hatfield and Richard Huseman's "The Job Incumbent Survey: An Approach to Identifying Communication Training Needs" (Buchholz, *Communication Training and Consulting,* 133-40). The authors wisely caution that "using the results of a job incumbent survey as the only basis for decisions about training program content assumes that respondents are able to diagnose their own training needs and are willing to admit that they may have communication problems" (p. 139). The literature on the issue of how best to assess needs is surveyed in Michael Moore and Philip Dutton's "Training Needs Analysis: Review and Critique" (*Academy of Management Review* 3 [1978]: 532-45).

From management's point of view, a basic problem at this early stage is whether or not to hire an outside consultant at all or simply to use someone already on staff. The issues are discussed in three articles in a recent issue of *Technical Communication* (First Quarter 1983). W. Lee Garner's "Family Run or Hired Gun?" (8-10) argues against the hired gun; F. M. O'Hara, Jr., in "Hiring a Private Consultant" (10-11), offers a number of sensible tips, such as asking for the consultant's list of publications; and Stephen T. Moskey makes a strong case for hiring "College Instructors as Writing Consultants" (12-13). An excellent discussion of the advantages and disadvantages of hiring outside consultants to perform editorial functions is David L. Armbruster's "Hiring and Managing Editorial Consultants" (*Technical Communication* [Fourth Quarter 1986]: 243-46).

A strong "Case Against Hiring Outside Consultants" is made by Frank T. Wydra (*Training/HRD* [June 1980]: 24-25). Other tips for management thinking about hiring a consultant are in Henrietta Tichy's "Teaching in Industry: The Consultant-Instructor Speaks" (*Proceedings of the Society for Technical Communication,* 1972; reprinted in *Teaching Technical Writing and Editing: In-House Programs That Work,* edited by James G. Shaw, Washington, D.C.: Society for Technical Communication, 1976, pp. 5-11). Tichy offers some examples, from her personal experience, of encounters with misguided and ill-informed managers, examples that provide food for thought for both client and consultant.

There are many articles in the literature that describe specific courses—far too many to discuss or even list here. An annotated bibliography of articles describing courses is in L. W. Denton and W. E. Rivers's (1983) "Consulting and In-House Writing Courses: A Selected Bibliography" (in Buchholz, *Communication Training and Consulting,* 265–84). Here, I will discuss just a few of the most relevant and accessible articles on the subject.

Robert R. Rathbone presents his syllabus for a short course in technical writing in "The Main Ingredients for a Successful In-Plant Writing Course" (*Journal of Technical Writing and Communication* 4 [Fall 1974]: 323–30). Several other examples are in Buchholz's (1983) volume, *Communication Training and Consulting.* These range from Robert D. Gieselman's "The One-Day, In-House Writing Workshop" (205–12) to Joel P. Bowman and Bernadine P. Branchaw's "Conducting a Fifteen-Week Writing Program" (213–34). Additional course descriptions can be found in the volume edited by James G. Shaw (1976), *Teaching Technical Writing and Editing: In-House Programs that Work,* including Carver C. Linville's "Developing an In-House Writing Course for Engineers and Scientists" (12–20) and Max Weber's "Teaching an Effective Course in Technical Writing in Private Industry" (28–36). A more specific sort of course is described by Paul E. T. Jensen in "An In-Plant Proposal-Writing Workshop" (*IEEE Transactions on Engineering Writing and Speech* EWS-9, no. 2 [Dec. 1966]: 46–47). Though Jensen's article is twenty years old, it may be of special interest to teachers today because of the recent emphasis in college classrooms on team writing, a concept essential to Jensen's syllabus.

For those who have taught in-house courses or have encountered some problems—with management, for instance, or attendance and motivation—R. John Brockmann, Jr., provides answers to "Ten Practical Questions Often Asked by the Instructor-Consultant" (*The Technical Writing Teacher* 3 [Spring 1980]: 127–32). Brockmann also provides some bibliography on the topic.

Project Consulting

In project consulting, one is called on to help write, edit, and/or oversee production of specific documents. The move from teaching to project consulting involves a more significant reorientation: the consultant no longer plays the comfortable and familiar roles of lecturer, paper grader, or cheerleader (though those roles may be called for now and then)—instead, the consultant is now the outside expert, the hired gun, the practical problem solver. There are radically different roles to play, and some teachers will find them easier to perform than will others. Those who wish to make this sort of shift, however, will find the work usually more lucrative than training consulting, and they will find the experience invaluable when they return to the classroom.

A good argument for making the change is in Frederick W. Harbaugh's (1983) "Nontraining Consulting: Get Your Feet Wet" (Buchholz, *Communication Training and Consulting,* 65–70). Harbaugh (1983, p. 65) defines the difference between the two types of consulting thus: "Whereas training consulting typically involves systematic instruction, exercises, and feedback or evaluation, nontraining consulting typically involves a product such as a handbook, brochure, report, or proposal whose production typically requires such support services as researching, writing, and editing."

Harbaugh gives some specific hints on getting into the business, as does Peter B. Clarke (1983) in "Obtaining, Negotiating, and Pricing Your First Consulting Job" (Buchholz, *Communication Training and Consulting,* 89–101). Clarke is especially interesting on the perennial problem faced by new consultants concerning pricing their services. He suggests this formula for determining a fee:

> Here, then, is a formula for roughly figuring what you should charge: Annual salary you would receive if you worked full time (or annual salary you would like to receive for working full time) plus 65 percent of that for overhead plus 10 percent of the resulting sum for profit (after all, you're going into consulting to make a profit, aren't you?) divided by the number of days a year you can actually work:
>
> As an example, suppose your annual desirable salary is $28,000.
> Salary $28,000
> Overhead (65 percent) $18,200
>   Subtotal $46,200
> Profit (10 percent) $4,620
>   Subtotal $50,820
> Divided by workdays per year 200
> Daily fee you should charge $254

Clarke goes on to say that this fee is probably on the low side for most consultants. The formula does need some adjustments for market factors, but it remains a good starting point. Some good tips, especially for the consultant operating on a contract basis, are given by Patricia Caernarven-Smith and Anthony A. Firman in "Consultant, Freelancer, Contractor: Take Your Choice" (*Technical Communication* [Fourth Quarter 1986]: 218–23). A good discussion of the ins and outs of setting hourly fees is in Judith Gunn Bronson's "Ringmastering Your

Own Three-Ring Circus: Life as a Successful Biomedical Freelancer" (*Technical Communication* [Fourth Quarter 1986]: 224–32). A fuller and highly recommended discussion of the issue of pricing is in Robert E. Kelley's *Consulting: The Complete Guide to a Profitable Career* (New York: Charles Scribner's Sons, 1985). The inevitable problem of taxes is discussed in P. Goodman's "Estimating Taxes for the Self-Employed" (*Energy Engineering* 77, no. 2 [Feb./March 1980]: 56–57), although this is an area that changes constantly; probably no article or book can be as useful here as can an up-to-date accountant.

Several articles deal with the practical aspects of setting up in business for oneself as a communications consultant. Among them are Ron Blicq's "Starting into Part-Time Consulting" (*Proceedings of the 27th International Technical Communication Conference,* Washington, D.C.: Society for Technical Communication, 1980, p. R107) and Gene Schlaline's "The Technical Writer as Consultant" (*Technical Communication* [Fourth Quarter 1986]: 215–17). An excellent book-length discussion of the issues is by Robert Scott, *How to Set Up and Operate Your Office at Home* (New York: Charles Scribner's Sons, 1985).

There are numerous books available on consulting broadly conceived (as opposed to communication consulting specifically), but most deal with management consulting almost exclusively and are thus not very relevant to our present purpose. Out of all those books, however, two deserve special mention.

The first is a theoretical study, *Consultation,* by Robert R. Blake and Jane Srygley Mouton (Reading, Mass.: Addison-Wesley Publishing Co., 1976). The style used in the book is a little overcomplicated and jargon-ridden, but the book's main ideas and approaches to the issues make it worth a little extra work on the reader's part. Blake and Mouton emphasize *intervention* (rather than, say, help giving), and this can change the way one sees the whole dynamic of the consulting relationship and can significantly alter the way one approaches a client.

Blake and Mouton see five different kinds of intervention, and they argue that the basic question the consultant needs to ask is simply, What kind of intervention and when? For example, what the authors call *confrontation intervention* is needed when the consultant, physician-like, diagnoses that the organization is being stymied by a partly hidden set of values; in such a case, the consultant's job is value clarification. *Prescription intervention,* on the other hand, is called for when the client is at his or her wit's end about how to handle the problem and is unable to initiate any solution on his or her own initiative. Here the consultant's job is not to discuss or clarify but simply to prescribe answers. The medical metaphor is implicit throughout the book and helps to shed a rather different sort of light on the consultant-client relationship. The book may be too theoretical for some, but others will find its approach a thought-provoking one.

The second major book on consulting in general is Herman Holtz's *How to Succeed as an Independent Consultant* (New York: John Wiley and Sons, 1983). This book is the best discussion of the field of project consulting available, both because of its overall high quality and, just as important for our purposes here, because Holtz is himself a communications consultant. Thus, though his book is aimed at consultants of all types, most of his examples are drawn from his experience as a writer for industry and government. His skill in writing also, incidentally, makes for a highly readable book.

Holtz has chapters on many topics of interest—founding the practice, conducting the initial meeting with the client, negotiating and setting fees, various profit centers to exploit, and so on. Each of these chapters is greatly enriched by the author's many years of experience in the field. One particular strength is the book's emphasis on marketing. Many teacher-consultants seem not to give much thought to marketing their services at all, finding that often enough clients come to them based solely on their reputation in the community. Holtz suggests ways to go beyond that system, which, obviously, has its major drawbacks. He is especially good on the subject of packaging and presenting oneself, offering some provocative ideas, such as this: "One of the keys to successful marketing is discovering what it is that the client believes you are or wishes you to be. Or, to put it differently, what the client wishes to buy from you or believes you are selling. Until you have determined what the client really wishes to buy, you can't be sure of what you should say" (Holtz 1983, p. 23). Holtz goes on to give a great deal of practical advice on understanding the client's perceived needs and determining how—and whether—to attempt to meet them.

There are two excellent chapters on marketing, one of them devoted solely to marketing in the public sector. Here there is much good information on the byzantine requirements of federal, state, or local procurement systems. And there is an extremely informative chapter on proposal writing—that is, how to land the consulting contract in a competitive situation. (Harbaugh's "How to Write Winning Freelance Proposals" [*Technical Communication* Fourth Quarter 1986: 239–42] is another fine discussion of the issue, and it includes a valuable specimen proposal.) In short, Holtz's book is essential reading for the technical writing teacher who is thinking about setting up shop as a project consultant.

The ultimate question, though, is whether one should think about doing such a thing at all. Is it worth the time, trouble, and risk? Holtz is very encouraging, but one should also read the work of another very experienced consultant, Robert Hays, who stresses the difficulties in his "Communication Consulting: It's Gold, But It's Hard to Mine" (*The Technical Writing Teacher* 7, no. 2 [Winter 1980]: 53–55). Hays' (1980, p. 53) article brings up nearly every negative aspect conceivable concerning consulting, from dealing with "slovenly, surly, and incompetent clerks, drivers, and baggage handlers" at airports to the pains of dealing with the Internal Revenue Service after one is finally paid by tight-fisted clients. Another article that stresses the negative is M. E. Campbell's "Weeding the Garden: Or the Awful Things Consultants Must Deal With" (*Bulletin of the Association for Business Communication* 48, no. 3 [September 1985]: 1–3). Of course, some of the problems Hays and Campbell list exist no matter what profession one goes into, but their articles are very much worth reading nonetheless, as they imply a very important truth: consulting might well turn out to be much harder work than teaching, and it should be approached with some forethought about the risks and dangers.

Conclusion

This essay has made no attempt to discuss or even list all of the available literature on the broad field of consulting, but has instead focused on those articles and books that are likely to be of most immediate usefulness to the technical writing teacher, especially the teacher who is relatively new to the field. And the essay has tried to make the point that there is indeed a great deal of very useful material out there, material that the beginning consultant should not ignore. The literature is richest in descriptions of actual courses, and there will no doubt continue to be an audience eager to read more such descriptions. Some areas in which more research would be helpful include discussions of how to evaluate in-house courses and discussions of ethical concerns—such as the extent to which time spent consulting interferes with time for which one is already being paid as a teacher, a problem that has bothered many a dean. And there is very little literature available concerning the consultant's role in product liability issues, a field that grows more complex—and for the expert consultant, potentially more lucrative—all the time.

Nearly all the existing literature does, however, either imply or directly state one very important point: the technical writing teacher who does not try to get involved in some form of consulting is missing a great deal, both in terms of added income and in terms of professional development.

Bibliography

Armbruster, David L. 1986. "Hiring and Managing Editorial Consultants." *Technical Communication* Fourth Quarter 1986: 243-46.

Blake, Robert R., and Jane Srygley Mouton. 1976. *Consultation.* Reading, Mass.: Addison-Wesley Publishing Co.

Blicq, Ron. 1980. "Starting into Part-Time Consulting." In *Proceedings of the 27th International Technical Communication Conference,* p. R107. Washington, D.C.: Society for Technical Communication.

Bowman, Joel P., and Bernadine P. Branchaw. 1983. "Conducting a Fifteen-Week Writing Program." In *Communication Training and Consulting in Business, Industry, and Government,* edited by William J. Buchholz. Urbana, Ill.: American Business Communication Association.

Brockmann, R. John, Jr. 1980. "Ten Practical Questions Often Asked by the Instructor-Consultant." *The Technical Writing Teacher* 3 (Spring): 127-33.

Bronson, Judith Gunn. 1986. "Ringmastering Your Own Three-Ring Circus: Life as a Successful Biomedical Freelancer." *Technical Communication* Fourth Quarter 1986: 224-32.

Buchholz, William J. 1983. "Interviewing and Auditing Procedures for In-house Communication Seminars." In *Communication Training and Consulting in Business, Industry, and Government,* edited by William J. Buchholz. Urbana, Ill.: American Business Communication Association.

Caernarven-Smith, Patricia, and Anthony A. Firman. 1986. "Consultant, Freelancer, Contractor: Take Your Choice." *Technical Communication* Fourth Quarter 1986: 218-23.

Campbell, M. E. 1985. "Weeding the Garden: Or the Awful Things Consultants Must Deal With." *Bulletin of the Association for Business Communication* 48, no. 3 (Sept.): 1-3.

Clarke, Peter B. 1983. "Obtaining, Negotiating, and Pricing Your First Consulting Job." In *Communication Training and Consulting in Business, Industry, and Government,* edited by William J. Buchholz. Urbana, Ill.: American Business Communication Association.

Denton, L. W., and W. E. Rivers. 1983. "Consulting and In-House Writing Courses: A Selected Bibliography." In *Communication Training and Consulting in Business, Industry, and Government,* edited by William J. Buchholz. Urbana, Ill.: American Business Communication Association.

Garner, W. Lee. 1983. "Family Run or Hired Gun?" *Technical Communication* First Quarter 1983: 8-10.

Gieselman, Robert D. 1983. "The One-Day, In-House Writing Workshop." In *Communication Training and Consulting in Business, Industry, and Government,* edited by William J. Buchholz. Urbana, Ill.: American Business Communication Association.

Golem, Steven, and Thomas Inman. 1983. "A Questionnaire to Determine Barriers to Effective Communication." In *Communication Training and Consulting in Business, Industry, and Government,* edited by William J. Buchholz. Urbana, Ill.: American Business Communication Association.

Goodman, P. 1980. "Estimating Taxes for the Self-Employed." *Energy Engineering* 77, no. 2 (Feb./March): 56–57.

Harbaugh, Frederick W. 1983. "Nontraining Consulting: Get Your Feet Wet." In *Communication Training and Consulting in Business, Industry, and Government,* edited by William J. Buchholz. Urbana, Ill.: American Business Communication Association.

———. 1986. "How to Write Winning Freelance Proposals." *Technical Communication* Fourth Quarter 1986: 239–42.

Hatfield, John, and Richard Huseman. 1983. "The Job Incumbent Survey: An Approach to Identifying Communication Training Needs." In *Communication Training and Consulting in Business, Industry, and Government,* edited by William J. Buchholz. Urbana, Ill.: American Business Communication Association.

Hays, Robert. 1980. "Communication Consulting: It's Gold, But It's Hard to Mine." *The Technical Writing Teacher* 7, no. 2 (Winter): 53–55.

Holtz, Herman. 1983. *How to Succeed as an Independent Consultant.* New York, N.Y.: John Wiley and Sons.

Jensen, Paul E. T. 1966. "An In-Plant Proposal-Writing Workshop." *IEEE Transactions on Engineering Writing and Speech,* EWS-9, no. 2 (Dec.): 46–47.

Kelley, Robert E. 1985. *Consulting: The Complete Guide to a Profitable Career.* New York, N.Y.: Charles Scribner's Sons.

Linville, Carver C. 1976. "Developing an In-House Writing Course for Engineers and Scientists." In *Teaching Technical Writing and Editing: In-House Programs that Work,* edited by James G. Shaw. Washington, D.C.: Society for Technical Communication.

Lippet, R. 1959. "Dimensions of the Consultant's Job." *Journal of Social Issues* 15, no. 2: 5–12.

Meyer, Charles A. 1964. "Seminar on Writing Improvement Programs for Engineers: A Report." *IEEE Transactions on Engineering Writing and Speech* Dec.: 18–22.

Moore, Michael, and Philip Dutton. 1978. "Training Needs Analysis: Review and Critique." *Academy of Management Review* 3: 532–45.

Moskey, Stephen T. 1983. "College Instructors as Writing Consultants." *Technical Communication* First Quarter 1983: 12–13.

O'Hara, F. M., Jr. 1983. "Hiring a Private Consultant." *Technical Communication* First Quarter 1983: 10–11.

Pevey, Jo Lundy. 1985. "Preparing for the First Consulting Assignment." *Bulletin of the Association for Business Communicaton* 48, no. 2 (June): 42–44.

Rathbone, Robert R. 1974. "The Main Ingredients for a Successful In-Plant Writing Course." *Journal of Technical Writing and Communication* 4 (Fall): 323–30.

Rothwell, William J. 1983. "Assessing Attitudes about Organizational Communications." In *Communication Training and Consulting in Business, Industry, and Government,* edited by William J. Buchholz. Urbana, Ill.: American Business Communication Association.

Schlaline, Gene. 1986. "The Technical Writer as Consultant." *Technical Communication* Fourth Quarter 1986: 215–17.

Scott, Robert. 1985. *How to Set Up and Operate Your Office at Home.* New York, N.Y.: Charles Scribner's Sons.

Tichy, Henrietta. 1976. "Teaching in Industry: The Consultant-Instructor Speaks." In *Teaching Technical Writing and Editing: In-House Programs that Work,* edited by James G. Shaw. Washington, D.C.: Society for Technical Communication.

Weber, Max. 1976. "Teaching an Effective Course in Technical Writing in Private Industry." In *Teaching Technical Writing and Editing: In-House Programs that Work,* edited by James G. Shaw. Washington, D.C.: Society for Technical Communication.

Wydra, Frank T. 1980. "Case Against Hiring Outside Consultants." *Training/HRD* 1980 (June): 24–25.

8 Style and Technical Writing

James C. Addison, Jr.
Western Carolina University

Writing recently in "Style in Technical and Scientific Writing," Glenn J. Broadhead (1985) could still claim that "there has been no comprehensive bibliography of style in technical writing." His chapter partially corrects that omission. This article provides both more and less than one might expect from its title. It promises to be a comprehensive survey of the scholarship and the research, and Broadhead does refer to several hundred articles, books, and papers. Yet, in its very attempt at comprehensiveness, the survey departs from its immediate subject—style in technical and scientific writing—by bringing in extraneous matters and by omitting items that should have been included. Still, such objections are minor, considering the very real service Broadhead has rendered: providing the first comprehensive bibliography and literature survey in the new and relatively narrow, but expanding, field of style in technical and scientific discourse.

That this should be the first bibliography and literature survey should strike the reader as strange if not disturbing. Yet, when one considers Broadhead's summary observation that "an adequate theory of style in technical writing does not appear in general use at present," one realizes a primary reason for this lack. Quite simply, technical style as an area of inquiry has not enjoyed the kind of serious research and meticulous scholarship that has greatly benefited other areas—areas as new as discourse theory, for example. In fact, in much of what has been written on the subject, researchers are still grappling with the most basic of considerations: definitions of radical terms—"style," "technical," "scientific style," and so on. Is it any wonder, then, that a field so new, so underdeveloped still lags at quite a distance behind that of "literary style" (Klaus 1968; Freeman 1970; Chatman 1971) and that of "style in composition" (Corbett 1976)?

Faced with such substantial quantities of quality research in the fields of literary style and style in composition, would-be researchers in style in technical writing immediately encounter a problem: what amount of this research is relevant or directly applicable to their subject—and what amount is peripheral for a variety of reasons? Because there is no universal agreement on basic definitions—no clear demarcations showing where "writing" leaves off and where "technical writing" begins for instance, any decisions researchers make will likely be erroneous. They will either err on the side of inclusivity or, just as likely, on the side of exclusivity. Just what one decides to allow, to include—and just what one decides to exclude—become critical decisions, affecting as they do everything that comes after.

If this study errs, it probably does so on the side of exclusivity; that is, in striving to limit itself to style only as it applies to technical and scientific discourse, it omits something of real importance. The present study will not concern itself, for example, with style in business writing or with style manuals or guides. These areas have all been adequately covered in the literature, and useful, comprehensive surveys and bibliographies exist for them. Researchers desiring to know more about general theories of style are referred to articles by Louis T. Milic (1965, 1966). These standard works, as well as many other general treatments, are adequately covered by Broadhead and need no further elaboration here. For discussion of style guides and manuals (government, industrial, vocational, and others), refer to John A. Walter's (1971) "Style Manuals," Adrienne De Vergie's (1975) "English for Lawyers: A Bibliography of Style Manuals and Other Related Guides," and Caroline R. Goforth's (1985) "A Selection of Style Manuals." Relatedly, discussions of grammar, usage, and mechanics are included only when they have direct bearing on the larger issue of style in technical writing. Thus, by being so exclusive, this survey offers readers a usable body of information, limited by constraints of both choice and practicality.

Definitions

In "On Defining Style," Nils E. Enkvist (1964) provides a useful definition. Style, he writes, is a configuration of variable features (phonological, morphological, syntactic, lexical, and grammatical) found in a given context. Similarly, John M. Lannon (1985), in *Technical Writing,* provides a functional definition of technical writing. It is, he says, specialized information for the practical use of readers who have requested it. As such, it has a transactional function. Putting the two definitions together results in a definitional basis for the present study. Technical style may be seen as the selection and arrangement, by both writer and reader, of variable textual features within a context at once specialized, practical, and transactional. With such a definitional basis behind it, this examination of style and technical writing begins where it should—with history.

History

Just as there have been no bibliographies and no comprehensive surveys of this subject, there have been no histories. This is partly due to the relative newness of the field and its narrowness. Yet, while many of the histories of English literary style do not have direct bearing on the issues of technical and scientific style, some do. For instance, it is easy to see how R. F. Jones's ideas on how Baconian science redirected English prose style, producing a crisper, more straightforward expression, apply (Jones 1930, 1932). Similarly, James Paradis's (1983) "Bacon, Linneaus, and Lavoisier: Early Language Reform in the Sciences," shows how the contributions of Bacon, Linneaus, Lavoisier, and other scientists, which grew out of the scientific impetus for more precision in language, have led to an ongoing refinement of technical lexical systems (styles) today. Likewise, James Stephens's (1983) "Style as Therapy in Renaissance Science" and James P. Zappen's (1975) "Francis Bacon and the Rhetoric of Science" illustrate how scientific style gained in clarity and precision as the new science developed from the work of Bacon (1620), Kepler, Paracelsus, and others.

But just because there have been no histories of technical and scientific writing style should not imply that the field is without history. Just the opposite is true. At least since the time of Bacon, there has been an interest in how style functioned in technical documents. Two brief quotations, the first from Francis Bacon's (1620) *Novum Organum* and the second from Thomas Sprat's (1667) *History of the Royal Society,* will illustrate the tremendous historical interest in the ways in which style and specialized kinds of writing coexist and interact:

> There are also Idols formed by the intercourse and association of men with each other, which I call Idols of the Marketplace, on account of the commerce and consort of men there. For it is by discourse that men associate: and words are imposed according to the apprehension of the vulgar. And therefore the ill and unfit choice of words wonderfully obstructs the understanding.

Similarly, Sprat (1667) records that members of the society strove to return

> to the primitive purity, and shortness, which men delivered so many things, almost in equal number of words. They have exacted

from all their members a close, naked, natural way of speaking; positive expressions; clear sentences; a native easiness; bringing all things as near the mathematical plainness as they can; and preferring the language of Artisans, Countrymen, and Merchants before that of Wits and Scholars.

Treatments of Style in Technical Writing

In a 1982 review of Joseph M. Williams' (1981) *Style: Ten Lessons in Clarity and Grace,* Jack Selzer (1982) neatly summarizes how critics, writers, and researchers have dealt with style in technical writing, and in so doing, put his finger on some of the field's more demonstrable problem areas. His opening paragraph zeroes in on the problematical state of style in technical writing and effectively reveals sources of the difficulty:

> Take a look at the treatments of style in technical writing textbooks and manuals. Some textbooks ignore style completely. Some simply identify a good style with correctness—they provide short handbooks containing "common errors," drills and lists of frequently misused phrases. Others limit themselves to a short chapter filled with readability formulas, do's and don'ts, oversimplified prescriptions (like "use small words and short sentences"), and questionable generalizations ("use active voice whenever possible"). Most are long on precepts ("avoid jargon"; "keep your language simple"), long on exhortation ("be clear"; "be concise"), but short on real instructions. They often *describe* a good technical style, but they seldom do much to help students achieve it.

Selzer goes on to praise Williams's contribution as an excellent book that admirably "attends to both the complexity of technical style and the difficulties teaching it." In fact, *Style: Ten Lessons in Clarity and Grace* (Williams 1981) is probably the best researched and most effective of all texts on style and technical-scientific writing, even though much of what it presents focuses on microstructural elements (word and sentence levels) of discourse. Nevertheless, Williams's book may succeed in redefining the issue of technical style and in redirecting research away from reliance on prescriptive rules and toward fuller considerations of audience and discourse context. By doing so, it will help solve a problem that has been with technical style since its first consideration in the early texts (Rosner 1983).

Theory

Writing in the large shadow cast by Edward P. J. Corbett's (1976) remark that "we still lack a fully developed coherent theory of style,"

Broadhead (1985) has only recently concluded that "an adequate theory of style in technical writing does not appear to be in general use at present." Indeed, without a comprehensive general theory and agreement on some basic definitions, no fully adequate style studies of particular kinds of writing—legal, scientific, medical, or technical—are likely. Yet, good work is beginning to be done, as Williams's book attests, and more is on the horizon. What these effective recent researchers share is a set of underlying assumptions about the nature of technical writing and the meaning of style. Using such an integrated and agreed-on set, they can accomplish much more than can others, for whom the lack of a comprehensive general theory presents an insurmountable obstacle.

In addition to Williams, whose work is both theoretical and applied (Hake 1981), other important theorists such as Robert De Beaugrande describe how old and new information is distributed within slots in various kinds of texts and the implications of such arrangements for both audience and style (De Beaugrande 1977b, 1978). In his "Generative Stylistics: Between Grammar and Rhetoric," De Beaugrande (1977a) calls for a method of generative stylistics that will account for choices—stylistic, rhetorical, and contextual—and their impact on a text's effectiveness.

Other important theorists working with style and technical writing are R. A. Huddleston et al. (1968), whose *Sentence and Clause in Scientific English* derives from the work of Michael Halliday, a cohesion specialist, whose recent work involves a theory of networking within language. In their work, Huddleston et al. analyze scientific texts ranging through three strata to explain how various cohesion strategies work. They are especially interested in showing how these patterns of cohesiveness produce distinctive styles and how these affect readers.

Related to this theoretical work are Myrna Gopnik's (1973) *Linguistic Structures in Scientific Texts,* in which she analyzes biology texts, grouping them into three types, each possessing certain characteristic linguistic and stylistic features: Karel Bares's (1976) *Word Formation in English Technical Style,* in which she considers microstructures and microjunctures within technical discourse and their implication for style; Ruqaiya Hasan's (1964) *A Linguistic Study of Contrasting Features in the Style of Two Contemporary English Prose Writers;* and Michael Halliday's (1976) *Cohesion in English,* which presents a thorough accounting for cohesive ties within various kinds of texts and suggestions of stylistic effects achieved by manipulating such ties. More recently, the work of Richard D. Ramsey (1977, 1980) calls for a linguistic focus on technical writing to uncover useful approaches to style study; Robert

Graves and Alan Hodge (1979) examine in detail all kinds of prose and both develop and apply theoretical principles of clear style to them; Michael P. Jordan (1981) provides theoretical and practical analyses of cohesion techniques in technical writing; and Alan G. Gross (1984) explores scientific writing and concludes that traditional advice on style is often not the best editorial practice and that "stylistic changes are tactical choices made within the context of strategic presuppositions about the impersonal and descriptive nature of scientific prose," demonstrating the continuity of his work with earlier theoretical studies.

Methodology and Application

By far the vast majority of books and articles on style and technical writing have focused, not on theory—in fact, a rather rare concern—but on practical application: how to clear up a muddled, turbid style, how to determine a text's readability, and how to enliven dead prose. Most technical writing textbooks fall into this category, devoting a chapter perhaps, or just a few pages, to clear writing, clear style, or plain style. Unfortunately, most of these pronouncements have been highly prescriptive and do little to show the students *how* they might actually achieve a plainer style. In addition, nothing is typically said about why such a style is desirable or who desires it. Like the textbooks, the articles and longer works in this category have insufficient theoretical bases and fail to pursue either the underlying assumptions of their quick fix, recipe-like prescriptions or their logical implications.

Readability and Technical Writing Style

Writing in his conclusion, Broadhead (1985) provides this account of how readability has been tied to technical style:

> In sum, readability is well entrenched in the literature about technical writing—as a technique for audience analysis, as a set of norms based on that technique, and as a general equivalent for good or clear or simple writing. Its main limitations are that it fails to take into account the varying characteristics of audience needs and wishes; it ignores important aspects of linguistic structure and cohesion . . . ; and it does not consider the ultimate goal of style in writing—which is not merely to achieve speed, ease, or personal involvement, but rather to create understanding or comprehension of the information in the text. For these reasons,

readability as a stylistic norm has been challenged at two levels: first at the level of presentational style, by proponents of usability; second at the level of discourse style, by critics who for the most part view technical writing as a particular application of traditional rhetorical principles.

Basically, readability theory, stemming from a post–World War II campaign to rank textbooks by level of reading difficulty, has been seen either as a practical panacea for problems with technical writing style or as a misguided, unreliable, highly reductive means of achieving some homogeneity within technical texts.

Most readability formulas are based on microstructural relationships—word choice, word length, sentence length, and word familiarity—and thus are heavily prescriptive and easily quantifiable. Primary advocates of such an approach to technical and scientific writing are Rudolf Flesch (1948, 1951, 1958, 1962, 1974, 1980), John A. Miller (1948), Robert L. Shurter (1952), Robert Gunning (1964, 1968), Charles H. Vervalin (1980), Douglas Mueller (1980), George R. Klare (1969, 1974/1975, 1976, 1977), Stewart Docter (1961), John Gilliland (1972), Andrew K. Clark (1975), Eleanor M. Schenk (1977), Helen J. Schwartz (1980), Lloyd R. Bostian (1983), and James De George et al. (1984), and Gary A. Olson and Richard Ray (1984).

Yet, because readability formulas are based on microstructural relationships, some critics have faulted them. These antagonists claim that such mathematical expressions oversimplify the complexity of texts and seriously misrepresent the concept of text comprehension. Some of these critics—notably such pioneers as William H. Whyte, Jr. (1952), Stephen E. Fitzgerald (1953), Martin V. H. Prince (1955), and John S. Fielden (1959, 1982)—are simply suspicious of quantifying what had always been quite differently expressed. Others more recently have attacked readability formulas for their lack of validity and reliability and for their woefully inadequate accounting for the myriad influences on text comprehension. Typical of these critics are Bertram Bruce et al. (1981) and Jack Selzer (1981, 1983). By demonstrating the multitude of problems that come from applying readability formulas to technical texts, Selzer in particular draws attention to the often superficial advice promulgated by many textbooks on technical writing. He also surveys most of what has been done in readability and provides an extensive list of references as well as a guide to needed research. Still other critics find problems with the formulas but see genuine uses for them—for instance, in helping writers edit technical discourse. Into this group go Janice C. Redish (1981), Kenneth B. Powell (1981), Daniel L. Plung (1981, 1982), and Jeanne G. Barry (1981), all of whose articles appear in *IEEE Transactions on Professional Communication*.

The Plain Style as Ideal Norm

Perhaps the most echoed trait of technical writing style over the years has been that of plainness. The urging of such a style perhaps began with Francis Bacon, and it continues to exert strong influence on the literature today. Although there have been recent challenges to the idea of the plain style as the ideal norm for technical writing, it remains a persistent phenomenon as evidenced by the sheer number of its sponsors. These include Donald M. Crawford (1945), John R. Baker (1955), Herman M. Weisman (1959, 1985), John Durham and Paul Zall (1967), John H. Mitchell (1968, 1980), Herman A. Estrin (1971), J. L. Brogan (1973), Sir Ernest Gowers (1977), Michael Lipman and Russell Joyner (1979), David Jarmul (1981), Barbara S. Lynch and Charles F. Chapman (1980), and M. A. Zeidner (1982). Weissman (1985) sums up the plain style succinctly:

> Technical style is characterized by a calm, restrained tone; an absence of any attempt to arouse emotion; the use of specialized terminology; the use of abbreviations and symbols; and the integrated use of illustrations, charts, and diagrams to help explanation. Technical writing is characterized by exactness rather than grace or variety of expression. Its main purpose is to be informative and functional rather than entertaining. Thus, the most important qualities of technical writing style are clarity, precision, conciseness, and objectivity.

Departures from the Norm

Yet, even with this strong support, the plain style as an ideal norm for technical writing has recently come under siege. Most of the attacks have come from critics who fault what they claim is an oversimplified formula for plainness. This formula, they claim, reduces a very complex writing act—one of combining an awareness of purpose, stance, audience, language, and context—to a two-dimensional, simplistic misrepresentation. Critics whose work demonstrates this more sophisticated conception of the complexities of technical and scientific technical writing style and thus who depart from the doctrine of plain style as an ideal norm include several who are at the cutting edge of research and discovery.

Here one must mention Clyde W. Park's (1940) chapter on "Appropriate Style" in *English Applied in Technical Writing;* Reginald O. Kapp's (1957) *The Presentation of Technical Information,* with its innovative ideas about functional English; H. R. Clauser's (1961) "Writing Is for Readers"; Marshall Keith's (1967) "Informal Writing: Milestone or Millstone?"; and Thomas P. Johnson's (1966) *Analytical Writing: A Handbook for Business and Technical Writers,* in which the author admits unequivocally that "there is no one ideal style" for all technical or business writing. In addition, Albert J. Brouse's (1971) "Clarity in Science Writing Is Not Enough"; W. Earl Britton's (1972) "Personality in Scientific Writing," in which he discusses the charms of style and their applicability to the writing of science; Gertrude Smith's (1972) "Differences in the Thinking-Writing Process"; and George E. Schindler's (1975) "Why Engineers Write as They Do—Twelve Characteristics of Their Prose," in which he defends the prose of engineers and scientists, offer substantive reasons for their departing from the ideal norm of the plain style.

Other critics reacting against the plain style include Merrill D. Whitburn et al. (1978) in "The Plain Style in Scientific and Technical Writing"; Thomas L. Warren (1979) in "Style in Technical Writing"; and Joseph M. Williams (1979) in "Defining Complexity," a watershed article that explores the whole issue of discourse complexity and readers' reactions to it. In the 1980s, nontraditional contributions include Michael J. Marcuse's (1980) "Ethos in Technical Discourse: The Current State of the Question," a paper given at the annual Conference on College Composition and Communication; Dona M. Kagan's (1980) "Syntactic Complexity and Cognitive Style"; Marvin Rabinovitch's (1980) "Technical Writing's Last Stand"; John Kirkman's (1980) *Good Style: For Scientific and Engineering Writing,* a quite interesting account of technical style from a British perspective; and Freda F. Stohrer's (1981) "Style in Technical Writing," in which she demonstrates that many apparent flaws in technical discourse are in fact choices necessitated by considerations of audience, aim, subject matter, and context.

In addition, one should examine R. Battison and Dixie Goswami's (1981) "Clear Writing Today," a provocative assessment of the Document Design Center's findings on what constitutes clear writing; Daniel L. Plung's (1982) "Literary Communications: Adding Style to Professional Writing"; Richard D. Vick's (1982) thought-provoking article on style's effect on memory and comprehension, "Style in Technical Writing"; John S. Fielden's (1982) "What Do You Mean You Don't Like My Style?"; Daniel Marder and Dorothy M. Guinn's (1982) "Defensive Aesthetics for the Technical Writer"; and finally three textbooks, Ronald K. Messer's (1982) *Style in Technical Writing: A Text/Workbook* (a good approach to the subject because it adapts a balanced perspective and openly acknowledges that a writer's purpose determines technique), Robert W. Bly and Gary Blake's (1982) *Technical Writing: Structures, Standards, and Style* (a useful text which stresses the matching of technical style with the audience's needs), and most recently, David C. Leonard and Peter J. McGuire's (1983) *Readings in Technical Writing* (an effective text which treats style in relation to audience, effective arrangement, and readability, stressing their interrelationships.

Other Contributions to Technical Style

Into this rather sizable category fall the miscellaneous contributions to the literature on technical and scientific style. Some of these are valuable additions to the corpus of knowledge, simply placed here because they do not fit neatly into the other categories. Some are very narrow critical concerns—for instance, the passive with metaphor in science writing, with syntactic fluency. Other contributions, such as textbook chapters on style and traditional handbooks and style books, go here because they are typically hodgepodge collections with no specific focus and an inadequate theoretical base.

Textbooks and Style Books

Among texts, with their pertinent style sections identified, one finds Donald H. Menxel et al.'s (1961, pp. 71–98) *Writing a Technical Paper;* Richard W. Smith's (1963, pp. 13–28) *Technical Writing;* Richard Lloyd-Jones and Clarence A. Andrews' (1963, Section IV) *Technical and Scientific Writing;* and J. D. Thomas's (1965, Part 1) *Composition for Technical Students,* which includes a vigorous defense of the passive voice. Other useful textbooks are W. Stone and J. G. Bell's (1968) *Prose Style: A Handbook for Writers;* Dewitt C. Reddick's (1969) *Literary Style in Science Writing;* Virginia Tufte's (1971) unusual and interesting text, *Grammar as Style;* Robert Rathbone's (1972) *Communicating Technical Information,* a self-help guide for engineers; Richard Lanham's (1974) popular *Style: An Anti-Textbook;* Theodore A. Sherman and Simon S. Johnson's (1975) *Modern Technical Writing;* Charles H. Sides' (1984) *How to Write Papers and Reports About Computer Technology,* a self-help guide for computer professionals; A. J. Herbert's (1975) *The Structure of Technical English;* and J. C. Mathes and Dwight Stevenson's (1975) excellent text, *Designing Technical Reports: Writing for Audiences in Organizations*. Each of these includes discussions of the many factors affecting technical style.

The following books also warrant examination: William Strunk and E. B. White's (1975) *The Elements of Style;* *Newsweek's Writing Style and Effectiveness;* Earl G. Bingham's (1982) *Pocketbook for Technical and Professional Writers;* William D. and Deborah C. Andrews' (1982) *Write for Results;* Anne Eisenberg's (1982) *Effective Technical Communication;* Mary Lay's (1982) *Strategies for Technical Writing: A Rhetoric with Readings;* and James Miles et al.'s (1982) *Technical Writing: Principles and Practice.*

Just in the past few years, eight texts have appeared that address the issue of technical style: Michael H. Markel's (1984) *Technical Writing: Situations and Strategies;* Kenneth W. Houp and Thomas E. Pearsall's (1984) now classic *Reporting Technical Information;* Kevin J. Harty's (1985) *Strategies for Business and Technical Writing,* which contains a useful annotated bibliography; Patricia A. Robinson's (1985) *Fundamentals of Technical Writing;* Nancy Roundy and David Mair's (1985) *Strategies for Technical Communication;* John M. Lannon's (1985) *Technical Writing,* an intelligent, though largely prescriptive, treatment of style in relation to audience and context; James Sherlock's (1985) *A Guide to Technical Communication;* and finally Peter M. Sandman et al.'s (1985) *Scientific and Technical Writing.*

Articles

Two articles emphasizing the close kinship between grammar and technical style fall into this miscellaneous section: E. R. Spangler's (1956) "Modern Grammar and Its Application to Technical Writing" and Melvin F. Orth's (1978) "Striking Out: Poor Style and Grammar Still Abound in Technical Writing." Five articles that focus on grammatical voice in technical and scientific writing include John Kirkman's (1971) "What Is Good Style for Engineering Writing?" Richard D. Ramsey's (1980) "Grammatical Voice and Person in Technical Writing: Results of a Survey," Elizabeth Tebeaux's (1980) "What Makes Technical Writing Bad? A Historical Analysis," Donald Bush's (1981) "The Passive Voice Should Be Avoided—Sometimes," and Thomas L. Warren's (1981) intriguing survey, "The Passive Voice Verb: A Selected, Annotated Bibliography—Parts I–IV," one of the very few bibliographies of anything related to technical style.

Other articles—such as Michael Millard's (1972) "On the Improvement of Style in Technical Writing," Colin B. Elliott's (1976) "Must

Scientific English Be Dull?" David L. Borger's (1978) "Style and the Effective Engineer," Deborah V. Gross and Raymond F. Sis's (1980) "Scientific Writing: The Good, The Bad, and The Ugly," and Eric Ashby's (1982) "Where There's a Need for Some Style," an article which calls for improved government report style so that the public can understand numerous documents that bear directly on their lives—offer specific remedies for technical writing's ills. Two articles—John S. Harris's (1975) "Metaphor in Technical Writing" and Robert R. Hoffman's (1980) "Metaphor in Science"—concentrate on the use of metaphors in technical and scientific prose and on metaphor's unique ability to communicate effectively complex information.

Finally, the most theoretical work of Patricia Wright and her associates on cognition, usability of texts, text comprehension, and reader processing of technical information is contained in seven significant articles: Wright et al.'s "Five Skills Technical Writers Need" (1981); Wright's "Presenting Information in Tables" (1970), "Presenting Technical Information: A Survey of Research Findings" (1977), "Writing to Be Understood: Why Use Sentences?" (1971), and "Feeding the Information Eaters: Suggestions for Integrating Pure and Applied Research on Language Comprehension" (1978); Wright and Reid's "Written Information: Some Alternatives to Prose for Expressing the Outcomes of Complex Contingencies" (1973); and most especially, Wright's "Usability: The Criterion for Designing Written Information" (1980), a theoretical article that succeeds in drawing together much interdisciplinary discovery on style and its relation to text processing.

New Directions

In considering and evaluating what has been written about style in scientific and technical writing, the reader should not be surprised to find basic definitional problems existing. Such problems are growing pains of a field new to serious, systematic, interdisciplinary research of the kind just mentioned. In addition, such problems are common to relatively narrow areas whose unplowed fields are only now being tilled to any depth. But the reader and prospective researcher should also be aware that just beneath these surface disagreements and contentions lies the promise for ground breaking, revolutionary discovery. Such discovery, it appears likely, will come from important theorists who are able to bring to the problem expertise in a number of related fields. Patricia Wright, Rosemary Hake, Robert De Beaugrande, Michael Halliday, and others like them certainly belong in this group. Going in new directions and blazing new trails, their work is ever fraught with an inevitable sense of the emergent possibility of style.

References

Andrews, William D., and Deborah C. Andrews. *Write for Results.* Boston: Little, Brown, 1982.
Ashby, Eric. "Where There's a Need For Some Style." *Nature* 296 (1982): 495 ff.
Bacon, Francis. *"The New Organon" and Related Writings,* edited by F. H. Anderson. New York: Liberal Arts Press, 1960.
Baker, John R. "English Style in Scientific Papers." *Nature* 176 (1955): 851–52.
Bares, Karel. *Word Formation in English Technical Style.* Praha: Univerzita Karlova, 1976.
Barry, Jeanne G. "Computerized Readability Levels." *IEEE Transactions on Professional Communication* PC-24, no. 1 (1981): 45–46.
Battison, R., and Dixie Goswami. "Clear Writing Today." *Journal of Business Communication* 18, no. 4 (1981): 5–16.
Bingham, Earl G. *Pocketbook for Technical and Professional Writers.* Belmont, Calif.: Wadsworth, 1982.
Bly, Robert W., and Gary Blake. *Technical Writing: Structures, Standards, and Style.* New York: McGraw-Hill, 1982.
Borger, David L. "Style and the Effective Engineer." *Journal of Technical Writing and Communication* 8, no. 1 (1978): 53–57.
Bostian, Lloyd R. "How Active, Passive, and Nominal Styles Affect Readability of Science Writing." *Journalism Quarterly* 60 (1983): 635–40, 670.
Britton, W. Earl. "Personality in Scientific Writing." In *Proceedings of the 19th International Technical Communication Conference.* Washington, D.C.: Society for Technical Communication, 1972, pp. 71–76.
Broadhead, Glenn J. "Style in Scientific and Technical Writing." *In Research in Technical Communication: A Bibliographic Sourcebook,* edited by Michael G. Moran and Deborah Journet. Westbrook, Conn.: Greenwood Press, 1985.
Brogan, J. L. *Clear Technical Writing.* New York: McGraw-Hill, 1973.
Brouse, Albert J. "Clarity in Science Writing Is Not Enough." *Journal of Technical and Scientific Writing* 1 (1971): 73–78.
Bruce, Bertram, Andee Rubin, and Kathleen Starr. "Why Readability Formulas Fail." *IEEE Transactions on Professional Communication* PC-24, no. 1 (1981): 50–52.
Bush, Donald. "The Passive Voice Should Be Avoided—Sometimes." *Technical Communication* 28, no. 1 (1981): 19–20, 22.
Chatman, Seymour, ed. *Style in English Prose.* New York: Oxford University Press, 1971.
Clark, Andrew K. "Readability in Technical Writing—Principles and Procedures." *IEEE Transactions on Professional Communication* PC-18, no. 2 (1975): 6–70.

Clauser, H. R. "Writing Is for Readers." *STWP Review* 8 (1961): 12–17.
Corbett, Edward P. J. "Approaches to the Study of Style." In *Teaching Composition: Ten Bibliographic Essays,* edited by Gary Tate. Fort Worth, Tex.: Texas Christian University Press, 1976.
Crawford, Donald M. "On Engineering Writing." *Mechanical Engineering* 67 (1945): 607–9.
De Beaugrande, Robert. "Generative Stylistics: Between Grammar and Rhetoric." *College Composition and Communication* 28, no. 3 (1977a): 240–46.
———. "Information and Grammar in Technical Writing." *College Composition and Communication* 28, no. 4 (1977b): 325–32.
———. "Communication in Technical Writing." *Journal of Technical Writing and Communication* 8, no. 1 (1978): 5–15.
De George, James, Gary A. Olson, and Richard Ray. *Style and Readability in Technical Writing: A Sentence-Combining Approach.* New York: Random House, 1984.
De Vergie, Adrienne. "English for Lawyers: A Bibliography of Style Manuals and Other Related Guides." *College Composition and Communication* 26, no. 3 (Oct. 1975): 131–37.
Docter, Stewart. "Testing the Readability of Engineering Writing." *IEEE Transactions in Engineering Writing and Speech* 4, no. 3 (1961): 91–96.
Durham, John, and Paul Zall. *Plain Style.* New York: McGraw-Hill, 1967.
Eisenberg, Anne. *Effective Technical Communication.* New York: McGraw-Hill, 1982.
Elliott, Colin B. "Must Scientific English Be Dull?" *English Language Teaching Journal* 31 (Oct. 1976): 29–34.
Enkvist, Nils E. "On Defining Style." In *Linguistics and Style,* edited by N. E. Enkvist, J. Spencer, and M. J. Gregory. London: Oxford University Press, 1964.
Estrin, Harman A. "The Need for and the Improvement of Technical Writing." *Journal of Technical Writing and Communication* 1 (1971): 61–72.
Fielden, John S. "Writing Papers for Readability." *Mechanical Engineering* 81, no. 3 (1959): 46.
———. " 'What Do You Mean You Don't Like My Style?' " *Harvard Business Review* 60, no. 3 (1982): 128–38.
Fitzgerald, Stephen E. "Literature by Slide Rule." *Saturday Review* 36 (14 Feb. 1953): 15–16, 53–54.
Flesch, Rudolf. "A New Readability Yardstick." *Journal of Applied Psychology* 32 (1948): 221–33.
———. *How to Test Readability.* New York: Harper, 1951.
———. *A Way to Better English.* New York: Harper, 1958.
———. *How to Be Brief: An Index to Simple Writing.* New York: Harper, 1962.
———. *The Art of Readable Writing.* New York: Harper and Row, 1974.
———. *The ABC of Style.* New York: Harper and Row, 1980.
Freeman, Donald C., ed. *Linguistics and Literary Style.* New York: Holt, Rinehart and Winston, 1970.

Gilliland, John. *Readability.* London: University of London Press, 1972.

Goforth, Caroline R. "A Selection of Style Manuals." *Technical Communication* 32, no. 2 (1985): 44–48.

Gopnik, Myrna. *Linguistic Structure in Scientific Texts.* The Hague: Mouton Press, 1973.

Gowers, Sir Ernest. "Technical Prose: English or Techlish?" *Chemical Engineering Education* 11, no. 4 (1977): 154–59, 173.

Graves, Robert, and Alan Hodge. *The Reader Over Your Shoulder.* New York: Vintage Books, 1979.

Gross, Alan G. "Style and Arrangement in Scientific Prose: Rules Behind The Rules." *Journal of Technical Writing and Communication* 14 (1984): 241–53.

Gross, Deborah V., and Raymond F. Sis. "Scientific Writing: The Good, The Bad, The Ugly." *Journal of Veterinary Medical Education* 7, no. 3 (Fall 1980): 127–30.

Gunning, Robert. *How to Take the Fog Out of Writing.* Chicago: Dartnell, 1964.

———. *The Technique of Clear Writing.* New York: McGraw-Hill, 1968.

Hake, Rosemary. "Style and Its Consequences: Do As I Do, Not As I Say." *College English* 43 (1981): 433–51.

Halliday, Michael. *Cohesion in English.* London: Longman, 1976.

Harris, John S. "Metaphor in Technical Writing." *The Technical Writing Teacher* 2 (Winter 1975): 9–13.

Harty, Kevin J. *Strategies for Business and Technical Writing.* New York: Harcourt, Brace, Jovanovich, 1985.

Hasan, Ruqaiya. "A Linguistic Study of Contrasting Features in the Style of Two Contemporary English Prose Writers." Ph.D. diss., University of Edinburgh, 1964.

Herbert, A. J. *The Structure of Technical English.* New York: Longman, 1975.

Hoffman, Robert R. "Metaphor in Science." In *Cognition and Figurative Language,* edited by Richard P. Honeck and Robert R. Hoffman. Hillsdale, N.J.: Erlbaum, 1980, pp. 393–423.

Houp, Kenneth W., and Thomas E. Pearsall. *Reporting Technical Information.* New York: Macmillan, 1984.

Huddleston, R. A., E. D. Winter, and A. Henrici. *Sentence and Clause in Scientific English.* London: Communication Research Center, University College, 1968.

Jarmul, David. *Plain Talk: Clear Communication for International Development.* Mt. Rainier, Md.: Volunteers in Technical Assistance, 1981.

Johnson, Thomas P. *Analytical Writing: A Handbook for Business and Technical Writers.* New York: Harper and Row, 1966.

Jones, R. F. "Science and English Prose Style in the Third Quarter of the Seventeenth Century." *PMLA* 45 (1930): 977–1009.

———. "Science and Language in England of the Mid-Seventeenth Century." *Journal of English and German Philology* 31 (1932): 315–31.

Jordan, Michael P. "Some Associated Nominals in Technical Writing." *Journal of Technical Writing and Communication* 11 (1981): 251–63.

Kagan, Dona M. "Syntactic Complexity and Cognitive Style." *Applied Psycholinguistics* 1 (1980): 111–22.

Kapp, Reginald O. *The Presentation of Technical Information*. New York: Macmillan, 1957.

Keith, Marshall. "Informal Writing: Milestone or Millstone?" *IEEE Transactions in Engineering Writing and Speech* 10, no. 2 (1967): 39–40.

Kirkman, John. "What Is Good Style for Engineering Writing?" *Chemical Engineer* (Aug. 1971): 285–92. Also in *Chemical Engineer* (Sept. 1971): 343–45.

Klare, George R. *The Measurement of Readability*. Ames, Iowa: Iowa State Unversity Press, 1969.

———. "Assessing Readability." *Reading Research Quarterly* 10, no. 1 (1974): 62–102.

———. "A Second Look at the Validity of Readability Formulas." *Journal of Reading Behavior* 8 (1976): 129–52.

———. "Readable Technical Writing: Some Observations." *Technical Communication* 24, no. 2 (1977): 1–3, 5.

Klaus, Carl H., ed. *Style in English Prose*. New York: Macmillan, 1968.

Lanham, Richard. *Style: An Anti-Textbook*. New Haven: Yale University Press, 1974.

Lannon, John M. *Technical Writing*. Boston: Little, Brown, 1985.

Lay, Mary. *Strategies for Technical Writing: A Rhetoric with Readings*. New York: Holt, Rinehart and Winston, 1982.

Leonard, David C., and Peter J. McGuire. *Readings in Technical Writing*. New York: Macmillan, 1983.

Lipman, Michael, and Russell Joyner. *How to Write Clearly: Guidelines and Exercises for Clear Writing*. San Francisco: International Society for General Semantics, 1979.

Lloyd-Jones, Richard, and Clarence A. Andrews. *Technical and Scientific Writing*. Iowa City, Iowa: Iowa State University Press, 1963.

Lynch, Barbara S., and Charles F. Chapman. *Writing for Communication in Science and Medicine*. New York: Van Nostrand Reinhold, 1980.

Marcuse, Michael J. "Ethos in Technical Discourse: The Current State of the Question." Paper presented at the annual meeting of the Conference on College Composition and Communication, Washington, D.C., 1980. ERIC Document 188 221.

Marder, Daniel, and Dorothy M. Guinn. "Defensive Aesthetics for the Technical Writer." *Journal of Technical Writing and Communication* 12 (1982): 35–42.

Markel, Michael H. *Technical Writing: Situations and Strategies*. New York: St. Martin's, 1984.

Mathes, J. C., and Dwight W. Stevenson. *Designing Technical Reports: Writing for Audiences in Organizations*. Indianapolis: Bobbs-Merrill, 1975.

Menxel, Donald H., Howard M. Jones, and Lyle G. Boyd. *Writing a Technical Paper*. New York: McGraw-Hill, 1961.

Messer, Ronald K. *Style in Technical Writing: A Text/Workbook*. Glenview, Ill.: Scott, Foresman, 1982.

Miles, James, Donald Bush, and Allin Kaplan. *Technical Writing: Principles and Practices.* Chicago: SRA, 1982.

Milic, Louis T. "Theories of Style and Their Implications for the Teaching of Composition." *College Composition and Communication* 16, no. 2 (May 1965): 66–69.

———. "Against the Typology of Styles." In *Essays in the Language of Literature,* edited by Seymour Chatman and Samuel R. Levin. New York: Macmillan, 1966.

Millard, Michael. "On the Improvement of Style in Technical Writing." *Journal of Technical Writing and Communication* 2, no. 2 (1972): 147–53.

Miller, John A. "Technical Writing—An Easily Acquired Skill." *Civil Engineer* 18 (May 1948): 43–44, 80.

Mitchell, John H. *Writing for Technical and Professional Journals.* New York: John Wiley and Sons, 1968.

———. "Basic Writing Concepts for Scientists and Engineers." *The Technical Writing Teacher* 8 (1980): 3–6.

Mueller, Douglas. "Put Clarity in Your Writing." *Hydrocarbon Processing* 59, no. 6 (1980): 143.

Newsweek. Writing Style and Effectiveness. New York: *Newsweek,* 1981.

Olson, Gary A., and Richard Ray. *Style and Readability in Technical Writing: A Sentence-Combining Approach.* New York: Random House, 1984.

Orth, Melvin F. "Striking Out: Poor Style and Grammar Still Abound in Technical Writing." *IEEE Transactions on Professional Communication* PC-21, no. 2 (1978): 44–47.

Paradis, James. "Bacon, Linnaeus, and Lavoisier: Early Language Reform in the Sciences." In *New Essays in Technical and Scientific Communication: Research, Theory, Practice,* edited by Paul V. Anderson, R. John Brockmann, and Carolyn R. Miller. Farmingdale, N.Y.: Baywood Publishing, 1983.

Parks, Clyde W. *English Applied in Technical Writing.* New York: F. S. Crofts, 1940.

Plung, Daniel L. "Readability Formulas and Technical Communication." *IEEE Transactions on Professional Communication* PC-24, no. 1 (1981): 52–54.

———. "Literary Communications: Adding Style to Professional Writing." *The Technical Writing Teacher* 10, no. 1 (1982): 25–31.

Powell, Kenneth B. "Readability Guides Are Helpful If. . . ." *IEEE Transactions on Professional Communication* PC-24, no. 1 (1981): 43–45.

Prince, Martin V. H. "It Ain't Necessarily So: Short Words and Simple Sentences Are Not Necessarily the Clue to Clarity, Readability." *Chemical and Engineering News* 33, no. 34 (1955): 3513.

Rabinovitch, Marvin. "Technical Writing's Last Stand." *Technical Communication* 27, no. 3 (1980): 23–25.

Ramsey, Richard D. "Technical Writing, Stylistics and TG Grammar." *Journal of Technical Writing and Communication* 7 (1977): 333–45.

———. "Grammatical Voice and Person in Technical Writing: Results of a Survey." *Journal of Technical Writing and Communication* 10 (1980): 109–13.

Rathbone, Robert. *Communicating Technical Information.* Reading, Mass.: Addison-Wesley, 1972.

Reddick, Dewitt C. *Literary Style in Science Writing.* New York: Magazine Publishers Association, 1969, Chap. 2.

Redish, Janice C. "Understanding the Limitations of Readability Formulas." *IEEE Transactions on Professional Communication* PC-24, no. 1 (1981): 46–48.

Robinson, Patricia A. *Fundamentals of Technical Writing.* Boston: Houghton-Mifflin, 1985.

Rosner, Mary. "Style and Audience in Technical Writing: Advice from the Early Texts." *The Technical Writing Teacher* 11, no. 1 (1983): 38–45.

Roundy, Nancy, and David Mair. *Strategies for Technical Communication.* Boston: Little, Brown, 1985.

Sandman, Peter M., Carl S. Klompus, and Betsy G. Yarrison. *Scientific and Technical Writing.* New York: Holt, Rinehart and Winston, 1985.

Schenk, Eleanor M. "Technical Writer—Readability Formulas and the Nontechnical Reader." *Journal of Technical Writing and Communication* 7 (1977): 303–7.

Schindler, George E., Jr. "Why Engineers Write as They Do—Twelve Characteristics of Their Prose." *IEEE Transactions on Professional Communication* PC-18, no. 1 (1975): 5–10.

Schwartz, Helen J. "Teaching Stylistic Simplicity with a Computerized Readability Formula." In *Proceedings of the International Meeting of ABCA.* Washington, D.C.: N.p., 1980.

Selzer, Jack. "Readability Is a Four-Letter Word." *Journal of Business Communication* 18, no. 4 (1981): 23–24.

———. "Review of *Style: Ten Lessons in Clarity and Grace.*" *College Composition and Communication* 33, no. 1 (Feb. 1982): 76.

———. "What Constitutes a 'Readable' Technical Style?" In *New Essays in Technical and Scientific Communication: Research, Theory, Practice,* edited by Paul V. Anderson, R. John Brockmann, and Carolyn R. Miller. Farmingdale, N.Y.: Baywood Publishing, 1983, pp. 77–89.

Sherlock, James. *A Guide to Technical Communication.* Boston: Allyn and Bacon, 1985.

Sherman, Theodore A., and Simon S. Johnson. *Modern Technical Writing.* Englewood Cliffs, N.J.: Prentice-Hall, 1975.

Shurter, Robert L. "Let's Take the Straight Jacket Off Technical Style." *Mechanical Engineering* 74 (1952): 549–650.

Sides, Charles H. "Some Aspects of Syntax." *Technical Communication* 30, no. 1 (1983): 54–59.

———. *How to Write Papers and Reports About Computer Technology.* Philadelphia: ISI Press, 1984.

Smith, Gertrude. "Differences in the Thinking-Writing Process." *Journal of Technical Writing and Communication* 2 (1972): 19–32.

Smith, Richard W. *Technical Writing.* New York: Barnes and Noble, 1963.

Spangler, E. R. "Modern Grammar and Its Application to Technical Writing." *Journal of Chemical Education* 33 (1956): 61–64.

Sprat, Thomas. *History of the Royal Society,* edited by J. I. Cope and H. W. Jones. St. Louis: Washington University Press, 1966.

Stephens, James. "Style as Therapy in Renaissance Science." In *New Essays in Technical and Scientific Communication: Research, Theory, Practice,* edited by Paul V. Anderson, R. John Brockmann, and Carolyn R. Miller. Farmingdale, N.Y.: Baywood Publishing, 1983.

Stohrer, Freda F. "Style in Technical Writing." *Teaching English in the Two-Year College* 7 (1981): 217–22.

Stone, W., and J. G. Bell. *Prose Style: A Handbook for Writers.* New York: McGraw-Hill, 1968.

Strunk, William, and E. B. White. *The Elements of Style.* New York: Macmillan, 1975.

Tebeaux, Elizabeth. "What Makes Technical Writing Bad? A Historical Analysis." *IEEE Transactions on Professional Communication* PC-23, no. 2 (1980): 71–76.

Thomas, J. D. *Composition for Technical Students.* New York: Scribner's, 1965.

Tufte, Virginia. *Grammar as Style.* New York: Holt, Rinehart and Winston, 1971.

Vervalin, Charles H. "Checked Your Fog Index Lately?" *IEEE Transactions on Professional Communication* PC-23, no. 2 (1980): 87–88.

Vick, Richard D. "Style in Technical Writing." *The Technical Writing Teacher* 10, no. 1 (1982): 32–37.

Walter, John A. "Style Manuals." In *Handbook of Technical Writing Practices.* Vol. 1. Edited by Stello Jordan. New York: Wiley Interscience, 1971, pp. 1267–73.

Warren, Thomas L. "Style in Technical Writing." *The Technical Writing Teacher* 6 (1979): 47–49.

———. "The Passive Voice Verb: A Selected, Annotated Bibliography—Parts I-IV." *Journal of Technical Writing and Communication* 11 (1981): 226–34.

Weisman, Herman M. "Problems in Technical Style, Diction, and Exposition." In *Proceedings of the 1959 Institute in Technical and Industrial Communication.* Fort Collins, Colo.: Institute in Technical and Industrial Communication, 1959, pp. 31–41.

———. *Basic Technical Writing.* Columbus, Ohio: Merrill, 1985.

Whitburn, Merrill D., Marijane Davis, Sharon Higgins, Linsey Oates, and Kristene Spurgeon. "The Plain Style in Scientific and Technical Writing." *Journal of Technical Writing and Communication* 8 (1978): 349–58.

Whyte, William H., Jr. "The Prose Engineers." *Journal of Communication* 2, no. 1 (1952): 6–10.

Williams, Joseph M. "Defining Complexity." *College English* 40 (1979): 595–609.

———. *Style: Ten Lessons in Clarity and Grace.* Glenview, Ill.: Scott, Foresman and Co., 1981.

Wright, Patricia. "Presenting Information in Tables." *Applied Ergonomics* 1 (1970): 234–42.

———. "Writing to be Understood: Why Use Sentences?" *Applied Ergonomics* 2 (1971): 207–9.

———. "Presenting Technical Information: A Survey of Research Findings." *Instructional Science* 6 (1977): 93–134.

———. "Feeding the Information Eaters: Suggestions for Integrating Pure and Applied Research on Language Comprehension." *Instructional Science* 7 (1978): 249–312.

———. "Usability: The Criterion for Designing Written Information." In *Processing of Visual Language,* edited by Paul A. Kolers, et al. New York: Plenum, 1980, pp. 185–205.

Wright, Patricia, and F. Reid. "Written Information: Some Alternatives to Prose for Expressing the Outcomes of Complex Contingencies. *Journal of Applied Psychology* 57 (1973): 160–66.

Wright, Patricia, et al. "Five Skills Technical Writers Need." *IEEE* Transactions on Professional Communication PC-24, no. 1 (1981): 11–16.

Zappen, James P. "Francis Bacon and the Rhetoric of Science." *College Composition and Communication* 26, no. 3 (1975): 224–47.

Zeidner, M. A. "Physician, Heal Thyself." *The Technical Writing Teacher* 9 (Spring 1982): 186–87.

9 Professional Presentations

James R. Weber
Battelle Northwest
Richland, Washington

The initial problem in discussing professional presentations is identifying them. In fact, presentations are not one speech usage but a cluster of uses. Authors in the field define them by a bewildering number of criteria: by the aims of the presentations (usually, either informative or persuasive); by the context in which they are presented; by the audience addressed; by their scope; or by the techniques used in making the presentation. There is also a considerable variety of terms, some of which seem to be used interchangeably: oral reports, oral presentations, small-group presentations, management presentations, conferences, public speeches, or "talks."

Some attempts have been made to carve an order out of this variety. E. G. Bormann, for instance, has distinguished talks from public speeches, oral reports, and presentations (Bormann et al. 1982). He reserves the term *presentations* for multimedia events and "talks" for very short events followed by question and answer sessions. Although it is a valiant attempt, the advice contained in most resources on professional presentations is not affected by these fine distinctions. However, there are generally agreed-on distinctions. We may locate the nature of a presentation as either formal or informal, private (as in small-group sessions with verbal interactions), or public (one person addressing a group), as we might visualize with the following intersecting axes:

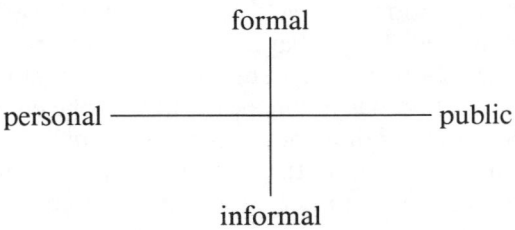

Public speeches, for instance, which are considered formal presentations, are given to audiences larger than the handful that may attend a small decision-making session. A "talk" may be an informal public presentation. A small-group presentation, though personal, may be considered formal if it is offered by a member of a lower organizational level to members of a higher level (vertically) or informal if it is offered on the same level (horizontally). The purposes of presentations vary among situations or professional communities, being informative in some instances (as with a research physician presenting findings to other researchers) or primarily persuasive in others (as with the same physician presenting the same material to a committee to obtain a grant). Thus, for our purposes, we may define a professional presentation as any speaking situation in which a professional seeks either to persuade or to inform an audience assembled to share information or reach decisions.

Until the 1960s, the dominant approach to professional presentations was as a kind of public communication, usually formal. But two major influences have strongly affected the textbook approaches to professional presentations: the changes in organizational theory and the rise of interpersonal theories of communication. Organizational theory influenced oral reporting by pointing out the importance of small decision-making groups in many organizations. Studies have identified variables that affect verbal communication in groups. The group size, the norms and degree of conformity within the group, the cohesiveness, the power structures, the work roles of the members, their personalities and status, and the task of the group as a whole—all these variables—affect the process of communication. (See, for instance, Bobby R. Patton and Kim Griffin's [1978] *Decision-Making Group Interaction*.) Interpersonal communication studies have also influenced oral reporting by focusing on the interactive nature of communication, pointing out that messages travel not in one direction only but in at least two (speaker to audience and audience to speaker). Moreover, communication is not only verbal but also nonverbal. Because interaction is more evident in person-to-person and small-group situations, these speaking situations have become the paradigms for interpersonal communication analysis, in teaching oral presentations as well as in general speech pedagogy. Gordon Wiseman and Larry Barker's (1967) *Speech-Interpersonal Communication* is representative of many other such works.

Since the mid-1970s, it has become clear that public communication is not the primary form of oral communication in most organizations. Informal oral communication in the form of small-group or two-person meetings (the interpersonal model) is much more common. Jon M.

Heugli and Harvey D. Tschirgi (1974) surveyed 101 business graduates in entry-level positions, asking about specific job duties and the communication skills they used to perform their jobs. Although oral communication was more frequent than written communication in their work, the respondents said that their most common speaking situations were personal and informal: in one-to-one meetings with a boss (vertical communication) or with fellow workers at the same level (horizontal). Listening skills were third most frequently used; fourth was persuasive speech skills in "selling ideas" to colleagues. Public appearances and speeches were infrequent among these entry level workers. Much the same emphasis on personal informal speaking skill was brought out for engineers, as Peter M. Schiff (1980) reported in *Engineering Education.* One-to-one talks with technically sophisticated personnel were the main vehicles for oral communication, followed by participation in a small group or a committee of technically knowledgeable people, and then by one-to-one talks with nontechnical personnel. Formal oral presentations were fourth among oral forms of communication—but only tenth among all communication skills, after counting various sorts of writing. Where there are technical developments to keep up with, it appears that formal presentations are more frequent. In short, in business and technical professions, oral presentations form only one part of an entire field of communication activities—one that may happen less frequently than more personal and more informal methods.

Most professionals, then, need interpersonal communication even more urgently than public-speaking skills. Textbooks, however, are only recently catching up to the professional community's actual needs. Michael S. Hanna (1978) did a study of the "most troublesome" communication situations in business and found that formal presentations ranked ninth among twelve troublesome settings. He concluded that such communication skills as motivating people, delegating authority, and listening should be stressed. Formal presentations, he advised, should be deemphasized in favor of conference leadership and participation. A later study done by Gerald M. Gibson and Ethel C. Glenn (1979) examining forty-nine business communication textbooks published between 1956 and 1979 concluded that these randomly selected texts overemphasized formal presentations at the expense of other communication needs, particularly one-to-one meetings and conference leadership.

Since the late 1970s, textbooks and articles on oral presentations have changed by giving less emphasis to public speaking but more to interpersonal and small-group communication skills. Skills that contribute to successful small-group sessions—listening, nonverbal communication, and group participation—share a place along with such public-speaking skills as preparation of materials, delivery strategies, and control of speaker anxiety. Recently, interviews, small decision-making groups, and individual conferences have taken their places as equals of formal presentations in textbooks. For instance, *Speech Communication in Business and the Professions* by Larry A. Samovar et al. (1981), despite a title that is reminiscent of an old speech communication approach, reflects the new balancing of communication needs. It is divided into three sections of approximately equal weight: public speaking, small-group discussion, and interviewing.

For teachers of oral communication, works of the past 25 years present a great variety of approaches, all of which may be useful to an eclectic teacher. Rather than categorize works by their dates, then, or their dominant theoretical influences, it seems better to divide them by their offerings—that is, by the sort of help they primarily offer to the student of oral presentations. To accomplish this, I have chosen the relatively constant rhetorical triad to describe speaking situations: a speaker, an audience, and a speaker's message. The works covered can be fit (with some overlapping, of course) into groups reflecting three dynamic relationships.

First, works emphasizing the speaker-audience relationship tend to present the bulk of their information in terms of audience analysis and the interpersonal aspects of oral presentations. They base their approaches on the interactive nature of speaking.

Second, works emphasizing the speaker-message relationship focus on methods of generating ideas, of organizing materials, or of achieving an oral style. They also discuss conference presentations and delivery of written speeches.

Third, works emphasizing the audience-message relationship provide information on an audience's apprehension of information, including the helpfulness of visual aids and the conduct of question and answer sessions.

The Speaker-Audience Relationship

Though the influence of organizational and interpersonal communication theories has been reflected in all recent approaches to oral presentations, it is most evident in works focusing on the speaker-audience dynamics. These works are less concerned with specific attributes of oral presentations and more with how oral presentations reveal elements of common communication patterns. For instance, interviews or discussion groups share with oral presentations the elements of the communication process itself, including encoding a message, analyzing an audience, and sending and receiving nonverbal messages. Thus, oral presentations are but a species of nonwritten communication and are often treated among other nonwritten kinds of communication in textbook discussions. Though some instructors do not see the value of theoretical approaches to oral reporting, regarding them as too general, the theory does make it possible to provide students a broad perspective on oral reporting—the goal advocated by Hanna and others.

Because of their broad coverage of communication uses, recent textbooks often rely on universal models of communication. *Communicating for Results: A Guide for Business and the Professions* by Cheryl Hamilton and Cordell Parker (1981) reflects the approximate weightings of many similar texts. These texts divide professional communication into three equally weighted sections: (1) theory of interpersonal communication, (2) interviewing and small-group skills (including informal oral presentations), and (3) public presentations (including formal oral presentations). Jerry W. Koehler and John I. Sisco (1981) divide the field into essentially formal (public) and informal (small conference) presentations, after an overview of the communication process. So, too, Malra Treece (1983) in *Communication for Business and the Professions* defines the communication process by referring to the Shannon-Weaver and Berlo models of interpersonal communication. She then covers oral presentations specifically by including small-group skills and nonverbal communication.

Textbooks that cover a comprehensive range of communication needs must usually reduce their treatments of any particular application. Thus, the coverage of oral presentations is necessarily limited. Theory and application must be balanced, then, in the best texts, but because the applications are numerous and varied, oral presentations have been deemphasized in favor of more frequently used kinds of communication.

Some works attempt not just to balance theory and application, with one on either side of the scale, but actually to draw one from the other. They make principles and applications interactive, just as they would be in a speech. Ernest Bormann et al. (1982) related theory to practical applications in *Interpersonal Communication in the Modern Organization* by giving each chapter both a theory and an applications section. The effect is to encourage students to apply the general principles to specific situations, an effect that may be easily lost when theory commands the beginning of the book and applications fill the later chapters. Its emphasis, as the title implies, is on the ways in which interpersonal factors shape organizational communication.

Roger Wilcox (1967) in his *Oral Reporting in Business and Industry* also used a balanced speaker-audience view of oral presentations. Indeed, if there were a citation index among textbooks covering oral reporting, this book would probably be the most quoted. Like Bormann, Wilcox balanced theory and application but seems to draw the principles from the midst of application rather than vice versa. He defines the aims of oral reporting as understanding and retention—both audience-centered goals. To attain these ends for an audience is the speaker's primary responsibility. "For in communication" he stresses, "it is not what we present that is important, but what our listener receives—what he understands, believes, and accepts" (Wilcox 1967, p. 13). For instance, structuring an oral report—clearly the responsibility of the speaker—becomes a project of mutual concern to speaker and to audience. It should concern a speaker because it concerns an audience. Like Theodore Clevenger (1966) in *Audience Analysis,* Wilcox considers audiences as reflexive thinkers whose rational thinking normally involves solving problems. Thus, the preparation of presentation should be guided, he advises, by making a problem common to speaker and audience.

Thomas H. Olbricht's (1968) *Informative Speaking* draws out the implications for language and thought contained in an audience-centered approach to presentations. Unlike Wilcox and Bormann, he limits himself to informative oral presentations. Like Wilcox, however, he stresses that it is the audience's understanding that determines whether communication is occurring, pointing out that such evaluative terms as accuracy, economy, and specificity may be different for various audiences. A speaker who holds a purely referential view of language, however, would see no difference among his own and an audience's use of these terms. Such a concern for speaking an audience's language is extremely helpful for a classroom of technically minded speakers. Olbricht's analysis lays bare one of the major contributions of the audience-centered, interpersonal approach: the assumption that a speaker cannot adequately prepare a message without anticipating what messages an audience will receive nor deliver a successful presentation without monitoring the audience's responses for evidence of the messages they are receiving.

The Speaker-Message Relationship

The speaker-message dynamic is the intrapersonal side of oral reporting. It includes the preparation and delivery of a presentation, as well as the practical advice that experienced speakers and teachers offer the novice. The speaker-message dynamic is largely pragmatic rather than theoretical. In these works, there is a minimum of organizational or communication theory, a maximum of helpful hints. Because this aspect dwells on the craft of speaking, it includes practical topics important to students making presentations: inventing and organizing ideas, making arrangements for the talk, controlling nervousness, or writing speeches for delivery. Indeed, the largest number of resources on oral presentations are speaker-message oriented.

Very often, problems in content and delivery of a presentation can be traced to a speaker's orientation to the message itself, not to the speaker's orientation to the audience. That is, speakers err by assuming that their message is unchangeable—that it cannot be adapted. A complex audience analysis makes little difference to a speaker who believes that his message can be put in only one way or must include only a certain set of examples. The speaker-message dynamic has probably brought out so much literature not only because it is practical but also because it includes the speaker-speaker dynamic, as well. It requires that a speaker ask, what do I know about this topic that I can offer to this audience? What do I want this talk to do? How flexible can I be in paraphrasing or in providing alternative examples? Focusing on the message, then, requires a speaker to form audience-related objectives and concentrate on a small set of important ideas. Presentations within an organization will probably need to take into account management objectives, requiring the speaker to keep one foot in the message and the other in his audience's concerns. (And, we hope, a foot out of his mouth, too.)

The better works on organizing presentations seem to share this concern for objectives and idea-based structure. W. A. Mambert's (1976) *Effective Presentations: A Short Course for Professionals* puts an emphasis on developing a structure around a speaker's objective. In particular, Mambert helps a speaker find the key ideas in a presentation with a series of heuristic exercises. He points out that developing an idea for oral presentation means translating ideas into a presentational form—being able, for instance, to conceive of an idea in purely sensory form, as in an effective visual aid, or to avoid the pitfalls in an audience's emotional response to a term or concept. Like the dramatist creating a play, the speaker must be able to conceive of ideas as being interactive. A similar approach to Mambert's is adopted by Kevin R. Daley (1980), who recommends that a speaker pay attention to controlling the information. In an informative presentation, it is a particular danger to let the information control the speaker. Daley suggests ideographs—pictographs that illustrate general ideas—as helpful visual aids as well as ways of replacing written notes or a manuscript. This emphasis on providing visuals for the speaker is an interesting concept in emphasizing the major ideas. However, Daley's enthusiasm for ideographs should be regarded with caution. Taking visual reminders to the podium might work for some speakers, but for many of us such icons simply create additional levels of inferencing during the talk, resulting in confusion and blank moments.

Part of a speaker's preparation is mastering the stages of the speech and the details of delivery well enough so that she can concentrate on the message. Presenting information before an astute audience is probably not the time to experiment with new, untried ways of encapsulating or remembering information. Thus, short, helpful articles on the speaking process can be extremely valuable in allowing speakers to see the process as a whole, without the fine details. They often contain sound advice that students and accomplished speakers alike are likely to remember. It is unlikely, for instance, that you could forget the mnemonic aid for organization: "Tell 'em what you're gonna tell 'em. Tell 'em. And tell 'em what you told 'em." Though this formula has driven writing teachers to distraction, oral presentations benefit from such a clear, expected rhythm. Thomas Sawyer's (1970) "Preparing and Delivering an Oral Presentation" and Max Weber's (1970) "Time to Improve Our Oral Presentations" both counsel a presenter on organizing and delivering a talk. Because of their mnemonic approaches, both are palatable forms of seasoned advice to offer classes in oral presentations. Robert Haakenson's (1974a, 1974b, 1974c) series of articles on preparing and presenting also offer advice in a readable, anecdotal style. J. Edwin Hollingworth's (1968) "The Oral Briefing: A Tool for More Effective Decision Making" emphasizes the limitations of the oral report, particularly the limits to which a speaker can reduce a message and still make it clear. When briefings fail, Hollingworth points out, it is generally because of the speaker's poor methods of preparing. All of these practical approaches have the advantage of being structured like oral presentations themselves, with the point emphasized through enumeration and illustration and punctuated with anecdotes and examples. By being short, they can put the emphasis on the speaker speaking rather than the speaker reading about speaking.

But there are also other, longer works that provide advice that is memorable and helpful. Harry Shefter's (1971) *How to Prepare Talks and Oral Reports* is among the best books that advises on preparing presentations. Though it contains slightly histrionic prose, the speaker's needs for memorable advice remain clearly in the forefront. For instance, Shefter advises speakers on supporting their ideas by introducing the trial lawyer's acrostic DESCEND, which stands for Describe, Extract (testimony or questions), State (facts), Clarify(by examples), Exhibit, Narrate, and Demonstrate. Other books, advising a speaker to do much the same thing, may spread their counsel over an entire chapter, expending in usefulness what they gain in exposition.

Admittedly, some information is just not adapted to memorizing, or worth it. Though there may be no point in memorizing lists of things to remember in arranging a presentation, a list may nonetheless be vitally helpful to consult. Some works provide just this sort of service to speakers—being reference works and silent valets. Jacqueline Dunkel and Elizabeth Parnham's (1985) *The Business Guide to Effective Speaking* is such a resource book. On the subject of speaking situations, for instance, they provide thirteen valuable questions to ask about a speaking situation before a speaker arrives (perhaps to be unhappily surprised). A speaker could ask, for example, "Can a room be changed to accommodate my needs? Can it be darkened, if necessary? Will people be drifting in and out as I speak?" Their chapter on the audience's impressions of a presenter's clothing contains tables of appropriate styles and colors for particular occasions.

Just as there were balanced, comprehensive approaches among the works emphasizing the speaker-audience interaction, so there are such balanced approaches in the practical speaker-message dynamic. Terry C. Smith's (1983) *Making Successful Presentations: A Self-Teaching Guide* and Marya Holcombe and Judith Stein's (1983) *Presentations for Decision Makers: Strategies for Structuring and Delivering Your Ideas* both cover small-group and public speaking, as well as considering the issues of organization, arrangements, and delivery that concern the presenter. I am more familiar with the Holcombe and Stein book and consider it my current choice for the Practical Presenter Award. It is, however, a book focusing largely on managerial presentations that require persuading an audience of the rightness of a particular solution to a problem. In their view, oral presentations recommend a course of action. They also hold that informative or technical presentations are better written than spoken. Although their philosophy of presenting includes only persuasive purposes, their practical advice is applicable to any presenter's purposes. Their lists and worksheets for organizing a talk are the products of considerable experience. Their version of the storyboard for organizing each section of the presentation provides space for the thesis statement for that section, the supporting ideas with their attending data (with space for a tiny version of the visual aid drawn in), and a transition sentence. Less iconic and mysterious than an ideograph, it can successfully take the place of an outline. Their treatment of visual aids, too, is particularly useful for a comprehensive text, teaching principles of good design by giving ample examples of good and poor design for overhead screens.

Besides those works that deal with the general needs of speakers for preparation and delivery, there are works that address specific issues in presentations. Special problems arise from the professional backgrounds of the audiences to whom presentations are made, the preparation of the presentation, or the speaker's anxiety level in delivery. Each of these issues affects the message that the speaker communicates.

Although most of the literature on oral presentations has been directed to speakers in management, not every audience is composed of managers. Journals in technical professions have sometimes helped educate their members about speaking, but textbooks have addressed the specific speaking needs of a particular professional community only infrequently. However, three books from the 1950s and 1960s, written for engineers, were directed at a particular professional community of listeners: John E. Dietrich and Keith Brooks' (1958) *Practical Speaking for the Technical Man,* Harold Weiss and J. B. McGrath's (1963) *Technically Speaking: Oral Communication for Engineers, Scientists, and Technical Personnel,* and Charles A. Ranous's (1964) *Communication for Engineers.* All three are actually comprehensive speech communication texts but with examples and hypothetical cases drawn from workplace settings that would be familiar to engineers. Dietrich and Brooks even condensed their information in each chapter into "formulas" that were meant to appeal to mathematically minded people. For example:

$$MYII = \frac{TI}{SA} + ASL$$

The diagram means Make Your Information Interesting (MYII) by incorporating Sensory Appeals (SA) into the Tools of Interest (TI) necessary to the speech, and then add Accurate and Stimulating Language (ASL).

These approaches may seem a little dated to us now and perhaps a little false not only because of their sexist language ("the technical man") but because they were written before the influx of interpersonal theory into communication textbooks. But their value lies in familiarizing the elements of presentations in the contexts of a profession—through examples and stories of engineers and scientists who were themselves presenters. Moreover, the Dietrich and Brooks example shows an attempt to provide mnemonics in a form palatable for engineers. The same desire to provide guidance for speakers in particular professions was behind the series of texts recently published by Scott, Foresman called the PROCOM series. There are texts for trial attorneys, corporate managers, engineers, office staff, government workers, military officers, physicians, and police officers. A general speaking guide, entitled *Professionally Speaking: A Concise Guide,* by Robert J. Doolittle (1984) emphasizes public speaking, while the other works concentrate on particular speaking situations common to each profession, thus dealing with more personal and informal situations.

Nearly every speaker in every profession must sometimes prepare a talk from a written work or even prepare a written speech. Although in informal presentations, speakers generally only outline their remarks, a practice that allows great flexibility, presentations that emphasize communicating information precisely and fully must often be written. How does a speaker make such a potentially stultifying situation into a more vibrant experience for an audience? Reading the written speech or presenting conference papers requires a sort of preparation of its own—often translating already written reports or articles into spoken presentations. Formal spoken presentations lie some place between formal written reports and informal spoken presentations in the amount of detail and complexity of ideas.

Although a great deal of information and a variety of approaches can be successful in a written report, oral reporting can suffer from complex organization or too much detail. Indeed, organizing and culling may be the most difficult part of a speaker's task. W. H. Auden once remarked that writing an opera libretto required that a poet put limits on the complexity of ideas because the music and drama impose limits on the audience's ability to understand. Oral reporting is a little like an opera libretto, requiring that a speaker carefully select the best information for an audience and the best means of conveying it to listeners. Thus, one of the most practical approaches to oral presentations may be to distinguish them from written reports.

Comparing written reporting to oral reporting, William E. McCarron (1981) actually uses the analogy of the novel versus the drama. McCarron points out that drama is limited by the ability of the audience to attend to the stimulation of the moment. Oral briefings, like drama, must be leaner and more emphatic than written material. Both, however, share the elements of rhetoric (such as the goals of persuading and informing), the need for clear delivery and organization, the use of graphic materials, and the quality of both being the medium of a message. The difference in the nature of feedback, however, is probably the most significant distinction for a speaker. Oral presentations involve immediate feedback. A speaker actually observes an audience processing information in the message—observes whether they are interested, quizzical, moved, or persuaded.

Presenters of academic papers are notorious for ignoring the interactive potential of their presentations. They may see themselves as "reading" a paper rather than presenting it. The magnum opus on conference presentations is B. A. Jones's (1964) "Presenting the Chemical Paper." Basing his suggestions on a survey of chemists who attended conferences, Jones notes that their primary criticism of oral presentations was that the papers had not been revised for presentation: they were journal articles, read in dusty library tones without noticeable modulation or enthusiasm. There were also criticisms about room arrangement, such as lighting being too dim or outside noise being too great. The conference goers were also unhappy with the quality of the visual aids and the lack of opportunity for question and answer sessions after a presentation. Jones's advice is to open conference presentations to interaction with an audience and a message; he emphasizes the presentational features of the report (the objectives, the main ideas, the visual components, and the problems appealing to an audience's interest).

The principle of interactive speaking might not only be used to rewrite conference presentations but also to guide corporate speech writing. Written speeches may be important policy statements in which every word is weighted; they may be presentations accompanying multimedia visual aids or sales presentations that have a "core" of ideas that allows flexibility in adapting the speech for various audiences. Craig Kallendorf and Carol Kallendorf (1980) suggest a system of topics for inventing ideas for corporate speeches. They reorganize the traditional Aristotelian topoi to create a series of heuristic questions, likely to be asked by an audience. This approach may be helpful to presenters of written material because their lack of flexibility in the speaking situation may be at least partially countered by a comprehensive method of anticipating questions. James J. Welsh's (1968) *The Speech Writing Guide: Professional Techniques for Regular and Occasional Speakers* offers a more comprehensive range of advice about such matters as time considerations, speaking arrangements, and the speech writer's relationship to the speaker.

Finally, we address an issue in making presentations that few speakers are really prepared for—controlling nervousness. Much has been said about this topic, but little to any definite, universal consequence. Most approaches to oral presentations include some advice about controlling nerves: take time by yourself before the presentation; breathe slowly and deeply; visualize the audience as friends; understand that the audience does not wish you evil. But the actual process of speaker anxiety has always seemed to be much more complex than the assumptions behind most of the advice. Speakers who are inordinately, dysfunctionally nervous are *afraid*—a condition not greatly aided by deep breathing. Even experienced speakers report sometimes suddenly feeling afraid in front of a group or exhibiting the physiological signs of fear, such as sweating, tightened muscles, or reduced respiration. An excellent analysis of research on the topic by William T. Page (1981), "Helping the Nervous Presenter: Research and Prescription," notes that there is a qualitative difference between phobic presenters and those with relatively normal levels of fear. The outlook for curing speaking phobia is actually better than that for relieving those of us with only the chronic jitters. Systematic desensitization, biofeedback sessions, or drugs used for reducing high blood pressure are all extremely effective for phobic speakers; normal speakers, however, must try to change the stress producers in their environments, such as their mental or physical states. One fascinating finding is that speaker fear is a reflexive phenomenon, growing more intense the more the speaker is aware that he or she is afraid. Page (1981, p. 17) offers two pieces of advice for anyone working with presenters:

> (1) Always assume that complaints about nervousness represent potentially serious problems, which may pose a threat to coursework or career success. Leave the ultimate determination of problem severity to a mental health professional.
> (2) Offer realistic assurance that nervousness problems are common and can be dealt with successfully in the long run, but avoid false promises about how nervousness automatically fades as a

result of practice or experience. Teaching with these directives in mind sets up an environment where presenters are most likely to learn long-term strategies for coping with nervousness.

The Audience-Message Relationship

Rather than focusing on the speaker's rapport with an audience or with the content of a presentation, the audience-message relationship involves an audience's understanding of a message and their opportunities to clarify it. Under the rubric audience-message, we may place such aspects of oral communication as nonverbal feedback, listening, audiovisual aids, and question and answer sessions. Because nonverbal feedback and listening are considered interpersonal communication skills, however, they fall outside the immediate concerns of this essay. Question and answer sessions, which allow an audience a direct opportunity to clarify and respond to a message, are common parts of the public component of oral presentations. For our purposes, audiovisual aids may be considered in the audience-message domain because of their power to draw an audience's attention away from a speaker's presence and into the speaker's information.

"It would be wrong to imply," Robert Haakenson (1974a) acknowledges, "that a-v aids are good *per se*. Properly used, they strengthen the impact of the talk; improperly used, they detract." This wise attitude points out that audiovisual aids are easily misused. Even experienced speakers sometimes overlook the potential for distracting an audience with visual stimuli that are meant simply to inform or dazzle. A colleague relates the story of watching a well-known author of a job placement text ruin an otherwise interesting multimedia presentation by trying to write on a blackboard in a darkened room with phosphorescent chalk. The effect would have been striking: a slide projection was showing at the same time that the speaker was writing out visible information on a chalkboard. But his fingers picked up some of the phosphorescent chalk dust so that very shortly all that the audience cared to watch was his gesturing, glowing hands in the darkness.

Works focusing on the mechanics of presenting visuals can help a speaker avoid such unanticipated problems. Although it omits glowing chalk, *Presenting Yourself* by Michael Kenny (1982) is an objective-based text that is excellent for presenters planning multimedia events or slide presentations. Sponsored by Eastman Kodak, the book covers a range of contingencies in preparing and structuring the heavily "visual" talk: selecting proper media and equipment, integrating script and visuals, considering an audience's physical needs, presenting away from home, and equipping a presentation room. It discusses the mechanics of visual presentations in detail, including the advantages, disadvantages, and requirements of various media. However, it is heavily weighted toward slide presentations, a rather inflexible form of aid, and does not cover principles of design. Other works, too, have excellent sections on the mechanics of visuals. George A. Magnan's (1970) *Using Technical Art: An Industry Guide* includes a long chapter on "Effective Visuals for Presentations and Briefings." Magnan is less sales oriented than Kenny is and more directed to providing maximum assimilable information in visuals—often the goal in technical presentations.

Problems in the mechanics of visual presentations seem to result as often from a foggy idea of what constitutes visual information for an audience as from ignorance of equipment or room layout. There are probably only a handful of basic principles that most presenters need in approaching their visual aids. Wilcox (1967, pp. 151–54) offers five essentials with clear rationales in *Oral Reporting in Business and Industry:* visuals should serve a need, play a subordinate role to the verbal message, be adapted to the listening-viewing situation, have a professional appearance, and be practical to use. The practicality of visual aids deserves to be emphasized, though. The most valuable visual aid a presenter has to offer, after all, is himself or herself.

Most management and technical presentations use charts or graphs, a need now met by various kinds of software. However, most software cannot prevent clutter or information misapplied by using an inappropriate graphic. Thus, I recommend that students consult works on designing visual aids. Two excellent books provide readable advice on charts and graphs: Gene Zelazny's (1985) *Say It with Charts: The Executive's Guide to Successful Presentations* approaches structuring presentations around effective graphics and Robert Leffert's (1981) *How to Prepare Charts and Graphs for Effective Reports* emphasizes charts that can be prepared by hand or by computer.

The field of instructional media is also a valuable resource in visual design for presenters. It includes books on helping teachers create visuals to supplement their verbal instruction. Though most of these books are meant for classroom instruction, some are clearly applicable to other oral presentations. One short introduction to pragmatic design, *Designing for Visual Aids* by Andrew Wright (1970), points out that the major criterion for the appropriateness of a visual aid is its fidelity to the speaker's objective. The book's three sections explain the concept of objectives, consider the types of media, and discuss design principles. Wright uses two approaches to choosing content for a visual aid—approaches much different from communication texts. A speaker, he notes, could follow up the potential of a design element in a visual aid, exaggerating a visual analogy, for instance, or using a verbal suggestion in the speech to create a memorable picture. Another approach is for a speaker to balance the degrees of realism and symbolism necessary to communicate a message. Showing the layout of the inside of an aircraft, for instance, requires more symbolism than realism if your purpose is to show how the seats are disposed and the flight attendants' quarters are laid out. A photograph would be more realistic than a cutaway drawing but less fitting to the purpose.

Thinking visually is a way of ensuring that unimpeded and unambiguous messages reach an audience. The approach in Ralph E. Wileman's (1980) *Exercises in Visual Thinking,* although directed to teachers, can also help oral presenters visualize their messages. His position on choosing particular media is unusual; he holds that "most media ... have the potential to accommodate the visual aspect of a message" (Wileman 1980, p. 20). In other words, most speakers can probably use mundane technology in delivering their messages in slides, charts, or overhead projectors. It seems to be true that visual messages are not often bungled because of lack of a visual technology. Instead, they suffer from the wrong use of the available technology. Visual aids are either misused (as in the case of the phosphorescent chalk) or misapplied to produce low-information or confusing visuals. Then, the biggest problem for a speaker may not be in choosing the right equipment but in using the available equipment to the greatest advantage. Wileman provides a self-teaching format composed of problem-solving exercises, very similar to the situations confronting oral presenters or lecturers.

Although visuals encourage an audience to be momentarily passive in its reception of a message, the question and answer session bring out their participation, often in unexpected ways. A question and answer session is clear evidence of whether a presentation has been truly interactive. A lack of questions quite often means a lack of interest. Anticipating the problems and opportunities in question and answer sessions is half the battle in becoming comfortable with fielding questions from an audience. Novice speakers are often surprised that many audiences must be encouraged or even primed to ask questions while others have an abundance of questions, some even embarrassing or sharp. In either case, a speaker confident in his or her message is well advised to invite an audience to take notes in preparing for their questions at the end of a presentation. Audiences that listen to a presentation are more likely to find their questions answered and more likely to ask intelligent questions. Two articles by Robert Haakenson,

"The Q&A Period Can Make or Break Your Talk" (1974c) and "Oral Communication: Answering Audience Questions" (1974b) counsel speakers to encourage questions with an invitation early in the talk and by reading an audience's responses during the presentation.

Thomas Gordon's (1978) *L.E.T.—Leadership Effectiveness Training* discusses "active" listening as a way of decoding a message, that is, reaching through a question to the questioner's real concerns. Knowing that people often ask questions rather than reveal their opinions in public can help a speaker disarm hostile, potentially damaging questions. A book written in 1977 for women newly entering the public arena, *Speaking Up* by Janet Stone and Jane Bachner (1977), covers the problems of outright or vaguely hostile questions. As others who have dealt with loaded questions have done, their advice largely is to direct the questioner to information about the topic—that is, to the support the speaker has mustered for the message. On advice for those speakers who lead question and answer sessions, Frederick C. Dyer et al. (1972) also suggest that threats to a leader's poise be handled by knowing the audience's concerns beforehand and by focusing on the messages, that is, on substance, whenever possible.

Conclusion

The topic of audience response to a message leads us full circle, back to considering the other dynamics of the triad: the speaker-audience and the speaker-message relationships. Indeed, teachers of oral presentations should reflect all three dynamics, adopting a balanced, pragmatic view that accounts for the needs of both speaker and audience and counsels a speaker toward a clear, complete message.

Despite the changes in the status of oral presentations in articles and textbooks during the last twenty-five years, it is clear that they still merit inclusion for business and technical communication teachers. The question may arise, why have oral presentations survived at all in the curriculum if they are used much more infrequently than other sorts of communication? Two reasons seem to justify an important place for teaching presentations. First, the studies of frequency do not tell the whole story of the importance of oral presentations. They can be highly influential in ways that telephone conferencing or one-to-one meetings cannot be because they can back up opinion with a combination of personal presence and evidence. They may be especially important for the lower-to-higher direction of organizational communication because they are potent ways for technicians or middle managers to influence more powerful members of the organization. Second, oral presentations demand the formal thinking and speaking skills that are profitably applied to other forms of communication. Bormann et al. (1982, p. 195) justifiably defend their emphasis on presentations because, they say, "if you learn the principles of preparing and delivering the important messages, you will learn the same skills and information you need for the less complicated and important oral reports that you will have to give."

References

Bormann, Ernest, Ralph G. Nichols, William S. Howell, and George L. Shapiro. *Interpersonal Communication in the Modern Organization.* Englewood Cliffs, N.J.: Prentice-Hall, 1982.
Clevenger, Theodore. *Audience Analysis.* Indianapolis: Bobbs-Merrill, 1966.
Daley, Kevin R. "Presenting Your Viewpoint." *Chemical Engineering* 87 (1980): 287–90.
Dietrich, John E., and Keith Brooks. *Practical Speaking for the Technical Man.* Englewood Cliffs, N.J.: Prentice-Hall, 1958.
Doolittle, Robert J. *Professionally Speaking: A Concise Guide.* Glenview, Ill. Scott, Foresman, 1984.
Dunkel, Jacqueline, and Elizabeth Parnham. *The Business Guide to Effective Speaking.* Seattle: Self-Counsel Press, 1985.
Dyer, Frederick C., Thornton B. Moore, and John M. Dyer. "How to Handle Yourself and Others During Question and Answer Sessions." *The Journal of Business Communication* 9 (1972): 19–24.
Gibson, Gerald M., and Ethel C. Glenn. "Oral Communication in Business Textbooks: A Twenty-Four Year Survey." *The Journal of Business Communication* 19 (1979): 39–49.
Gordon, Thomas. *L.E.T.—Leadership Effectiveness Training.* New York: Wyden, 1978.
Haakenson, Robert. "Audio-Visual Aids Bolster Your Talk." In *Effective Communication for Engineers,* edited by R. Haakenson. New York: McGraw-Hill, 1974a.
———. "Oral Communication: Answering Audience Questions." In *Effective Communication for Engineers,* edited by R. Haakenson. New York: McGraw-Hill, 1974b, pp. 75–77.
———. "The Q&A Period Can Make or Break Your Talk." In *Effective Communication for Engineers,* edited by R. Haakenson. New York: McGraw-Hill, 1974c, pp. 72–74.
Hamilton, Cheryl, and Cordell Parker. *Communicating for Results: A Guide for Business and the Professions.* Belmont, Calif.: Wadsworth Publishing, 1981. (Also available in a second edition, 1987.)
Hanna, Michael S. "Speech Communication Training Needs in the Business Community." *Central States Speech Journal* 29 (1978): 163–72.

Heugli, Jon M., and Harvey D. Tschirgi. "An Investigation of Communication Skills: Application and Effectiveness at the Entry Job Level." *The Journal of Business Communication* 12 (1974): 24–25.

Holcombe, Marya, and Judith Stein. *Presentations for Decision Makers: Strategies for Structuring and Delivering Your Ideas.* Belmont, Calif.: Lifetime Learning, 1983.

Hollingworth, J. Edwin. "The Oral Briefing: A Tool for More Effective Decision Making." *Management Review* 57 (1968): 2–11.

Jones, B. A. "Presenting the Chemical Paper." *The Journal of Chemical Documentation* 4 (1964): 131–40.

Kallendorf, Craig, and Carol Kallendorf. "A New Topical System for Corporate Speechwriting." *The Journal of Business Communication* 2 (1980): 3–14.

Kenny, Michael. *Presenting Yourself.* New York: John Wiley, 1982.

Koehler, Jerry W., and John I. Sisco. *Public Communication in Business and the Professions.* St. Paul, Minn.: West, 1981.

Leffert, Robert. *How to Prepare Charts and Graphs for Effective Reports.* New York: Barnes and Noble, 1981. (Hardcover title: *Elements of Graphics.*)

Magnan, George A. *Using Technical Art: An Industry Guide.* New York: John Wiley, 1970.

Mambert, W. A. *Effective Presentations: A Short Course for Professionals.* New York: John Wiley, 1976.

McCarron, William E. "Oral Briefing versus Technical Report: Two Approaches to Communication Problems." In *Courses, Components, and Exercises in Technical Communication,* edited by Dwight W. Stevenson. Urbana, Ill.: National Council of Teachers of English, 1981.

Olbricht, Thomas H. *Informative Speaking.* Glenview, Ill.: Scott, Foresman, 1968.

Page, William T. "Helping the Nervous Presenter: Research and Prescriptions." *The Journal of Business Communication* 22 (1981): 9–19.

Patton, Bobby R., and Kim Griffin. *Decision-Making Group Interaction.* New York: Harper and Row, 1978.

Ranous, Charles A. *Communication for Engineers.* Boston: Allyn and Bacon, 1964.

Samovar, Larry A., Stephen W. King, and Myron W. Lustig. *Speech Communication in Business and the Professions.* Belmont, Calif.: Wadsworth, 1981.

Sawyer, Thomas. "Preparing and Delivering an Oral Presentation." *Technical Communication* 17 (1970): 4–7.

Schiff, Peter M. "Speech: Another Facet of Technical Communication." *Engineering Education* 71 (1980): 180–81.

Shefter, Harry. *How to Prepare Talks and Oral Reports.* New York: Pocket Books, 1971.

Smith, Terry C. *Making Successful Presentations: A Self-Teaching Guide.* New York: John Wiley, 1983.

Stone, Janet, and Jane Bachner. *Speaking Up.* New York: McGraw-Hill, 1977.

Treece, Malra. *Communication for Business and the Professions.* Boston: Allyn and Bacon, 1983.

Weber, Max. "Time to Improve Our Oral Presentations." *Technical Communication* 17 (1970): 6–11.

Weiss, Harold, and J. B. McGrath. *Technically Speaking: Oral Communication for Engineers, Scientists, and Technical Personnel.* New York: McGraw-Hill, 1963.

Welsh, James J. *The Speech Writing Guide: Professional Techniques for Regular and Occasional Speakers.* New York: John Wiley, 1968.

Wilcox, Roger. *Oral Reporting in Business and Industry.* New York: Prentice-Hall, 1967.

Wileman, Ralph E. *Exercises in Visual Thinking.* New York: Hastings House, 1980.

Wiseman, Gordon, and Larry Barker. *Speech-Interpersonal Communication.* San Francisco: Chandler, 1967.

Wright, Andrew. *Designing for Visual Aids.* London: Studio Vista, 1970.

Zelazny, Gene. *Say It with Charts: The Executive's Guide to Successful Presentations.* Homewood, Ill.: Dow Jones-Irwin, 1985.

II Genres in Technical Communication

10 Annual Reports, Brochures, and Newsletters

John W. Ferstel
University of Southwestern Louisiana

The communications teacher who tends to cover the usual staples of technical writing textbooks will find that annual reports, brochures, and newsletters can provide students with further examples of and insight into professional writing in the business and technical environment. Despite their diversity of forms and objectives, all three types of communication fulfill important needs in business, with the latter two—brochures and newsletters—frequently having specialized roles in technical communication as well.

As this essay will demonstrate, the sources available to the teacher or researcher who wishes to explore any of these types of professional communications actually span a number of different fields beyond technical writing, such as public relations, sales promotion, marketing, and journalism. In addition to the interdisciplinary nature of these types of writing, the fact that samples of each are readily obtainable from large businesses and professional associations makes a further argument for their inclusion in the professional communication course.

The present essay surveys the research and discussion conducted since about 1960. The level of sophistication in the writing of annual reports, brochures, and newsletters has risen so rapidly in the last 25 years that much work done before this period is simply antiquated and in no way representative of our state of knowledge and expertise today.

Due to their distinctive uses and formats, each of these three types of professional communications will be discussed separately in this chapter.

Annual Reports

Since the Baltimore and Ohio Railroad produced the first annual report in 1827, its form and purpose has evolved considerably from a simple financial statement into a polished, legally regulated document that corporations spend hundreds of thousands of dollars each year to create, produce, and distribute. The communications teacher will find a large body of material in business and trade publications about the annual report, including information on its early development, its objectives, and its recent innovations and achievements. In addition, there is also a growing number of audience research studies by private business associations that delineate the effectiveness of the annual report in terms of its accessibility and overall usefulness to particular reader groups. "How-to" books and articles can also assist the instructor in appreciating the mechanics and considerations that go into the creation of an annual report. Finally, several fine articles can provide the teacher with suggestions on how to use the annual report in a communications class.

The writing teacher with little or no familiarity with the annual report's role in business will find several works that can provide a historical perspective for recent changes. Elizabeth R. Floyd's *Preparing the Annual Report* (1960) presents the results of a survey that outlines the organizational and procedural practices of over 278 companies in producing their annual reports at the end of the 1950s. Based on the same survey, she also indicates the typical contents of 100 annual reports and analyzes the significance of the data given. Floyd's work also includes a fifty-page section of exhibits from annual reports of that era.

Since the Securities and Exchange Commission (SEC) changed the guidelines for annual reporting considerably in 1974 and again, to a lesser extent, in 1979, an understanding of the state of the annual report before and after these changes is illuminating. Richard A. Lewis's article, "Tomorrow's Annual Report: Paragon of Communication" (1972), provides a concise review of the annual report as it was conceived and written in the 1960s and early 1970s. It also includes a brief review of the progress of the annual report as it has evolved in this century. Arlene Hershman's "And Now: The 'Gutsy' Annual Report" (1975) discusses the SEC changes that were mandated in the 1974 reports, especially the inclusion of a 5-year summary of operations and the new "management analysis" section that required companies to comment on their financial data. Perhaps the best overall introduction to the annual report is Herbert E. Meyer's "Annual Reports Get An Editor," which traces the legal requirements for the annual report since 1934 and shows in some detail how the annual report has changed in scope and content since the 1974 SEC regulations went into effect.

Audience surveys of readers of annual reports are another category of source material for the communications teacher. Several organizations, publications, and scholars have conducted such surveys from time to time to determine who reads annual reports and what readers think of them. Both private organization studies as well as academic studies agree that both individual investors as well as professional investors rate annual reports as the single most important written source of information for making investment decisions. Kenneth S. Most and Lucia S. Chang's "How Useful Are Annual Reports?" (1979) confirmed this in a study of Florida investors which also noted that financial analysts rated the importance of annual reports even higher than investors did. A more recently published international study of individual investors, institutional investors, and financial analysts in the United States, Britain, and New Zealand is Lucia S. Chang, Kenneth S. Most, and Carlos W. Brain's "The Utility of Annual Reports: An International Study" (1983), which also demonstrated the importance which readers placed on the annual report in making investment decisions. As to what readers look at in the annual report, John Costello reports in "What's Read Most in Annual Reports" (1976) that a study by a New York investor relations firm indicated that the sections most read by small investors are the earnings per share, the letter to the stockholder, the statistics, and future prospects.

Nevertheless, communications teachers should be aware of the mixed attitudes that readers have toward annual reports. Srully Blotnick's "Take Your Report and . . ." (1983) points out that some studies indicate as few as 3 percent of all shareholders read their annual reports. In one study, even when a postage-paid reply card was enclosed, only 15 percent said they had studied the report. Also, of interest in this regard were the results of a private survey published in "Professional Investors Critical of Annual Reports" (1985). According to a national survey released by Hill and Knowlton, Inc., a New York City–based public relations firm, 73 percent of individual investors believe that annual reports play down bad financial news or attempt to hide unpleasant news in the data sections in the back of the reports.

The small number of individual investors who actually read the annual reports and the negative criticism that they give these reports may be related to the language used. Robert L. Heath and Greg Phelps (1984) reported in their article, "Annual Reports II: Readability vs. Business Press," that a 1981 annual report survey of twenty firms from the Fortune 500 list indicated that most reports are written on the "difficult" or "very difficult" reading level in all sections. Yet, Thomas L. Means (1981) in his "Readability: An Evaluative Criterion of Stockholder Reaction to Annual Reports" had contended several years earlier that stockholders' attitudes and readability levels are not related because stockholders have familiarized themselves with business jargon; therefore, standard readability formulas are not good predictors of investor attitudes. Certainly, more research in this area is needed.

Despite the audience studies undertaken by academic researchers and other organizations, Marianne Paskowski (1981) points out in "Stifling the Yawn: Annual Reports Awaken to New Audiences" how few individual companies bother to conduct surveys of their stockholders to measure the effectiveness of their annual reports.

In addition to the aforementioned sources for a historical perspective on the annual report, teachers will find the trade magazine articles on trends in annual report writing and design quite useful. Usually, these articles appear in the summer or early fall issues after their authors have had the time to review the new crop of annual reports that arrived on their desks in late April or May. Two instructive articles are Peg Dardenne's "Emerging Trends in Annual Reports" (1977), which discusses briefly some of the innovations for the 1976 reports, and "The Annual Report 1978: Thick and Innovative" (1979), which notes that annual reports for that year increased in size as many companies used some of the extra space to discuss their views on corporate social responsibility as well as key political and environmental issues. Two other notable articles that offer a look at developments in annual report writing and design are William P. Dunk's (1980) "28 Trends in Annual Reports," which contains a handy list of recent changes and Janet Dyer's (1981) "Predictable: The Watchword for the 1980 Reports," which provides a sampling of the 1980 reports, with some brief background commentary. More recently, Sid Cato's (1985) "The Annual Report: Here I Come, World: Report from an AR Watchdog" presents a rather detailed look at current trends in annual reports based on early arrivals. He also makes several predictions on the future development of the annual report as a communication tool.

In 1983, three key articles appeared that analyzed the uses of language in the 1982 annual reports by companies that had experienced difficulties due to the sluggish economy. These articles provide especially lucid examples for the communications instructor who wishes to focus on diction and style in the annual report. William D. Lutz (1983) demonstrates in "Corporate Doublespeak: Making Bad News Look Good" how language is used to deny responsibility for economic losses or to deny that such losses have even been incurred. In a similar vein, Milton Moskowitz's (1983) "The 1982 Annual Reports: A Potpourri for the Corporate Watchdog" critiques a dozen annual reports from the viewpoint of language, quoting examples of especially candid and well-written sentences from some and turgid and somewhat deceptive instances of language from others. Lastly, Edward O. Raynolds's (1983) "Annual Report Update: 1983 Reports Face New Challenges" is a brief but worthwhile overview of the new requirements for an effective annual report in a weak economy, including comments on the audience, content, and design needs for this new climate.

Three valuable articles for the teacher interested in looking at the design and pictorial elements of annual reports are recommended. Johnny R. Johnson et al.'s (1980) "Pictures that Lie: The Abuse of Graphs in Annual Reports" is a good primer on fair and unfair graphic presentations with some useful examples for the classroom. Jon Herrmann (1981), a senior graphic designer, presents an expert's look at both pedestrian and innovative design in recent annual reports in "Questioning the Slick But Tiresome Traditions of Annual Report Design." And in "The Costly New Look in Annual Reports," Arlene Hershman and G. Bruce Knecht (1981) provide an insider's view of the cost and design of annual reports by some of the major outside consulting firms that specialize in annual reports.

For an even more elaborate insider's view of the creation of annual reports, the communications teacher can read *Speaking Out on Annual Reports* (S. D. Scott 1977), a collection of observations and critiques of the annual report business by fifty writers, designers, printers, and planners. Although some of the advice is repeated by more than one contributor, the work provides considerable and worthwhile advice about putting together an annual report. For those unable to locate this book, Leo J. Northart's (1979) "What They're Saying About Annual Reports" includes a good sampling of some of the contributors' statements in the book.

Finally, one of the most recent trends in annual reports involves the use of an entirely different medium: video. Robert Levy's (1981) "Televising Annual Reports" reports on the Emhart Corporation's pioneering use of videotape to present its annual report. It began broadcasting a twenty-six-minute adaptation of its written annual report to its stockholders in Connecticut via cable networks with its 1979 report. And with its 1980 report, it also began making videocassettes available to its stockholders; in addition, these videocassettes have been shown at regional stockholders' meetings.

Several organizations and publications regularly assess the best annual reports produced each year. For example, *Institutional Investor* publishes a usually unsigned article on the "best" annual reports of the year in its September issue each year. The choices represent the judgment of financial analysts in the business commmunity. The two most recent articles were "The Best Annual Reports" (1985) and "Top Reports of 1985" (1986). Similarly, each year since 1940, *Financial World,* a financial trade publication, has sponsored an industry-wide judging of annual reports from nearly 1,000 corporations and presents numerous individual awards at a formal banquet to those firms with outstanding works. The professional communications instructor will usually find a preview article of the judging process in the June or July issue of the magazine followed by an article announcing the winners of the awards in the middle or late October issue. A recent example is R. B. Harris's (1984) "1984 Annual Report Awards: The Art of Corporate Communication." In 1979, the American Society for Personnel Administration began bestowing international awards to the two companies each year whose annual reports best reflect an emphasis on the contributions of their employees to corporate progress. Articles by Scott Dever announcing these awards and analyzing the achievement of the winners appeared in the July issues of the society's publication, *Personnel Administrator,* in 1980 and 1981. A representative article is Dever's (1980) "Mason Award Winners for 1980: Annual Reports and the Human Approach." Since 1981, the publication has not published an article on the Mason Award Winners, but interested teachers may still wish to obtain the list of winners from the society directly after their June convention (American Society for Personnel Administration, 606 N. Washington Street, Alexandria, VA 22314).

How-to articles and books can also provide the professional communication instructor as well as the student with some important insights on the mechanics and considerations that go into the creating of an annual report. Five articles and two books represent some of the best advisory material in this area. Both Walter G. Barlow's (1965) "Annual Reports and Annual Report Writing" and Alfred B. Smedley's (1975) "Is the Annual Report a Corporate Dinosaur?" discuss the overall conceptualizing of the annual report. Barlow's paper, despite its age, offers sound advice on the need for careful language and good graphics based on detailed research of investor response. Drawn from his own research on reader comprehension, his study makes several specific recommendations on layout and writing style. Similarly, Smedley's brief article is valuable for its emphasis on audience identity and needs in planning an annual report. Herbert C. Rosenthal's (1980) examples of good and poor writing in annual reports in "Scorecard for 1979 Annual Reports" also suggest lines of analysis for classroom study. And both John P. Brion's (1975) "Getting Ready for Annual Reports" and Elizabeth R. Turpin's (1980) "Annual Reports: A Fertile Field for Imaginative Graphics" provide concise checklists for the report writer in the areas of content and graphics. Turpin's comments on the visual impact of the report fit nicely with the emphasis in many technical writing textbooks on the importance of integrating the text with appropriate graphics.

For book-length works on annual report creation, the researcher will find relatively few. For overall planning of the annual report, Frances A. Koestler's (1969) *Creative Annual Reports* is still a seminal guide. In the area of graphic design Richard A. Lewis's (1971) *Annual Reports* is unsurpassed both in its systematic design checklist (PERT) and its use of numerous examples of good graphic design in annual reports.

In addition to corporations, many other nonprofit organizations issue annual reports. Two specialized articles in this area can be recommended here. Irving I. Rimer's (1975) "How the Non-Profits Do It" briefly discusses some of the specific concerns of the annual report for the nonprofit organization and distinguishes them from those of the corporate annual report. Likewise, James E. Fowler's (1977) "The Many Facets of Association Annual Reports" outlines the uses, contents, and objectives of association reports in contrast to corporate ones.

Although academe's interest in the annual report has lagged behind that of business and industry, there are some worthwhile materials for the communications teacher to use with annual reports. These can be classified into three categories: journal articles, textbook chapters and exercises, and other resources.

Four articles provide ideas that can easily be adapted by the communications instructor. Robert W. Rasberry's (1978) "A Quick and Simple Guide to Understanding Annual Reports" introduces the two-page student guide that is given to students at Southern Methodist University's School of Business Administration. The guide briefly outlines the typical sections in the annual report and explains the purpose of each. Edward G. Thomas's (1978) "The Corporate Annual Report: A Basic Resource in the Written Communication Course" contains a number of suggestions for using the annual report in conjunction with assignments in letter, memorandum, and report writing. Especially useful are his suggested topics for analytical papers based on student reading of annual reports. Of equal note is William V. Ruch's (1979) "The Corporate Annual Report as a Teaching Aid in Business Communication Classes," which suggests a comprehensive series of inspections of a single annual report from its accompanying packaging and cover letter through its graphics, format, and writing style. His suggestions can be used as either in-class exercises or as the basis for out-of-class reports. Another fine article that provides a checklist of questions and an outline of the major parts of the annual report, with special emphasis on audience analysis, is Pamela S. Rooney and Eileen B. Evans's (1983) "Using Annual Reports to Strengthen Business Communication Students' Understanding of Audience."

Recent technical and business communication textbooks only occasionally focus on the annual report. Charles T. Brusaw et al.'s (1982) *Handbook of Technical Writing* includes a five-page entry under "Annual Reports," which discusses the overall concerns of content, audience, tone, and artwork. William M. Schutte and Erwin R. Steinberg's (1983) *Communication in Business and Industry* briefly suggests a student assignment in analyzing the graphics, layout, and design of an annual report. Perhaps the most instructive use of the annual report is found in Thomas Pearsall and Donald Cunningham's (1985) *How to Write for the World of Work*. The authors present the president's letter to policyholders of a large insurance company, which they have marginally annotated to illustrate the analytical and persuasive strategies used in the document. Together with their introductory material on analytical reports, Pearsall and Cunningham's commentary offers the student an excellent model for his or her own study of the text of an annual report's letter to the stockholders.

The communications teacher who seeks further textbook material and exercises on annual reports will generally find a more consistent focus on annual reports in public relations textbooks. Typical of this trend is the brief discussion of the usual sections found in an annual report by Fraser P. Seital (1984) in *The Practice of Public Relations.* More interesting is Doug Newsom and Tom Siegfried's (1981) chapter on annual reports in *Writing in Public Relations Practice,* which emphasizes style, audience, contents, and theme of the annual report with examples from some recent reports. A more detailed chapter on annual reports can be found in Robert T. Reilly's (1982) textbook, *Public Relations in Action,* which discusses the contents of the standard report and illustrates each section with an example.

Other resources may also assist the professional communications teacher in planning a course segment around the annual report. The availability of annual reports is worth noting in this regard. Each year, between the end of April and the beginning of June, annual report cooperative advertisements can be found in such publications as the *New York Times, Forbes,* the *Wall Street Journal, and Barron's.* Teachers and students can send for dozens of annual reports by simply filling out and sending in a few forms. In addition, many university libraries subscribe to the *Q-Master Index* (Q-Data Corporation), which is a microfiche collection of business reports from foreign as well as American companies; it includes many annual reports. It is updated frequently and provides a wide assortment of corporation reports. And, at least one corporation publishes its own educational edition of its annual report. Since 1973, Armstrong World Industries, Inc., has published each year a special annotated, eight-page supplement for its annual report that contains definitions and explanations of basic terms as well as a student quiz. Armstrong provides over 100,000 copies of its annual report and supplement each year without cost to teachers, schools, and universities. Interested instructors may order the annual report and supplement in bulk quantities by contacting Armstrong's Corporate Information Division (Armstrong World Industries, Inc., P.O. Box 3001, Lancaster, Pa. 17604). For the instructor who wishes to keep up on future developments in annual report writing, the winter issue of *Public Relations Review* contains a separate heading for "Annual Reports" in its annual bibliography. And finally, for the last word on annual reports, there is Sid Cato's Newsletter on Annual Reports, a monthly publication written by a veteran annual report consultant and general industry watchdog. Instructors may wish to request a sample copy from the publisher (Sid Cato Communications, Inc., 1814 N. Lincoln Park West, Chicago, IL 60614).

Brochures

The term "brochure" refers most specifically to a fancy, printed document with a strong emphasis on the visual element. Yet, many professionals use the term more casually and interchangeably with "folder" or "leaflet." And outside of the guides on brochure design published by printing companies, the amount of material available to the professional communications teacher is rather modest at best.

Herman Holtz (1983) in *Persuasive Writing* categorizes brochures in the business and technical world into four general categories according to the purpose of each: (1) general sales, (2) product, (3) announcement, and (4) capability. What should be evident is that the business or technical brochure refers most commonly to a type of sales message or marketing vehicle that informs the public or other industries about a firm's services or products.

The communications teacher who is relatively unfamiliar with the writing and production of brochures may wish to consult first some standard textbook treatments of the brochure. Edward L. Nash's (1982) *Direct Marketing* presents a brief overview of the purpose, audience, format, and content of the direct mail sales brochure. A similar discussion of the promotional/sales/informational brochure in terms of its concept, accuracy, and design is available in Doug Newsom and Tom Siegfried's (1981) *Writing in Public Relations Practice*. One of the few technical writing texts that the communications teacher might wish to consult for this subject is Philip Kolin and Janeen L. Kolin's (1985) brief coverage of brochures in their chapter on "Technical Sales Literature" in *Models for Technical Writing*.

Several papers and articles about brochures provide more detailed insights into the considerations and concerns in creating brochures. David J. Chestnut's (1969) panel presentation, "Brochures—Four Points of View," illustrates the varying perspectives of the manager, copywriter, artist, and printer on preparing the promotional brochure that is used to help the sales of an industrial device or service. More recently, Judith H. Marcus's (1982) "The Abstract Art of Brochure Writing" offers some sound advice for the technical editor in mediating between the technical contributor and the intended reader of the technical brochure. L. R. Bowers's (1950) "Good Technical Bulletins: Their Composition and Distribution" is still useful for its assistance in distinguishing between brochures and other types of technical literature, such as catalogues, bulletins, and data sheets. And James A. Mann and John B. Ketchum's (1984) "Multi-Use: Reshaping Technical Material" demonstrates how a technical document might be revised into other forms (including the technical brochure) for different purposes and different audiences.

Two other works discuss particular types of technical brochures used in specific industries. "Companies Put New Zip in Old Sales Tool" (1960) still presents a good overview of the types and uses of technical brochures. Despite its outdated statements on the costs of brochure production, it contains excellent background material for teachers and students on the inception, development, and distribution of technical brochures in the chemical industry. H. L. Turner's (1966) "The Technical Capability Brochure" illustrates how a technical brochure can be used to advertise the use of facilities within a large federal agency. Turner stresses the knowledge required on the part of the technical writer and the appropriate writing style necessary to communicate effectively with a specific audience.

Finally, John B. Moffett et al. (1985) discuss recent developments in the use of computer technology in the preparation of texts and graphics for brochures in "Technical Brochure Preparation."

The best and one of the few books devoted solely to brochure writing and design is Gerre Jones's (1976) *How to Prepare Professional Design Brochures*. Based on his years of experience as a designer of architectural and engineering capability brochures, Jones covers all of the basics of the brochure in detailed chapters. In the preface, Jones recounts how he decided to write this book after finding not a single work in the Library of Congress that focused on "how to produce a brochure." Communications instructors will find especially useful his discussions of "Why Most Brochures Are Ineffective," "The First Layout," and "Writing."

Suggestions for using the brochure in a professional communications course include Della A. Whittaker's (1978) "Preparing a Brochure from the Student's Technical Report" and Jean M. Swaino's (1985) "Teaching Illustration Throughout the Technical Writing Course." Whittaker explains how she has her technical writing students turn their technical reports into brochures. She provides an outline of the steps in brochure design and notes that several of her working students have had their brochures published by their employers. Swaino related how she used a college career day as a realistic problem for a class exercise on brochure (pamphlet) design. Both teachers and students who lack access to samples of technical brochures should pick up issues of *Industrial Design* and *Business Marketing*. Each issue of these two publications contains reader service cards that can be sent in to obtain free brochures on industrial products and services.

Newsletters

The newsletter, like the annual report, has gradually evolved in this century into an important communication vehicle with its own standards for writing style and format. And like the brochure, today's newsletter can be found in almost every type of enterprise. Howard Penn, the publisher of *The Newsletter on Newsletters,* divides all newsletters into four categories:

- Subscription
- Organizational
- Franchise
- Public relations

The professional communications teacher will find technical and business newsletters in all of these categories. For example, subscription newsletters often provide technical advice and information to consumers or other professionals in a specific field. And public relations newsletters for industry frequently serve the dual function of disseminating technical information about a new product or service while at the same time promoting it to a potential customer, much the same way as does the brochure.

Most of the sources for the communications teacher can be classified as either how-to books and articles or case studies on how a specific newsletter was created to fill a special need. The instructor unfamiliar with the world of newsletters can best begin by consulting Howard P. Hudson's (1982) *Publishing Newsletters,* an authoritative overview of the modern newsletter that began with the Whatley-Eaton Report in 1918 and was popularized several years later with the founding of the *Kiplinger Washington Letter.* Hudson, who is president of the Newsletter Clearinghouse, lucidly outlines all of the major considerations in producing a commercial newsletter, from the analysis of a potential audience and managing of the editorial content through the establishment of a writing style and an appropriate design for the publication. And some time spent checking the third edition of *The Newsletter Yearbook/Directory* (Hudson 1981) will indicate the extent to which the newsletter has penetrated every corner of the business and technical world.

In addition to Hudson's volume, there are several excellent guides to newsletter publishing and production that have varying focuses. Mark Beach's (1982) *Editing Your Newsletter* (second edition) offers a thorough explanation for designing, writing, and producing many types of newsletters. He includes numerous sample pages from current newsletters, including business ones. LaRae H. Wales's (1975) *A Practical Guide to Newsletter Design and Editing* is also a fine introduction to the general newsletter written by a practicing technical editor. For insight into the uses of promotional newsletters, the communications instructor may consult Herman Holtz's (1983) discussion in *Persuasive Writing.* For information on in-house newsletters, Robert Newcomb and Marg Simmons's (1956) *Developing Effective Supervisory Newsletters: A Guide to Better Communication* is still one of the most comprehensive and useful works.

Two shorter works that review the concerns and mechanics of business or technical newsletters are Janet H. Potvin's (1982) "Eight Steps to Better Newsletters" and Stephen E. Arnold's (1979) "Newsletters, from the Management Side." Potvin concisely covers the entire gamut of considerations in editing a newsletter for a technical society. Arnold discusses the dimensions of the employee newsletter with emphasis on planning and credibility. He recommends that an attitude survey be taken before planning and emphasizes the importance of establishing a tone in the publication, "with a minimum of dogma, pontification, and condemnation." He also provides a useful checklist against which to measure a newsletter. Equally valuable are Arnold's discussion of trends to watch for in the newsletters of the 1980s.

Specific case studies of newsletters may afford the best background for both the professional communications teacher and the student who wishes to understand the actual needs of the workplace that a newsletter can serve. W. H. Puder's (1961) "Publishing the Weekly Technical News Bulletin" discusses the creation of an in-house weekly technical newsletter for a subsidiary of Western Electric to provide news on technical research and developments among the organization's separate divisions. Puder covers editorial objectives, sources of information, and ways to judge the effectiveness of such a publication. Similarly, Dewey E. Olson's (1966) "The Information Profile" describes an in-house technical information newsletter at an International Business Machines research facility that was designed to keep engineers abreast of new developments in their fields. He also suggests ways of adapting this newsletter to other companies.

Other articles that provide practical examples of the technical communication function of the newsletter include J. H. Smyth's (1965) "The Research and Development Newsletter" and Hyman Olken's (1972) "The Internal Technical Newsletter—Versatile Communication Tool." Smyth explains the Budd Company's *R/D Newsletter,* which was created to inform company management about the developments of research units. Special attention is focused on the news-gathering role of the editor as well as the need to balance editorial content from issue to issue to maintain reader interest. Olken's article describes the monthly in-house technical newsletter that evolved in the Electronics Engineering Department of Lawrence Livermore Laboratory. The editor found that he could improve the publication's reader interest considerably by highlighting a different department's work each month. Furthermore, he explains how he has turned the newsletter into a recruiting device for the company by sending copies to local college departments of electrical engineering.

Materials and pedagogical aids for teaching the newsletter are extremely limited for the professional communications instructor. One may wish to consult Hudson's (1982) *Publishing Newsletters* for a list of communications publications that periodically feature articles on newsletter writing and design. Public relations textbooks occasionally include mention of the types and objectives of newsletters as does Newsom and Siegfried's (1981) *Writing in Public Relations Practice.* For classroom ideas Paul Ashdown's (1975) "A Newsletter Writing Project in an Industrial and Technical Writing Course" is of interest here. Ashdown briefly suggests a project for technical writing students in which a student researches, writes, and produces a limited circulation newsletter in his or her chosen field. Such an endeavor provides a way for the instructor to give the student "a feeling for the texture and function of technical information [that] can be transmitted to the general communicator while doing justice to the integrity of the technical subject and the informational values of the reporter" (Ashdown, p. 12).

Conclusion

As this survey illustrates, new opportunities in the teaching of professional communication do exist for the instructor who chooses to use annual reports, brochures, or newsletters in the classroom. Perhaps the unique blending of journalism and professional communication inherent in all of these forms has caused many educators to consider them outside their usual pedagogical concerns. Nevertheless, a perusal of the sources cited here clearly demonstrates the importance that such publications might well have in their students' future work environments. A careful reassessment of the proper place for these three types of writing in the communications course syllabus may well be needed.

Bibliography

Annual Reports

"The Annual Report 1978: Thick and Innovative." *Business Week,* 16 April 1979, 114–18.

Barlow, Walter G. "Annual Reports and Annual Report Writing." *STWP Proceedings* 12th Annual International Technical Communication Conference. 20–22 May 1965. New York: Society of Technical Writers and Publishers, 22 May a.m. Section, pp. 1–14.

"The Best Annual Reports." *Institutional Investor,* Sept. 1985, 94–96, 98, 100.

Blotnick, Srully. "Take Your Report and. . . ." *Forbes,* 15 Aug. 1983, 128–29.

Brion, John P. "Getting Ready for Annual Reports." *Financial Executive,* Nov. 1975, 39–41.

Brusaw, Charles T., Gerald J. Alfred, and Walter E. Oliu. *Handbook of Technical Writing.* 2d ed. New York: St. Martin's, 1982.

Cato, Sid. "The Annual Report: Here I Come, World: Report from an AR Watchdog." *Public Relations Quarterly* 30, no. 1 (1985): 17–21.

Chang, Lucia S., Kenneth S. Most, and Carlow W. Brain. "The Utility of Annual Reports: An International Study." *Journal of International Business Studies* 14, no. 1 (1983): 63–84.

Costello, John. "What's Read Most in Annual Reports." *Nation's Business,* Feb. 1976, 6, 8.

Dardenne, Peg. "Emerging Trends in Annual Reports." *Public Relations Journal* 33, no. 9 (1977): 8, 48.

Dever, Scott. Mason Award Winners for 1980: "Annual Reports and the Human Approach." *Personnel Administrator,* July 1980, 63–67.

———. "The Individual Within the Corporation." *Personnel Administrator,* July 1981, 60–63.

Dunk, William P. "28 Trends in Annual Reports." *Public Relations Journal* 36, no. 8 (1980): 10–13.

Dyer, Janet. "Predictable: The Watchword for the 1980 Reports." *Public Relations Journal* 37, no. 8 (1981): 9–10.

Floyd, Elizabeth R. *Preparing the Annual Report.* New York: American Management Association, 1960.

Fowler, James E. "The Many Facets of Association Annual Reports." *Public Relations Journal* 33, no. 9 (1977): 20–22.

Harris, R. B. "1984 Annual Report Awards: The Art of Corporate Communication." *Financial World,* 31 Oct.–13 Nov. 1984, 38–39.

Heath, Robert L., and Greg Phelps. "Annual Reports II: Readability vs. Business Press." *Public Relations Review* 10, no. 2 (1984): 56–62.

Hermann, Jon. "Questioning the Slick but Tiresome Traditions of Annual Report Design." *Industrial Design,* March-April 1981, 40–45.

Hershman, Arlene. "And Now: The 'Gutsy' Annual Report." *Dun's Review,* March 1975, 53–55, 88, 90.

Hershman, Arlene, and G. Bruce Knecht. "The Costly New Look in Annual Reports." *Dun's Review,* June 1981, 62–65.

Johnson, Johnny R., Robert R. Rice, and Roger A. Roemmich. "Pictures that Lie: The Abuse of Graphs in Annual Reports." *Management Accounting* 62, no. 4 (1980): 50–56.

Koestler, Frances A. *Creative Annual Reports.* New York: National Public Relations Council of Health and Welfare Services, 1969.

Levy, Robert. "Televising Annual Reports." *Dun's Review,* Nov. 1981, 105–6.

Lewis, Richard A. *Annual Reports.* Zurich: Graphis Press, 1971.

———. "Tomorrow's Annual Report: Paragon of Communication." *Public Relations Journal* 28, no. 2 (1972): 6, 11–12, 47–51.

Lutz, William D. "Corporate Doublespeak: Making Bad News Look Good." *Business and Society Review* 44 (1983): 20–25.

Means, Thomas L. "Readability: An Evaluative Criterion of Stockholder Reaction to Annual Reports." *Journal of Business Communication* 18, no. 1 (1981): 25–33.

Meyer, Herbert E. "Annual Reports Get an Editor." *Fortune,* 7 May 1979, 210–12, 216, 220, 222.

Moskowitz, Milton. "The 1982 Annual Reports: A Potpourri for the Corporate Watchdog." *Business and Society Review* 46 (1983): 20–25.

Most, Kenneth, and Lucia S. Chang. "How Useful are Annual Reports?" *Journal of Accountancy* 148, no. 3 (1979): 111–13.

Newsom, Doug, and Tom Siegfried. *Writing in Public Relations Practice.* Belmont, Calif.: Wadsworth, 1981.

Northart, Leo J. "What They're Saying About Annual Reports." *Public Relations Journal* 35, no. 8 (1979): 10–15.

Paskowski, Marianne. "Stifling the Yawn: Annual Reports Awaken to New Audiences." *Industrial Marketing,* March 1981, 66–68, 70.

Pearsall, Thomas, and Donald Cunningham. *How to Write for the World of Work.* 3d ed. New York: Holt, Rinehart and Winston, 1985.

"Professional Investors Critical of Annual Reports." *Journal of Accountancy* 159, no. 1 (1985): 28, 32.

Q-Data Corporation. *Q-Master Index.* St. Petersburg, Fla.: Q-Data Corporation. Updated annually.

Rasberry, Robert W. "A Quick and Simple Guide to Understanding Annual Reports." *ABCA Bulletin* 41, no. 2 (1978): 34–36.

Raynolds, Edward O. "Annual Report Update: 1983 Reports Face New Challenges." *Public Relations Journal* 39, no. 11 (1983): 40–41, 44.

Reilly, Robert T. *Public Relations in Action.* Englewood Cliffs, N.J.: Prentice-Hall, 1982.

Rimer, Irving I. "How the Non-Profits Do It." *Public Relations Journal* 31, no. 9 (1975): 24–25.

Rooney, Pamela S., and Eileen B. Evans. "Using Annual Reports to Strengthen Business Communication Students' Understanding of Audience." *ABCA Bulletin* 46, no. 4 (1983): 5–9.

Rosenthal, Herbert C. "Scorecard for 1979 Annual Reports." *Public Relations Journal* 36, no. 8 (1980): 14–16.

Ruch, William V. "The Corporate Annual Report as a Teaching Aid in Business Communication Classes." *ABCA Bulletin* 42, no. 12 (1979): 1–3.

Schutte, William M., and Erwin R. Steinberg. *Communication in Business and Industry.* New York: Holt, Rinehart and Winston, 1983.

S. D. Scott Printing Co., comps. *Speaking Out on Annual Reports: Commentaries by 50 Experts on the Organization and Creation of Annual Reports.* New York: S. D. Scott Printing Co., 1977.

Seital, Fraser P. *The Practice of Public Relations.* Columbus, Ohio: Merrill, 1984.

Smedley, Alfred B. "Is the Annual Report a Corporate Dinosaur?" *Public Relations Journal* 31, no. 9 (1975): 21–23.

Thomas, Edward G. "The Corporate Annual Report: A Basic Resource in the Written Communication Course." *ABCA Bulletin* 41, no. 2 (1978): 29–34.

"Top Reports of 1985." *Institutional Investor,* Sept. 1986, 278–80, 283–84.

Turpin, Elizabeth R. "Annual Reports: A Fertile Field for Imaginative Graphics." In *Proceedings of the 27th International Technical Communication Conference.* Washington, D.C.: Society for Technical Communication, 1980, pp. G33–G35.

Brochures

Bowers, L. R. "Good Technical Bulletins: Their Composition and Distribution." *Journal of Chemical Education* 27 (1950): 565–66.

Chestnut, David J. "Brochures—Four Points of View." In *Proceedings of the 16th International Technical Communication Conference*. Washington, D.C.: Society for Technical Communication, 1969, pp. A29–A43.

"Companies Put New Zip in Old Sales Tool." *Chemical and Engineering News* 38, no. 33, 15 Aug. 1960, 34–36.

Holtz, Herman. *Persuasive Writing*. New York: McGraw-Hill, 1983.

Jones, Gerre. *How to Prepare Professional Design Brochures*. New York: McGraw-Hill, 1976.

Kolin, Philip, and Janeen L. Kolin. *Models for Technical Writing*. New York: St. Martin's, 1985.

Mann, James A., and John B. Ketchum. "Multi-Use: Reshaping Technical Material." *IEEE Transactions on Professional Communication* PC-27, no. 2 (1984): 85–88.

Marcus, Judith H. "The Abstract Art of Brochure Writing." In *Proceedings of the 29th International Technical Communication Conference*. Washington, D.C.: Society for Technical Communication, 1982, pp. W74–W77.

Moffett, John B., Stephen G. Smith, and S. J. De Amicis. "Technical Brochure Preparation." *IEEE Transactions on Professional Communication* PC-28, no. 2 (1985): 17–20.

Nash, Edward L. *Directing Marketing*. New York: McGraw-Hill, 1982.

Newsom, Doug, and Tom Siegfried. *Writing in Public Relations Practice*. Belmont, Calif.: Wadsworth, 1981.

Swaino, Jean M. "Teaching Illustration Throughout the Technical Writing Course." *The Technical Writing Teacher* 12, no. 1 (1985): 29–31.

Turner, H. L. "The Technical Capability Brochure." In *Proceedings of the 13th International Technical Communication Conference*. Washington, D.C.: Society for Technical Communication, 1966, Paper 71, pp. 1–10.

Whittaker, Della A. "Preparing a Brochure from the Student's Technical Report." In *Proceedings of the 25th International Technical Communication Conference*. Washington, D.C.: Society for Technical Communication, 1978, pp. 385–86.

Newsletters

Ashdown, Paul. "A Newsletter Writing Project in an Industrial and Technical Writing Course." *The Technical Writing Teacher* 2, no. 3 (1975): 12–13.

Arnold, Stephen E. "Newsletters from the Management Side." In *Proceedings of the 26th International Technical Communication Conference*. Washington, D.C.: Society for Technical Communication, 1979, pp. M15–M18.

Beach, Mark. *Editing Your Newsletter*. 2d ed. Portland, Oreg.: Coast to Coast Books, 1982.

Holtz, Herman. *Persuasive Writing*. New York: McGraw-Hill, 1983.

Hudson, Howard P. *Publishing Newsletters.* New York: Charles Scribner's Sons, 1982.

Hudson, Howard P., ed. *The Newsletter Yearbook/Directory.* 3d ed. Rhinebeck, N.Y.: The Newsletter Clearinghouse, 1981.

Newcomb, Robert, and Marg Simmons. *Developing Effective Supervisory Newsletters: A Guide to Better Communication.* New York: American Management Association, 1956.

Newsom, Doug, and Tom Siegfried. *Writing in Public Relations Practice.* Belmont, Calif.: Wadsworth, 1981.

Olken, Hyman. "The Internal Technical Newsletter—Versatile Communication Tool." *Technical Communication* 19, no. 4 (1972): 14–16.

Olson, Dewey E. "The Information Profile." *STWP Review* 13, no. 3 (1966): 6–8.

Potvin, Janet H. "Eight Steps to Better Newsletters." *IEEE Transactions on Professional Communication* PC-25, no. 4 (1982): 204–10.

Puder, W. H. "Publishing the Weekly Technical News Bulletin." *STWP Review* 8, no. 2 (1961): 24–27.

Smyth, J. H. "The Research and Development Newsletter." *STWP Review* 12, no. 3 (1965): 2–4.

Wales, LaRae. *A Practical Guide to Newsletter Design and Editing.* Ames, Iowa: Iowa State University Press, 1975.

11 Instructions, Procedures, and Style Manuals

Sherry G. Southard
East Carolina University

Instructions and Procedures

What are instructions? Obviously, they are how-to-do-something information—instructions, procedures, directions, training manuals, operator manuals, service manuals, specifications, and instructions for assembling products. Even with all of these "how-to" documents, the question seems fairly simple until one begins to think about warranties, policy manuals, company or school handbooks, insurance policies, leases, loans, cookbooks, and the endless number of forms that must be completed. All of these documents are instructions or contain instructions. For some of the documents such as income tax forms, though, their primary purpose is to obtain information, not to convey instructions. However, if the instructions in a document are not clear, even though they serve a secondary function, the document will not be a means of obtaining the information sought. Because instructions have become an integral part of our lives, knowing how to write them is important both for teachers of technical communication and for those involved in business, technical, and scientific writing.

Beginning with the first technical communication textbooks written in the early 1920s, most have included a section about the writing of instructions. Although *Technical Manual Writing and Administration,* a book-length work about writing military manuals by Thomas Walton (1968), was written in 1968, it is only since the early 1980s that there have been other books of note entirely about the writing of instructions. Along with these books has come an increase in the number of articles on the subject. Also, since the early 1980s, as would be expected with the impact of computers on our lives, many of the books and articles about the writing of instructions deal with writing for the field of computer science.

Articles about the writing of instructions have normally been short and based on personal experience; few present the results of empirical research or refer to other related research. This situation has been changing. For example, in September 1978, the American Institutes for Research began the Document Design Project (DDP), a project to enable writers to produce public documents whose prose and design are clear and simple. All publications produced as a part of the DDP are based on theoretical and applied research, and they contain information valuable to those writing instructions; however, they are not readily accessible and are not specifically about instructions.

In addition to presenting the results of their own empirical research, people involved in the writing of instructions are applying the relevant research from other fields such as linguistics, applied psychology, graphics, instructional design, and art and design. In addition to books in these fields such as *Designing Instructional Text* by James Hartley (1985), *Designing Usable Texts* edited by Thomas M. Duffy and Robert Waller (1985), and *Typographic Design: Form and Communication* by Rob Carter et al. (1985), those who write instructions should read journals such as *Journal of Applied Psychology, Journal of Educational Psychology, Human Factors, Information Design Journal, Ergonomics,* and *Applied Ergonomics*. A word of warning—technical communicators must be careful how they use the theory and research contained in these books and journals. In "A Reader's View of Text and Graphics: Implications for Transactional Text," Philip Rubens (1986, p. 74), cautions readers about how they use the theory and research he presents concerning graphics, a relatively new field: "do not rely too heavily on the discussion of studies throughout this essay as substantive evidence for mandating certain graphic techniques. Instead, read widely, talk to colleagues in other departments, and seek out practitioners as well as researchers." Technical communicators should also apply his advice to the use of research from other fields and the writing of instructions; they should not generalize blindly. And, more importantly, they should verify the research from other fields by conducting their own research using instructions. Even then, they should not assume that the results of research on instructions to assemble a product will be the same as those to repair the product or the results for instructions found in an operator manual the same as for those in a standards and procedures manual.

In this chapter, I have not indicated sections contained in technical writing textbooks. Normally, I exclude information about the writing of instructions for the field of computer science (see "Computer Documentation" by Charles H. Sides, in this volume); however, because so much of what is written about computer documentation, especially in regard to visual format, is applicable to the writing of instructions for other areas, I sometimes refer to such information. Like it or not, anyone wanting to be up-to-date about the writing of instructions, no matter what the subject area, must read works about writing for computers.

In this bibliographical essay, I first cover sources about methodology. Following that section, I discuss general works focusing on the writing of instructions, both articles and the book-length works that I have arbitrarily excluded from the category of textbooks. Included in this section on general works are those on the writing of standards and procedures and the writing of specifications—two important types of how-to discourse. I then briefly survey sources providing information about audience analysis and style as related to the writing of instructions. After those sections, I cover works about formatting instructions—a matter particularly crucial if technical communicators are to write effective instructions. Finally, I conclude with information about style manuals, which contain instructions especially important to those in technical communication.

Methodology

Although there have been many works of methodology about teaching technical and scientific writing, little has been written specifically about how to teach students or those in the corporate world to write instructions. In "Teaching the Writing of Instructions," Donald H. Cunningham and John H. Mitchell (1981) provide three assignments, but more importantly, they discuss the strategies involved as students write to an identifiable audience, master a format related to on-the-job writing, and use appropriate graphics. Even though they are referring primarily to the formatting of the prose, their view that "the directions section is perhaps best discussed prescriptively as a problem of layout" (Cunningham and Mitchell 1981, p. 141) is similar to current ideas about the importance of the physical appearance of instructions, including both the prose and nonprose elements. Mary M. Lay (1982), in "Procedures, Instructions, and Specifications: A Challenge in Audience Analysis," suggests assignments for each of the three communications tasks. Another article dealing with methodology is William Coggin's (1980) "A Hands-On Project for Teaching Instructions."

Several authors discuss how to teach students to write a process description and, in doing so, point out differences between a process description and instructions—a difference not always clear to students:

G. Ronald Dobler (1977) in "Teaching the Process Theme to Freshman Technical Writing Students Through Field Experiences," Roger E. Masse and Patrick M. Kelly (1979) in "The Process of Teaching Description of a Process," and Marion K. Smith (1979) in "Teaching Process Description: Reporting and Directing."

At this point in the development of technical and scientific writing as an academic discipline, I believe that learning to write instructions more effectively is a matter of becoming aware of the information contained in the literature and then applying that knowledge. Teachers of technical communication should themselves become knowledgeable so that they can convey that knowledge to their students. In addition, they should have students complete some basic assignments about the writing of instructions, assignments similar to those suggested by the authors just mentioned. Using case studies based on typical instructions, students should analyze and revise instructions; they should also find people or companies that need instructions written and then write them as part of their classroom work. Although Elizabeth Tebeaux (1985), in "Redesigning Professional Writing Courses to Meet the Communication Needs of Writers in Business and Industry," discusses the changes needed in basic professional writing courses, the changes she suggests are applicable to courses in which students learn to write instructions. See also Paul V. Anderson's (1985) "What Survey Research Tells Us About Writing at Work," in which he explores what survey research has disclosed about the writing people do on the job.

General Works

A good way to begin to learn about instructions is to consult appropriate entries in two handbooks: *Handbook of Technical Writing Practices* edited by Stello Jordan (1971) and *Handbook of Technical Writing* by Charles T. Brusaw et al. (1982). Then one can proceed to general works about the writing of instructions.

Elizabeth Harris (1983), in "A Theoretical Perspective on 'How To' Discourse," presents a theoretical overview of instructions based on semiotically based discourse theory, focusing on the discourse level (the actual) rather than the linguistic level (the potential) because how-to writing involves the ways language is actually used in real situations. Defining how-to discourse as "whole pieces of writing that exist to instruct their readers in the performance of some physical or intellectual task," Harris (1983, p. 139) attempts to answer the question, "what is it exactly?" She examines how-to writing from three main perspectives—discourse semantics, discourse syntactics, and discourse pragmatics.

Harris views how-to discourse as different from referential discourse. However, because of its focus on the reader's activity, it does not qualify as persuasive discourse either. Therefore, she labels it "a special kind of persuasion, used primarily to effect readers' performances of tasks" (Harris 1983, p. 154). One might ask why how-to discourse has to be categorized as either referential or persuasive discourse. Why not consider it how-to discourse?

In "Revising Functional Documents: The Scenario Principle," Linda Flower et al. (1983) discuss the results of empirical research designed to investigate what readers need to be able to understand functional documents, which include regulations, contracts, manuals, and procedures—all documents that people read to do something. By using reading-aloud protocols (tape-recorded transcripts) in their first study, they discovered that instead of paraphrasing the information in the regulation, readers created scenarios. Thus, "functional prose should be structured around a *human agent* performing *actions* in a particularized *situation*" (Flower et al. 1983, p. 42). The results of this study also suggested that writers should structure text according to the specific answers for which readers are searching. In a second study, they discovered that expert writers do use the scenario principle to meet their readers' needs; these writers provide human focus in their sentences and in their headings. Using the results of their research, Flower et al. (1983) provide specific guidelines that enable revisers to apply the scenario principle to functional documents.

According to Janice C. Redish et al. (1985) in "Making Information Accessible to Readers," to make a document as useful as possible, writers must write reader-centered documents and focus on the documents as a whole—on their organization, not on their words and sentences. As they discuss how to organize, write, and design documents so that readers can find information readily, they normally explain in terms of instructions. First, they illustrate what makes information inaccessible, and then after discussing how to analyze audience, purpose, and content, they present eight specific techniques for making information accessible. Finally, they indicate why many documents still have inaccessible information, suggest what teachers can do, and outline needed research.

In "Four Principles for Designing Instructions," Patricia Baggett (1983) presents principles for designing multimedia instructions, those combining visual and verbal material with actual practice. These principles were primarily derived from and tested on assembly tasks; other researchers are urged to investigate the possibilities of generalizing them to other types of tasks. Throughout, she describes the empirical experiments on which she bases the principles. In "Behavioral Research and the Technical Communicator," Patricia Wright (1978) relates the results of some human behavioral experiments to the problems of the technical writer. Her research deals with verbal explanations, numerical tables, and instructions for operating appliances. See also "Analyze the 'What' Before You Write the 'How to' " by Forrest G. Allen (1974).

In addition to these articles, three general book-length works about the writing of instructions are *Writing and Designing Operator Manuals* by Gretchen H. Schoff and Patricia A. Robinson (1984), *Creating Technical Manuals: A Step-by-Step Approach to Writing User-Friendly Instructions* by Gerald Cohen and Donald H. Cunningham (1984), and *An Introduction to Technical Publishing* by Anthony H. Firman (1983). Even though these books are written to technical experts and writers and editors, rather than to technical communication teachers, the authors present information that people teaching students how to write effective instructions must have. The books themselves are how-to books about how to write instructions. All of the authors organize their information according to the process involved; sometimes they include tips for those supervising the process or cover aspects of production such as choosing bindings, paper, and ink.

As the title suggests, *Writing and Designing Operator Manuals* by Schoff and Robinson (1984) contains information about the writing of instructions for operators of products. Information about the major steps in writing such a manual is organized according to those steps: planning; analyzing the user; choosing organizational and writing strategies; coordinating format, references, and mechanics; and creating visuals. They do cover matters related to the printing of the manual, but only briefly. However, in the first and last chapters of the book, they discuss management techniques that will help supervisors in directing the process of producing a manual. In addition, they provide information about what they call special topics: safety messages, service manuals, manuals for international markets, and manual production.

Their information about writing safety messages and writing manuals for international markets is reliable and one of the few readily available sources of such important information. A crucial factor in the financial success of a company may be the effectiveness of its safety warnings— whether they are well written or designed well. As a result of product liability law, manufacturers must warn product users against any hazards; if manufacturers fail to do so in the instructions for the product, they can lose product liability suits. (For additional information about writing cautions and warnings, see "Safety Labels: What to Put in Them, How to Write Them, and Where to Place Them" by Chris

Velotta [1987].) Companies that want to sell their products outside the United States must provide manuals for the products written in the appropriate native language. Their success in the international market may depend largely on whether their translated manuals are usable.

At first, one might suspect that *Creating Technical Manuals: A Step-by-Step Approach to Writing User-Friendly Instructions* by Cohen and Cunningham (1984) is just about the writing of instructions for the field of computer science—the title contains the phrase "user-friendly" and, for those not familiar with the name Gerald Cohen, the back cover announces that he has worked for over twenty years for a nationally known company that produces computers. Although their last chapter is about writing for the world of computers, Cohen and Cunningham provide information about writing instructions for any commercial product (assembling, shipping, installing, operating, or repairing the product) or about performing any procedure. They have written their book for people with little or no experience in writing manuals (whether they are primarily writers and editors or technical experts) as well as for writers who are both technically trained and experienced in writing manuals (people they designate as rare exceptions, however).

The book might be termed a generic manual about writing manuals. Providing plan sheets that help writers create manuals from scratch, Cohen and Cunningham show readers how to collect the necessary information, how to select and organize key data from that information, and how to structure the information for the intended audience. They present these plan sheets because of the difficulties writers encounter when facing blank sheets of paper or empty video display screens, but they urge writers to remember the principles of effective communication behind those plan sheets so that they can write manuals using plain English and effective graphics. The major sections of the book concern developing a procedure that works, explaining what the product or procedure is, explaining how to use the product or procedure, explaining how to fix the product, mapping the manual, and writing for the world of computers. They do not include information for management or for those involved with the printing of the manual.

Although the title is *An Introduction to Technical Publishing,* Firman's (1983) focus is technical manuals. He covers the entire process of preparing a manual from the first planning involved until the manual reaches the user (planning, creation, production, and reproduction—all of which involve management). The book, however, is an introduction and is not meant to be exhaustive in any area; in fact, some sections are quite short (for example, his discussion of analyzing the audience is only one page). Appendix A, "An Introduction to Psycholinguistics," contains rules related to the prose to help writers create manuals that are easy to read, understand, and remember. Appendix B, "An Introduction to Psychographics," covers rules for creating illustrations that are easy to understand and remember—rules that supplement those of good design. In both appendices, Firman presents commentary and an example for each rule.

Examples and descriptions of three types of how-to communications are presented by Lay (1982) in "Procedures, Instructions, and Specifications: A Challenge in Audience Analysis." Little has been published about the writing of standards and procedures, that is, the policies and standards established by organizations and the procedures for implementing those standards. In "Using Systems Analysis Techniques in the Development of Standards and Procedures," Joann T. Hackos (1985) discusses the reasons for and current problems in writing procedures, presents two case studies, and recommends some guidelines for procedures writers. Although in "Making Information Accessible to Readers," Redish et al. (1985) deal with all types of instructions, their discussion sometimes refers specifically to procedural manuals. Three other articles that provide a start for those writing procedures are "Developing a Policy Manual" by Terry W. Smith (1982), "Procedure Writing and Corporate Management: Thinking, Writing, and Speaking for Internal Coordination," by Jamie Vink (1983), and "The Procedure Writer as a Catalyst for Implementing Change" by Leo R. Lunine (1976).

In "A History of Specifications: Technical Writing in Perspective," Tim Whalen (1985) explains this special type of instructions by discussing their history; in "Clarifying Specifications," Whalen (1982) reduces the development of specifications to manageable, step-by-step units. "Status of Technical Manual Specifications and Standards" appears in each issue of *Technical Communication;* in addition, the Society for Technical Communication has published a *List of Specifications and Standards Pertaining to Technical Publications* (Kleinman 1983). See also "Effective Specification Writing" by Martin Freir (1975) and "Writing for the Government" by Robert S. Kellner (1985).

Audience Analysis

The authors of the books discussed in the preceding section present information about analyzing the users for instructions, although only Schoff and Robinson (1984) cover the subject in detail (nineteen pages). They provide a checklist of questions pertaining to the personal characteristics of the user, the conditions under which the audience will be using the manual, and the information desired by the user. Their discussion of how to obtain user feedback covers both theory and application, with the examples provided making the theory easy to understand.

In "Procedures, Instructions, and Specifications: A Challenge in Audience Analysis," Lay (1982) describes the audiences for these three documents; for each type, the audience must participate in an operation, but the specific purpose and, therefore, audience for each is unique. Analyzing audience, purpose, and content is the subject of one section in "Making Information Accessible to Readers," by Redish et al. (1985).

In *Audience Analysis and Response* (1983), Patricia Caernarven-Smith presents audience analysis techniques particularly suitable for those writing instructions. She provides a lengthy checklist of questions to be asked about audiences (once on pp. 65–67 and again on pp. 174–76) and discusses these questions in detail with examples. The chapter "Responses Based on Human Learning and Understanding" is valuable because, as she indicates, writers can respond to their users only if those writers know how people take in, process, and use information.

Prose Style

As I indicated earlier, most technical writing textbooks contain sections or chapters about the writing of instructions, usually short and usually with emphasis on writing the prose part of instructions. Some of the standard do's including using chronological order, putting one instruction in a sentence, writing short sentences, keeping syntax parallel, using consistent terminology, retaining definite and indefinite articles, listing conditions separately, using second person imperative, placing the verb first, separating instructions from informational material, using present tense, and using active voice. Some of the standard do not's include avoiding nominalizations, noun strings, wordiness, difficult words, abstract words, and several negatives.

Daniel Felker et al. (1981), in "Principles for Organizing Text" and "Principles for Writing Sentences," provide useful information for anyone writing instructions, although the authors assume that most readers will be professionals in business, government, law, medicine, or related fields who write or supervise the production of public documents (such as product warranties, insurance policies, loan agreements, government rules and regulations, and income tax instructions and forms). They base all recommendations on empirical research and provide bibliographies; a description of each guideline is followed by the sections "explanation and illustration," "other related principles," "qualifications," and "what the research says." The book is an excellent demonstration of what the authors advocate. In "Revising Functional Documents: The Scenario Principle," Flower et al. (1983), provide specific guidelines that enable revisers to apply the scenario principle (a principle they derive from empirical research) to prose in functional documents.

Of the three books discussed earlier in the section "General Works," only *An Introduction to Technical Publishing* (Firman 1983) contains a separate section about good prose style for instructions: "An Introduction to Psycholinguistics" (pp. 125–32). However, throughout *Creating Technical Manuals: A Step-by-Step Approach to Writing User-Friendly Instructions,* Cohen and Cunningham (1984) stress the fact that manuals should be written in plain English. According to them, most manuals are written in technical manual English, "a language found only in written form and only in technical or instructional literature" (Cohen and Cunningham 1984, p. 20) and a language with too much passive voice and too many abstract words, especially words naming products and procedures. Schoff and Robinson provide little information about writing prose for instructions. They suggest using parallel structure, active voice, and the appropriate language level which involves the correct amount of technical terminology and the correct tone.

Jan Robbins (1983, pp. 146–56) provides guidelines applicable to writing the prose in instructions when she summarizes the research on psycholinguistics: "Psycholinguistics." In *Style: Ten Lessons in Clarity and Grace,* Joseph M. Williams (1985) very briefly discusses writing prose for audiences that can understand only the clearest and simplest language possible. The examples he uses make his information understandable, and the examples are often instructions.

In "A History of Specifications: Technical Writing in Perspective," when Tim Whalen (1985, p. 235) mentions the prose in specifications, he points out that for persons not familiar with that type of how-to discourse, "the special emphasis given to the formal structure of the language is puzzling, even perplexing." Specification language consists of "a codified set of agreed-on passages from preceding legal codes which have been passed along into our own" (Whalen 1985, p. 236), and modifications in the language occur only in the passages dealing with emerging technology.

Formatting

Visual format has become extremely important for all types of technical communication because people have become accustomed to learning visually. However, the physical appearance of both the prose and illustrations is especially crucial in the writing of instructions. People read these documents in order to do something; whether they can complete a task or not and how easily and quickly they can complete the task frequently depends on the formatting. In addition, instructions contain crucial information not contained in other technical communications—cautions and/or warnings and troubleshooting charts. Writers can use format to emphasize this information so that their readers do not overlook it.

Format is sometimes defined very narrowly to mean the organization of a document, such as "Assembling Your Stereo," "Using Your Stereo," and "Caring For Your Stereo." Most broadly defined, format refers to any aspect related to the physical appearance of a document. It involves, among other matters, the typography and physical arrangement of the words of a document, the visual appearance of the illustrations, and the layout and design of both the words and illustrations.

There has been some research concerning format, but most of it has dealt with technical documents in general, rather than instructions specifically. Also, current research about format often applies to writing for the field of computer science. Furthermore, particularly for matters concerning format, technical communicators need to draw much more than they have on research in other related subjects such as reading, cognitive psychology, instructional design, graphics, and art and design.

Researchers have tried different methods of displaying text. Robert Horn (1976) in *How to Write Information Mapping* shows writers how to make content and structure clearer to readers by using "information mapping," a technique for organizing and spacing text. Technical communicators have adapted his technique in various ways in the writing of instructions.

"Research in Technical Communication" (1985), a special issue of *Technical Communication,* contains several articles providing information related to the formatting of instructions. Printed documents are the subject of Philippa J. Benson's "Writing Visually: Design Considerations in Technical Publications," while on-line displays are the concern of Philip Rubens and Robert Krull in "Application of Research on Document Design to Online Displays." However, the guidelines suggested by Rubens and Krull have implications for printed documents. According to Benson (1985, p. 35), the roles of writers and designers are merging, as they should be, because "the results of usability tests of documents are providing concrete evidence that readers find documents most usable when the visual aspects of a document support the hierarchy of the information in a text." The information in her article is particularly suitable for novices to the field of document design, but experienced writers and designers can also benefit. Her reference list provides sources of research in fields related to technical communication.

In "The Changing Image of Technical Communication," a special section in *Technical Communication* edited by Roger Grice (1984), several employees describe the dramatic revolution technical communication is undergoing at IBM's Data Systems Division laboratory in Kingston, N.Y.—"a revolution in the way [they] convey information and the forms that the information is taking" (Grice 1984, p. 4). Although the information is directed toward writing for computers, some of it applies to the writing of any instructions.

All three of the books discussed earlier (*Writing and Designing Operator Manuals* [Schoff and Robinson 1984], *Creating Technical Manuals* [Cohen and Cunningham 1984], and *An Introduction to Technical Publishing* [Firman 1983]) contain information about format. Also, research about formatting as well as visuals is presented by Walter Moody and the IBM Corporation (1983) in "Psychographics." In addition, several publications from the Document Design Center contain information about format and provide bibliographies: "Typographic Principles" and "Graphic Principles" by Felker et al. (1981), "Human Factors" by Andrew Rose and Lee Gregg (1980), and "Typography/Graphics" by Cheryl Olkes (1980).

Although Philip M. Rubens (1986, p. 73) in "A Reader's View of Text and Graphics: Implications for Transactional Text" discusses the broad category of texts "intended to perform a function," he provides theoretical information relevant to the formatting of instructions. He first surveys the theory and research as applied to creating a "visual grammar" and then considers three significant areas of graphic activities (layout, typography, and illustrations). Throughout, he points out ways his information could be useful for teachers and practitioners. He takes into account relevant research from other fields, which is indicated in his bibliography. Similarly, Thomas E. Pinelli et al. (1986) do not focus on instructions in "A Survey of Typography, Graphic Design, and Physical Media in Technical Reports." However, technical communicators can benefit from their summaries of the experimental and theoretical literature concerning typography (composition method, type style, type size, and margin treatment), graphic design (layout and imposition of material on the page), and physical media (paper, ink, and binding methods). Also their reference list indicates research sources from other related fields.

While some research is suggesting that instructions should consist of almost equal amounts of prose and illustrations, some writers and editors are experimenting with a format that uses a smaller amount of prose or almost no prose at all. A format that indicates visually with a minimum number of words the operating and maintenance procedures for complex weapons systems is described by Benjamin D. Meyer (1986) in "The ABCs of New-Look Publications." The format was developed for new recruits in the military, persons with no technical background or only a semitechnical one. Rather than indicating how a system operates, the manual guides users step-by-step so that they can locate a problem and replace a part or assembly. To make sure that the text and illustrations interact, the manual consists of text/ illustration units or modules similar to storyboard panels used to plan film or videotape productions. These new-look publications, though quite effective for certain users, are expensive.

The reasoning behind functionally oriented maintenance manuals (FOMMs) is similar to that for the new-look publications. FOMMs contain block diagrams that indicate the functional relationship of components in the system, rather than sections on theory of operation and diagrams that indicate the physical location of components. In other words, FOMMs present troubleshooting procedures visually. Information about FOMMs can be found in the following sources: "Functionally Oriented Maintenance Manuals" (1985) and "Improving FOMM Troubleshooting" by Raymond Q. Little and Michael S. Smith (1983).

In "Word-Free Setup Instructions—Stepping into the World of Complex Products," Charles Gange and Amy Lipton (1984) describe the process they used to develop word-free setup instructions for a complex product. Increasingly, instructions are used by readers whose native language is not English. Because word-free instructions are a way of bypassing language problems, they are particularly effective for these users. See also "Technical Manuals—A Visual Vacuum" by Don E. Bissell (1977) and "Cartoons Can Add Punch to Your Technical Manual" by John W. Trimble (1976).

Good but Not Readily Available Sources

Two good sources of information about the writing of instructions are the annual proceedings volume for the International Technical Communication Conference (ITCC), published by the Society for Technical Communication, and materials published by the Document Design Center, including the newsletters *Simply Stated* and *Simply Stated in Business*. Some of these sources, however, are not readily accessible.

Papers in the *ITCC Proceedings* are short (four pages or less) and the quality varies greatly. Beginning in 1982, articles appearing in the *ITCC Proceedings* are included in "ATTW Annual Bibliography." Also entries in the *ITCC Proceedings* from 1968 through 1980 are listed in an *Annotated Bibliography on Technical Writing, Editing, Graphics, and Publishing 1966-1980* (Carson et al. 1983). Information about acquiring copies of papers in the *ITCC Proceedings* can be obtained from Interlibrary Loan (Edmond Low Library, Oklahoma State University, Stillwater, Okla. 74078). Edmond Low Library is the archive for documents published by STC. Currently, the library has copies of the following proceedings: 14th (1967) to 19th (1972), 23rd (1976), 25th (1978), and 27th (1980, volume 2) to the present. In addition, some of the papers in the *ITCC Proceedings* can be obtained through the ERIC Document Reproduction Services.

Materials published by the Document Design Center contain both theoretical and practical information that is well written, well researched, and current. *Simply Stated,* a monthly newsletter distributed to almost 14,000, first appeared as *Fine Print* in November 1979 with a distribution of 400, and the bimonthly *Simply Stated in Business* began in August 1983. Beginning in 1983, entries in *Simply Stated* are included in "ATTW Annual Bibliography." Though the articles in these two newsletters are quite short, usually under 1,000 words, reading them is an excellent way of staying current with theoretical research related to the writing of instructions (and other types of documents) and, especially, of obtaining practical information from people in the corporate world.

For example, "Illustrations for Procedural Instructions" (1982) presents the results of research of Cornell University on how people use instructions to assemble an object from specific parts. In one study, subjects used various combinations of prose text and line drawings; in a later study, the cognitive styles preferred by the subjects were matched with different formats. In contrast to such theoretical articles, practical information about the writing of instructions appears in a series of articles in *Simply Stated in Business* concerning plain English projects that companies have developed. One article in the series (January 1984) contains information about Westinghouse's handbook about product safety labels—a handbook to help their engineers and product designers write cautions and warnings. Another article (May-June 1985) summarizes revisions that Zenith made in the operating guides for their color televisions.

In the February 1986 issue, *Simply Stated* began a new feature called "Research Note," which presents the results of experimental research that dispels myths. For example, although most people believe that it is as easy to read from a computer screen as from paper, it is not. David A. Schnell (February 1986) summarizes the research and then indicates several ways to present information on a computer screen so that it is easier to read. The information given concerns the field of computers, but, again, as in many cases, some of the findings are relevant to other subject areas.

Other recommended Document Design Center publications related to the writing of instructions include Andrew M. Rose and Louis A. Cox's (1980) *Following Instructions,* V. Melissa Holland and Andrew M. Rose's (1980) *Understanding Instructions with Complex Conditions,* Andrew Rose and Lee Gregg's (1980) "Human Factors," Cheryl Olkes's (1980) "Typography/Graphics," Holland and Andrew Rose's (1981) *A Comparison of Prose and Algorithms for Presenting Complex Instructions,* and Daniel B. Felker et al.'s (1981) *Guidelines for Document Designers.* A few of these were described earlier in the sections on prose style and formatting.

Persons interested in being placed on the mailing list for the newsletters should contact the Document Design Center (American Institutes for Research, 1055 Thomas Jefferson Street, N.W., Washington, D.C. 20007). Many issues of *Simply Stated* and *Simply Stated in Business* are in Edmond Low Library; information on acquiring copies of articles can be obtained from Interlibrary Loan. Some of the other Document Design publications can be purchased from the Document Design Center, while others are available through the ERIC Document Reproduction Service.

Style Manuals

Style manuals present a specialized type of instructions—instructions telling authors how to prepare manuscripts for publication. Style manuals or authors' guides cover editorial style and format as opposed to prose style. An area that seems to be of great concern to everyone is the proper way to document: the procedures used within the text and the format used for reference lists. Also of concern are matters such as what size margins should be and whether to double-space; in addition, guidelines related to usage and grammar are normally included in style manuals. Examples of style manuals include *The Chicago Manual of Style* (University of Chicago Press 1982), *Words Into Type* (Skillin et al. 1974), and *U.S. Government Printing Office Style Manual* (GPO 1973).

Teachers of technical communication should clearly understand which works are properly called style manuals. In spite of their name, style manuals do not cover extensively the stylistics involved in writing the prose of a manuscript. They are not works that are primarily about grammar and usage or about how to improve one's writing. Joseph M. Williams's (1985) *Style: Ten Lessons in Clarity and Grace* and Robert A. Day's (1983) *How to Write and Publish a Scientific Paper* are not style manuals because the first one provides guidelines mainly about what constitutes good and bad prose style and the second covers the prose style, organization, and content appropriate for papers in certain subject areas. The primary purpose of these authors is not to provide information about editorial style and format. Although the list is short, a current list of books about improving written English appears in *The MLA Style Manual* by Walter S. Achtert and Joseph Gibaldi (1985, pp. 3–4).

In this section about style manuals, I discuss their evolution and content, general works about them, and the selection of a style manual.

Evolution and Content

In "A Review of Style Guides," Dorothy D. Jones (1973) provides historical background about style guides as well as factors influencing their development, information that is included, and ways to improve format. Her title is slightly misleading because she never reviews specific style guides as her title suggests and as she admits she originally intended to do. Nonetheless, she enables one to understand what style guides are and how they have evolved.

In the introduction of *Style Manuals of the English-Speaking World: A Guide,* John B. Howell (1983) discusses the evolution of contemporary style manuals from guides issued by German printers in 1608, 1653, and 1673 and the first printer's manual in English, Joseph Moxon's (1683) *Mechanik Exercises.* He also comments on what he believes is a move to "the standardization of bibliographic entries at the international level" (Howell 1983, p. xiii) and predicts that many organizations will adopt *American National Standard for Bibliographic References* or the international version, *Uniform Requirements for Manuscripts Submitted to Biomedical Journals,* as their guide.

A useful text about preparing a style guide is Rudy Domitrovic's (1977) *How to Prepare a Style Guide.* Although the contents of style guides vary greatly, most cover three areas: language or text treatment, graphic arts, and formats and specifications. According to Domitrovic, if the guide is oriented toward writers and editors, it may cover only the first area, including subsections about editing, rhetoric, spelling, punctuation, compounding, capitalization, abbreviations, numerals, signs and symbols, references, tables, and figures.

General Works

In *Style Manuals of the English-Speaking World: A Guide,* Howell (1983) annotates (1) general manuals for commercial publishers, government printing, term papers and theses, and university presses and (2) subject manuals for twenty-five areas, such as agriculture, chemistry, newspapers and news magazines, and mathematics. For each of these subject areas, he groups entries according to whether they contain general guidelines about preparing manuscripts (general style) or guidelines used by a specific journal (journal style). Finally, in two appendices, he annotates style manuals for the subject areas of disabled people and nonsexist language; these guides indicate ways writers can avoid stereotyping handicapped persons and females, particularly the stereotyping that occurs because of the language used. For each style manual, including those in the appendices, Howell gives a bibliographical citation, describes the contents, and explains the bibliographical style used. Sometimes he evaluates the manual.

Howell's book is limited to manuals written in English; however, for anyone who is interested, he references a multilingual bibliography of style manuals which "lists 359 entries in English, French, Russian, Spanish, German, Bulgarian, Danish, Polish, and Czech" (Howell 1983, p. vii): *Bibliography of Publications Designed to Raise the Standard of Scientific Literature* (United Nations Educational, Scientific, and Cultural Organization 1963).

Gerald J. Alred et al. in *Business and Technical Writing: An Annotated Bibliography of Books, 1880-1980* (1981, pp. 197-200) list style guides that are very limited in their publication: (1) industry and society style guides and (2) government and military style guides. Although these style guides are unavailable through standard means, they can be traced using the information provided.

Caroline R. Goforth's (1985) "A Selection of Style Manuals" provides useful information, but she does not focus on style manuals. Throughout the chapter, she intermingles information about works that are style manuals with information about ones that cover grammar, usage, prose style (writing better), organization and content, and some combination.

Selection of a Style Manual

Teachers of technical communication should explain to their students how to determine what style guide to follow. Of course, while students are in school, they will follow the guidelines issued by each of their teachers—often guidelines that pertain only to what size the margins should be, whether to double-space, and how to document. Technical communication teachers should have students follow the style manuals used in the students' majors; for example, biology students should use the latest edition of *CBE Style Manual: A Guide for Authors, Editors, and Publishers in the Biological Sciences* (CBE 1983).

After students graduate, they will follow the style guide prepared by their employer or by the journal or publishing house to which they are submitting their manuscripts. Persons working for employers outside of the academic environment may follow a style guide developed specifically for their situation: for example, those working for Bell Laboratories, Langley Research Center in Hampton, Va., and NCR Corporation. Such style guides may be complete enough to be used alone or may be used with another style manual or with more than one other style manual. In other cases, persons in the corporate world rely solely on style manuals other than their own. Some journals provide guidelines for authors, usually published yearly in one of the issues; others refer authors to a specific style manual. Likewise, publishing houses may have their own style manuals or may refer authors to a specific manual.

Those teaching technical communication should have students use the latest editions appropriate for their fields. Below I indicate some style manuals of which teachers should be aware.

- *American National Standard Guidelines for Format and Production of Scientific and Technical Reports* (ANSI 1974)
- *An ASME Paper* (ASME 1982)
- *CBE Style Manual: A Guide for Authors, Editors, and Publishers in the Biological Sciences* (CBE 1983)
- *The Chicago Manual of Style* (University of Chicago Press 1982)

- *Handbook and Style Manual for ASA, CSSA, and SSSA Publications* (ASA, CSSA, and SSSA 1977)
- *Handbook for Authors of Papers in American Chemical Society Publications* (ACS 1978)
- *Manual for Authors and Editors: Editorial Style and Manuscript Preparation* (AMA 1981)
- *A Manual for Authors of Mathematical Papers* (AMS 1980)
- *The MLA Style Manual* (Achtert and Gibaldi 1985)
- *Publication Manual of the American Psychological Association* (APA 1983)
- *Style Manual for Guidance in the Preparation of Papers* (AIP 1978)
- *Suggestions to Authors of the Reports of the U.S. Geological Survey* (U.S. Geological Survey 1978)
- *U.S. Government Printing Office Style Manual* (GPO 1973)
- *Words Into Type* (Skillin et al. 1974)

Although *The MLA Style Manual* (Achtert and Gibaldi 1985) has been used primarily by those in English and other liberal arts fields, I have included it because so many teachers of business, technical, and scientific writing are housed in English departments, and, more importantly, because the revised documentation system included in the 1985 edition is now similar to that often used in business, technical, and scientific fields.

Bibliography

Instructions and Procedures

Allen, Forrest G. "Analyze the 'What' Before You Write the 'How to.'" *Industrial Education* 63 (1974): 34–36. (Reprinted in *The Practical Craft: Readings for Business and Technical Writers,* edited by W. Keats Sparrow and Donald H. Cunningham. Boston: Houghton, 1978, pp. 201–7.)

Anderson, Paul V. "What Survey Research Tells Us About Writing at Work." In *Writing in Nonacademic Settings,* edited by Lee Odell and Dixie Goswami, New York: Guilford, 1985: 3–83.

Anderson, Paul V., R. John Brockmann, and Carolyn R. Miller, eds. *New Essays in Technical and Scientific Communication: Research, Theory, Practice.* Farmingdale, Mass.: Baywood, 1983.

"ATTW Annual Bibliography." *Technical Writing Teacher.* Appears annually.

Baggett, Patricia. "Four Principles for Designing Instructions." *IEEE Transactions on Professional Communication* PC-26, no. 3 (1983): 99–105.

Benson, Philippa J. "Writing Visually: Design Considerations in Technical Publications." In Pinelli, pp. 35–39.

Bissell, Don E. "Technical Manuals—A Visual Vacuum." *Technical Communication* 24, no. 3 (1977): 9–11.

Brusaw, Charles T., Gerald J. Alred, and Walter E. Oliu. *Handbook of Technical Writing.* 2d ed. New York: St. Martin's, 1982.

Caernarven-Smith, Patricia. *Audience Analysis and Response.* Pembroke: Firman Technical Publications, 1983.

Carson, Helen V., Ruth Hersch Mayo, Theresa A. Philler, and Douglas J. Schmidt, comps. *Annotated Bibliography on Technical Writing, Editing, Graphics, and Publishing 1966–1980.* Washington, D.C.: Society for Technical Communication, 1983.

Carter, Rob, Ben Day, and Philip Meggs. *Typographic Design: Form and Communication.* New York: Reinhold, 1985.

Coggin, William. "A Hands-On Project for Teaching Instructions." *Technical Writing Teacher* 8, no. 1 (1980): 7–9.

Cohen, Gerald, and Donald H. Cunningham. *Creating Technical Manuals: A Step-by-Step Approach to Writing User-Friendly Instructions.* New York: McGraw-Hill, 1984.

Cunningham, Donald H., and John H. Mitchell. In "Teaching the Writing of Instructions." In Stevenson, pp. 136–43.

Dobler, G. Ronald. "Teaching the Process Theme to Freshman Technical Writing Students Through Field Experiences." *Technical Writing Teacher* 5, no. 1 (1977): 22–25.

Duffy, Thomas M., and Robert Waller, eds. *Designing Usable Texts.* Orlando, Fla.: Academic, 1985.

Felker, Daniel B., ed. *Document Design: A Review of the Relevant Research.* Washington, D.C.: American Institutes for Research, 1980.

Felker, Daniel, Frances Pickering, Veda R. Charrow, V. Melissa Holland, and Janice C. Redish. *Guidelines for Document Designers.* Washington, D.C.: American Institutes for Research, 1981. (This publication contains chapters and bibliographies referred to individually in the text: "Principles for Organizing Text" (pp. 7–24), "Principles for Writing Sentences" (pp. 25–70), "Typographic Principles" (pp. 71–88), "Graphic Principles" (pp. 89–105), and bibliographies for each chapter (pp. 109–17).

Firman, Anthony H. *An Introduction to Technical Publishing.* Pembroke: Firman Technical Publications, 1983.

Flower, Linda, John R. Hayes, and Heidi Swarts. "Revising Functional Documents: The Scenario Principle." In *New Essays in Scientific Communication: Research, Theory, Practice,* edited by P. V. Anderson, J. Brockmann, and C. R. Miller. Farmingdale, Mass.: Baywood, 1983, pp. 41–58.

Freir, Martin. "Effective Specification Writing." *Technical Communication* 22, no. 2 (1975): 14–16.

"Functionally Oriented Maintenance Manuals." Special section. *Technical Communication* 32, no. 3 (1985): 6–13.

Gange, Charles, and Amy Lipton. "Word-Free Setup Instructions—Stepping into the World of Complex Products." In Grice, pp. 17-19.

Grice, Roger, ed. "The Changing Image of Technical Communication." Special section. *Technical Communication* 31, no. 3 (1984): 1-19.

Hackos, Joann T. "Using Systems Analysis Techniques in the Development of Standards and Procedures." *IEEE Transactions on Professional Communication* PC-28, no. 3 (1985): 25-30.

Harris, Elizabeth. "A Theoretical Perspective on 'How To' Discourse." In *New Essays in Scientific Communication: Research, Theory, Practice*, edited by P. V. Anderson, J. Brockmann, and C. R. Miller. Farmingdale, Mass.: Baywood, 1983, pp. 139-55.

Hartley, James. *Designing Instructional Text*. 2d ed. New York: Nichols, 1985.

Holland, V. Melissa, and Andrew M. Rose. *Understanding Instructions with Complex Conditions*. Document Design Project, Technical Report 5. Washington, D.C.: American Institutes for Research, 1980.

———. *A Comparison of Prose and Algorithms for Presenting Complex Instructions*. Document Design Project, Technical Report 17. Washington, D.C.: American Institutes for Research, 1981.

Horn, Robert. *How to Write Information Mapping*. Lexington, Mass.: Information Resources, 1976.

"Illustrations for Procedural Instructions." *Simply Stated,* May 1982, 1, 3-4.

ITCC Proceedings. Annual Proceedings. Washington, D.C.: Society for Technical Communication, 1954.

Jordan, Stello, ed. *Handbook of Technical Writing Practices*. 2 vols. New York: Wiley-Interscience, 1971.

Kellner, Robert S. "Writing for the Government." In *Research in Technical Communication: A Bibliographic Sourcebook,* edited by Michael G. Moran and Debra Journet. Westport, Conn.: Greenwood, 1985, pp. 427-39.

Kleinman, Joseph M., comp. *List of Specifications and Standards Pertaining to Technical Publications*. Washington, D.C.: Society for Technical Communication, 1983.

Lay, Mary M. "Procedures, Instructions, and Specifications: A Challenge in Audience Analysis." *Journal of Technical Writing and Communication* 12, no. 3 (1982): 235-42.

Little, Raymond Q., and Michael S. Smith. "Improving FOMM Troubleshooting." *Technical Communication* 30, no. 1 (1983): 20-24.

Lunine, Leo R. "The Procedure Writer as a Catalyst for Implementing Change." *Technical Communication* 23, no. 4 (1976): 10-11.

Masse, Roger E., and Patrick M. Kelly. "The Process of Teaching Description of a Process." *Technical Writing Teacher* 7, no. 1 (1979): 15-18.

Meyer, Benjamin D. "The ABCs of New-Look Publications." *Technical Communication* 33, no. 1 (1986): 16-20.

Moody, Walter, and the IBM Corporation. "Psychographics." In Caernarven-Smith 1983, pp. 163-67.

Odell, Lee, and Dixie Goswami, eds. *Writing in Nonacademic Settings*. New York: Guilford, 1985.

Olkes, Cheryl. "Typography/Graphics." In *Document Design: A Review of the Relevant Research,* edited by Daniel R. Felker. Washington, D.C.: American Institutes for Research, 1980, pp. 103–10, 163–66.

Pinelli, Thomas E., ed. "Research in Technical Communication." Special issue. *Technical Communication* 32, no. 4 (1985): 1–52.

Pinelli, Thomas E., Virginia M. Cordle, and Robert McCullough. "A Survey of Typography, Graphic Design, and Physical Media in Technical Reports." *Technical Communication* 33, no. 2 (1986): 75–80.

Redish, Janice C., Robbin M. Battison, and Edward S. Gold. "Making Information Accessible to Readers." In *Writing in Nonacademic Settings,* edited by Lee Odell and Dixie Goswami. New York: Guilford, 1985, pp. 129–53.

Robbins, Jan. "Psycholinguistics." In Caernarven-Smith 1983, pp. 146–56.

Rose, Andrew, and Louis A. Cox. *Following Instructions.* Document Design Project, Technical Report 4. Washington, D.C.: American Institutes for Research, 1980.

Rose, Andrew, and Lee Gregg. "Human Factors." In *Document Design: A Review of the Relevant Research,* edited by Daniel R. Felker. Washington, D.C.: American Institutes for Research, 1980, pp. 95–102, 159–61.

Rubens, Philip. "A Reader's View of Text and Graphics: Implications for Transactional Text." *Journal of Technical Writing and Communication* 16, no. 1–2 (1986): 73–86.

Rubens, Philip, and Robert Krull. "Application of Research on Document Design to Online Displays." In Pinelli, pp. 29–34.

Schoff, Gretchen H., and Patricia A. Robinson. *Writing and Designing Operator Manuals.* Belmont, Calif.: Lifetime Learning, 1984.

Simply Stated. Monthly newsletter. Washington, D.C.: American Institutes for Research, July-August 1980. (Journal first appeared as *Fine Print* in Nov. 1979.)

Simply Stated in Business. Bimonthly newsletter. Washington, D.C.: American Institutes for Research, August 1983.

Smith, Marion K. "Teaching Process Description: Reporting and Directing." *Technical Writing Teacher* 6, no. 2 (1979): 43–46.

Smith, Terry W. "Developing a Policy Manual." *Personnel Journal* 61, no. 6 (1982): 446–49.

"Status of Technical Manual Specifications and Standards." Appears in each issue. *Technical Communication.*

Stevenson, Dwight W., ed. *Courses, Components, and Exercises in Technical Communication.* Urbana, Ill.: National Council of Teachers of English, 1981.

Tebeaux, Elizabeth. "Redesigning Professional Writing Courses to Meet the Communication Needs of Writers in Business and Industry." *College Composition and Communication* 36, no. 4 (1985): 419–28.

Trimble, John W. "Cartoons Can Add Punch to Your Technical Manual." *Technical Communication* 23, no. 1 (1976): 10–11.

Valotta, Chris. "Safety Labels: What to Put in Them, How to Write Them, and Where to Place Them." In *Legal and Ethical Issues in Technical*

Communication, edited by Stephen Doheny-Farina. (Special issue of *IEEE Transactions on Professional Communication* PC-30, no. 3 (1987): 121–26.)

Vink, Jamie. "Procedure Writing and Corporate Management: Thinking, Writing, and Speaking for Internal Coordination." *Journal of Technical Writing and Communication* 13, no. 4 (1983): 349–53.

Walton, Thomas. *Technical Manual Writing and Administration.* New York: McGraw-Hill, 1968.

Whalen, Tim. "Clarifying Specifications." *Technical Communication* 29, no. 2 (1982): 8–10.

———. "A History of Specifications: Technical Writing in Perspective." *Journal of Technical Writing and Communication* 15, no. 3 (1985): 235–45.

Williams, Joseph M. "Special Problems." In *Style: Ten Lessons in Clarity & Grace.* 2d ed. Edited by Joseph M. Williams. Glenview, Ill.: Scott, Foresman and Co., 1985, 96–109.

Wright, Patricia. "Behavioral Research and the Technical Communicator." *Technical Communication* 25, no. 2 (1978): 6–12.

Style Manuals

Achtert, Walter S., and Joseph Gibaldi. *The MLA Style Manual.* New York: Modern Language Association, 1985.

Alred, Gerald J., Diana C. Reep, and Mohan R. Limaye, comps. *Business and Technical Writing: An Annotated Bibliography of Books, 1880–1980.* Metuchen, N.J., and London: Scarecrow, 1981.

American Chemical Society (ACS). *Handbook for Authors of Papers in American Chemical Society Publications.* Washington, D.C.: American Chemical Society, 1978.

American Institute of Physics (AIP) Publications Board. *Style Manual for Guidance in the Preparation of Papers.* 3d ed. Edited by David Hathwell and A. W. Kenneth Metzner. New York: American Institute of Physics, 1978.

American Mathematical Society (AMS). *A Manual for Authors of Mathematical Papers.* 7th ed. Providence, R.I.: American Mathematical Society, 1980.

American Medical Association (AMA). *Manual for Authors and Editors: Editorial Style and Manuscript Preparation.* 7th ed. Chicago: American Medical Association, 1981.

American National Standards Institute (ANSI). *American National Standard Guidelines for Format and Production of Scientific and Technical Reports.* New York: American National Standards Institute, 1974.

American Psychological Association (APA). *Publication Manual of the American Psychological Association.* 3d ed. Washington, D.C.: American Psychological Association, 1983.

American Society of Agronomy (ASA). *Handbook and Style Manual for ASA, CSSA, and SSSA Publications.* Rev. ed. Madison, Wis.: American Society of Agronomy, Crop Science Society of America, Soil Science Society of America, 1976.

American Society of Mechanical Engineers (ASME). *An ASME Paper.* New York: American Society of Mechanical Engineers, 1982.

Council of Biology Editors (CBE) Style Manual Committee. *CBE Style Manual: A Guide for Authors, Editors, and Publishers in the Biological Sciences.* 5th ed. Bethesda, Md.: Council of Biology Editors, 1983.

Day, Robert A. *How to Write and Publish a Scientific Paper.* 2d ed. Philadelphia: ISI, 1983.

Domitrovic, Rudy. *How to Prepare a Style Guide.* Washington, D.C.: Society for Technical Communication, 1977.

Goforth, Caroline R. "A Selection of Style Manuals." In *Research in Technical Communication: A Bibliographic Sourcebook,* edited by Michael G. Moran and Debra Journet. Westport, Conn.: Greenwood, 1985, pp. 454–68.

Howell, John B. *Style Manuals of the English-Speaking World: A Guide.* Phoenix: Oryx, 1983.

Jones, Dorothy D. "A Review of Style Guides." *IEEE Transactions on Professional Communication* PC-16, no. 1 (1973): 18–22.

Moxon, Joseph. *Mechanik Exercises.* London: 1683.

Skillin, Marjorie E., and Robert M. Gay. *Words Into Type.* Based on studies by Marjorie E. Skillin, Robert M. Gay, and other authorities. 3d ed. Englewood Cliffs, N.J.: Prentice-Hall, 1974. (Fourth edition by Thomas L. Warren is forthcoming.)

United Nations Educational, Scientific, and Cultural Organization, comp. *Bibliography of Publications Designed to Raise the Standard of Scientific Literature.* Paris: N.p., 1963.

U.S. Geological Survey. *Suggestions to Authors of the Reports of the United States Geological Survey.* 6th ed. Washington, D.C.: U.S. Government Printing Office, 1978.

U.S. Government Printing Office (GPO). *U.S. Government Printing Office Style Manual.* Rev. ed. Washington, D.C.: U.S. Government Printing Office, 1973.

University of Chicago Press. *The Chicago Manual of Style.* 13th ed. Chicago: University of Chicago Press, 1982.

Williams, Joseph M., ed. *Style: Ten Lessons in Clarity & Grace.* 2d ed. Glenview, Ill.: Scott, Foresman and Co., 1985, pp. 96–109.

12 Proposals: The Process and the Document

Alice E. Moorhead
Hamline University

A proposal is at the center of a process involving a firm and a client, where both seek to share equitably the risks and responsibilities of solving problems. A proposal is the means for closing the gap between what is and what ought to be through exacting participation and agreement between parties. Whether presenting a business plan in search of capital, recommending that a prospective client purchase a product or service, competing for a government contract, or seeking funding for a nonprofit educational project, the medium is the same—a proposal.

Available resources on proposal writing have increased in volume and in scope in the past twenty years. Not only are there more books and articles on proposals, but these are more diverse in source and focus than in the past. In addition, proposal literature reflects a shift from a document orientation to a process orientation. Once considered variations of technical reports, proposals are now considered as functionally different discourses, generated as part of a larger communication system—a process of procurement and project management. Within this system, proposals serve technical and marketing functions as technical sales documents. Current literature—from technical and organizational communication to marketing and procurement management—reflects a greater emphasis on the proposal process, strategies, and preparation in addition to the features of a proposal document.

To put proposal literature in context, the framework for this article outlines the significant aspects of the proposal process and the proposal document. What follows is a four-part survey of the principal aspects:

1. A classification of proposals, a survey of comprehensive proposal texts, and an evolution of proposals

2. The proposal process, including the solicitation, procurement, and contract stages

3. The proposal document, including structure, format, and production considerations
4. Proposal research and education for proposal writers

Classification, Survey, and Evolution

A Classification of Proposals

Proposals are the most diverse, effective communicative tool currently available for gaining others' endorsement and business. Proposals can be classified in several ways: as solicited or unsolicited; as internal or external; as government or commercial; and as offers for products or services. There are, however, two distinct functional categories of proposals: research and implementation.

A research proposal, such as a proposal by an academic institution to the National Science Foundation, is an offer to address a problem. An implementation proposal (often referred to as a technical proposal) is an offer to solve a problem. This distinction is rarely stated, but a few texts, including Ammon-Wexler and Carmel's (1978) *How to Create a Winning Proposal* and Larson's (1976) *How to Write a Winning Proposal,* attempt to clarify and address both categories.

Research and development (R and D) proposals are often unsolicited study offers, whereas technical proposals are more often solicited. R and D proposals represent a distinct and separate literature, reflecting many discipline requirements and addressing the research needs of academic and nonprofit institutions as well as some areas of industry. In *How to Prepare a Research Proposal,* Krathwohl (1966) suggests ways to seek funds for behavioral science research, while in *The Art of Writing Successful R and D Proposals,* Orlich and Orlich (1977) offer direction for preparing proposals for educational institutions and community action groups. Mattice's (1974, pp. 5–17) "The Research Proposal by an Academic Institution" supplies a thoughtful rationale and guidelines for securing financial support for research projects.

The following authors' works offer good introductions to technical and military R and D proposals: Whalen's (1982a, pp. 36–38) "Grant Proposals: A Rhetorical Approach"; Hillman's (1978) *Art of Winning* series, including *The Art of Winning Government Grants;* and Kimball and Long's (1972, pp. 106–8) "Technical Management Notes." Several large universities publish their own R and D guides for grant writing.

Since implementation (or technical) proposals represent the greatest volume of government and commercial practice, this article focuses on its literature. Implementation proposals are solicited offers for products or services, which are either sealed bids or involve competitive negotiation. Sealed bid procurement limits the communication between a firm and a client, whereas competitive negotiation engages a firm and a client in communication about plans, ideas, and problems as well as costs (which is not permitted in sealed bids). For a discussion of solicited versus unsolicited and sealed bid versus competitively negotiated proposals, see procurement management and organizational buying literature, including Corey's (1978) *Procurement Management: Strategy, Organization, and Decision Making;* Webster and Wind's (1972) *Organizational Buying;* Levitt's (1965) *Industrial Purchasing Behavior: A Study of Communications Effects.*

Proposals can be external, between a firm and a client, or internal, between divisions in an organization. Few sources distinguish external from internal proposals, but an interesting treatment of audience analysis specifically for internal proposals—with implications for external proposals—can be found in Herrstrom's (1983, pp. 101-7) "A Matrix of Audience Responses for the Internal Proposal."

The most common category of proposals today is the selectively competitive, external, solicited proposal offering products and professional services. This category of proposal usually consists of a written document and an oral presentation with a question and answer period. The written proposal falls into three subproposal sections: technical, management, and cost.*

A Survey of Comprehensive Proposal Texts

A growing resource on proposal writing, comprehensive texts provide a systematic introduction to the proposal process and document. Two older but noteworthy texts are Clarke's (1962) *How to Prepare Effective Engineering Proposals* and Mandel and Caldwell's (1962) *Proposal and Inquiry Writing: Analysis, Techniques, Practice.* Clarke's text was one of the first comprehensive handbooks on proposal writing from the engineer's perspective, while Mandel and Caldwell's is more a textbook than a handbook, emphasizing technique and practical application with less on theory and conjecture.

Over the next twenty years, several comprehensive texts supplemented, and in some cases replaced, previous ones. Holtz and Schmidt (1981) develop and illustrate in their informative textbook, *The Winning*

---

* The technical approach is the key to the technology or engineering proposal; often the entire discourse is loosely referred to as a "technical proposal." In fact, the proposal should include all three parts—the technical, management, and financial sections. To refer to the entire discourse as a technical proposal is not incorrect, but it is misleading. For this article, the term "proposal" refers to the entire discourse.

Proposal: How to Write It, a communicative approach to proposal writing for commercial and government clients. Loring and Kerzner (1982) in *Proposal Preparation and Management Handbook* expand on the proposal management function with a definitive organizational approach. Both include useful bibliographies, yet Loring and Kerzner provide separate listings for proposal preparation, project management, and competitive bidding. Representing marketing resources, Beveridge and Velton (1982, pp. 45-51) in *Positioning to Win: Planning and Executing the Superior Proposal* argue for client-based marketing strategies for proposals in terms of the "discriminator discipline," which identifies the best reasons for a client to select one firm over another.

Two other comprehensive texts provide important treatments of proposals. In *Preparing Contract-Winning Proposals and Feasibility Reports,* Whalen (1982b) presents a knowledgeable discussion of a communication process for developing technically persuasive documents. The most recent, and perhaps best, proposal text, Stewart and Stewart's (1984) *Proposal Preparation,* offers an in-depth study of proposal procedures, including a thorough discussion of each stage and component of the proposal process and document, with reasonable guidelines for coordinating the preproposal stage, which is often neglected in other texts. The Stewart and Stewart reference text is not the only one to include sample proposals or a broad scope, but its case study work is certainly an exceptional approach to illustrating how proposals evolve.

Two periodical sources, an anthology of previous articles and a special issue, represent valuable collections of recent writing and bibliographies on proposals: Society for Technical Communication's (1973) *Proposals and Their Preparation* and the "Special Issue on Developing Proposals" (1983) in *IEEE Transactions on Professional Communication.* Both offer essays on the management of the proposal process, proposal strategies, preparation, and format. The important journals concerned with the communication implications of the proposal include *Journal for Technical Writing and Communication, Technical Communication, The Technical Writing Teacher,* and *IEEE Transactions on Professional Communication.*

Occasionally, engineering and business journals include articles on proposal writing; these articles typically focus on the proposal document. More and more, the wealth of resources on the proposal process can be found in organizational communication and marketing literature. Comprehensive sources have the advantage of addressing both the proposal process and the proposal document based on commercial and government practice; each will be cited when referring to particular aspects of the proposal.

Evolution of Proposals

In the past forty years, proposals have evolved into a time-honored business practice of "formalized propositions," according to Smith (1968, p. 9) in "An Introduction to Proposals." Smith explains how the modern proposal process follows procedures that evolved in the aerospace industry. In the early procurement of aircraft, government buyers were able to defer investing until they saw a demonstration of performance adequate to meet their requirements. Eventually, the design and development of electronic air transportation and advanced weapons required so much time and money that no firm could afford to risk the effort without some assurance that the client (i.e., the government) would in fact buy. The client, in turn, did not want to commit to a product that would not do the job.

In "The Billion-Dollar Proposal Industry," Murray (1966) provides an anecdotal survey on the growing importance and sophistication of proposals, which anticipates a current, popular belief that a proposal is a technical and sales document. Ireland (1967) in *How to Prepare Proposals that Sell* reinforces this belief in an early, systematic approach to integrating the marketing and sales function into technical proposals. Ireland is concerned specifically with writing government proposals, which he claims require more advanced skills than writing commercial proposals.

The move toward formalizing the proposal process came out of a mutual need on the part of clients and firms to communicate explicit assurances about both products and services in a written proposal. Wittreich (1966, pp. 127–38) in "How to Buy/Sell Professional Services" clarifies the key differences between proposals for products or services. Products are tangible and easier to understand than services. According to Wittreich (1966), a client needs to know exactly "what services are we going to get" from a firm if a proposal is accepted (p. 127); a firm needs to specify exactly "what services we are willing to offer" to a client if a proposal is accepted (p. 130). The nature of professional services, in contrast to products, accelerated the demand for a more explicit, regularized proposal process.

The proposal process has evolved into today's complex communication system to manage the risks and responsibilities involved in soliciting contracts. Federally contracted expenses, which in any year exceed $100 billion, are generally determined through negotiated procurement. Holtz and Schmidt (1981, p. xv) cite that 5 out of every 100 federal employees are engaged full-time in making and managing government procurements—or over 130,000 government buyers. Whether involving a government or commercial client, the proposal process has evolved because clients can define the tasks to be accomplished, request proposals and bids from among competing firms, and select confidently the most qualified firm with the most appropriate bid for the client's project. The proposal process positions control for procurement with a client, the one who solicits and pays for the goods and services.

The Proposal Process

A proposal process is designed not only to solicit contracts and select vendors but to coordinate the communication between a client and a firm, while both strive to protect their own best interests to the full extent of the law. A short introduction to this process can be found in Plotkin's (1970, pp. 36–38) "Preparing a Proposal, Step-by-Step." The proposal process has evolved into a fairly predictable series of stages, specifically, the solicitation (preproposal), procurement (proposal), and contract (postproposal) stages. Throughout the proposal process, several constituents deserve note and reference.

In the solicitation stage, a client defines problems, plans projects, and screens and selects qualified firms for the proposal stage. Early communication between a firm and a client is stressed in marketing literature on the proposal process. During this preliminary stage of the process, a client makes a Request for Qualifications (RFQ) and all interested firms submit a Statement of Qualifications (SOQ) to create a short list of firms eligible to submit proposals based on a client's Request for Proposals (RFP).

These steps, along with activities known as "courting clients" and "prewiring jobs," are necessary. Coxe's (1983) *Marketing Architectural and Engineering Services* offers one of the most detailed introductions to a marketing response to the solicitation stage, emphasizing the need for a firm to become increasingly more credible, even invaluable, to a potential client. In Hough's (1980, pp. 2–4) "Effective Proposal Preparation—Part I" the emphasis is on the importance of a firm researching projects early—even before clients know they have a problem or project. For detailed discussion of RFQ and SOQ sequences as miniatures of the proposal process, see Loring and Kerzner's (1982, pp. 1–35) Chapter 1, "Preproposal Work," and Stewart and Stewart's (1984, pp. 11–29) Chapter 2, "Preproposal Marketing and the Decision to Bid."

Before pursuing any project, a firm designates a proposal team responsible for writing the proposal to solicit a desirable project. Several sources highlight the contributions of individuals from engineering, management, or marketing on a proposal team, but many point to the importance of teamwork, including DeGeorge's (1969, pp. 122–26) "Ingredients for Successful Proposals"; Martin's (1971, pp. 969–1027) "The Roles and Responsibilities of Management and Supervision"; Woelfle's (1975, pp. 31–34) "The Role of the Engineer in Preparing Proposals." For thorough discussions of proposal team members see Ammon-Wexler and Carmel (1978), Loring and Kerzner (1982); Mandel and Caldwell (1962); and Stewart and Stewart (1984).

Proposal management also becomes the responsibility of the proposal team. In spite of its years, Smith's (1960, pp. 28–30) "Organizing a Complex Technical Proposal Effort" presents the classic systems personnel approach to proposal management. Whitesell (1971, pp. 1103–58) in "Role and Scope of Technical Writing Activities" indicates the technical writer provides coordination of all proposal efforts. Again, most comprehensive texts include discussion of proposal management.

A critical responsibility of a proposal team is to conduct a "Go/No Go" decision, weighing the advantages and disadvantages of pursuing a client's project based on a proposal request. Go/No Go decisions must be based on systematic criteria, otherwise a firm would pursue all projects indiscriminately and either acquire more work than it could accomplish or win unprofitable contracts. This decision methodology has become quantitative and qualitative, as in DeWitt's (1982, pp. 1–3) "Proposal Go/No Go Decision Methodology" and McConochie's (1981, pp. 3–5) "How to Be Selective in Pursuing Work."

The RFP details, to greater or lesser degrees, the requirements necessary for a competing firm to respond with a qualifying proposal as well as establishes the criteria for review of proposals and the deadlines. The client's RFP is an important factor a firm considers when deciding whether or not to pursue a project; however, more evidence exists on interpreting RFPs than on writing them. An exception, Epstein's (1983, pp. 1109–11) "Procurement Without Problems: Preparing the RFP" provides general guidelines for designing and responding to RFPs for automated systems. In "Proposal Heartburn: Out in the Open," LaFlash (1984, pp. 54–56) insists that government acquisition is supposed to be a reciprocal partnership, but there is a lack of awareness by the people who administer the massive and complex RFPs. Additional coverage of RFPs appears in Whalen; Loring and Kerzner; and Stewart and Stewart.

The RFP signals the end of the solicitation stage and the beginning of the procurement stage. During the procurement stage, each eligible firm receives a client's RFP, prepares a proposal based on its strategy to win, makes a presentation, and faces review and evaluation before a contract award is announced.

Strategies for proposals have increased in number and sophistication in the past ten years to match the increasing number and worth of proposals. Professional proposal consultants, such as Hyman Silver, market their philosophies and techniques through seminars as much as through publication. Several marketing organizations provide both conference proceedings, newsletters, and journals to promote proposal strategies. A typical example would be Spaulding's (1982, pp. 14–15) "The Proposal: Microcosm of the Design Project," which draws its strategy from what a firm knows best—managing projects.

Other sources develop strategies to compete with the constraints within a proposal process: limited time; coordination of proposal team members representing several conflicting disciplines; enormous production costs; and proprietary and legal consequences. James E. Tracey (1974, 1982, 1983), a respected proposal authority, advocates the Sequential Thematic Organization of Proposals technique in several articles.

Many argue for a "storyboard" approach to proposals, which coordinates different, modular proposal sections prepared by different people. Several works discuss the merits of storyboarding, including Englebret's (1972, pp. 115–19) "Storyboarding—A Better Way of Planning and Writing Proposals"; McClure's (1984) "Planning and Writing a Page-Limited Proposal"; and Larson's (1976, pp. 21–23) Chapter 7, "The Storyboard Approach to Proposal Preparation."

Marketing resources are responsible for streamlining the proposal process into ongoing communication between a firm and a client, which can be misunderstood by technical and management staff. Marketing, often confused with sales, deals with *what* you sell while selling deals with *how* you sell it. A fundamental marketing strategy is strengthening a shared commitment during the proposal process between a firm and a client, which previews the commitment during the project. In Kliment's (1977) *Creative Communication for a Successful Design Practice,* he outlines the advantages of and techniques for good communication as good business. The following offer sound theoretical and practical techniques, respectively, for proposals as marketing tools: Wilson's (1972) *The Marketing of Professional Services* and D'Elia et al.'s (1980) *The A/E Marketing Handbook: A User's Manual.* For a broader marketing approach, examine the Jones's (1973) *How to Market Professional Design Services.*

In marketing research, the state of the art text on proposals is perhaps Beveridge and Velton's (1982) *Positioning to Win: Planning and Executing the Superior Proposal.* The authors base their strategies on their proposal management experience in the aerospace industry. Beveridge and Velton's (1982, pp. 147-49) strategy, "competitive convergence," means identifying and exploiting discriminators (strengths and weaknesses in proposal offers, as perceived by a client) to shift a firm's proposal closer to answering for a client, "Why should I accept your offer?" Hill (1985) in "How to Work Win Strategies into Your Proposals" specifies how to track winning arguments throughout a proposal, encouraging a client to adopt the arguments to support contract award decisions. Another good source for "winning" strategies is Breedlove's (1983, pp. 25-27, 39) "How to Improve Your Proposals: The Winning Process."

Along with proposal strategies, a firm needs to adopt strategies for presentations, a frequent prerequisite in a procurement process. Holtz and Schmidt's (1981, pp. 115-44) text provides strategies tailored both for proposals and for presentations in Chapter 9, "The Evolution of Strategies." Several works on oral presentations are relevant points of departure in the study of proposal presentations, including Wilcox's (1977) *Communication at Work: Writing and Speaking;* Eadie and Sincoff's (1977, pp. 205-17) "Technical Communication in Written and Oral Modes"; Estrin and Monohan's (1978, pp. 49-53) "Effective Oral Presentation of Scientific and Technical Information"; and Sawyer's (1979, pp. 28-30) "Preparing and Delivering an Oral Presentation."

Once the proposal strategy is developed into a proposal, most firms conduct a "red team" review to anticipate and resolve any problems with the firm's offer before submitting the document to a client. Most comprehensive texts provide checklists to conduct self-reviews of proposals; however, the client review process is difficult to predict. Proposal evaluation criteria are usually specified in the RFP, yet when and how a client reviews a proposal to reach a contract award decision is neither necessarily universal nor systematic. Dibner (1983, pp. 1-2), after changing his role from private consultant to government client, reveals how clients review competing proposals in "The Selection Process: A View from Both Sides."

On evaluation, there is no one source adequately treating both commercial and government procedures, the latter being the most regulated yet most elusive. An exception, the Stewart and Stewart's

(1984, pp. 215–38) text, offers a solid evaluation chapter, including clarification of source evaluation versus source selection as well as details on evaluation factors, scheduling, scoring, debriefing, and protest appeals. To locate sources that define what constitutes responsive and nonresponsive proposals, see Whalen's (1982b, pp. 12–19) Chapter 3, "Essential Criteria in Proposals: Business and Government Preferences"; Stewart and Stewart's (1984, pp. 239–49) Chapter 11, "A Few Key Elements for Success"; and Holtz and Schmidt's (1981, pp. 65–78) Chapter 6, "Common Faults and Failures."

The contract stage begins once a client has ranked all the proposals and presentations and awarded the contract to one firm. The development of the contract agreement is the result of important policies and decisions established during the solicitation and procurement stages and permits the contract stage to proceed without serious delays.

A proposal, once offered and accepted, is a legal contract. Several sources provide a solid introduction to the contract stage, such as Firmage's (1980) *Modern Engineering Practice: Ethical, Professional, and Legal Aspects;* Tilly's (1971, pp. 1159–92) "Contracting and Subcontracting"; Loring and Kerzner (1982); Holtz and Schmidt (1981); and Mandel and Caldwell (1962). For legal implications of a proposal, refer to Moorhead's (1985, pp. 68–72) "Legal Implications of a Proposal: A Frozen Document"; Cushman's (1983) *Avoiding Liability in Architecture, Design and Construction: An Authoritative and Practical Guide for Design Professionals;* and Vaughn's (1977) *Legal Aspects of Engineering.*

The proposal process is complicated by factors not typical of similar technical communication processes. Each proposal process presents unique challenges and obstacles to each participant managing the communication exchanges between a client and the competing firms to promote problem solving and informed decision making. A proposal process is complicated because it must be flexible to adapt to a firm's changing knowledge about a client's needs. Nearly all literature on the proposal process assumes a firm's perspective rather than a client's, but a few sources are exceptions. The U.S. Environmental Protection Agency's (1976) *Resource Recovery Plant Implementation: Guides for Municipal Officials—Procurement* offers guidelines for a client involved in a proposal process. Two key functions frame this Environmental Protection Agency manual's models and instructions: the process of system procurement and competitive negotiation. In addition, Whalen's (1982b) and Beveridge and Velton's (1982) books are written from a firm's perspective, yet both texts attempt to direct a firm's proposal activities based on a client's point of view.

The Proposal Document

A proposal communicates persuasively the nature of the product or service offered, inspires confidence in its source, and influences a prospective client to choose one proposal instead of another. A proposal is not an advertisement that requires a client to be in the right place at the right time to be influenced. It is not a marketing brochure that a client automatically tosses into the circular file with so many others. It is not a salesperson who may be relegated to dealing with people unauthorized to make a contract award. Geared to decision makers, a proposal is an offer for consideration—a formal business proposition that commands a high degree of attention and respect. Proposals respond specifically to a problem, address a client's needs, and promise to fulfill its expectations.

A proposal is not an informative report. The terms "proposal" and "report" are not interchangeable, yet most traditional textbooks treat the proposal as a variation of technical report writing. At the end of a job, a firm writes a report, but to get a job, a firm writes a proposal. A proposal is the forecast; the report is the result.

More specifically, a proposal is not a recommendation report. In *Technical Writing: Process and Product,* Stratton (1984, p. 326) points out that "a proposal is similar to a feasibility recommendation report in that it deals with a solution to a technical problem, but it differs from the recommendation report in that it focuses on a single solution rather than alternative solutions and it goes beyond a discussion of *what* should be done to include information on *how* much it will cost." In Whalen's (1982b) book, he notes that a feasibility study is paid for by the client (proposals are paid for by the firm) and are often more thorough than a proposal, but neither document is a guarantee of a substantive contract. A potential client has no obligation to anyone who competes for any contract; nor is a client obligated to choose any one of the proposals.

Most standard technical writing textbooks written in the past ten years include at least a few pages on the features of a proposal document; the discussion is usually general, but some texts offer much more detail. Several texts and essay collections on technical writing provide useful introductions to the proposal, among them, Houp and Pearsal's (1984) *Reporting Technical Information,* DeBakey's (1978) "The Persuasive Proposal," Ulman's (1972) "Proposals," and Reisman's (1962) "The Technical Proposal."

For a current marketing approach to proposal documents, consult Creel's (1978) "Proposal Preparation," Emerson's (1977, pp. 7–8)

"Structure Determines Content: A Mini-Paradigm for Use in Proposal Writing," Richard's (1971, pp. 62–64) "Brush Up on Your Proposal Preparation," and Kuhns's (1967, pp. 26–28, 38–40) "What Is a Proposal?"

The proposal document consists of three principal sections: technical (what a firm is proposing), management (the proof that a firm can deliver), and cost (the estimated cost). In *Guidelines for Report Writers: A Complete Manual for On-the-Job Report Writing* Blicq (1982) supplies a useful pyramid approach to structuring technical reports, which is particularly appropriate for proposals. For an introduction to all three proposal components, see Hillman's (1981) *The Art of Writing Business Reports and Proposals* as well as the book by Ammon-Wexler and Carmel (1978). A detailed account of each proposal component can be found in the works of Stewart and Stewart (1984) and Loring and Kerzner (1982).

The technical section, the key to a proposal, analyzes the client's problem as described in the RFP and argues for a proposed solution. It presents, in orderly engineering design details, the most advantageous approach to a client's problem. The technical proposal needs to convey the technical features in a scope of work in terms beneficial to a client otherwise a firm leaves a client to interpret these. Thorough discussions of the technical proposal appear in Seisler's (1983, pp. 58–60) "Proposal Writing: Approaching the Approach"; Stewart and Stewart's (1984, pp. 98–124) Chapter 6, "The Work Statement as the Basis for the Technical Proposal"; and Loring and Kerzner's (1982, pp. 165–212) Chapter 6, "The Technical Proposal: Scope of Work, Specifications, Standards, and Scheduling."

The management section also presents an argument, citing the caliber of a firm's personnel assigned to a project and communicating assurances for scheduling, cost controls, and guarantees to maintain communication and involvement with a client throughout a project. This section argues for a firm's capability of providing a client with the requested expertise based on a firm's previous successful projects as well as its current understanding of this client's needs and wants. Detailed discussions of the management section, or statement of understanding, are provided in Stewart and Stewart's (1984, pp. 125–54) Chapter 7, "The Organization and Management Proposal: The Work Element, Project Plan, Organization, and Personnel"; Loring and Kerzner's (1982, pp. 213–56) Chapter 7, "The Management Proposal: Program Management, Company History, Facilities, and Controls"; and Mandel and Caldwell's (1962, pp. 80–90) Chapter 3, "The Commercial and Management Proposal."

The cost section provides a detailed cost analysis and projection of expenses to justify the costs for a client. For many reasons, this section of a proposal receives considerable client attention, offering a convenient, though limited, means to compare competing firms' offers. Unless this section is examined along with the level of effort offered in the technical proposal section, a client can award a contract to the lowest bidder yet not receive the needed work. The cost section also specifies legal qualifications committing the degree of risk and responsibility a firm is willing to assume if awarded the contract. For cost proposals, see Stewart and Stewart's (1984, pp. 155-76) Chapter 8, "The Cost Proposal: Credibility, Estimating, and Documentation"; Loring and Kerzner's (1982, pp. 257-301) Chapter 8, "The Cost Proposal: Pricing and Profit Strategy"; Ammon-Wexler and Carmel's (1978, pp. 7.1-7.5) Chapter 7, "The Pricing Component: Presenting Cost and Contractual Details."

Although some sections of a proposal are more technical or more persuasive, all sections of a proposal require "technical persuasion." As a technical sales document, a proposal must fulfill the RFP requirements but must also provide a client with a persuasive argument that it can adopt to justify its contract decision. In "Rhetoric, Persuasion, and the Technical Communicator," Sachs (1978, pp. 14-15) argues that technical persuasion involves all choices in proposals—not only in content and means but also in format, arrangement, and presentation of technical data.

Certain persuasive language and rhetorical forms increase the effectiveness of proposals, according to McAlister (1985, pp. 129-31) in "Preparing a Persuasive Proposal"; Corey (1975, pp. 2-5) in "The Persuasive Technical Proposal: Rhetorical Form and the Writer"; and Smith (1975, pp. 12-14) in "Use Rhetoric for Better Technical Proposals." Most articles referring to technical persuasion in proposals focus more on a rhetoric of style, but Whalen's (1982b, pp. 33-36) Chapter 6, "Technical Persuasion" suggests this strategy extends beyond these concerns to include a proposal term's commitment to a potential project in terms of a proposal offer. Also see Beveridge and Velton's (1982, pp. 136-51) Chapter 10, "Argumentative Headlines and Competitive Theses—Get What Matters Up Front For Maximum Effect," and Holtz and Schmidt's (1981, pp. 219-42) Chapter 13, "Writing Persuasively."

Proposals are edited for cohesion and persuasiveness by the proposal writers and marketing personnel on a proposal team. Not only the technical, management, and cost proposals, but the other proposal components require editing, including a letter of transmittal, an executive summary, a problem statement, schedules, résumés, references, and appendix materials. Two particular proposal components deserve consideration: Performance Evaluation Review Technique (PERT) or Program Evaluation Procedure (PEP) charts and boilerplate material.

Elaborate, specialized flow charts, common to proposals and engineering projects, are PERT or PEP charts. Originally, PERT charts for the Navy and PEP charts for the Air Force were created as effective management tools for planning and evaluating progress in the development of complex weapon systems. These charts display the schedule for monitoring thousands of items, which operate together as a network of events contributing to the completion of a complex project. The flow chart, or network, is a graphic representation of the events showing sequence and interrelationships to follow progress from one event to another as well as to predict time involved to move from one event to the next.

Today, PERT and PEP charts in proposals provide both a firm and a client with an important visual representation of how proposed projects will be executed. Mandel and Caldwell's (1962, pp. 226-38) text includes an important reprint, Philip Klass's "PERT/PEP Management Tool Use Grows." Additional resources on the use of PERT charts include Whalen's (1980) article and Ireland's (1967) text. Firms use PERT charts in proposals and presentations to demonstrate to a client how a complex project will operate; firms also use PERT charts with storyboarding techniques, to organize their own proposal production.

To save time, cut costs, and meet deadlines, proposals are often partially composed of "boilerplate" text (any reusable material) and "off-the-shelf," or "standard," sections (regularly reused larger units of text). Debate arises among proposal writers on how boilerplate materials should be included in a proposal, yet the debate usually centers on when and why. At its best, boilerplate represents quality, accurate evidence gleaned from debriefings; provides an ideal launching point for a proposal; and maximizes a time-efficient and cost-effective use of proposal team effort. At its worst, it represents outdated, potentially flawed evidence; exaggerates a lack of cohesion in the proposal; and exposes lazy and unimaginative proposal team effort. In "Prescriptions for Using Boilerplate," Hays (1983, pp. 60-62) offers a concise examination of the advantages and disadvantages of boilerplate writing for proposals. Loring and Kerzner's (1982) text plus Whalen's (1982b) devote entire sections to boilerplate, including lists of proposal sections likely to become boilerplate material—perhaps firm histories, résumés, previous project summaries, and standard federal forms 254 and 255.

Although many firms use boilerplate materials, smart firms try to avoid submitting boilerplate and never repeat the RFP language in a proposal. Tailored proposals, individualized to each particular client's needs and wants, are the objective whenever time and information permits. Nevertheless, as more firms computerize their client marketing data, access to boilerplate versions of this information becomes indispensable in preparing proposals. Creel and Young (1983, pp. 1–12) compiled in *The Computer vs. Preprints* the survey data reflecting the use of the computer to replace and revise off-the-shelf marketing materials. Their survey indicated that 93 percent of all firms computerize their boilerplate materials. It is doubtful that boilerplate will ever disappear from proposals, but more firms are using boilerplate selectively rather than because it is available (p. 6).

Advice on editing proposals is a common subject for many technical communication articles and most comprehensive texts concerned with proposals, yet the focus on editing has shifted recently to production concerns, specifically the role of computers and word processing for proposals. Proposals, unlike company brochures and product bulletins, are intended for only limited distribution. Frequently, only six or eight copies will be all a client requires. Add to this the number that a firm wishes to distribute internally, usually not more than ten or twenty, even for a large firm. Production concerns for proposals is not quantity but quality.

A number of recent resources explore a document design orientation to producing technical writing, and proposals are often the most important test of these technological advances. Mali and Sykes (1985) develop and illustrate the distinction between printing and producing documents in *Writing and Word Processing for Engineers and Scientists: How to Get Your Message Across in Today's High Technology World*. This text describes strategies for report and proposal writers to use computers throughout the writing process, not just to produce a clean, final copy.

High-quality, competitive proposals produced under deadline pressures demand automation. Another plan for computerized text management is included in Dressel et al.'s (1983, pp. 63–68) "ASAPP: Automated Systems Approach to Proposal Production." The use of computers and word processing for proposals will increase, maximizing the effectiveness of boilerplate materials while tailoring entire proposals for specific clients.

Proposal Research and Call for Education

There is very little primary research on proposals, and there are few experimental studies. Access to actual proposals is limited to a firm and a client due to the fierce competition between firms and time-bound quality of proposal offers. This restriction makes research difficult yet even more interesting. Some industries, such as the aerospace industry, are more secretive about their proposals than others are. The aerospace industry has been preparing proposals longer than other businesses and has developed the most sophisticated proposal process strategies of all. For the sake of study, it is almost impossible to examine these documents (not to mention to study communication in a proposal process), regardless of the age or the cost of a project, simply because the industry is protective of its proposals—for content, form, and clients' internal security (for example, that of the defense department). Ironically, only actual proposals serve to advance our understanding of how proposals and the proposal process functions, yet actual proposals are what researchers often lack.

One experimental study of proposals, cited in Dycus's two articles—"The Relative Effectiveness of Proposal Approaches—An Experimental Study" (1975, pp. 9–11) and "Relative Efficacy of One-Sided vs. Two-Sided Communication in a Simulated Government Evaluation of Proposals" (1976, pp. 787–90)—presents a loosely controlled experiment concerning different approaches to proposal use depending on the demographic and psychological make-up of a review committee. This is an interesting prospect for research, but designing and evaluating proposals for hypothetical rather than actual situational contexts results in misleading results and application. On the other hand, articles such as Lipson's (1983, pp. 41–53) "Theoretical and Empirical Considerations for Designing Openings of Technical and Business Reports" suggest promising directions for testing actual proposals.

Occasionally, commercial and government procurement practices permit limited access to proposals. When I conducted a year's field study of a consulting engineering firm and its proposal practices, I was permitted almost unlimited access to documents, meetings, client and firm personnel, yet my thesis (Moorhead 1984), "The Rhetorical Design and Function of the Proposal," did not nearly represent all the evidence I gathered because the firm partners restricted certain evidence and conclusions to protect their clients and the firm's interests.

The education of a proposal writer is often on the job, but there is a need for instruction to prepare future proposal writers. A call for proposal writing instruction is supported in Rainey's (1974, pp. 30–39) "Proposal Writing—A Neglected Area of Instruction" and in Smith's (1976, pp. 113–22) "Education for Proposal Writers." Rainey surveys corporate executives, while Smith assesses the requirements of proposal writers in the aerospace industry; both suggest how educational institutions can better prepare students. For a specific application, see

Norman and Young's (1984, pp. 1–9) "Using Peer Review to Teach Proposal Writing," which develops and illustrates how students can work in groups as review teams for proposals. For presentations, see Hand's (1975, pp. 18–21) "Technical Speech: A Need for Teaching and Research."

Conclusion

The literature of proposal writing will grow and expand. Proposals are important enough that the unpublished, restricted proposal evidence will surface—even in abbreviated form—because the demand to prepare successful proposals can only increase. Every year proposals cost firms hundreds of thousands of dollars and many staff production hours, while contracts buy ten times that amount. A handshake or a telephone call was once enough to arrange business between parties. Once there were fewer firms competing and clients and firms were more familiar with each other. Today, accountants, lawyers, and consultants use proposals to present their offers to potential clients. As problems, solutions, and choices become more complex for commerce, the more often the proposal will organize the efforts.

Bibliography

Ammon-Wexler, Jill, and Catherine Carmel. *How to Create a Winning Proposal.* Santa Cruz, Calif.: Mercury Communications Corporation, 1978.

Anderson, Barbara. "Writing Responsive Proposals." *The Editorial Eye,* March 1985, 1–3.

Betsinger, Signe T. "Ten Tips for Timely Proposals." *Tech Talk* 28, January 1987, 1–2. (Society for Technical Communication's Twin Cities Chapter Newsletter.)

Beveridge, James M., and Edward J. Velton. *Positioning to Win: Planning and Executing the Superior Proposal.* Radnor, Pa.: Chilton Book Co., 1982.

Blicq, Ron S. *Guidelines for Report Writers: A Complete Manual for On-the-Job Report Writing.* Englewood Cliffs, N.J.: Prentice-Hall, 1982.

Breedlove, Kendall H. "How to Improve Your Proposals: The Winning Process Part I and II." *National Defense* 67, no. 384 (January 1983): 25–27, 39; and *National Defense* 67, no. 385 (February 1983): 17–21.

Clarke, Emerson. *How to Prepare Effective Engineering Proposals: A Workbook for the Proposal Writer.* River Forest, Ill.: TW Publishers, 1962.

Considine, Barney M. "Writing Proposals to Win Large Contracts" and "Your Career as a Proposal Professional." *Tech Talk* 28, January 1987, 1–3. (Society for Technical Communication's Twin Cities Chapter Newsletter.)

Corey, E. Raymond. *Procurement Management: Strategy, Organization, and Decision-Making.* Boston: CBI Publishing, 1978.

Corey, Robert L. "The Persuasive Technical Proposal: Rhetorical Form and the Writer." *Technical Communication* 22, no. 4 (Fourth Quarter 1975): 2–5.

Coxe, Weld. *Marketing Architectural and Engineering Services.* New York: Van Nostrand Reinhold, 1983.

Creel, Diane C. *Proposal Preparation.* Marketing Information Report No. 2. Alexandria, Va.: Society for Marketing Professionals, 1978.

Creel, Diane C., and William W. Young. *The Computer vs. Preprints: Can the Computer Completely Replace Your Off-the-Shelf Marketing Materials?* Marketing Information Report No. 5. Alexandria, Va.: Society for Marketing Professional Services, 1983.

Cushman, Robert F. *Avoiding Liability in Architecture, Design and Construction: An Authoritative and Practical Guide for Design Professionals.* New York: Wiley-Interscience, 1983.

DeBakey, Lois. "The Persuasive Proposal." In *Directions in Technical Writing and Communication.*, edited by J. R. Gould. Farmingdale, N.Y.: Baywood, 1978.

DeGeorge, William. "Ingredients for Successful Proposals." *Machine Design* 41 (April 1969): 122–26.

D'Elia, Sandy, Jim Ricereto, and Margaret Spaulding. *The A/E Marketing Handbook: A User's Manual.* Newington, Conn.: A/E Marketing Journal, 1980.

DeWitt, Dennis. "Proposal Go/No Go Decision Methodology." *Society for Marketing Professional Services* 7 (June 1982): 1–3.

Dibner, David R. "The Selection Process: A View from Both Sides." *Society for Marketing Professionals* 8 (April 1983): 1–2.

Dressel, Susan, James S. Euler, Susan A. Bagby, and Sherry A. Dell. "ASAPP: Automated Systems Approach to Proposal Production." *IEEE Transactions on Professional Communication* PC-26, no. 2 (June 1983): 63–68.

Dycus, Robert D. "The Relative Effectiveness of Proposal Approaches—An Experimental Study." *Technical Communication* 22, no. 1 (First Quarter 1975): 9–11.

———. "Relative Efficacy of One-Sided vs. Two-Sided Communication in a Simulated Government Evaluation of Proposals." *Psychological Reports* 38 (1976): 787–90.

Eadie, William F., and Michael Z. Sincoff. "Technical Communication in Written and Oral Modes." *Journal of Technical Writing and Communication* 7, no. 3 (Third Quarter 1977): 205–17.

Emerson, A. D. "Structure Determines Content: A Mini-Paradigm for Use in Proposal Writing." *Technical Communication* 24, no. 3 (Third Quarter 1977): 7–8.

Englebret, David. "Storyboarding—A Better Way of Planning and Writing Proposals." *IEEE Transactions on Professional Communication* PC-15, no. 4 (Dec. 1972): 115–18.

Epstein, Susan Baerg. "Procurement Without Problems: Preparing the RFP." *Library Journal* 108 (1983): 1109–11.

Estrin, Herman A., and Edward J. Monohan. "Effective Oral Presentation of Scientific and Technical Information." *IEEE Transactions on Professional Communication* PC-21, no. 2 (June 1978): 49–53.

Firmage, David A. *Modern Engineering Practice: Ethical, Professional, and Legal Aspects.* New York: Garland Press, 1980.

Frederickson, Lola. "A Checklist for Proposal Esthetics." *Tech Talk* 28, January 1987, 3. (Society for Technical Communication's Twin Cities Chapter Newsletter.)

Greenly, Robert B. "Technical Writing and Illustrating Strategies for Winning Government Contracts." *IEEE Transactions on Professional Communication* PC-28, no. 2 (June 1985): 7–12.

Hand, Harry E. "Technical Speech: A Need for Teaching and Research." *IEEE Transactions on Professional Communication* PC-18, no. 1 (March 1975): 18–21.

Hays, Robert. "Prescriptions for Using Boilerplate." *IEEE Transactions on Professional Communication* PC-26, no. 2 (June 1983): 60–62.

Helgeson, Donald V. *Handbook for Writing Technical Proposals That Win Contracts.* Englewood Cliffs, N.J.: Prentice-Hall, 1985.

Herrstrom, David S. "A Matrix of Audience Responses for the Internal Proposal." *The Technical Writing Teacher* 10 (Winter-Spring 1983): 101–7.

Hill, James W. "How to Work Win Strategies into Your Proposals." In *IEEE Professional Communication Society Conference Record 1985.* New York: IEEE Publishing Service, pp. 175–79.

———. "The Proper Structuring and Use of Strategies, Outlines, and Theme Statements for Technical Proposals." In *IEEE Professional Communication Society Conference Record 1986.* New York: IEEE Publishing Service, pp. 267–77.

Hillman, Howard. *The Art of Winning Government Grants.* New York: Vanguard, 1978.

———. *The Art of Writing Business Reports and Proposals.* New York: Vanguard, 1981.

Holtz, Herman. *The Consultant's Guide to Proposal Writing.* New York: John Wiley and Sons, 1986.

Holtz, Herman, and Terry Schmidt. *The Winning Proposal: How to Write It.* New York: McGraw-Hill, 1981.

Hough, Michael R. "Effective Proposal Preparation—Part I." *A/E Marketing Journal* 7 (Nov. 1980): 2–4.

Houp, Kenneth W., and Thomas E. Pearsal. *Reporting Technical Information.* New York: Macmillan, 1984.

Ireland, Stanley H. *How to Prepare Proposals that Sell.* Chicago: Dartnell Corporation, 1967.

Jones, Gerre L. *How to Market Professional Design Services.* New York: McGraw-Hill, 1973.

Kimball, G. Warren, and G. Allison Long, Jr. "Technical Management Notes." *IEEE Transactions on Engineering Management* EME19, no. 3 (Aug. 1972): 106–8.

Kliment, Stephen. *Creative Communication for a Successful Design Practice.* New York: Whitney Library of Design, 1977.

Krathwohl, David. *How to Prepare a Research Proposal.* Syracuse, N.Y.: Syracuse Bookstore, 1966.

Kuhns, Carl F. "What Is a Proposal?" *Research/Development* 18 (Aug. 1967): 26–28; (Sep. 1967): 38–40.

LaFlash, Judson. "Proposal Heartburn: Out in the Open." *Countermeasures* (Sept. 1984): 54–56.

Larsen, Michael. *How to Write a Book Proposal.* Cincinnati: Writer's Digest Books, 1985.

Larson, Virginia. *How to Write a Winning Proposal.* Carmichael, Calif.: Creative Book Co., 1976.

Levitt, Theodore. *Industrial Purchasing Behavior: A Study of Communications Effects.* Boston: Harvard Graduate School of Business Administration, 1965.

Lipson, Carol S. "Theoretical and Empirical Considerations for Designing Openings of Technical and Business Reports." *Journal of Business Communication* 20 (Winter 1983): 41–53.

Loring, Roy J., and Harold Kerzner. *Proposal Preparation and Management Handbook.* New York: Van Nostrand Reinhold, 1982.

Mali, Paul, and Richard W. Sykes. *Writing and Word Processing for Engineers and Scientists: How to Get Your Message Across in Today's High Technology World.* New York: McGraw-Hill, 1985.

Mandel, Siegfried, and David L. Caldwell. *Proposal and Inquiry Writing: Analysis, Techniques, Practice.* New York: Macmillan, 1962.

Marcus, Judith H. "Proposal Management in a Small Organization—Everyone's Responsibility." In *Proceedings of the 31st International Technical Communications Conference,* Seattle, Wash. Washington, D.C.: Society for Technical Communication (1984): MPD69–MPD71.

Martin, Arthur C. "The Roles and Responsibilities of Management and Supervision." In *Handbook of Technical Writing Practices,* edited by Stello Jordan. New York: Wiley-Interscience, 1971, pp. 969–1027.

Mattice, Douglas A. "The Research Proposal by an Academic Institution." *Journal of Technical Writing and Communication* 4, no. 1 (Winter 1974): 5–17.

McAlister, James. "Preparing a Persuasive Proposal." *Machine Design* 57, no. 4 (Feb. 21, 1985): 129–31.

McClure, George F. "Planning and Writing a Page-Limited Proposal." In *IEEE Professional Communication Society Conference Record 1984.* New York: IEEE Publishing Service, pp. 103–5.

McConochie, Carol. "How to Be Selective in Pursuing Work." *A/E Marketing Journal* 8 (Jan. 1981): 3–5.

Moorhead, Alice E. "The Rhetorical Design and Function of the Proposal." Ph.D. diss. University of Michigan, 1984.

———. "Legal Implications of a Proposal: A Frozen Document." In *IEEE Professional Communication Society Conference Record 1985*. New York: IEEE Publishing Service, pp. 68–72.

Moran, Michael G. "Using Student Experience to Teach the Technical Proposal." *The Technical Writing Teacher* 11 (Spring 1984): 199–200.

Murray, Thomas J. "The Billion-Dollar Proposal Industry." *Dun's Review* 87 (Jan. 1966): 40–41, 71–72, 77.

Norman, Rose, and Marynell Young. "Using Peer Review to Teach Proposal Writing." *The Technical Writing Teacher* 12 (Winter 1984): 1–9.

Orlich, Donald C., and Patricia Rend Orlich. *The Art of Writing Successful R and D Proposals*. Pleasantville, N.Y.: Redgrave, 1977.

Plotkin, Harris M. "Preparing a Proposal, Step-by-Step." *Journal of Systems Management* 23 (Feb. 1970): 36–38.

Rainey, Bill G. "Proposal Writing—A Neglected Area of Instruction." *Journal of Business Communication* 11 (Summer 1974): 30–39.

Reisman, S. J. "The Technical Proposal." In *A Style Manual for Technical Writers*, edited by S. J. Reisman. New York: Macmillan, 1962.

Richard, Paul. "Brush Up On Your Proposal Preparation." *Electronic Design* 19 (Oct. 1971): 62–64.

Sachs, Harley. "Rhetoric, Persuasion, and the Technical Communicator." *Technical Communication* 25 (Fourth Quarter 1978): 14–15.

Sawyer, Thomas M. "Preparing and Delivering an Oral Presentation." *Technical Communication* 26, no. 1 (First Quarter 1979): 4–7.

Seisler, Jeffrey M. "Proposal Writing: Approaching the Approach." *IEEE Transactions on Professional Communication* PC-26, no. 2 (June 1983): 58–60.

Smith, Eric. "Organizing a Complex Technical Proposal Effort." *IRE Transactions on Engineering Writing and Speech* EWS-3, no. 1 (April 1960): 28–30.

Smith, Frank R. "An Introduction to Proposals." *Technical Communications* 15, no. 1 (First Quarter 1968): 9–11.

———. "Use Rhetoric for Better Technical Proposals." *Technical Communication* 22, no. 3 (Third Quarter 1975): 12–14.

———. "Education for Proposal Writers." *Journal of Technical Writing and Communication* 6, no. 2 (1976): 113–22.

Society of Technical Communication Anthology Series No. 1. *Proposals and Their Preparation*. Washington, D.C.: Society for Technical Communication, 1973.

Spaulding, Margaret. "The Proposal: Microcosm of the Design Project." *Society for Marketing Professional Services* 7 (Oct.-Nov. 1982): 14–15.

"Special Issue on Developing Proposals." Edited by J. Brand. *IEEE Transactions on Professional Communication* PC-26, no. 2 (June 1983).

Stewart, Rodney D., and Ann L. Stewart. *Proposal Preparation*. New York: John Wiley and Sons, 1984.

Stratton, Charles R. *Technical Writing: Process and Product*. New York: Holt, Rinehart and Winston, 1984.

Tilly, Vernon F. "Contracting and Subcontracting." In *Handbook of Technical Writing Practices,* edited by Stello Jordan. New York: Wiley-Interscience, 1971, pp. 1159–92.

Tracey, James R. "Managing-Editing A STOP Proposal: The Technical Editor As Bookbuilder." In *Proceedings of the 21st International Technical Communications Conference.* St. Louis, Mo.: Society for Technical Communication (1974): 157–64.

———. "The Practice of STOP." In *IEEE Professional Communication Society Conference Record, 1982,* 10–13.

———. "The Theory and Lessons of STOP Discourse." *IEEE Transactions on Professional Communication* PC-26, no. 2 (June 1983): 68–78.

Ulman, Joseph N., Jr. "Proposals." In *Technical Reporting,* edited by J. N. Ulman, Jr., and J. R. Gould. New York: Holt, Rinehart and Winston, 1972.

U.S. Environmental Protection Agency. *Resource Recovery Plant Implementation: Guides for Municipal Officials—Procurement.* Washington, D.C.: U.S. Government Printing Office, 1976.

Vaughn, Richard C. *Legal Aspects of Engineering.* Dubuque, Iowa: Kendall-Hunt, 1977.

Webster, Frederick E., Jr., and Yoram Wind. *Organizational Buying.* Englewood Cliffs, N.J.: Prentice-Hall, 1972.

Whalen, Tim. "Keeping Proposals on Target." *Consulting Engineer* 54, no. 5 (May 1980): 90.

———. "Grant Proposals: A Rhetorical Approach." *ABCA Bulletin* 45, no. 1 (March 1982a): 36–38.

———. *Preparing Contract-Winning Proposals and Feasibility Reports.* New York: Pilot Books, 1982b.

———. "Renewal: Writing the Incumbent Proposal." *IEEE Transactions on Professional Communication* PC-28, no. 2 (June 1985): 13–16.

———. "Proposal Costs: Meeting the Milestones on Time, on Budget." *IEEE Transactions on Professional Communication* PC-29, no. 3 (Sept. 1986a): 25–28.

———. "Proposals in the Aftermath: Postmortems." *Technical Communication* 33 (1986b): 81–83.

———. "A Training Checklist for Engineering Proposals." *The Technical Writing Teacher* 13 (Winter 1986c): 18–22.

Whitesell, Carl F. "Role and Scope of Technical Writing Activities." In *Handbook of Technical Writing Practices,* edited by Stello Jordan. New York: Wiley-Interscience, 1971, pp. 1103–58.

Wilcox, Roger P. *Communication at Work: Writing and Speaking.* Boston: Houghton Mifflin, 1977.

Wilson, Aubrey. *The Marketing of Professional Services.* London: McGraw-Hill Book Co. (UK) Ltd., 1972.

Wittreich, Warren J. "How to Buy/Sell Professional Services." *Harvard Review* 1966 (March-April): 127–38.

Woelfle, Robert M. "The Role of the Engineer in Preparing Proposals." *IEEE Transactions on Professional Communication* PC-18 (March 1975): 31–34.

13 Technical Advertising and Sales

Mary M. Lay
Clarkson University

Two types of sources provide the professional communication teacher with suggestions on how technical advertising and sales should be developed in the field and taught in the classroom. I use the term *professional communication* teacher because in advertising and sales, distinctions between technical and business writing detract from the main issues and because many decisions in advertising and sales go beyond writing to format, design, and other general communication principles. The source with which communication teachers feel most comfortable is the professional communication journal or bulletin, which usually contains persuasive pieces on teaching approaches and practical classroom assignments. The second source may be more unfamiliar to teachers but is often more useful in such a specialized and contemporary classroom unit; that source is the professional journal in marketing, advertising, or sales management. The articles in these journals tend to be very practical; the "My Favorite Assignment" offerings in communication journals are matched in marketing and sales journals with such standards as "Copy Chasers" in *Industrial Marketing*.

Although technical advertising and sales are interdependent, communication teachers may separate sales letter assignments from advertising copy assignments. In turn, marketing professionals usually distinguish their thoughts on print advertising from those on sales letters and direct mail campaigns. Although in this analysis I follow this division, with the current emphasis on situational writing assignments, teachers may wish to link copywriting and letter assignments. Because writers in professional marketing journals offer the broader range of information on sales and advertising, I begin each section with an analysis of them.

Technical Advertising

Teachers who are unfamiliar with the principles of advertising marketing and copywriting may want to begin their study with a classic account of "scientific" advertising written before the mid-1960s. Claude C. Hopkins's (1966) *Scientific Advertising* offers practical rules along with personal mottoes. His suggestions hold true today: the rule "address the people you seek, and them only" corresponds to modern market segmentation. His call for specificity in copy and his warning that visuals should be used only when they present a "better selling argument" than the same amount of space set in type introduce the reader to the personal, direct style of most articles in marketing magazines. "The Copy Chaser Rules: What Makes Good Business Industrial Advertising" (1982) offers a review of similar principles to those that appeared as early as 1937 in *Industrial Marketing.*

Although some professionals see little difference between consumer advertising and technical advertising, others support the trend toward specialization. The communication teacher will understand the heuristic justification for this specialization: since the end result or function of technical advertising is different, the techniques must be different. For example, a consumer might be expected to remember a particular brand of dish detergent in the supermarket, but if a technical advertisement is successful, a sophisticated sales force will be invited to call on an identifiable, highly educated management. However, many experts argue that the differences between technical and nontechnical advertising are not great. Ernest Dichfer's (1973) "Psychology in Industrial Marketing: Industrial Buying Is Based on Same 'Only Human' Emotional Factors that Motivate Consumer Market's Housewife" proposes that the same illusions and irrationality used to sell consumer products are essential in technical advertising; wood, as opposed to plastic, "lives," Dichfer offers as an example of general persuasive style. In contrast, "From Inconsequential Clerk to Specialist in Communications: The Ad Manager Grows Up" (1976) chronicles the growth of ad specialization, while Burton Schellenback's (1975) "Back to Basics: Tie in Your Ads with Your Business Aims" analyzes the differences between advertisements designed by five kinds of businesses. Professional communication teachers might ask students to collect and analyze "consumer" and "technical" advertisements and to assess what differences in style and approach they find. Four more sources give the teacher an overview of the controversy. Joseph A. Bellizzi and Jacqueline J. Mohr (1985) analyze "Technical Versus Nontechnical Wording of Industrial Print Advertising," while Bellizzi and Robert E. Hite (1986a,

p. 120) in their "Improving Industrial Advertising Copy," decide that "technical copy is useful in presenting technical information, but due to the informational needs and background of various audiences, industrial advertisers should reevaluate one-copy-for-all strategies." While Bellizzi and his colleagues argue for style based on situation, George N. Havens (1986), in "Industrial Advertising Grows in Scope, Status, and Strategic Value," traces the reasons why technical and nontechnical advertising might appear more similar than different. Havens studies how various socioeconomic impacts have changed industrial advertising. Such factors as strategic planning, consumerization, new media options and programming strategies, highly focused programs, extended product benefit, and worldwide communications have contributed to the evolution of an industrial ad that looks much like a consumer ad; "Today's operating premise is that people in executive suites or engineering departments are also consumers who respond to both *intellectual* and *emotional* appeals," Havens (1986, p. 165) concludes. Finally, Bellizzi and Hite (1986a) explore some unique professional advertisements in their "Consumer Attitudes Toward Accountants, Lawyers, and Physicians with Respect to Advertising Professional Services."

Two articles that give teachers an overview of industrial marketing and advertising are Robert Woods's (1982) "Industrial Ads: The Focus Gets Sharper" and Bellizzi and Julie Lehrer's (1983) "Developing Better Industrial Advertising." Woods's article covers everything from budgets to reader analysis, while Bellizzi and Lehrer note the major steps in developing industrial ads, successful copy techniques such as case histories and testimonials, stylistic suggestions, and layout and media selection. For those who wish an overview of advertising in general, Richard W. Pollay's (1985) "The Subsiding Sizzle: A Descriptive History of Print Advertising, 1900–1980" offers a content analysis of 2,000 ads from 10 of the largest selling magazines, decade by decade, with a focus on fads, trends, tactics, and style of print ads, and copy characteristics and layout, as well as rhetorical strategies such as ethos, pathos, and logos.

The many professional marketing articles that address the specific challenge of language in technical advertising generally fall into two categories: those that give practical suggestions about word usage from experienced advertising writers and those that offer in-depth analyses of style and vocabulary by those affiliated with academe. In the first category, the "Copy Chasers" department in *Industrial Marketing* regularly reviews industrial advertising copy. For example, in the February 1983 issue, the journal praised Foxboro for using a case history to promote its process control systems. They found that the headline had two powerful elements—a "how to" promise and "specific performance data"—to gain the attention of the engineer who might want process control system information. Since these reviews are brief and concrete, a teacher might want to ask each student to analyze and present one to the class. Robert Stone (1980), in "Long Narrative Copy: A Marketer's View," interviews John Caples of Batten, Barton, Durstine and Osborn on the style of direct mail advertising, and William D. Tyler (1979), in "Top Industrial Ads Tip Sales, Reflect Solid Ad Principles," discusses the successful combination of headline and copy in a specific ad. Reva Korda (1979) as creative head of Ogilvy and Mather, in "How to Break the Rules: Heresies About Writing Copy," shows how one ad breaking typical rules brought company sales up. Richard F. Beltramini and Vincent L. Blasko's (1986) "An Analysis of Award-Winning Advertising Headlines" details words and approaches that attract reader attention.

Other recommended articles by professional advertisers concentrate on narrow aspects of style. For example, Howard G. Sawyer (1979) in "About Repetition and Pronoun Use" and Dick Jackson (1978) in "Bridges Are the Links to Make Copy Flow" discuss how repetition and connectors sell the product or service to the reader. Jackson (1978, p. 61) gives a list of connectors that "warm up body copy, and help it flow smoothly like body temperature cognac, into the consumer's brain." In a longer article with examples of ads, Fred Poppe and Fred Messner (1978), in "To Succeed, Ads Must First Engage the Business Reader," illustrate how "stoppers" in copy and art engage the reader. Because these articles in *Advertising Age* address both industrial and consumer ads, the teacher will find the illustrations useful to show to students. For a reaffirmation that, as teachers of professional communication, we teach style that professional advertisers dictate, Bruce B. MacMillan's (1985, p. 75) "Seven Ways to Improve Your Writing Skills," repeats such sound writing rules as "use live verbs that convey action" and "put the most important point up front."

Finally, in the category of advertisers offering specific advice, I would suggest eight more articles. Irwin W. Tyson (1975, p. 12), in " 'Tell Me Quick and Tell Me True. . .': A Cynical Look at Business," criticizes businesses that try to tell "how our horseshoe nails make a richer life for Americans" rather than talking to management about what the business can do for the user. John C. Harrison (1974), in "To Write Better Ads, Ask Better Questions," stresses that a copywriter must get information for advertising copy not from data sheets but from people who know the product best; Harrison's suggestions will give students direction on research. A more in-depth look at industrial advertising research can be found in Peter J. Roggemann's (1985) "From Strategy to Communications: A Case Study of Advertising Research in Action." Roggemann (1985, p. RC-13), a vice-president of Manufacturer's Hanover Trust, assesses how financial marketers describe their customers and how as a result of this audience analysis "the star of the advertising is the customer, not the institution. The products are represented, not for their own sake, but as tools for the customer to use to achieve personal goals." J. G. Bronson's (1972) "Basic Source Document—An Analgesic for Technical Advertisers" proposes that technical people furnish advertising copywriters with not only data but also interpretations of that data so that the product will not be misrepresented. William D. Tyler (1975), in "Top Industrial Ads Feature Product Benefits, Demos, Problem Solving," as his title suggests, analyzes the strategy in the copy and format of several industrial ads; students would benefit from seeing the ads Tyler duplicates in his article before they read his analysis. Although the sixth article addresses the design, testing, tone, and style of direct mail ads, because the author interviews an experienced writer about style, Robert Stone's (1977) "Leading Direct Response Writer Shares His Copywriting Secrets" belongs in this recommended group of professional journal articles. For teachers who have classes with medical students or technical writing majors interested in medical writing, Gail Dearing's (1979) paper, "Role of the Medical Writer in the Pharmaceutical Industry and Advertising Agencies," reviews the various styles and formats used by pharmaceutical companies and the way the technical writer can transform medical vocabulary into persuasive copy. Finally, David A. Aaker and Donald E. Bruzzone (1985) cite sixteen copy characteristics or advertising approaches that increase or decrease irritation in the television viewers. While most of the 524 commercials analyzed are general consumer commercials, the products include everything from soap to batteries, and the authors show how irritation levels depend on product class and socioeconomic level.

In the second category of in-depth analysis of language, three articles lead the field. All are more complex and less accessible to the student than those in the first category, but they will increase the teacher's background knowledge of technical advertising. Fred Kopf (1978) finds that industrial advertisements contain two levels of language: the "native" dialects of the technical experts and the "deep structure" of the language that tells the reader how his or her problems matter. In "Industrial Language Is Whole New Dialect," Kopf (1978, p. 52) states that "the best industrial advertising is written in a language whose surface structure talks to the reader in his own dialect, but whose deep structure does the more important job: It makes human contact." In a well-referenced article that advocates technical terminology, Rolph E. Anderson and Marvin A. Jolson (1980) discuss ads that use nontechnical, partially technical, or technical language. In their study of the impact of these vocabularies, "Technical Wording in Advertising: Implications and Segmentation," they include copies of the ads they studied in the article. In a similar article, Sam J. Bruno (1974) discusses the level of vocabulary in thirty ads from airlines, automobiles, and finance companies, fifteen of which address business and industrial users and fifteen household consumers. Although Bruno's (1974) conclusions are predictable, that the general readability is more difficult in industrial than in consumer ads, teachers who read "A Readability Comparison Between Industrial and Consumer Advertising Copy" could share Bruno's readability formulas with their students. M. Carole Macklin et al. (1985) also discuss readability formulas in technical advertisements in "Is It Always as Simple as 'Keep It Simple'?"

Although most articles on industrial marketing and advertising concentrate on style, for the teacher who wants students to experiment with format and design, I suggest Jacalyn Langenthal's (1979) "Is Your Ad Format on Target?" Although this article runs only two pages, Langenthal analyzes the ad formats from Witco Chemical Corporation and offers four excellent suggestions for industrial advertising design. For the teacher who wants a thorough background on general advertising design, Richard M. Schlemmer's (1976) *Handbook of Advertising Art Production* covers everything from paper to type. For the teacher who wants more samples of industrial advertisements, *Advertising Age* offers fifty Raytheon ads in their January 30, 1984, issue while their January 23, 1984, issue contains the Kelly Award Winners from 1983, with the best magazine ads from that year printed and analyzed briefly.

Three articles address the growing concern with achieving a positive corporate image through advertising. Since most companies now use the media extensively to promote their image, students and teachers should look at corporate image strategies. Cecelia Reed (1984) justifies a corporate ad campaign in "Corporate Image Advertising"; Lewis C. Winters (1986) uses Chevron to illustrate how to improve the "social conduct image" of the corporation in "The Effect of Brand Advertising on Company Image: Implications for Corporate Advertising"; and Robert L. Heath and Richard A. Nelson (1985) offer an excellent review of current advertising case law and regulatory decisions of the Federal Trade Commission, the Federal Communications Commission, and the Internal Revenue Service as they affect image/issue campaigns by corporations attempting to overcome negative news coverage in

"Image and Issue Advertising: A Corporate and Public Policy Perspective."

Unfortunately, despite the breadth of subjects covered in professional marketing journals, few sources in professional communication journals help the teacher design units and courses in technical advertising. However, the teacher who combines articles from both types of journals has an excellent start. Since advertising copywriting depends on persuasive and provocative style, students might benefit from rethinking their use of adjectives and verbs. "How to Develop Ideas" (1970) in the *ABCA Bulletin* offers a checklist of features and associations that promote a product and suggests how students and teachers can develop their own lists. Should the teacher want to define technical advertising as direct mail advertising, John T. Maguire (1971) includes a course outline, sample assignments, and examples in "An Outline for a Course: Part III." The fifty-page article provides the teacher with complete course materials for direct mail marketing of consumer and industrial products. Perhaps the best textbook available for teachers who need to design a course in technical advertising is Philip W. Burton's (1983) *Advertising Copywriting*. Burton's text provides a comprehensive look at advertising with three chapters devoted to direct mail and mail order copy and two to advertising for business, the professions, and agriculture. Although Burton does little with design, he offers examples from both the print and electronic media and bases his suggestions for copy on sound marketing and research principles.

The Link between Technical Advertising and Sales

Again, the separations between advertising and sales are artificial, although sometimes necessary when teachers design units and assignments. The sources that address the link between the two fields provide teachers with transitional units or bases for simulation for multiple assignments.

The teacher might start with George Risley's (1972) sixth and seventh chapters in *Modern Industrial Marketing*. Risley ranks various forms of advertising and sales promotion by tasks and analyzes types of salespeople and customer buying behavior. Although many industrial marketing texts provide such background material, Risley's graphics are particularly accessible. Also Manoj K. Agarwal et al. (1986) have collected in *Readings in Industrial Marketing* essays that address all aspects of industrial marketing.

Three journal articles discuss the unique connections between advertising and sales in technical industries. Marianne Paskowski's (1981)

"Industrial Advertising: It Ain't What It Used to Be, 'Thank Goodness' " proposes that the real difference between industrial and consumer advertising is not in the advertising but in the sales approach; the main function of technical advertising today is to pave the way for the salesperson. Don Breech (1973), in "How to Produce Advertising that Works with Your Sales Force," provides examples of the relationship between advertising and sales in direct mail ads. A concrete approach to language in advertising and sales appears in Ernest Zucker's (1976) "The Role of Technical Literature in Marketing Communications at Stelco: Standards and Style." Zucker demonstrates how at Stelco the "dramatic" style of advertising copywriters and the too often "dull" style of technical people can be reconciled.

The next three articles offer personal suggestions and checklists on advertising sales so common in the professional marketing journal. John Caples (1975), in "50 Things I Have Learned in 50 Years in Advertising," and Ralph Zeuthen (1975), in "Top-Notch Writing Offers Your Product or Idea a Better Chance," have created excellent checklists on copy, clients, and accounts in advertising and sales. Robert Stone's (1974) "How to Create Good Direct Mail and Print Advertising" discusses the copy, research, tone, and style essential to direct mail—the type of advertising that might take the place of the sales force (see also Stone's [1977] "Leading Direct Response Writer Shares His Copywriting Secrets"). To understand how sales and advertising are linked in an advertising campaign, Prodeep K. Korgaonkar et al. (1986) focus on awareness, attitude, and sales as the goals of all advertising campaigns. The authors cover product characteristics analysis, agent-client relations, media selection, competition, market research, resources, and messages and creativity, all illustrated in comprehensive charts, in "Successful Industrial Advertising Campaigns." Although these and other articles address consumer as well as industrial advertising and sales, they provide the teacher with a view of what the most successful professionals suggest.

Finally, one magazine has gathered the winners of such advertising awards as the Effie, given by the American Marketing Association. *Ads Magazine* (1983) displays award-winning print and electronic media ads from this country and others; the print ads are published in full color and the radio commercials appear on a plastic soundsheet insert. Teachers should request volume 2, issue number 6 (July-August 1983), of *Ads Magazine* to obtain a superior source of examples.

Communication educators in their suggestions for classroom assignments and units also recognize the essential link between technical advertising and sales. Carol H. Adams (1977, p. 4), in "My Favorite

Assignment: Persuading the Customer," tells how students can develop an ad campaign based on a ten-point sales checkpoint evaluation that includes such criteria as "did the group refrain from giving price until they had created value?" Her suggestions address both oral and written work and include such aspects as packaging the product. Evelyn Morris (1981), in "My Favorite Assignment: Using Ads to Teach Sales Writing," emphasizes the difference between physical characteristics of products and psychological advertising approaches. In her analysis of the product, prospects, and selling points, Morris demonstrates how to convert these physical characteristics into user benefits and how students learn from such activities as preliminary marketing meetings. Cheryl A. Halper (1980) carries product analysis into specific technical selling with a four-point sales strategy in "Using Magazine Ads to Teach Sales Writing." All three of these articles provide the teacher with teaching approaches as well as specific assignments. Perhaps the best theoretical link between advertising and sales can be gleaned from Annette N. Shelby's (1986) "The Theoretical Basis of Persuasion: A Critical Introduction." In her coverage of persuasive strategies that extend beyond traditional models or the classical rhetorical paradigm, the motive-goal approach, and the psychological structure, Shelby covers a wide range of practical persuasive strategies. Using learning theory, consistency theory, and functional theory, Shelby illustrates through a thorough literature review and some concrete illustrations how most professional communication can be persuasive.

Technical Sales

Since in the classroom, technical sales assignments usually focus on letter writing, in this section, I concentrate on sources that promote ways to improve or teach the sales letter. Overall balance of sources reverses in the field of technical sales, as professional communication journals provide a greater resource for suggestions than do professional marketing journals.

Although Stone's (1972) "Here Are Some Ways You Can Write a Better Sales Letter" is somewhat flip, the article is also one of the few marketing journal articles that offer practical suggestions on letter writing. Sig Rosenbloom's (1977) "Ten Secrets of Better Sales Letters" is equally as informative for students. Rosenbloom's three-phase writing plan and his practical tips reinforce the "you attitude" that most communication teachers advocate. Two other articles from professional marketing journals, which both students and teachers might appreciate, are "Letters that Sell" (1974) and "On Writing a Sales Letter" (1962) from *The Royal Bank of Canada's Monthly Letter.* The first article proposes three formulas for letters: a sales approach, a logical approach, and a rhetorical approach; the second covers salesmanship, appeal, and style.

A paper that proposes a definite link between promotional literature for technical products and a strong sales force is F. T. Van Veen's (1968) "Technical Sales Promotion Writing." Another conference paper that teachers of sales writing may find useful is H. Olken's (1968) "Role of the Technical Writer in Marketing and Sales Promotion." Olken advocates the demonstration of user benefits to sell the product. Conference papers in the ITCC *Proceedings* naturally combine the thoughts of professional marketing experts and professional communication teachers, since the audience for this conference consists of both.

Even though most business and technical writing texts have chapters on the sales letter, three "My Favorite Assignment" articles in communication journals help the teacher prepare to teach these units. Iva M. Hatfield's (1978) "Writing a Sales Message" is clever and unique. Hatfield designs a series of letters to sell "short men's products" to demonstrate the necessity for euphemisms. Carolyn C. Dolecheck's (1980) "Communication Students—Sales Letter Consultants for Small Business Firms" contains some excellent suggestions for students writing real letters for local firms. Finally, Helen Carl (1981), in "Demonstration Writing: Sales and Collection Letters," outlines a two-week, eleven-assignment unit on sales campaigns. These three articles help the teacher go beyond textbook assignments and stress a realistic link between student assignments and specific business situations.

Three articles offer communication teachers an excellent theoretical basis for teaching sales writing. Daniel L. Plug (1980), in "Writing the Persuasive Business Letter," models a strategy of "motivated sequence" after the natural thought processes identified by John Dewey (1910) in *How We Think.* Plug turns Dewey's five-step process into five steps in persuasive writing to convince, stimulate, and actuate the reader. Using Plug's ideas, students can promote their products and services in a pattern that corresponds with the reader's decision-making process. Harry W. Smith, Jr. (1974), in "An Analytical Approach to the Development of Technical Sales Literature," categorizes the common functions of technical sales literature to demonstrate that "form follows function." Smith illustrates typical specifications for typical functions; for example, in buyer reference literature available sizes, capacities, and variations are "vital." Smith discusses the entire package of sales literature: the physical appearance, the specific visuals, the copy, and the budget. These two articles will also convince the teacher to design assignments and choose textbooks that challenge students to produce sales communications in realistic and varied situations. The third article, Michael P. Jordan's (1986) "Co-Associative Lexical Cohesion in Promotional Literature," although more challenging to comprehend and adapt to the classroom, uses technical advertising as well as sales literature to analyze the linguistic structure of comparison. Teachers will find useful theoretical information in this article on the style of comparative advertising and product promotion. Jordan (1986, p. 33) also uses his study to create a "developing paradigm of technical writing."

To complete the overview on the controversy between those who believe that technical advertising is unique and those who propose that little difference exists between technical and consumer advertising, the communication teacher should consider two more articles on industrial sales. Bellizzi and Paul A. Cline (1985) discuss the pro's and con's of using a salesforce with technical training, such as an engineering background, and provide a model to determine the relationship between information exchange and salesforce characteristics in "Technical or Nontechnical Salesmen?" John E. Swan et al. (1985), in "How Industrial Salespeople Gain Customer Trust," analyze the degree of technical knowledge necessary for industrial sales.

For the teacher who wishes to provide students with assignments that address selling specific products, Liz Murphy's (1985) "Market or Perish" explores how colleges market themselves, an interesting product with which to start student discussion. However, for those professional communication teachers who have computer science students in the classroom, three articles analyze how to sell the personal computer. The March 5, 1984, issue of *Advertising Age* offers an introductory essay and several other short articles on marketing the personal computer. Richard Kern (1986) describes the "battle" between the selling and educational process in computer marketing as well as overcoming buyer hesitancy in "Fighting Buyer Resistance in the PC Market." Finally, A. Coskun Samli and James Wills (1986), in "Strategies for Marketing Computers and Related Products," provide three models for computers and high-technology marketing.

Persuasive Communication Models

In this final section, I recommend five articles for the teacher who desires more information on how communication in general fits in technical advertising and sales. Dan H. Robertson (1974), in "Communications and Sales Force Feedback," considers the salesperson a vital link in a two-way communication system between company and potential consumer. Robertson calls for formal communication channels inside and outside the company. Swan and Charles M. Futrell (1978), in "Does Clear Communication Relate to Job Satisfaction and Self-Confidence Among Salespeople?", prove that communication is a key function of management and that, to be effective, management must establish maximum communications with the salesforce. Although readers will find Swan and Futrell's thesis predictable, most can appreciate their thorough bibliography.

Ronald D. Michman and Lynn Harris (1977) set up a coordinated, formal, channel-of-distribution communications system in "The Development of Marketing Channel Communication Models." They provide charts to illustrate the relationship between transfer of goods and services and the exchange of information. Although complex, these models are clear and consist of both microcommunication and macrocommunication systems with positive outcomes listed. Chapter 10, "Industrial Marketing Communications," in Frederick E. Webster, Jr.'s (1979), *Industrial Marketing Strategy* is based on the ADVISOR (*Ad*vertising *I*ndustrial Products: *S*tudy of *O*peration *R*elationships) studies at the Massachusetts Institute of Technology. Webster advocates strategic decision making and helps with media selection. Finally, Peter M. Chisnall (1977), in Chapter 11, "Marketing Communications," in *Effective Industrial Marketing,* adapts Wilbur Schramm's source-receiver communication model to marketing feedback. Chisnall discusses audience analysis and feedback as well as budgeting and includes a sample communications package from International Telephone and Telegraph. All five of these articles or chapters are worth the professional communication teacher's time.

In a final comment on this review of literature, I stress that successful technical advertising and sales teaching should embrace both what communication experts and marketing experts have to offer. Although professional communication teachers have been more outspoken about classroom sales assignments and approaches, the marketing experts lead the field in technical advertising. Now that many experts recognize some distinct characteristics of technical advertising, communication teachers who develop teaching units in advertising in particular should share their ideas and increase the pedagogical literature on technical advertising.

Bibliography

Aaker, David A., and Donald E. Bruzzone. "Causes of Irritation in Advertising." *Journal of Marketing* 49 (Spring 1985): 47-57.

Adams, Carol H. "My Favorite Assignment: Persuading the Customer." *ABCA Bulletin* 40 (Dec. 1977): 4.

ADS Magazine 2 (July-Aug. 1983). D & L Publishing Services, Inc.

Agarwal, Manoj K., Philip C. Burger, and David A. Reid, eds. *Readings in Industrial Marketing.* Englewood Cliffs, N.J.: Prentice-Hall, 1986.

Anderson, Rolph E., and Marvin A. Jolson. "Technical Wording in Advertising: Implications and Segmentation." *Journal of Marketing* 44 (Winter 1980): 57-66.

Bellizzi, Joseph A., and Paul A. Cline. "Technical or Nontechnical Salesmen?" *Industrial Marketing Management* 14 (1985): 69-74.

Bellizzi, Joseph A., and Robert E. Hite. "Consumer Attitudes Toward Accountants, Lawyers, and Physicians with Respect to Advertising Professional Services." *Journal of Advertising Research* 26 (June-July 1986a): 45-54.

———. "Improving Industrial Advertising Copy." *Industrial Marketing Management* 15 (1986b): 117-22.

Bellizzi, Joseph A., and Julie Lehrer. "Developing Better Industrial Advertising." *Industrial Marketing Management* 12 (Feb. 1983): 19-23.

Bellizzi, Joseph A., and Jacqueline J. Mohr. "Technical Versus Nontechnical Wording of Industrial Print Advertising." In *Educator's Proceedings* 50. Edited by R. W. Belk, Robert Peterson, Gerald S. Albaum, Morris B. Holbrook, Roger A. Kerin, Karesh K. Malhotra, and Peter Wright. Chicago, Ill.: American Marketing Association, 1984, 171-75.

Beltramini, Richard F., and Vincent L. Blasko. "An Analysis of Award-Winning Advertising Headlines." *Journal of Advertising Research* 26 (April-May 1986): 48-52.

Breech, Don. "How to Produce Advertising that Works with Your Sales Force." *Industrial Marketing* 58 (March 1973): 34-36.

Bronson, J. G. "Basic Source Document—An Analgesic for Technical Advertisers." *Technical Communication* 19, no. 1 (First Quarter 1972): 14-16.

Bruno, Sam J. "A Readability Comparison Between Industrial and Consumer Advertising Copy." *Journal of Business Communication* 11 (Winter 1974): 32-41.

Burton, Philip W. *Advertising Copywriting.* 5th ed. Columbus, Ohio: Grid Publishing, 1983.

Caples, John. "50 Things I Have Learned in 50 Years in Advertising." *Advertising Age* 46 (Sept. 22, 1975): 47-48.

Carl, Helen. "Demonstration Writing: Sales and Collection Letters." *ABCA Bulletin* 44 (March 1981): 23-24.

Chisnall, Peter W. *Effective Industrial Marketing.* New York: Longman, 1977.

"The Copy Chaser Rules: What Makes Good Business Industrial Advertising." *Industrial Marketing* 67 (Dec. 1982): 51-52.

Dearing, Gail. "Role of the Medical Writer in the Pharmaceutical Industry and Advertising Agencies." In *Proceedings of the 26th International Technical Communications Conference,* Los Angeles, Calif., 1979. Society for Technical Communication. Paper W43-W45.

Dichfer, Ernest. "Psychology in Industrial Marketing: Industrial Buying Is Based on Same 'Only Human' Emotional Factors that Motivate Consumer Market's Housewife." *Industrial Marketing* 58 (Feb. 1973): 14, 16, 18.

Dolecheck, Carolyn C. "Communication Students—Sales Letter Consultants for Small Business Firms." *ABCA Bulletin* 43 (March 1980): 9-10.

"From Inconsequential Clerk to Specialist in Communications: The Ad Manager Grows Up." *Industrial Marketing* 61 (June 1976): 107.

Halper, Cheryl A. "Using Magazine Ads to Teach Sales Writing." *ABCA Bulletin* 43 (Dec. 1980): 22-30.

Harrison, John C. "To Write Better Ads, Ask Better Questions." *Industrial Marketing* 59 (Feb. 1974): 78, 80.

Hatfield, Iva M. "Writing a Sales Message." *ABCA Bulletin* 41 (June 1978): 8.

Havens, George N. "Industrial Advertising Grows in Scope, Status, and Strategic Value." In *Readings in Industrial Marketing,* edited by Manoj K. Agarwal, Philip C. Burger, and David A. Reid. Englewood Cliffs, N.J.: Prentice-Hall, 1986. pp. 164-68.

Heath, Robert L., and Richard A. Nelson. "Image and Issue Advertising: A Corporate and Public Policy Perspective." *Journal of Marketing* 49 (Spring 1985): 58-68.

Hopkins, Claude C. *Scientific Advertising.* Chicago: Advertising Publications, 1966.

"How to Develop Ideas." *ABCA Bulletin* 33 (Nov. 1970): 14.

Jackson, Dick. "Bridges Are the Links to Make Copy Flow." *Advertising Age* 49 (July 24, 1978): 61.

Jordan, Michael P. "Co-Associative Lexical Cohesion in Promotional Literature." *Journal of Technical Writing and Communication* 16, no. 1-2 (1986): 33-53.

Kern, Richard. "Fighting Buyer Resistance in the PC Market." *Sales and Marketing Management* 36 (Jan. 13, 1986): 42-44.

Kopf, Fred. "Industrial Language Is Whole New Dialect." *Advertising Age* 49 (June 12, 1978): 52, 56.

Korda, Reva. "How to Break the Rules: Heresies About Writing Copy." *Advertising Age* 50 (March 5, 1979): 47-48.

Korgaonkar, Prodeep K., Danny N. Bellenger, and Allen E. Smith. "Successful Industrial Advertising Campaigns." *Industrial Marketing Management* 15, no. 2 (May 1986): 123-28.

Langenthal, Jacalyn. "Is Your Ad Format on Target?" *Industrial Marketing* 64 (Sept. 1979): 75-76.

"Letters that Sell." *The Royal Bank of Canada's Monthly Letter* 55 (May 1974).

Macklin, M. Carole, Norman T. Bruvoid, and Carol L. Shea. "Is It Always as Simple as 'Keep It Simple'?" *Journal of Advertising* 14, no. 4 (1985): 28–35.

MacMillan, Bruce B. "Seven Ways to Improve Your Writing Skills." *Sales and Marketing Management* 134 (March 11, 1985): 75–76.

Maguire, John T. "An Outline for a Course: Part III." *ABCA Bulletin* 34 (March 1971): 1–50.

Michman, Ronald D., and Lynn Harris. "The Development of Marketing Channel Communication Models." *Journal of Business Communication* 15 (Fall 1977): 29–39.

Morris, Evelyn. "My Favorite Assignment: Using Ads to Teach Sales Writing." *ABCA Bulletin* 44 (Dec. 1981): 29.

Murphy, Liz. "Market or Perish." *Sales and Marketing Management* 134 (May 13, 1985): 50–53.

Olken, H. "Role of the Technical Writer in Marketing and Sales Promotion." In *Proceedings of the 15th International Technical Communications Conference,* 1968, Paper W-1.

"On Writing a Sales Letter." *The Royal Bank of Canada's Monthly Letter* 43 (March 1962).

Paskowski, Marianne. "Industrial Advertising: It Ain't What It Used to Be, 'Thank Goodness.' " *Industrial Marketing* 66 (May 1981): 76, 78.

Plug, Daniel L. "Writing the Persuasive Business Letter." *Journal of Business Communication* 17 (Spring 1980): 45–49.

Pollay, Richard W. "The Subsiding Sizzle: A Descriptive History of Print Advertising, 1900–1980." *Journal of Marketing* 49 (Summer 1985): 24–37.

Poppe, Fred, and Fred Messner. "To Succeed, Ads Must First Engage the Business Reader." *Advertising Age* 49 (June 12, 1978): 25, 30, 32, 34.

Reed, Cecelia. "Corporate Image Advertising." *Advertising Age* 55 (Jan. 23, 1984): M9, M28.

Risley, George. *Modern Industrial Marketing.* New York: McGraw-Hill, 1972.

Robertson, Dan H. "Communications and Sales Force Feedback." *Journal of Business Communication* 11 (Winter 1974): 3–9.

Roggemann, Peter J. "From Strategy to Communications: A Case Study of Advertising Research in Action." *Journal of Advertising Research* 52 (Aug.-Sept. 1985): RC11–RC14.

Rosenbloom, Sig. "Ten Secrets of Better Sales Letters." *Sales and Marketing Management* 118 (May 16, 1977): 36–38.

Samli, A. Coskun, and James Wills. "Strategies for Marketing Computers and Related Products." *Industrial Marketing Management* 15 (1986): 23–32.

Sawyer, Howard G. "About Repetition and Pronoun Use." *Advertising Age* 50 (June 18, 1979): 68.

Schellenback, Burton. "Back to Basics: Tie in Your Ads with Your Business Aims." *Industrial Marketing* 60 (Sept. 1975): 86, 88.

Schlemmer, Richard M. *Handbook of Advertising Art Production.* 4th ed. Englewood Cliffs, N.J.: Prentice-Hall, 1976.

Shelby, Annette N. "The Theoretical Bases of Persuasion: A Critical Introduction." *Journal of Business Communication* 23 (Winter 1986): 5-29.

Smith, Harry W., Jr. "An Analytical Approach to the Development of Technical Sales Literature." *Journal of Technical Writing and Communication* 4 (Summer 1974): 207-15.

Stone, Robert. "Here Are Some Ways You Can Write a Better Sales Letter." *Advertising Age* 43 (Jan. 3, 1972): 55-56.

———. "How to Create Good Direct Mail and Print Advertising." *Advertising Age* 45 (Sept. 2, 1974): 30, 32-33.

———. "Leading Direct Response Writer Shares His Copywriting Secrets." *Advertising Age* 48 (June 13, 1977): 53.

———. "Long Narrative Copy: A Marketer's View." *Advertising Age* 51 (Aug. 25, 1980): 48.

Swan, John E., and Charles M. Futrell. "Does Clear Communication Relate to Job Satisfaction and Self-Confidence Among Salespeople?" *Journal of Business Communication* 15 (Summer 1978): 39-52.

Swan, John E., I. Frederick Trawick, and David W. Silva. "How Industrial Salespeople Gain Customer Trust." *Industrial Marketing Management* 14 (1985): 203-11.

Tyler, William D. "Top Industrial Ads Feature Product Benefits, Demos, Problem Solving." *Advertising Age* 46 (July 14, 1975): 91-92.

———. "Top Industrial Ads Tip Sales, Reflect Solid Ad Principles." *Advertising Age* 50 (Aug. 27, 1979): 41-42.

Tyson, Irwin W. "'Tell Me Quick and Tell Me True...': A Cynical Look at Business." *Public Relations Journal* 30 (Nov. 1975): 12.

Van Veen, F. T. "Technical Sales Promotion Writing." In *Proceedings of the 15th International Technical Communications Conference*, 1968. Society for Technical Communication. Paper W-2.

Webster, Frederick E., Jr. *Industrial Marketing Strategy.* New York: John Wiley, 1979.

Winters, Lewis C. "The Effect of Brand Advertising on Company Image: Implications for Corporate Advertising." *Journal of Advertising Research* 26 (April-May 1986): 54-59.

Woods, Robert. "Industrial Ads: The Focus Gets Sharper." *Sales and Marketing Management* 128 (April 26, 1982): 37-52.

Zeuthen, Ralph. "Top-Notch Writing Offers Your Product or Idea a Better Chance." *Advertising Age* 46 (April 21, 1975): 65.

Zucker, Ernest. "The Role of Technical Literature in Marketing Communications at Stelco: Standards and Style." In *Proceedings of the 23rd International Technical Communications Conference*, Society for Technical Communication, 1976, p. 157.

14 Letters and Memorandums

Nancy (Fitzgerald) Brown
Mount Wachusett Community College
Gardner, Massachusetts

Letters

The most significant skill demanded by businesses everywhere is the ability to communicate. In a recent survey of over 2,000 businesses, the ability to communicate was chosen above ambition, drive, education, experience, self-confidence, and good appearance (Langemo and Modlin 1986).

Letter and memorandum (or memo) writing certainly is at the top of the list of communication skills. In fact, over 76 million letters are written in American businesses each day. These 1986 business letters cost $8.52 each to generate and, according to analyst Sylvia Porter, many executive originated letters are now costing $20 to $30 each (Langemo and Modlin 1986).

Every letter that is mailed and every memo that is disbursed intercompany requires a copy for the file and normally copies for other individuals, and clarity and conciseness are demanded. Clarity and conciseness, however, evolve following careful analyzing, planning, and structuring. Teaching a student to compose the message can begin with stressing the importance of the writing situation as stated here. The ensuing instruction needs to examine the equally important aspects of an effective message. These aspects will be discussed in the rest of this paper.

Analysis and Communication Psychology

Dumont and Lannon (1985, p. 29) explain in *Business Communications* that "communication will fail if you ignore your audience's needs." Just as advertisements are prepared to appeal to certain audiences, business messages are prepared to appeal to certain readers. Guidelines are given throughout Dumont and Lannon's (1985, p. 30) book to help the student understand "human nature with its ways of reasoning, its habits, desires, and emotions."

"To know your audience" is a concept that is stressed in nearly all communication textbooks. Blicq (1976) in *On the Move: Communication for Employees* compares examples of warm, personal writing to cold, impersonal approaches to a reader. Adelstein (1971) in *Contemporary Business Writing* maintains the need for a writer's awareness for tone. Adelstein (1971, p. 26) states, "The business writer must plan his work, select his words, adapt his ideas, choose his style and direct his message to a particular person or group with a special educational, economic, social and cultural background and interest."

Dumont and Lannon's (1985, p. 27) *Business Communications* lists deliberate questions that the audience may have. The students who know their audience can anticipate such questions or others and will be better able to tailor their messages to the readers' needs.

Murphy and Hildebrandt (1984, p.48) explain that readers are "usually more concerned about themselves than about you or the company you represent." The authors contrast the "we attitude" to the "you attitude" by illustrating how the "you" or "your" can keep the reader in the message tactfully until the end. In addition, the authors offer situations in which it is advisable *not* to use "you." The examples and explanations presented help the students to write with the reader-oriented concept.

This element of business writing requires much attention. The ability to empathize and write with the "you perspective" puts new demands on the college student's writing. Goeller (1974, p.3) in *Writing to Communicate* claims, "Big words, long, involved sentences and lots of punctuation may impress the English professor but they simply turn off the business executive."

At one time, the student's objective was to write to impress; the writing was for the writer to demonstrate knowledge or literary talents. Business writing, however, places other demands on the students. They must now write for the reader and make decisions about feelings and attitudes and word connotation.

One of the best sources for displaying appropriate tones for business messages is Wolf and Kuiper's (1984) *Effective Communication in Business*. The communication student needs to identify positive, personal business writing. *Effective Communication in Business* (1984) provides examples of constructive tones, illustrating as well those ingredients that produce destructive tones. The chapter applications furnish abundant exercises to help the student apply the proper tone. In addition, individual sentence revision exercises offered in this text provide excellent practice in transforming the negative and impersonal into the positive and personal (pp. 84-96). Murphy and Hildebrandt (1984) also present beneficial examples and exercises to help the student accent the positive. To be successful, the reader-oriented message must show "what you can do for him or her." Here the authors contrast the negative and unpleasant to the positive and pleasant (Murphy and Hildebrandt 1984, p. 51).

Other factors affecting the tone of the message are word choice and connotation. Again, the college student has learned to write to impress— to expose an elegant vocabulary of long words. Again, the business executive has no time for such. Executives want to understand the purpose of the message as quickly as possible. The mission of the communication instructor, therefore, is to simplify that vocabulary for the written message. Murphy and Hildebrandt's (1984) *Effective Business Communications* provides guidelines to help the student to compose concrete, convincing messages. The numerous examples demonstrate the ability "to use specific facts and figures, to put action in your verbs, and to choose vivid, image building words" (Murphy and Hildebrandt 1984, p. 87).

Rudolph Flesch on Business Communication: How to Say What You Mean in Plain English (Flesch 1974) is a compact text with an explicit title. The book offers an overview of communication instruction. Flesch sets a style for the first-time communication teacher to fall back on, providing a casual review for the experienced teacher as well. As Flesch explains his ideas and experiences concerning letter and memo writing, he offers a sixty-word blacklist. The outdated or unclear vocabulary that is selected to appear in Flesch's blacklist gives the student a vocabulary list to avoid when creating concise and stimulating messages. As well, each word is discussed in the following twenty-three pages of the text to help the student understand the reasons for their unacceptance and to become aware of the principle of clear, concise word usage (Flesch 1974, pp. 72-95).

In addition to simplifying the word, the business writer needs to know word context and tone. Once more, audience awareness is stressed as Wolf and Kuiper in *Effective Business Communications* (1984) discuss denotations, connotations, and contexts as ingredients of message tone (p. 85). Dumont and Lannon's (1985, pp. 74-78) *Business*

Communications also contributes excellent discussion and examples of appropriate tone through word usage.

Clarity and Conciseness

In the mid-eighteenth century, the great English letter writer Lord Chesterfield lectured his son:

> The first thing necessary in writing letters of business is extreme clearness and perspicuity; every paragraph should be so clear and unambiguous that the dullest fellow in the world may not be able to mistake it, nor obliged to read it twice in order to understand it. (Adelstein 1969, p. 208)

Achieving the elements for clarity, that is, completeness, grammatical agreement, correct pronoun reference, and parallel structure, can be a difficult project for the communications instructor. If the approach is to review these areas of grammar, then Dumont and Lannon's (1985, pp. 64–99) *Business Communications* section "Revising for a Readable Style" will accomplish the task. In addition, this text offers an appendix on grammar, if reference is needed throughout the course regarding problem areas highlighted through the students' writing projects.

In two chapters of *Effective Business Communications* in which Murphy and Hildebrandt (1984, p. 66) discuss the seven C's of the business writing principles—completeness, conciseness, consideration, concreteness, clarity, courtesy, and correctness—specific ways to help make a message clear are illustrated:

1. Choose short familiar conversational words.
2. Construct effective sentences and paragraphs.
3. Achieve appropriate readability.
4. Include examples and illustrations, and other visual aids when desirable.

Himstreet and Baty (1981, pp. 52–58) approach the discussion of clarity through explanations of phrases, euphemisms, parallelisms, redundancies, and cliches. Although most communications texts suggest that business messages be written in a conversational tone, these units of encoding emphasize the necessity of coherence and help to avoid the pitfalls that could arise when writing in a conversational tone.

Wolf and Kuiper's (1984) *Effective Communication in Business* is another superior source for reviewing these elements of clarity. The section "Communication Criteria and Message Effectiveness" is a comprehensive and thorough presentation. This text, too, offers a reference section for more elaborate coverage of the rules of modern

English grammar. Yet, with proper guidance the student should come to the business communications class with competency in grammar. This, of course, would be advantageous for the instruction of writing logical and coherent sentences.

Another direction to help to make meaning clear is the list of transitions and the relationships they signal offered in Dumont and Lannon's (1985) *Business Communications.* The categorized lists give the student easy reference for developing fluency in sentence and paragraph structure. In addition, polished, easy-to-read sentences are discussed in the section "Revising for Readable Style" (Dumont and Lannon 1985, pp. 61-92). Active and passive voice further develop clarity and stress emphasis. The positive and negative components of each are presented in this chapter, with clear explanations and examples.

Although conciseness is stressed through the use of shorter words and shorter sentences, clarity must be maintained. Dawson (1969) in *Business Writing—A Situational Approach* states, "It is the writer's obligation to tailor a business message so that it may be absorbed in a time consistent with its importance." Examples indicate how a first copy message may be edited to save words, presenting information directly and without repetition.

Outdated or verbose expressions and needless jargon are the worst offenders of clarity and conciseness. Effective use of technical terms among specialists can save time and is appropriate. However, only confusion can arise from inappropriate use. Goeller (1974, pp. 72-83) in *Writing to Communicate* presents "Jargonese—How to Eliminate It from Your Writing." Goeller (1974, p. 74) begins with a series of definitions:

> If you've heard it or read it at least one hundred times before—it's Jargonese.
> If it sounds impressive but doesn't make any sense—it's Jargonese.
> If it takes 50 words to say what can be said in 10—it's Jargonese.

Wolf and Kuiper in *Effective Communication in Business* (1984) condense many needlessly wordy terms into concise equivalents. These practical examples listed in the section, "Communication Criteria and Message Effectiveness" give the business communications student a fingertip reference for editing verbose text and creating more concise writing (Wolf and Kuiper 1984, pp. 41-58).

Organization

Another decisive factor warranting the message to be understood on the first reading is organization. Dumont and Lannon (1985, p. 47) in

Business Communications state, "As with decisions about content, a writer's decisions about organization are guided by the audience's expectations." One section, "Organizing Good Paragraphs," offers discussion and examples of writing the topic sentence to paragraph unity and logical development (Dumont and Lannon 1985, pp. 46-56). Additional sections explain the various classifications of letters and the organizational plan to follow. In response to considering a reader's reaction to a message, a direct or indirect organizational plan is suggested. Examples and explanation support these plans throughout several chapters. Consequently, as the students write specific messages, for example, inquiries, special requests, or refusals, the plans provide an excellent direction to follow. Murphy and Hildebrandt (1984, p. 97) state that "the order in which you present your ideas is often as important as the ideas themselves." Four basic organizational plans—the direct request, good news, bad news, or persuasive request—are discussed briefly in one section and more specifically in other sections. By applying the direct (deductive) approach for direct request and good news plans and the indirect (inductive) approach for bad-news and persuasive request plans, the students are given a flexible guide to decide the best organization and content of each message.

In *Communication for Management and Business,* Sigband and Bell (1986, pp. 142-62) focus on planning and organizing to achieve an order that is logical and psychologically effective. Explaining the value of an outline, as well as analyzing specific examples, helps to emphasize the need to the students to compose an outline prior to the final draft.

Wolf and Kuiper in *Effective Communication in Business* (1984) distinguish between building-block and whole-into-parts methods of planning, organizing, and developing business messages. The chapter "Planning, Organization, and Development of Business Messages" provides detailed techniques for developing data lists into message drafts (Wolf and Kuiper 1984, pp. 62-79).

Wolf and Kuiper explain the communication-by-objectives message planning steps to help the students determine the totality of the message before they plan its details. The authors explain the whole-into-parts method of perception, requiring the student to consider the audience, to determine the purpose, and to develop a logical outline of relevant topics. This third step of the whole-into-parts method is to develop an appropriate outline by putting the topic list items into inductive order (specific to general) or into deductive order (general to specific). In all, the whole-into-parts method of planning, developing, and organizing a business message has nine steps to produce a message that is ready for signature and transmission (Wolf and Kuiper 1984, p. 64).

Special considerations for paragraphs and sentences are illustrated as well. Throughout the whole-into-parts method, empathy is again the guide in creating the business message. The authors suggest that effective paragraph length is more the result of empathy for the reader than of arbitrary line quotas. "The same is true of sentence length and whole message length; empathy is a reliable, profitable guide" (Wolf and Kuiper 1984, p. 76). The examples of opening and closing sentences display a reader-oriented tone. Excellent illustrations of contrasting the effects of opening and closing sentences clarify the relevant but antagonistic to the relevant and empathetic.

Himstreet and Baty (1981, p. 84) also emphasize the necessity of putting an outline on paper before beginning to write any message. An excellent discussion of the inductive and deductive sequencing of ideas is presented, giving the student the ability to present ideas "with less effort, more effect and greater confidence."

Letters and the Law

Once all is said and signed, occasionally legal questions develop— namely, negligence (by those who write without due care), liability (for the letters of the staff), and defamation (from the law of libel and slander). Janner (1977) has produced *The Businessman's Guide to Letter Writing and to the Law on Letters*. Dumont and Lannon (1985) in *Business Communications* consider this subject area as well. In *Business Communications,* Appendix B, "Legal Issues," informs the student of the basic legal principles. The object is to bring this knowledge to a logical solution of legal problems as they arise in business communications. Other sources for the nonspecialist are also recommended.

Message Transmission

Proper format enhances the business message, and Wolf and Kuiper's (1984) *Effective Communication in Business* provides complete, up-to-date information to achieve logical message format. The section "Effective Appearance of Business Messages" impressively covers the features of letter and memorandum final drafts.

Dumont and Lannon (1985, p. 127) in *Business Communications* also defend the appearance of a message declaring, "A letter's appearance should not call attention to itself. Otherwise, it distracts the reader from the letter's content and hurts your image or your firm's." Burtness and Hulbert (1985) also give complete information for the student to produce favorable reactions, using correct letter parts, styles, and stationery. Many students feel distraught with the idea of producing the effective message and creating the "letter perfect" image. The above-mentioned texts consider this effort and give precise information to achieve the positive results.

Electronic Mail

The efficient and rapid method of computer-based message systems is changing the way businesses operate and is increasing the quality of communication. Words, numbers, or pictures can be sent at the speed of light throughout the world. In telecommunications, the message will be received and recorded magnetically by the target computer. The message can then be read on a video display terminal or can be printed in hard copy form (Burtness and Hulbert 1985). This asynchronous method for transferring information within a building or around the world provides immediate response and effectively ends "telephone tag," the frustrating, time-consuming game where two callers never talk because one or the other is out of reach of the telephone. They waste time returning one another's calls but never connect (Dumont and Lannon 1985, p. 161).

According to Stein and Yates (1983), electronic mail promises to reshape the communication system in many organizations: "Managers will have to understand the mechanics and characteristics of the new medium if they are to use it effectively—to avoid its pitfalls and exploit its advantages. And those who teach communication skills must be prepared to train them." They claim the new style of communication falls between a telephone call and a memorandum, in both formality and detail of explanation. "What results is a message that is less formal and less inhibited in style than a traditional communication but more structured than a phone call" (Stein and Yates 1983).

Although electronic mail speeds up the metabolism of a business and saves time, misuse can interfere with the medium's usefulness. Stein and Yates (1983) indicate "the speed of the mode, its perceived informality and its frequently poor editing facilities encourage a user to send out first drafts without due consideration to logical structure and grammar, as well as to tone."

Another area of concern is that inappropriate or irresponsible copying is encouraged, as well as that excessive copies are made due to the ease with which communications can be sent. In addition, since most CRT screens hold only twenty-four lines of text while the typewritten page holds fifty-four, the communications instructor must emphasize the need for more conciseness and structure for the electronic message than for the typed messages. "Given the size of the screen and the nature of the scanning function, as well as the general difficulty of reading on a screen, users must now, more than ever structure their material with the reader in mind" (Stein and Yates 1983).

The unique opportunities electronic mail offers can greatly increase the speed and quantity of communication in business. Communication instructors must help the students to understand both the benefits and the dangers of electronic communication and to overcome the latter. Also, the ability to write English and to interpret what is read will be even more important in the age of electronic communication.

Memorandums

The discussion thus far about business messages has included both the letter and the memorandum. Although many of the concepts for communicating the business messages remain the same for both, memorandum writing has some special qualities. Auren Uris's (1975) *Memos for Managers* highlights some important facts about within-company communication:

> When you write a memo, you're doing at least three things all before your associates:
> 1. You're moving ahead on the subject of the communication itself.
> 2. You're showing your degree of mastery of one of the most important management skills—the ability to put thoughts into writing.
> 3. You're exposing your personality—the kind of person you are.

Obviously, the person who becomes adept at handling the memorandum not only increases his or her effectiveness but also improves the chances for recognition and advancement within a company. Uris's *Memos For Managers* presents a thorough study on memorandums from "The Memo as a Tool and Trumpet" to "When Not to Write a Memo." Examples in "Memos for Every Occasion" point out the good and bad aspects of memorandum writing further to sharpen awareness of effective memorandums.

Himstreet and Baty (1981) stress that the memorandum is the most used report format in business. Its aim should be informal, unpretentious, and concise. "Because memorandums are messages for informal use in the organization, personal pronouns are acceptable" (Himstreet and Baty 1981, p. 353). The authors also explain that deductive order is preferable if the message is informative. In addition, memorandum messages are written on a logical rather than a psychological basis (Himstreet and Baty 1981, p. 356).

Although these differences between letters and memorandums exist, the preparation of memorandums is an organizational and adaptational task much like letter planning. According to Himstreet and Baty (1981, p. 360) a good memorandum is a brief report—it calls for great attention to organization and to detail.

Brock's (1974) *How to Communicate by Letter and Memo* states the essential differences between letters and memorandums:

1. The business letter is a subjective piece of writing, whereas the memo is typically objective.
2. The memo, an internal communication, is more management oriented and, hence, the letter is more public relations oriented.

Brock discusses memorandums with these differences in mind, explaining his views of the essential five stages of memorandum preparation: planning, gathering information, organizing, outlining, drafting and editing.

Memorandum reports, another major means of written communication, cover any topic important to the firm's operations. Common types include informational, recommendation, justification, progress, periodic, and survey reports. Dumont and Lannon (1985) in *Business Communications* present examples of each and suggest ways to present all information impartially and concisely and in a format that guides the reader through the report. The chapter applications provide practical situations for each type of report. The students gain awareness of the various types of reports they may write on any workday.

The chapter "Proposals" evaluates the elements of a good proposal. Whether in business, science, industry, government, or education, proposals are written for decision makers. To help students to be successful and to convince the decision makers that suggestions, projects, or service proposals are worthwhile, Dumont and Lannon (1985, pp. 434–75) present guidelines to develop what might be the student's most important writing activity.

The internal memorandum report is discussed in Wolf and Kuiper's (1984) *Effective Business Communications* as well. The section "Reports as Decision Aids" stresses the application of clarity, conciseness, accuracy, and empathetic tone, along with the additional research and writing skills needed to produce effective reports. The authors describe a communications-by-objectives approach in a ten-part work plan to help the student develop objective, understandable memorandum reports (Wolf and Kuiper 1984, p. 292).

Conclusion

Business people and administrators are experiencing a "pinch" on profits and on budgets because of the steadily increasing volume of records and because of soaring record costs. Today, every inch of paper in filing cabinets costs an average of $300 to create and $13.97 per year to store—filing a single-page letter is over $1 (Langemo and Modlin 1986). In addition, the volume of paper in American offices has more than doubled in the last 10 years, a rather disturbing contradiction to the once-claimed paperless office.

Still, however, the electronic age is revolutionizing many organizations. "The Office in the Year 2000," as prepared by Mitchell (1986), lists predictions that will affect business communication instruction from every direction:

1. All those working in offices will have display terminals with multifunction capabilities (voice, data, word image, and video processing activities) at their fingertips.
2. Any incoming correspondence that is not transmitted electronically will be converted to a digitized format via laser scanners and input into the electronic filing system. The documents will then be accessed via display terminals for action.
3. Documents created in-house will be dictated to the voice actuated display terminal.
   a. Words will appear on the individual's terminal display for editing and revision by the author or support staff member.
   b. Words will be run through a dictionary and a grammar syntax validator before the final draft is ready for distribution.
   c. Documents will be sent via electronic mail anywhere in the world.
   d. Duplicate copies will be automatically filed in the optical disk storage system.
4. All mail and messages (to include voice mail) will be stored in "electronic mailboxes" that individuals can access at any time.
5. Voice communications will be conducted via the display terminals.
   a. The receiver can identify the caller and the purpose of the call.
   b. The receiver decides whether to talk or to take a message by pushing a few buttons.
6. Business trips will become less necessary through full-motion video teleconferencing in two, three, or a dozen locations.
7. While businesses will maintain a headquarters office complex for central control, more office work will be done by work

group clusters in distributed office complexes in outlying areas that are specially wired and outfitted.

To send messages and to retain one for the file, the skilled communicator must know how to outline, draft, and perfect each message so that it fits the purpose and suits the medium. Skilled business communicators will ensure personal success as well as the success of the company in which they are employed. Individuals who strive to acquire language facility and who incorporate the art of human relations into their writing will attain the level of skill and will gain the confidence necessary for successful business writing. Moreover, no matter how extensive or elaborate a communication system may be, effective communication still depends on each individual who functions within the organization.

References

Adelstein, Michael E. *Contemporary Business Writing.* New York: Random House, 1971.

Blicq, Ron. *On the Move: Communication for Employees.* Englewood Cliffs, N.J.: Prentice-Hall, 1976.

Brock, Luther A. *How to Communicate by Letter and Memo.* New York: McGraw-Hill, 1974.

Burtness, Paul S., and Jack E. Hulbert. *Effective Business Communications.* 8th ed. Cincinnati: South Western Publishing Co., 1985.

Dawson, Presley C. *Business Writing—A Situational Approach.* Belmont, Calif.: Dickenson, 1969.

Dumont, Raymond A., and John M. Lannon. *Business Communications.* Boston: Little, Brown, 1985.

Flesch, Rudolf. *Rudolf Flesch on Business Communications: How to Say What You Mean in Plain English.* New York: Barnes and Noble, 1974.

Goeller, Carl. *Writing to Communicate.* New York: New American Library, 1974.

Himstreet, William C., and Wayne M. Baty. *Business Communications.* 6th ed. Belmont, Calif.: Kent, 1981.

Janner, Greville (Ewan Mitchell, pseud.). *The Businessman's Guide to Letter Writing and to the Law on Letters.* 2d ed. London: Business Books, 1977.

Langemo, Mark, and Gail G. Modlin. "Records Management and Microcomputers: The Cutting Edge." 1986 Business Education Institute, Suffolk University.

Mitchell, Bill. "The Office in the Year 2000." Office Automation Consultant, University of Wisconsin–Eau Claire, 1986.

Murphy, Herta A., and Herbert W. Hildebrandt. *Effective Business Communications.* 4th ed. New York: McGraw-Hill, 1984.

Sigband, Norman B., and Arthur H. Bell. *Communication for Management and Business.* Glenview, Ill.: Scott, Foresman, 1986.

Stein, Judith, and JoAnne Yates. "Electronic Mail—How Will it Change Office Communication? How Can Managers Use it Effectively?" In *Information Systems and Business Communication,* edited by R. Beswick and A. Williams. Urbana, Ill.: Association for Business Communication.

Uris, Auren. *Memos for Managers.* New York: T. Y. Crowell,1975.

Wolf, Morris, and Shirley Kuiper. *Effective Communication in Business.* Cincinnati: South Western Publishing Co., 1984.

Additional Sources

Listed below are some sources, including a summary of each, for additional, up-to-date information for the instruction of letter and memorandum writing.

Andera, Frank. "Important Implications of Letter Mail Automation and Word Processing on Today's Written Communication." *Bulletin of the Association for Business Communication,* Sept. 1985, 45–49.

Shows how communication instructors can provide leadership in demonstrating how the cost of producing an average business letter can be reduced through the use of technology.

Bell, James D. "The Indirect Empathic Approach to Claim Letters." *Journal of Education for Business,* Oct. 1985, 11–15.

In discussing letter-writing methods for business communication classes, explains that claim letter formats other than the direct approach are not only legitimate, but also effective and suggests that the approach selected should depend on the circumstances surrounding the claim.

Booher, Dianna. "Writing More But Enjoying It Less?" *Training and Development Journal,* Nov. 1984, 48–51.

Discusses five steps to help pare and improve the writing training program's proposals, letters, memorandums, and course brochures: consider the audience; anticipate special problems; outline the message functionally; develop the first draft; and edit for clarity, content, conciseness, style, and grammar.

Brent, Douglas. "Indirect Structure and Reader Response." *Journal of Business Communication,* Spring 1985, 5–8.

Argues that the practice of delaying bad news in business letters by using buffer sentences is misguided, for it is based on a false notion of how people read. Suggests structuring letters on the type of argument and situation rather than palatability of the message.

Casady, Mon J. "Practice What You Preach about Goodwill Messages." *Bulletin of the Association for Business Communication,* Dec. 1985, 6–9.

Suggests ways for students to experience the impact of written messages and for teachers to promote good public relations through the use of goodwill messages. Examples include the use of verbal compliments and personal business letters.

Dieterich, Dan. "Real Readers for Real Writers." *Bulletin of the Association for Business Communication,* June 1986, 28–29.

States that writing must be taught in a way that interests and involves students and prepares them for life outside the writing classroom. Gives examples of appropriate assignments, including writing a letter of complaint and writing job application letters and resumes.

Feinberg, Susan, and Irene Pritzker. "An MBA Communication Course Designed by Business Executives." *Journal of Business Communication,* Fall 1985, 75–83.

Reports on writing skills business executives consider important areas of focus in business correspondence: logic, clarity, and brevity instead of grammar, diction, and paragraph structure.

Giovannini, Mary, and Milton F. Miller. "Teaching Business Communications: A Comparison of Teaching by the Traditional Writing and the Word Processing Methods." *Journal of Studies in Technical Careers,* Winter 1984, 21–28.

This study set out to determine the effect of teaching business communications by a traditional writing method and a word processing method on students' attitudes and cognitive achievements. No significance was found between treatment groups on the combined mean scores of the letter-writing problems.

Hansford, John W. "Letter Perfect." *Currents,* Oct. 1984, 26–29.

Effective fund-raising letters balance an eye-catching appearance with an action-getting appeal. Discusses some helpful hints to consider when planning direct mail letters, including making the letter attractive, using language skillfully, planning the text, and considering copy formulas.

Jablin, Fredric M., and Kathleen Krone. "Characteristics of Rejection Letters and Their Effects on Job Applicants." *Written Communication,* Oct. 1984, 387–406.

Describes the structural and content characteristics of actual employment rejection letters and analyzes their impact on applicants' feelings about themselves and about the letters. Concludes that few of the letter characteristics affected applicants' feelings about themselves but that a number were related to their perceptions of the letters.

Kilpatrick, Retha H. "International Business Communication Practices." *Journal of Business Communication,* Fall 1984, 33–44.

Surveyed one hundred corporations to identify and analyze current practices in writing international letters. Analyzed data relative to language, letter format, writing style, and communication skills needed by foreign correspondents.

Moran, Michael G. "Writing Business Correspondence Using the Persuasive Sequence." *ABCA Bulletin* 47, no. 2 (1984): 24–27.

Discusses the five steps in the persuasive sequence used by Joseph Priestley in his scientific writing and adapted for use in teaching business communication.

Reep, Diana C. "The Manager's Message—Teaching the Internal Memo." *ABCA Bulletin* 47, no. 1 (1984): 11–13.

Outlines a unit on teaching business communication students the complexities of writing in-house memorandums.

Trace, Jacqueline. "Teaching Resume Writing the Functional Way." *Bulletin of the Association for Business Communication,* June 1985, 34–41.

Cites reasons why resume writing is a legitimate subject in a business or technical writing course. Discusses advantages and components of the functional resume, the skills identification workshop, and last-minute tips for writing effective resumes.

Waltman, John L., and Steven P. Golen. "Resolving Problems of Invention in Persuasive Letters." *ABCA Bulletin* 47, no. 2 (1984): 19–20.

Offers a technique designed to help business communication students write sales letters and letters of application.

15 Reports, Papers, and News Releases

Brenda Johns
University of Cincinnati

When we consider these three genres for the purpose of evaluating what has been written about them recently, it becomes clear that a shared feature of the three is that all are used for communicative purposes to report to different audiences the results of research in science and technology. Another feature that we might consider as linking them is the fact that all may originate with the scientist or engineer, whereas other types of technical writing may be by science writers or public relations personnel assigned to translate the work of scientists and engineers for a more general audience. The news release may differ from the technical paper and the technical report in the extent to which the scientist or engineer may keep the format of the technical report. Because a newspaper editor may want to keep scientific news consistent with the format of other news and because the readership of a newspaper in which scientific and technical discoveries are reported is more diffuse than the readership of a company report, it is necessary to address the question of what the writer must know to meet the requirements of idiomatic writing for each genre while striving simultaneously to gauge the proficiency of his or her reader (or listener, if it is an oral report) in sifting through "technical" information.

Works devoted in part or wholly to all three genres address several issues. At the most trivial level, though, are books and articles devoted to questions centering on what it is one does in writing the three types of technical documents considered here. Thus, my emphasis will be on the writer and audience in these three genres because there is a wealth of material covered in excellent bibliographies that is concerned with many works on technical reports and papers that are minimally different from each other and on "how-to" guides that stress mechanical accuracy, adherence to the prescribed format for reports, etc. I suspect that this emphasis reflects a shift in composition research from writing as product or documents to an evaluation of writing as process. I would assert that books in this period on the three genres do address the greater world of writer-audience relations, but this theme has been masked because of the need to get scientists and engineers to think about writing at all and to produce intelligible documents.

I will treat the following concerns for each genre: What works focus on making explicit what the writer must bring to the task at hand to communicate? How are these genres learned? Which works focus on figuring out how to communicate effectively with different audiences? Above and beyond the questions I raise here, what is central to an understanding of how the three genres are realized as communicated products of writers in schools and industry?

Technical Reports

A recent bibliographic article on technical reports by Stanton (1985, pp. 285–311) does a good job of summarizing many of the major issues involved in the format of technical reports and also gives a good comprehensive bibliography of works on technical reports covering the period from 1960 to the present. Although Stanton recognizes that the technical report has been broadly defined, she redefines it for the purpose of her essay as "the engineering report of some length which provides a solution to an engineering problem with a view to what management needs to know." Seeing technical reports as a subset of other reports, she goes on to state her task in covering reports: "This bibliographical essay discusses studies in reports of all lengths, in all forms, and in most special fields other than law and medicine" (Stanton 1985, pp. 286–87).

While Stanton does a good job of placing technical reports in the context of other documents, a theme I discern in books on technical reports and papers is the question of how best to teach the form of the report and the question of how the audience needs determine the form of the report. Stanton maintains, "The problem-solving technique, developed by systems analysis, is the current trend and seems to be a good one, but the method has not been integrated into report-writing theory. Nevertheless, it appears to be the only approach to the writing process that is likely to supersede some authors' lame and stultifying insistence on outlining as the invention method of choice" (Stanton 1985, p. 296).

While several authors may advocate outlining in the preparation of a technical report, a common purpose has also been to prepare the writer of the technical report to consider the relationship between writer and audience, something that in the preparation of a paper would seem as vital as outlining or other devices. Ranous (1964, pp. 90–91) talks about the engineering report as specialized communication between engineers: "Consequently the main treatment of the subject makes no concessions to those who are untrained in engineering and few to those engineers who have not professionally considered a similar type of problem."

Mathes and Stevenson (1976) thoughtfully present some rhetorical goals in technical reporting and differ from many other sources in the extent to which the engineer is considered an active writer as part of an organization. They recognize the changed nature of the task, as compared with Ranous (1964): "Almost every report has a complex audience. To meet the needs of these audiences efficiently, the writer must design a report structure with two components. The first component addresses audiences interested in general information; the second component addresses audiences interested in particulars" (Mathes and Stevenson 1976, p. 45).

Shearing and Christian (1965) spend a fair amount of time (four chapters out of seven) persuading young research scientists of the need for prewriting. They ask among other things, "WHAT do the readers already know about the subject?... WHEN AND WHERE will the report be read?" (Shearing and Christian 1965, p. 133).

Probably the most forceful statement on writer-audience relations in technical report writing is by Williams (1983, p. 12): he characterizes the report writer as a "game-player." He continues, "Other than deployment of stylistic devices and rhetorical strategies, the conventional format would seem to offer little scope for play. But if one conceives of it as a game structure, a format comes alive as a challenge to the writer's skills as player and communicator."

Many other articles and books address the question of the report writer and prewriting tasks that may help focus writing. Among these are Michaelson's (1981) "How to Define Quality in Engineering Manuscripts," in which he assesses the characteristics of readers and discusses style and organizational strategies. This work builds on a previous Michaelson (1968) article, "Structure, Content, and Meaning in Technical Manuscripts," in which he analyzes what things make technical reports good.

Other short articles dealing with rhetoric and the technical report are Whittaker's (1980) "Write for Your Reader" and Hissong's (1978) "Write and Present Persuasive Reports."

Stanton very conveniently arranges books on technical reports according to whether they are good textbooks, provide information above and beyond format of the technical report, etc. Several books can be singled out for the useful information they provide on the writer and audience. An anthology by Leonard and McGuire (1983), *Readings in Technical Writing,* discusses, for students and professionals, such things as "What Management Wants in the Technical Report" and gives sample report texts with questions for students to discuss about the rhetoric of reports.

Weiss's (1982) *The Writing System for Engineers and Scientists* exhorts the reader to care about the way in which reports may be used for persuasion but ties this persuasion to practical consequences. Weiss (1982, p. 93) says, "Understand: If you will not learn to motivate your readers, then you will probably not get very far in business, industry, or government."

Stanton notes that we need to find out more about the writing process, as regards technical reports. One study that should cause researchers to think about what kinds of research can be pursued on how one writes a technical report was done by Stohrer and Pinelli (1981). In helping to develop a technical report format for the National Aeronautics and Space Administration, the authors surveyed various organizations and asked about their reports. The study explains what they discovered.

Technical Papers

A technical paper differs from a technical report in that it may not be intended for communication to supervisors or to the general public. Rather, it seems to be a way of acquainting the author's peers with current research findings. In many sources, scientific and technical papers are considered the same. For example, in Menzel et al.'s (1961) *Writing a Technical Paper,* the audience for the book is considered to be scientists and technical writers or those who will present to the public the results of research. This further clouds the issue in that it takes into account science journalism, but there are many good ideas in this work.

Day's (1979, p. 3) *How to Write and Publish a Scientific Paper* maintains that a scientific paper must meet the test of valid publication; that is, it must, among other things, be published "in a journal or other source document which is readily available within the scientific community." Day's definition of a scientific paper is by far the most stringent of those that use "scientific" and "technical" interchangeably, but which, in both cases, refer to those papers giving research findings.

The scientific or technical paper may also be defined rhetorically. Mitchell's (1968) *Writing for Technical and Professional Journals* is typical in building a case for the objectivity of scientific writing. He says, "Perhaps the only way to differentiate between informative and persuasive writing, and thus to determine appropriate stylistic techniques, is to determine the purpose of a specific piece of writing. Writers of both types present and explain facts. The informative writer, however, does so objectively. He exposes, as it were, data for consideration" (Mitchell 1968, p. 156).

On the other hand, Weiss (1982, pp. 116–17) states, "This I do know: The structure of a scientific paper is inherently persuasive. It starts with a thought-provoking problem and ends with a conclusion (even though it is usually called a 'discussion')."

Apart from the differences in emphasis on persuasion or on giving information, most books and articles on the subject contain sections on the format of the scientific paper. Mitchell (1968) discusses the form of a complete journal article. Monroe's (1980) *Effective Research and Report Writing in Government* offers suggestions on how to conduct research and to present findings in a paper.

But it is Trelease (1951) who, in *The Scientific Paper*, sets forth the basis for the scientific paper in research. He states, "The final and in some respects the most important stage in any scientific investigation is the preparation of the results for publication. After a scientific or technical worker has done a good piece of research work, he should present it to his colleagues in the best possible form" (Trelease 1951, p. v).

Other sources also focus on the way in which research presented in the technical or scientific paper contributes to the success of such publications. These sources serve as textbooks either for students of technical writing in colleges or for engineers and scientists on the job. Among them are Jones's (1981) *Writing Scientific Papers and Reports*, in which several chapters are devoted to placing scientific papers within traditional rhetorical modes like classification, analysis, and definition.

Tredennick and Shimamoto (1981), in "On Systematic Generation of Scientific Papers," take a funny look at the shortcomings of writing the scientific paper. They admonish the writer to "change plain positive statements into negative statements that say the same thing. Instead of 'It is wet,' use 'It is not dry' " (Tredennick and Shimamoto 1981, p. 125). A more serious attempt to teach the vocabulary of scientific papers is found in the work of Menzel et al. (1961). They devote several chapters to the question of language in scientific and technical papers: Chapter 6, on jargon, is particularly good. This work also includes examples of bad writing with clearer alternatives as well as examples from published papers.

Technical News Releases

The news release differs from the other genres treated here in that its content is subject to much more extensive revision by the editors of the publication to which it is directed. Also, its content is subject to journalistic considerations such as newsworthiness of the information presented. Because a news release often informs a more general audience than do other technical publications, sometimes adjustments must be made in content and language. A number of books and articles deal with the question of how to prepare news releases and, further, how engineers or writers for a company may use this source of publicity effectively to promote new products or research developments.

Schoenfeld (1963), in *Publicity Media and Methods: Their Role in Modern Public Relations,* discusses the general context for the presentation of scientific and technical information. He states, "[T]he science writer must not become so immersed in the relatively timeless aura of the laboratory that he forgets that his stories must be relatively timely. ... They must report events which 'make a difference now' " (Schoenfeld 1963, pp. 119–20). He talks about the news release in the context of other public relations strategies and discusses its format, showing how it may be transformed into a feature magazine article for both local and national circulation.

Kowal (1980), in "Responsible Science Reporting in a Technological Age," discusses the role of the science writer as the person responsible for the dissemination of technical or scientific news. "He or she must report news from the frontiers of scientific research and development, present all sides fairly when issues of the merit and application of the scientific enterprise are questioned, and put the information in the context of public policy and implications for the everyday world" (Kowal 1980, p. 313).

In *Industrial Publicity,* Quinlan (1983, pp. 2–3) defines the characteristics of the news release for the company: "The news release is the most important and useful form of publicity; much of your publicity efforts will be directed toward producing releases. Written in a terse, vigorous style, the news release announces something that is important, useful, and—as the name implies—new. If you want to convey information not related to announcing a new development, you should consider another form, such as a letter, bulletin, brochure, or manual."

In conjunction with the more general discussion of format, most sources on news releases stress the fact that an article submitted to a newspaper has a specific format governed by traditional principles of newswriting. Thus, Sperber and Lerbinger (1982, p. 40), in *Manager's Public Relations Handbook,* say, "Keep your writers ever mindful of the news dictum that the lead paragraphs must contain, in order of importance 1. What? 2. Who? 3. Where? 4. When? 5. Why? 6. How?" Adams (1965), in *Handbook of Practical Public Relations,* also mentions the importance of these points.

A primary concern in several of the sources on technical news releases is that the technical writer learns the exact format of the news release because it may well be a new format for the writer. St. Thomas's (1956), *How to Get Industrial and Business Publicity* gives examples of how to prepare releases, defines different types of releases a company may wish to send, and includes sample news releases. Among these news releases is the product story, the type that is most likely to be a technical news release.

Quinlan (1983, pp. 27–39), in discussing the format of news releases, also talks about the role of graphics, especially in Chapter 3, "Illustrating the Product Press Release." Furthermore, Quinlan provides the most details on different types of publications to which publicity may be sent; he invites readers to think of new product tabloids and trade periodicals in addition to newspapers and radio and television stations.

Perhaps the most important difference in the technical news release, however, is that it may well be either the writing of an engineer designated to send out information for a company or, as is becoming more common, the work of a company's public relations department. Most sources on news releases seem to agree that in the preparation of a news release, as opposed to other technical genres, the writer must be flexible and more willing to adjust to the needs of newspaper editors. These adjustments include not only the sensitivity to audience demanded in adhering to the newspaper format rather than that of a technical report but also the recognition that a newspaper editor may change a news release. Adams (1965, pp. 42–43) puts it this way: "If he [the editor] changes the lead, or develops the story beyond its original scope, he is trying to make the story of greater interest to his own particular readers. Unless the story has been truly mangled, the public relations representative has no right to complain. His function is not to write for the newspaper: his function is to draw the story to the newspaper's attention. Even though his story may be completely rewritten, he has accomplished his purpose."

Taken separately, each genre—technical reports, technical papers, and technical news releases—presents challenges to the person who would write about technology. But one important item that these genres share is the fact that they are perhaps the most important means of disseminating technological information to the widest audience.

Bibliography

Adams, Paul R. *Handbook of Practical Public Relations.* New York: Thomas Y. Crowell Company, 1965.

Day, Robert A. *How to Write and Publish a Scientific Paper.* Philadelphia: ISI Press, 1979.

Hissong, Charles. "Write and Present Persuasive Reports." *IEEE Transactions on Professional Communication* PC-21, no. 4 (Dec. 1978): 150–52.

Jones, W. Paul. *Writing Scientific Papers and Reports.* Dubuque, Iowa: Wm. C. Brown, 1981.

Kowal, Thomas. "Responsible Science Reporting in a Technological Age." *Journal of Technical Writing and Communication* 10, no. 4 (1980): 308–19.

Leonard, David C., and Peter J. McGuire, eds. *Readings in Technical Writing.* New York: Macmillan, 1983.

Mathes, J. C., and Dwight Stevenson. *Designing Technical Reports.* Indianapolis: Bobbs-Merrill, 1976.

Menzel, Donald H., Howard M. Jones, and Lyle G. Boyd. *Writing a Technical Paper.* New York: McGraw-Hill, 1961.

Michaelson, Herbert. "Structure, Content, and Meaning in Technical Manuscripts." *Technical Communications* 15, no. 2 (Second Quarter 1968): 15–18.

———. "How to Define Quality in Engineering Manuscripts." *Journal of Technical Writing and Communication* 11, no. 3 (1981): pp. 245–50.

Mitchell, John. *Writing for Technical and Professional Journals.* New York: John Wiley and Sons, 1968.

Monroe, Peter C. *Effective Research and Report Writing in Government.* New York: McGraw-Hill, 1980.

Moran, Michael, and Debra Journet, eds. *Research in Technical Communication.* Westport, Conn.: Greenwood Press, 1985.

Quinlan, Gerald R. *Industrial Publicity.* New York: Van Nostrand Reinhold, 1983.

Ranous, T. R. *Communication for Engineers.* Boston: Allyn and Bacon, 1964.

Schoenfeld, Richard. *Publicity Media and Methods: Their Role in Modern Public Relations.* New York: Macmillan, 1963.

Shearing, William, and Thomas Christian. *Reports and How to Write Them.* London: George Allen and Unwin, 1965.

Sperber, David C., and Robert M. Larbinger. *Manager's Public Relations Handbook.* Reading, Mass.: Addison-Wesley, 1982.

Stanton, Judith P. "Technical Reports." In *Research in Technical Communication,* edited by M. Moran and D. Journet. Westport, Conn.: Greenwood Press, 1985.

Stohrer, Freda F., and Thomas E. Pinelli. "Marketing Information: The Technical Report as Product." In *Technical Communication Perspectives for the Eighties.* NASA Conference Publication 2203, Part 1, 1981, pp. 33–42.

St. Thomas, Richard. *How to Get Industrial and Business Publicity.* Philadelphia: Chilton Company, 1956.

Tredennick, C., and I. Shimamoto. "On Systematic Generation of Scientific Papers." *IEEE Transactions on Professional Communication* PC-24, no. 3 (Sept. 1981): 124–27.

Trelease, Gerald. *The Scientific Paper.* Baltimore: The Williams and Willis Company, 1951.

Weiss, Edmund. *The Writing System for Engineers and Scientists.* Englewood Cliffs, N.J.: Prentice-Hall, 1982.

Whittaker, Della. "Write for Your Reader." *IEEE Transactions on Professional Communication* PC-23, no. 4 (Dec. 1980): 170–71.

Williams, Robert I. "Playing with Format, Style, and Reader Assumptions." *Technical Communication* 30, no. 3 (Third Quarter 1983): 11–13.

16 Computer Documentation

Charles H. Sides
Northeastern University

One definition of computer documentation is that it "is all the reproducible, human-usable material that describes the development of the [computer] product and describes the result of that development so that the product can be used effectively and transferred or converted to other environments if appropriate.... [It] serves five important functions: management communications, task-to-task communications, instructions and reference, quality assurance information, and historical reference" (National Bureau of Standards 1984, pp. 5–6). This view is the organizing principle of *Guideline for Software Documentation Management* (National Bureau of Standards 1984), which is one of the best places to begin a study of computer documentation. In this publication, there is a wealth of material, succinctly presented, on development documentation, product documentation, documentation responsibilities, the documentation life cycle, and widely agreed on documentation standards. Such a global view is also echoed in *How to Write Papers and Reports About Computer Technology* (Sides 1984). While that view is in the broadest applications correct, to apply it in this essay would cause numerous overlaps with other essays in this collection. So for the purpose of clarity, I will treat only specifications, computer manuals, and on-line documentation.

William L. Benzon (1981), in "The Computer and Technical Communication," presents a history of the emergence of computer technology in the technical communication profession. In this article, he contends that advances in computer technology will narrow the gap between writing computer programs and documenting them. As a result, Benzon suggests that future technical writers will be writing programs as well as writing documentation, at least in the software field. In fact, this trend can already be seen in the newspaper advertisements for software technical writers. Almost every advertisement specifies some sort of software knowledge as a requirement for the job, whether it is a knowledge of the C programming language, Unix operating system environments, Cobol, or whatever.

In "What Is Good Documentation?", Jim Howard (1981) addresses the issue of documentation specifically, defining it in terms of the types of information it usually presents, the audiences who use it, and the types of uses to which they are likely to put it. In a *Computerworld* editorial, titled "Responsible Documentation" (1982), the editors point out ways of improving documentation. Taken together, these two articles provide a good background into what is at issue in the field of computer documentation, and they do it from a perspective of what is happening on the "front lines."

More and more companies are treating documentation as part of their product development. The wisdom of this is self-evident: it saves time in producing documentation, thereby saving money, and it generally leads to better documentation. It does, however, require a rethinking of the technical communicator's responsibilities. Writers are finding themselves involved with a computer product from design to production, rather than being brought in after production to put together the documentation. A technical writer at Lotus Development Corporation points out that often she writes "fairy tales" before the design of a product based on the company's understanding of customer wants. Then, in many cases the developers design the product accordingly. This is still a radical method for developing software, and even Lotus does not use it all the time; but it does indicate what is at stake and what is ahead in documentation. Such a change in responsibilities means much more information to be organized in planning a document. There are a number of resources for learning methods of handling such organization. Thomas Gildersleeve's (1977) *Organizing and Documenting Data Processing Information* is excellent. It presents a variety of information-gathering and organizational strategies for writers. An earlier book by the same author, *Decision Logic Tables and Their Practical Application in Data Processing* (Gildersleeve 1976), is equally good, but much more narrow. In it, the author shows how to design decision logic tables and how to use them. This presents a good introduction to data processing in general, and as a byproduct, a good introduction to a particularly useful scheme for organizing documentation activities. Decision logic tables are also commonly used graphics in computer documentation. Along the same line is Harry Katz's (1977) *An Introduction to the HIPO Method.* HIPO, or *H*ierarchy *I*nput *P*rocess *O*utput, has been used at International Business Machines for years as a means of organizing information or activities that will be described in procedural manuals. It is especially useful for organizing complex, multifaceted material.

Another excellent introduction to a variety of topics concerning computer documentation is the entire fourth quarter 1980 issue of *Technical Communication*. This quarterly journal of the Society for Technical Communication frequently has articles that deal with matters relevant to computer documentation, but this particular issue was completely devoted to the subject.

Lastly, "A Model Documentation Course" (Sides 1982) describes a course that was developed at Clarkson University by Terrence Skelton and further enhanced there by John Brockmann and Charles H. Sides. This course has since been transported with changes to a variety of industries and government agencies around the world.

Specifications

Specifications are the precursors to the design and development of computer products. Well-written specifications are also the precursors to computer manuals. Tim Whalen (1955), in "A History of Specifications: Technical Writing in Perspective," provides an overview of specifications from Babylonia in 3300 B.C.E. to the present. He makes an arguable case for specifications as the precursors of technical writing.

One of the truisms of computer product design and development is unfortunately that specifications are not always written as well as they should be. David F. Crown (1976), in "Ten Commandments of Writing Readable Specs," presents a concise explanation of how to write better specifications. Martin Freier (1975) does much the same thing in "Effective Specification Writing," but from a technical writer's perspective. Together, the two provide a good introduction to writing specifications, and the latter is but one article in an entire issue of *Technical Communication* devoted to specifications.

The relationship between the skills needed to write good specifications and those required to write good manuals can be seen in Bernice E. Casey's (1981) "The Impact of the Technical Communicator on Software Requirements." In this article she points out that software engineering and technical writing espouse a structured approach to product development. As a result, technical writers have more to offer software engineers than merely writing and editing. Specifically, technical writers can aid software engineers in audience analysis, functional analysis, human factors research, and requirement specification writing. This article shows the increasing concern that technical writers be involved in the design and development of the computer product and not just in the end-of-job writing alone.

Daniel Teichrow and Ernest A. Hershey's (1977) "PSL/PSA: A Computer-Aided Technique for Structural Documentation and Analysis of Information Processing Systems" is excellent for showing the specifics of how documentation can be generated throughout the design and development stage of computer products. The authors describe a technique for computer-aided documentation during the requirements specification stage and the functional specification stage. Throughout, they emphasize structured documentation as a means of improving system development.

Two recent books also provide chapters on specification writing: *How to Write Papers and Reports About Computer Technology* (Sides 1984), which describes an approach to specification writing derived from the author's consulting work at Raytheon Corporation, and *Writing and Analyzing Effective Computer System Documentation* (Stuart 1984), which includes chapters on requirement specifications, functional specifications, and design specifications.

Finally, J. D. Root (1971), in "Specification Writing: Precursor to Better Manuals," presents the case for specifications being directly responsible for improving the usefulness of computer manuals.

Computer Manuals

Computer manuals include a variety of documents: user manuals, reference manuals, maintenance manuals, hardware manuals, and software manuals. Each of these generates specific concerns for technical writers, but all of them have areas in common as well. Valerie Antoine (1985), in "The Software Documentor: A New Specialist," examines the new sense of professionalism in software technical writing. She provides an excellent overview of the kinds of information used by software documentors, the tasks a software documentor might perform, and the types of documents generated by software documentors. Of particular interest is the fact that this article stresses the use of flow charts and HIPO diagrams.

One of the best introductions to the field of document design is Daniel B. Felker's (1980) *Document Design: A Review of the Relevant Research*. This is a valuable resource for all types of documents, not just those produced in the computer industry. For example, some of the areas covered in this collection of essays are psycholinguistics, cognitive psychology, instructional research, readability research, human factors research, and analyses of typography and graphics. The materials in this collection have applications for the instructor and the researcher alike.

In "Computer Software Documentation," Joseph Petito (1974) presents an early discussion of the need for having writers involved in the design phase. Frank Clark (1983), in "Software Documentation: A Major Problem," shows that solutions to problems identified by Petito ten years earlier still have not been implemented by many companies.

One attempt over the past decade to deal with the problems of computer documentation has been the company policies and procedures manual. John Harper (1976), in *Data Processing Documentation: Standards, Procedures, and Applications,* describes the activities that should occur in data processing documentation, how they should be performed, and what documents should be produced as a result. This book is particularly good for describing the interaction between management and writers. A briefer, but valuable source of information about policies and procedures manuals is Stephen M. Goldfarb's (1981) "Policies and Procedures Manuals: A Writer's Primer."

There are a number of good textbooks and guidebooks for both college courses and industrial seminars in documentation. Most of these share fairly standard material on audience analysis and writing techniques, but each book presents computer documentation from a different viewpoint, that of the writer's individual experience in industry. Lucia McKay and Monet Thomson's (1984) *Soft Words and Hard Words: A Common Sense Guide to Creative Documentation* is essentially a guide for computer professionals. The book offers advice on topics that range from the use of words, style, and punctuation to reading paths through a manual, multimedia documentation (the interrelationship between hard copy manuals and on-line documentation), top-down design for manuals, audience questionnaires, format issues such as headers and footers, editing, the production process, software for technical writers, and time and cost estimates. The book provides some excellent information that is difficult to find in most textbooks, for example, the material on time and cost estimates.

John O'Rourke's (1976) *Writing for the Reader* has been the standard writing resource at Digital Equipment Corporation for more than a decade. It is basically a compilation of past technical writing wisdom, borrowing heavily from the likes of Kenneth Houp and Thomas Pearsall's (1986) *Reporting Technical Information* and J. C. Mathes and Dwight Stevenson's (1976) *Designing Technical Reports,* among others. Nonetheless, it is a good summary of technical writing practices.

Joan Van Duyn's (1982) *The DP Professional's Guide to Writing Effective Technical Communication* is also an industry professional's guidebook. It is best for its chapters on "Mechanics of Data Processing Graphics," "Writing the Systems Study," "Writing Policy and Standards Manuals," and "Writing and Selling Technical Articles for Publication." Charles H. Sides's (1984) *How to Write Papers and Reports About Computer Technology* is similar in that it, too, is a guide for industry professionals. It is most noted for its chapters on "How to Write Specifications," "How to Make Presentations," and "How to Write Proposals."

Christine Browning's (1983) *Guide to Effective Software Technical Writing* is a brief "how-to" guide for professional technical writers. It is especially useful for chapters on "Reference Manuals," "How to Write Heads," and "Readability." R. John Brockmann's (1986) *Writing Better Computer Documentation* is good for its treatment of alternatives for presenting procedural information, particularly playscript and information mapping. Loeb and Woolever's (1990) *Writing for the Computer Industry* focuses on both manuals and the documents that accompany their development. It includes material on hardware documentation, a topic that has not been discussed nearly enough. Ann Stuart's (1984) *Writing and Analyzing Effective Computer System Documentation* is good for identifying the stages and documents of system development.

Finally, Sandra Pakin and Associates puts out a very useful book, despite its elephantine title—*Documentation Development Methodology* (Pakin 1978). There are good chapters on "Project Planning," "Managing the Review Process," and "Field Testing," as well as groups of chapters on "Graphics" and "Production." The book covers the entire scope of computer documentation and does it better than the title would suggest.

Probably the most common computer documentation, at least for public consumption, is the user manual. Although each of the previous sources has material that is useful for writing these documents, there are good resources specifically written about user manuals. Frank Whitehouse's (1973) *System Documentation* presents a variety of methods for documenting procedures: this book is especially good for its treatment of flow charts and decision logic tables. Jan Snyders (1981), in "User Manuals that Make Sense," suggests using more visuals in user manuals. Susan J. Grimm (1981), in "EDP User Documentation: The Missing Link," points out the importance of user documents as part of the computer product. This short article was a predecessor to her book *How to Write Computer Manuals for Users* (Grimm 1982). This book is chronologically arranged into the steps of researching, writing, producing, and updating a user manual. It is particularly useful for the chapters on updating manuals.

A relatively new book, Edmund Weiss's (1985) *How to Write a Usable User Manual,* presents the preparation of user documents in a radically different way from many of the other sources considered so far. This book, written as a companion to *How to Write Papers and Reports About Computer Technology* (Sides 1984), suggests that documents can be planned and written as modules. This top-down design process is particularly useful because it replicates the process used in designing the computer product about which the manuals are written. There are especially good chapters about storyboarding and modularization.

Another book that also espouses the modular approach to documentation is Richard Zaneski's (1982) *Software Manual Production Simplified.* This book includes material about creating a documentation policy, developing standards for manuals, accessing data sources, preparing manuals, reviewing manuals, and maintaining manuals. There are good sections on artwork in manuals and the writer-printer relationship, two areas many sources gloss over or omit entirely.

Usability can be designed in from the start, and it can be ensured at the finish. Editing for usability is the subject of Candace Soderston's (1985) "The Usability Edit: A New Level." She suggests that usability testing can be used as a means of aiding revision of documents and that it should occur iteratively throughout the development of documents.

On-line Documentation

On-line documentation is an area of current interest. Opinions on whether it should replace the printed page (and if it ever can) vary widely, not to mention opinions on how such documentation should be designed. There is more material published about this subject every month, and much of it is good. The main sources for this material are the IEEE publications, especially the *IEEE Transactions on Professional Communication* and the *IEEE Transactions on Software Engineering.* These two journals would be worth examining on a regular basis.

As to whether on-line documentation can replace the printed page, Annette N. Bradford (1984) points out the important differences between the two in "Conceptual Differences Between the Display Screen and the Printed Page." In this article, she discusses the differences in usability and design methods for both the page and the screen.

A particularly good source is William Fetter's (1965) *Computer Graphics in Communication.* Although the focus of this very early book is primarily on engineering, it is excellent for matching media to communication needs. It shows ways to incorporate computer-generated graphics into reports and manuals, display screens, and training videotapes. This was a forerunning study of modern CAD/CAM systems. It enabled engineers to produce orthogonal projections on screen and led to such technologies as flight simulators, as well as CAD systems for ships, aircraft, spacecraft, and automobiles. For additional early information about this subject, see I. E. Sutherland's (1963) "Sketch Pad— A Man/Machine Graphical Communications System," T. E. Johnson's (1963) "Sketch Pad III: A Computer Program for Drawing in Three Dimensions," and D. T. Ross and S. Coons's (1961) "Investigations in Computer-Aided Design."

An excellent source for understanding what is at issue in on-line documentation is A. Monk's (1984) *Fundamentals of Human-Computer Interaction.* Two chapters are especially useful: Chapter 2, "Extracting Information from Printed and Electronically Presented Text," and Chapter 9, "Dialogue Design: Characteristics of User Knowledge." Chapter 2 includes materials on the cognitive psychology of reading, the reading process, eye movement, perceptual span in reading, legibility (line length, capitals, and type size), and special problems in reading from CRT displays. Chapter 9 deals with the future of voice recognition systems.

A similarly useful source is Stephen E. Engel and Richard E. Granda's (1975) *Guidelines for Man/Display Interfaces.* This is a superb explanation of the display terminal as the interface between software and users; it is based on human factors and psychological principles (feedback, short-term memory, and reinforcement), experimental studies, and user comments. The report includes guidelines for display formats, frame contents, command language, recovery procedures, user entry techniques, and response time requirements.

Jessie M. Heines (1984), in *Screen Design Strategies for Computer-Assisted Instruction,* presents issues about on-line documentation in the field of computer-assisted instruction (CAI). This book is intended primarily for the designers of CAI systems. It focuses on the special characteristics of computer-driven screens, explores what the computer-video medium can do, and presents the pro's and con's of a large number of display techniques. It includes chapters about standard screen components, visual symbols, menus, text displays, and screen design tools such as text and graphics editors. It also stresses standards for CAI style.

The issue of standards and guidelines for on-line documentation is the subject of *Documentation Standards and Procedures for Online Systems* (Rubin 1979). This book contains useful information on project planning (including user requests, cost estimation, feasibility studies, and hardware resource estimates), documentation aids such as HIPO, job control language standards, data base organization, and man-machine dialogue. The book is also good for specifications.

The following sources address specific concerns of on-line documentation. Richard Krull and Philip Rubens (1984), in "An Eye-Motion Study of Online Information," present the results of a study using eye movements as an indicator of the reading process for on-line information. Raymond C. Houghton (1984), in "Online Help Systems: A Conspectus," reviews the important aspects of this particular type of on-line documentation, specifically comprehensiveness and ease of use.

The advocates of on-line documentation tout it as the inevitable future. Whether that proves to be true, perhaps the best way to end this essay is to consider some of the recent resources that describe futuristic systems for documentation, some of which are already in use. T. R. Girill and Clement H. Luk (1985) describe a documentation aid in "Document: An Interactive, Online Solution to Four Documentation Problems." A. S. Neal and R. M. Simons (1984) describe another aid in "Playback: A Method for Evaluating the Usability of Software and Its Documentation." A very useful source is *Directions in Human-Computer Interaction* (Badre and Schneiderman 1982). Of particular interest is Chapter 3, "System Message Design." This chapter includes such matters as specificity, constructive guidance, positive tone, user-adapted style, and appropriate format. It is encouraging that these issues are basically the same ones that have been advocated over the years with respect to printed documentation. Other chapters include "Artificial Intelligence," "Investigations of Natural Terminology for Command and Query Languages," "Designing Chunks for Sequentially Displayed Information," and "Information Highlighting on Complex Displays."

Finally, Richard A. Bolt (1984), in *The Human Interface,* explores the future of computers. He includes descriptions of voice and gesture interfaces and eye contact interfaces to manage the display of images and information. Such systems are presently being used by the totally disabled, such as those with cerebral palsy and quadriplegics. Although there is not much in this book about technical writing, the implications for the future of documentation are obvious.

Is technology moving toward paperless documentation? Definitely. Are we there yet? Not even close. It is hard to tell what the future of technical writing will be. This essay has been an attempt to examine what the present of computer documentation is and especially how that present is related to the recent past. Trends in documentation are changing rapidly; using this essay as a foundation, readers should be able to stay abreast of those trends.

References

Antoine, Valerie. "The Software Documentor: A New Specialist." *Technical Communication* 32, no. 3 (1985): 16-18.

Benzon, William L. "The Computer and Technical Communication." *Journal of Technical Writing and Communication* 11, no. 2 (1981): 103-8.

Bolt, Richard A. *The Human Interface*. Belmont, Calif.: Lifetime Learning Publications, 1984.

Bradford, Annette N. "Conceptual Differences Between the Display Screen and the Printed Page." *Technical Communication* 31, no. 3 (1984): 13-16.

Brockmann, R. John. *Writing Better Computer Documentation*. New York: Wiley-Interscience, 1986.

Browning, Christine. *Guide to Effective Software Technical Writing*. Englewood Cliffs, N.J.: Prentice-Hall, 1983.

Casey, Bernice E. "The Impact of the Technical Communicator on Software Requirements." *Journal of Technical Writing and Communication* 11, no. 4 (1981): 361-72.

Clark, Frank. "Software Documentation: A Major Problem." *Computerworld* 17, no. 9 (Feb. 28, 1983): 5-6.

Crown, David F. "Ten Commandments of Writing Readable Specs." *Specification Engineering* 35, no. 3 (1976): 54-57.

Engel, Stephen E., and Richard E. Granda. *Guidelines for Man/Display Interfaces*. IBM Technical Report TR 00.2720. Poughkeepsie, N.Y.: Poughkeepsie Laboratory, Dec. 1975.

Felker, Daniel B., ed. *Document Design: A Review of the Relevant Research*. Washington, D.C.: American Institutes for Research, 1980.

Fetter, William. *Computer Graphics in Communication*. New York: McGraw-Hill, 1965.

Freier, Martin. "Effective Specification Writing." *Technical Communication* 22, no. 1 (1975): 14-16.

Gildersleeve, Thomas. *Decision Logic Tables and Their Practical Application in Data Processing.* Rochelle Park, N.J.: Hayden Book Co., 1976.

———. *Organizing and Documenting Data Processing Information.* Rochelle Park, N.J.: Hayden Book Co., 1977.

Girill, T. R., and Clement H. Luk. "Document: An Interactive, Online Solution to Four Documentation Problems." *Communications of the ACM* 28, no. 3 (March 1985): 300–311.

Goldfarb, Stephen M. "Policies and Procedures Manuals: A Writer's Primer." *Computerworld* 15, no. 37 (Sept. 14, 1981): ID 9.

Grimm, Susan J. "EDP User Documentation: The Missing Link." *IEEE Transactions on Professional Communication* PC-24 (1981): 79–83.

———. *How to Write Computer Manuals for Users.* Belmont, Calif.: Lifetime Learning Publications, 1982.

Harper, John. *Data Processing Documentation: Standards, Procedures, and Applications.* Englewood Cliffs, N.J.: Prentice-Hall, 1976.

Heines, Jessie M. *Screen Design Strategies for Computer-Assisted Instruction.* Bedford, Mass.: Digital Press, 1984.

Houghton, Raymond C. "Online Help Systems: A Conspectus." *Communications of the ACM* 27, no. 2 (Feb. 1984): 126–33.

Houp, Kenneth, and Thomas Pearsall. *Reporting Technical Information.* New York: Macmillan, 1986.

Howard, Jim. "What Is Good Documentation?" *Byte* 6, no. 3 (March 1981): 132–50.

Johnson, T. E. "Sketch Pad III: A Computer Program for Drawing in Three Dimensions." In *AFIPS Conference Proceedings, 1963 Spring Joint Computer Conference.* Baltimore: Spartan Books, 1963, 347–53.

Katz, Harry. *An Introduction to the HIPO Method.* New York: Van Nostrand Reinhold, 1977.

Krull, Richard, and Philip Rubens. "An Eye-Motion Study of Online Information." In *Proceedings of the Annual Symposium on Usability.* Kingston, N.Y.: International Business Machines Corporation, 1984, pp. 9–18.

Loeb, Helen, and Kristin Woolever. *Writing for the Computer Industry.* Englewood Cliffs, N.J.: Prentice-Hall, 1990.

Margolis, Neal. "Responsible Documentation." *Computerworld* 16, no. 4 (Jan. 25, 1982): ID 7–16.

Mathes, J. C., and Dwight Stevenson. *Designing Technical Reports.* New York: Bobbs-Merrill, 1976.

McKay, Lucia, and Monet Thomson. *Soft Words and Hard Words: A Common Sense Guide to Creative Documentation.* Culver City, Calif.: Ashton-Tate, 1984.

Monk, A. *Fundamentals of Human-Computer Interaction.* New York: Harcourt, Brace, Jovanovich, 1984.

National Bureau of Standards. *Guideline for Software Management.* FIPS Publication 105. Gaithersburg, Md.: National Bureau of Standards, June 6, 1984.

Neal, A. S., and R. M. Simons. "Playback: A Method for Evaluating the Usability of Software and Its Documentation." *IBM Systems Journal* 23, no. 1 (1984): 82–96.

O'Rourke, John. *Writing for the Reader.* Maynard, Mass.: Digital Software Publications, 1976.

Pakin, Sandra. *Documentation Development Methodology.* Chicago: Sandra Pakin and Associates, 1978.

Petito, Joseph. "Computer Software Documentation." *Journal of Technical Writing and Communication* 4, no. 1 (1974): 117–20.

Root, J. D. "Specification Writing: Precursor to Better Manuals." In *Proceedings of the 18th International Technical Communications Conference,* Section 5–6. Washington, D.C.: Society for Technical Communication, 1971.

Ross, D. T., and S. Coons. "Investigations in Computer-Aided Design." Report 8436–IR-2. Boston: Massachusetts Institute of Technology, Nov. 1961.

Rubin, Martin L. *Documentation Standards and Procedures for Online Systems.* New York: Van Nostrand Reinhold, 1979.

Schneiderman, Ben, and Albert Badre, eds. *Directions in Human-Computer Interaction.* Norwood, N.J.: Ablex Publication Corporation, 1982.

Sides, Charles H. "A Model Documentation Course." *ABCA Bulletin* 45, no. 2 (June 1982): 26–29.

———. *How to Write Papers and Reports About Computer Technology.* Philadelphia: ISI Press, 1984.

Snyders, Jan. "User Manuals that Make Sense." *Computing Decisions* (April 1981): 127 ff.

Soderston, Candace. "The Usability Edit: A New Level." *Technical Communication* 32, no. 1 (1985): 16–18.

Stuart, Ann. *Writing and Analyzing Effective Computer System Documentation.* New York: Holt, Rinehart and Winston, 1984.

Sutherland, I. E. "Sketch Pad—A Man/Machine Graphical Communications System." In *AFIPS Conference Proceedings, 1963 Spring Joint Computer Conference.* Baltimore: Spartan Books, 1963, 329–46.

Technical Communication 27, no. 4 (Fourth Quarter 1980). Special issue on Computer Manuals.

Teichrow, Daniel, and Ernest A. Hershey. "PSL/PSA: A Computer-Aided Technique for Structural Documentation and Analysis of Information Processing Systems." *IEEE Transactions on Software Engineering* 3, no. 1 (Jan. 1977): 41–48.

Van Duyn, Joan. *The DP Professional's Guide to Writing Effective Technical Communication.* New York: Wiley-Interscience, 1982.

Weiss, Edmund. *How to Write a Usable User Manual.* Philadelphia: ISI Press, 1985.

Whalen, Tim. "A History of Specifications: Technical Writing in Perspective." *Journal of Technical Writing and Communication* 15, no. 3 (1985): 235–46.

Whitehouse, Frank. *System Documentation.* London: Business Books, 1973.

Zaneski, Richard. *Software Manual Production Simplified.* New York: Petrocelli Books, 1982.

17 Medical Science and Technology

Barbara Gastel
University of California, San Francisco

Writing about medical science and technology (in this essay, termed "biomedical writing") has much in common with writing about other science and technology, and indeed with expository writing in general. Thus, many general works on scientific and other writing can aid in teaching biomedical writing, and many books and articles on biomedical writing overlap considerably with more general works. However, some matters are specific to biomedical writing, and a literature on them exists.

The first part of this essay deals with that literature. It begins by identifying materials to consult regarding stylistic conventions in biomedical writing. Next, it discusses sources of guidance for writing such items as case reports and accounts of clinical trials. Finally, it briefly notes some writings about the interface between biomedical journals and the popular press.

The rest of the essay deals with sources that address more general aspects of writing but do so in a biomedical context. These aspects are the structuring of scientific papers, the writing of review articles, peer review of scientific literature, preparation of grant proposals, ethical issues in scientific communication, readability, and prose style. Many sources mentioned in this section have authors prominent in biomedical publishing, appeared in highly regarded biomedical journals, or both and thus may be especially credible to students in biomedical fields. Also, many contain biomedical examples that may be useful in teaching.

Because this essay is written mainly to aid in teaching, it focuses largely on works that are readily accessible and have substantial reference lists. Most of the sources cited deal with writing that is by and for physicians and biomedical scientists, but some discuss writing for the public. The essay is intended to aid both in preparing courses specifically on biomedical writing and in recommending works to students in biomedical fields who are taking more general writing classes.

Stylistic Conventions in Biomedical Writing

Among bibliographic resources for teachers and students are those on stylistic matters specific to biomedical writing. In general, conventions for writing about medical science and technology have not been highly standardized: formats for citing and listing references vary among biomedical journals, as do preferences with respect to other stylistic matters, and until recently nearly each of these journals had entirely its own requirements regarding the way in which manuscripts were to be prepared. However, well-established conventions do exist for nomenclature in some biomedical fields, and, recently, uniformity in other respects also has increased.

Most notably, in 1978 a group of editors from major English-language biomedical journals decided on uniform requirements for preparing manuscripts for submission. By 1982, when the International Committee of Medical Journal Editors (1982) (into which the former group evolved) published these "Uniform Requirements for Manuscripts Submitted to Biomedical Journals" in their current form, over 150 journals had agreed to receive manuscripts prepared following these requirements; the number is now at least 300 (Huth 1987a, *Medical Style and Format: An International Manual for Authors, Editors, and Publishers,* p. 179). Items addressed in these requirements include content and format of title page, abstract, and text; style of references (known as "Vancouver style," after the site of the 1978 meeting); preparation of tables and illustrations; reporting of units of measurement; and use of abbreviations and symbols.

The committee states that "the requirements are instructions to authors on how to prepare manuscripts, not to editors on publication style." Indeed, among journals agreeing to the uniform requirements, many convert references to their own formats (Porcher 1986). The committee also notes that authors submitting papers to journals must consult those journals' own instructions to authors regarding such matters as what topics are suitable for publication and what types of papers (e.g., original articles, literature reviews, or case reports) may be submitted.

Over the years, collections of various biomedical journals' instructions to authors have been published. The U.S. Department of Health, Education, and Welfare issued such a compilation in 1979; more recent such volumes include those prepared by Harriet R. Meiss and Doris A. Jaeger (1980) and by Banes (1984). Of course, for authors submitting manuscripts for publication, consulting such volumes cannot replace carefully inspecting journals and reading their most recent instructions.

Nevertheless, such compilations can serve as initial resources and may aid in acquainting students with such instructions' existence and nature. Also of possible use in discussion how to match manuscript and journal is a table in which Lynn T. Staheli (1986) lists twenty prominent medical journals and for each notes items such as circulation, citation rate, percentage of submitted manuscripts rejected, time taken for publication, average length of articles, and average numbers of tables and figures per article.

As noted earlier, conventions regarding style in biomedical writing have not been highly standardized. Thus, although no single authoritative guide exists, parties well established in the field have published style manuals. One such volume is the style manual of the American Medical Association (AMA) (Barclay et al. 1981), now in its seventh edition; this manual serves as the style guide for the journals published by the AMA, and it also can aid those writing about medical science and technology for courses and for other publications. Another resource is the *CBE Style Manual: A Guide for Authors, Editors, and Publishers in the Biological Sciences* (CBE Style Manual Committee 1983), published by the Council of Biology Editors; now in its fifth edition, this manual is intended for authors, editors, and publishers in the various biological sciences, including medical science. A recent addition is *Medical Style and Format* by Edward J. Huth (1987a), who edits the major journal *Annals of Internal Medicine*.

Specifically, biomedical matters addressed in these three manuals (each of which also addresses general aspects of scientific writing and of prose style) include conventions regarding nomenclature and style in various biomedical fields. The AMA style manual contains a portion (Barclay et al. 1981, pp. 61–72) focusing on clinically related nomenclature; the *CBE Style Manual* (CBE Style Manual Committee 1983) includes lengthy sections on conventions in microbiology (pp. 170–85) and in chemistry and biochemistry (pp. 214–26); and the manual by Huth (1987a) deals with nomenclature of drugs (pp. 127–29), anatomic structures (pp. 130–31), and diseases (pp. 131–32), as well as conventions regarding style in bacteriology, cardiology, chemistry (including biochemistry), endocrinology, genetics, hematology, immunology, mycology, oncology, parasitology and medical entomology, pharmacology, psychiatry, pulmonary medicine, radiology, and virology (pp. 211–59). The latter two sources list many references on nomenclature and related matters.

The manuals from the AMA and by Huth (1987a) also deal with other items specific to biomedical writing. For example, the former (Barclay et al. 1981) contains portions on abbreviations for clinical, technical, and general terms (pp. 46–52); on medical and other terms that are often misused (pp. 101–8); and on "medicalese and jargon" (pp. 109–10). The latter (Huth 1987a) includes material on formats for case series articles and case reports (pp. 45–47), the Vancouver style for citations and references (pp. 177–210), use of SI units for reporting clinical and laboratory data (pp. 288–320), and abbreviations and unabbreviated terms to use when listing journal titles in bibliographic references (pp. 321–37).

Learning to write about medical science and technology involves not only becoming acquainted with appropriate guidelines on style, but also becoming aware of what content to include. For writing in the clinical realm, issues include the following: When is publishing a case report justified? What should and shouldn't a case report include? What information on methods and other items should appear in accounts of clinical trials?

The case report has been called "the archetypal medical article" (Roland 1968, p. 83), and written accounts of cases date back to ancient times (Riley 1975, p. 79). Today, case reports, though common, are generally less highly regarded than papers reporting experiments; journal editors state that many case reports submitted to them say little that is new and worthwhile. In "Case Reports and Medical Progress," however, Ross J. Simpson, Jr., and Thomas R. Griggs (1985) note that case reports can still be of value. They argue that such reports can suggest fruitful hypotheses for scientific investigation and indeed may help yield new paradigms in medicine.

When is publishing a case report justified? In teaching biomedical writing, this question may be worth discussing both for its own sake and as a means to consider the more general question of what makes findings publishable. Useful vehicles for such discussion may include taxonomies of case reports. The *New England Journal of Medicine* published one such taxonomy, categorizing cases as "the oddity," "the new variant on an old theme," "the untoward effect," and "the new principle" ("The Case Report," 1967). *How to Write and Publish Papers in the Medical Sciences* by Huth (1982, pp. 58–61) presents a more detailed classification, which includes three types of cases that can merit publication in first-rank journals and several sorts that rarely deserve such a fate.

If writing a case report does seem justified, what information should be included and in what order? Over the years, various articles and book chapters have addressed this matter. Sources that appear both useful and accessible include "The Case Report" by Charles G. Roland (1968), "The Case Report. I. Guidelines for Preparation" by Lois DeBakey and Selma DeBakey (1983), and the relevant section of Huth's (1982, pp. 61–63) *How to Write and Publish Papers in the Medical Sciences.* Also, the *Journal of the American Dental Association* has published an article on preparing dental case reports (Croll 1981).

Publishing case reports and other writing in which individual patients are described or in which photographs of them are printed poses issues regarding confidentiality. Readings that could stimulate discussion of these issues include two letters to editors: one (Murphy and Dull 1973) in which two physicians object that a case report contained facts enabling identification of a specific scientist as the patient and one (Morgan 1985) in which a patient herself protests publication of a psychiatric case report from which colleagues readily identified her. "Informed Consent for Research Publication of Patient-Related Data" by Jeffrey C. Murray and Roberta A. Pagon (1984) explores the issues more deeply and offers suggestions for obtaining valid informed consent to publish such items as case reports and patients' photographs.

In addition to writing about individual patients and small groups, medical authors sometimes review large series of cases. In "Don't Look Back! The Perils of Retrospection," Roy A. Meals (1978) humorously describes the tribulations of performing such a study. Three formats for presenting case series are briefly discussed in Huth's (1982, pp. 67–68) *How to Write and Publish Papers in the Medical Sciences.*

Although case reports have long abounded, accounts of controlled clinical trials, in which patients are allocated to treatment and control groups and outcomes are compared, have become common only recently. As more and more clinical trials have been done, researchers have studied the quality of the resulting papers, and guidelines regarding content have been published. These studies and recommendations may interest teachers and students of biomedical writing.

One such study (DerSimonian et al. 1982) assessed the frequency with which eleven important aspects of design and analysis were reported in papers that four major medical journals published on clinical trials. (In part because human subjects are involved, clinical trials often are complex to conduct, and unless methods used are described sufficiently, readers cannot adequately evaluate the conclusions.) The researchers found that omissions were common, and they recommended that editors give authors lists of key items to report. The eleven items in their own paper might serve as such a list.

Another study (Meinert et al. 1984) also indicated that articles on clinical trials often omit some important types of information. The report of this study discusses what content, both methodological and other, to include in papers on clinical trials. It contains a table listing this content (Meinert et al. 1984, p. 334).

Free-standing guidelines for reporting on clinical trials also have been published. An early set ("Guidelines for Reporting Clinical Trials") appeared in the *Journal of the American Dental Association* in 1973; these guidelines were developed for reporting periodontal research, and because of their broad applicability, the journal printed them. Recently issued guidelines for reporting on clinical trials include two sets appearing in cancer journals (Zelen 1983; Simon and Wittes 1985). Teachers and students may wish not only to consult such guidelines but also to review a proposed schematic format for presenting results of clinical trials (Hampton 1981).

Clinical trials, by their nature, rely heavily on statistical methods. Such methods also are basic to much other medical research. In 1983, Douglas G. Altman et al. published an article entitled "Statistical Guidelines for Contributors to Medical Journals." This article, which appeared in the *British Medical Journal,* states what statistical information various sections of medical research papers should include and how that information should be presented. An upcoming version of the "Uniform Requirements for Manuscripts Submitted to Biomedical Journals" (International Committee of Medical Journal Editors 1982) may contain a section on statistics.

Various types of medical articles, ranging from case reports to accounts of clinical trials, often deal at least in part with adverse effects of drugs and medical procedures. For readers to assess the validity and implications of the findings, the articles must contain the proper sorts of information. J. Venulet et al. (1982) of the pharmaceutical company Ciba-Geigy studied the completeness of articles on adverse drug reactions, especially with regard to data from which incidence can be calculated, and offered suggestions for writing such articles better. In 1984, individuals from drug companies, academia, drug-regulating agencies, medical and scientific journals, and the popular press met to discuss writing better reports of adverse drug reactions; the resulting guidelines for content ("Improving Reports of Adverse Drug Reactions," 1984) have been published. Also, Kenneth Flegel and Robert Oseasohn 1982) studied the quality of reporting adverse effects of diagnostic tests; the criteria used in their research may serve as guidelines for writing papers on such effects.

Reports on benefits and risks of treatments, as well as on other medical matters, are among the most newsworthy of scientific papers. Thus, not surprisingly, the interface between peer-reviewed journals and the popular press has been of particular concern in medicine. A controversial policy regarding this interface is the *New England Journal of Medicine*'s Ingelfinger Rule (named after Franz J. Ingelfinger, editor of the *Journal* from 1967 to 1977), which states that the *Journal* may refuse to publish a report because its content appeared in the popular press or elsewhere. Goals of this policy are to help ensure that research undergoes peer review before it is presented to the public and practitioners, that patients do not learn of findings before their physicians see the data, and that the *Journal* is newsworthy. Resources for discussing this heavily debated policy and related issues include articles in the *Journal* (Relman 1979, "An Open Letter to the News Media"; Relman 1981, "The Ingelfinger Rule"), *Annals of Internal Medicine* (1979, "The News Media and the Question of Prior Publication"), the *Journal of the American Medical Association* (McBride 1981), *Science* (Wade 1981), and *Time* (1980, "The Ingelfinger Rule").

General Aspects of Writing in a Biomedical Context

Thus far, this essay has focused mainly on sources of information on matters specific to biomedical writing. However, many teachers and students may also want to consult books and articles that address more general aspects of writing but do so in a biomedical context. The rest of this essay deals with such items.

In biomedical as in other fields, scientific papers normally follow the IMRAD format (*I*ntroduction, *M*aterials and Methods, *R*esults, and *D*iscussion) and are preceded by abstracts. Huth's (1982) *How to Write and Publish Papers in the Medical Sciences,* the second edition of which was in press while this essay was being written, includes a chapter (pp. 50–57) describing what each section of a biomedical research paper should contain; it also presents and discusses a medical example of a well-structured informative abstract (pp. 77–79). Guidelines, at least in part biomedically oriented, for writing the sections of a scientific paper also appear in the "Uniform Requirements for Manuscripts Submitted to Biomedical Journals" (International Committee of Medical Journal Editors 1982), the *CBE Style Manual* (CBE Style Manual Committee 1983, pp. 18–23), and *How to Write and Publish a Scientific Paper* by Robert A. Day (1983), who has had many years of publishing experience at the American Society for Microbiology and elsewhere. Also, *Scientific*

Writing for Graduate Students: A Manual on the Teaching of Scientific Writing (Woodford 1968) deals largely with the writing of scientific papers; its emphasis is somewhat biomedical, and as exercises for students, it contains three biomedical papers to edit, along with improved versions and explanations of the suggested changes.

In biomedical as in other fields, review articles also are common. Using eight criteria, Cynthia D. Mulrow (1987) analyzed fifty review articles in major American medical journals; she concluded that "current medical reviews do not routinely use scientific methods to identify, assess, and synthesize information" (Mulrow 1987, p. 485). The recommendations in Mulrow's article and in the accompanying editorial (Huth 1987b, "Needed: Review Articles with More Scientific Rigor") may well aid, for instance, in preparing students to write term papers.

Articles submitted to biomedical and other scientific journals normally undergo peer review. "Peer Review in Biomedical Publication," written by Ingelfinger (1974) while he was editor of the *New England Journal of Medicine,* discusses items such as problems in peer review, costs of review, and proposals to improve reviewing. Ingelfinger's suggestions include giving reviewers better and more uniform sets of guidelines. A useful set of such guidelines, containing a checklist, appears in the *CBE Style Manual* (CBE Style Manual Committee 1983, pp. 82–84). These guidelines may help students learn to review their own and others' papers critically and may aid teachers in correcting students' papers.

The Ingelfinger (1974) article called for research on peer review in biomedical journals. Since then, Stephen Lock, editor of the *British Medical Journal* and author of *Thorne's Better Medical Writing* (1977), has prospectively studied the review of over 1,500 consecutive articles submitted to his journal; a report of this research forms a chapter of Lock's (1985, pp. 56–71) monograph, *A Difficult Balance: Editorial Peer Review in Medicine.* Lock (1985, p. 66) notes that despite the difficulties inherent in investigating peer review, his study

> did produce four important results. The *BMJ* 'captured' four-fifths of the articles that were published in high impact factor general journals; consensus between readers was better, often much better, than by chance; as a result of the assessors' recommendations most of the articles we published were substantially changed; and the whole 'system', using editors, referee, and hanging committee, seemed to work—that is, each stage seemed to filter out the less acceptable papers, leaving better and better subsets.

Although Lock's monograph centers on peer review of articles for medical journals, it ranges widely, also addressing such subjects as peer review in other journals, basic problems in peer review, review of grant applications, and suggestions for improving peer review. Among the 281 references listed are many pertaining to the quality of biomedical writing.

Preparing research proposals that will fare well in peer review is of interest to many students of biomedical writing. One source of guidance in this regard is the brief book *Writing a Successful Grant Application* by Liane Reif-Lehrer (1982), a scientist who has reviewed grant applications for the National Institutes of Health. Another source is the booklet *Helpful Hints on Preparing a Research Grant Application to the National Institutes of Health* (U.S. Department of Health, Education, and Welfare 1986). Of the sources of further information listed at the end of the booklet, "NIH Grant Applications for Clinical Research: Reasons for Poor Ratings or Disapproval" by Janet M. Cuca (1983) may be especially helpful in avoiding common shortcomings.

In his book on peer review, Lock (1985) deals with some ethical issues in scientific publishing. Such issues are the focus of the brief article "Believing What You Read: Responsibilities of Medical Authors and Editors" by David L. Schiedermayer and Mark Siegler (1986), and they are among the many items touched on in *An Insider's Guide for Medical Authors and Editors* by Peter Morgan (1986), scientific editor of the *Canadian Medical Association Journal*. They are treated more extensively in "Ethics and Etiquette in Biomedical Communication" by DeBakey and DeBakey (1975) and in the entry "Communication, Biomedical. II. Scientific Publishing," which Lois DeBakey (1978) wrote for the *Encyclopedia of Bioethics*. The DeBakeys deal with many issues in these articles; their view that extensively editing a manuscript that will appear under another person's name is unethical (DeBakey and DeBakey 1975, p. 533) could engender lively classroom debate. Paired with the above entry in the *Encyclopedia of Bioethics* is one by DeBakey and DeBakey (1978) on "Communication, Biomedical. I. Media and Medicine."

One ethical obligation of those writing about medical science and technology is to write readably, especially when presenting information that health professionals and the public may need to make sound decisions affecting health. However, Daniel C. Spadaro et al. (1980), having determined readability levels of over 100 brochures and pamphlets intended for patients, concluded that such publications often are written at levels that are too advanced. T. M. Grunder (1980) assessed readability levels of consent forms that patients must sign before surgery and obtained even more striking findings: that these items were written at, or nearly at, graduate-school reading levels.

Various sources provide medically oriented guidance in writing readably. "Writing Readable Health Messages" by Diane Manning (1981) concisely presents measures to help ensure that health education materials not only are clear but also are appealing, so that they will indeed be read. The article by Spadaro et al. (1980), entitled "Assessing Readability of Patient Information Materials," presents four methods for estimating readability. In "Writing for Communication with the Public," Susan Okie (1984), a physician who has covered medicine for the *Washington Post* and written a health column for *Cosmopolitan Magazine,* advises her medical colleagues on writing for lay audiences.

Closely related to ease of reading are the basics of good writing style. Thus, students writing about medical science and technology can gain much from general handbooks of style. They may, however, especially enjoy, and find especially useful, those works containing biomedical examples. Among such works are *Why Not Say It Clearly: A Guide to Scientific Writing* by Lester S. King (1978), formerly senior editor of the *Journal of the American Medical Association; Dx & Rx: A Physician's Guide to Medical Writing* by physician John H. Dirckx (1977), a highlight of which is a "survey of grammar" that uses sentences on medical topics as illustrations; *Breathing Life into Medical Writing: A Handbook* by Anitra P. Sheen (1982); and *Brighter Writing for Dentistry* by Robert C. McGiffert (1982). Biomedically oriented guidance on basic writing style also appears in the various handbooks and textbooks of medical and scientific writing that were cited earlier in this essay.

Gearing the message to the audience is central to good communication. Although basics of biomedical writing overlap greatly with those of other writing, students in biomedical fields have distinctive needs and interests. Teachers of writing often can best serve these students by using and recommending sources that address matters specific to biomedical writing and that present more general aspects of writing in biomedical contexts. I hope that this essay has aided in identifying such sources.

References

Altman, Douglas G., Sheila M. Gore, Martin J. Gardner, and Stuart J. Pocock. "Statistical Guidelines for Contributors to Medical Journals." *British Medical Journal* 286 (1983): 1489–93.

Banes, Joan, comp. *The Medical and Scientific Authors' Guide: An International Reference Guide for Authors to More Than 500 Medical and Scientific Journals.* New York: Le Jacq Publishing, 1984.

Barclay, William R., M. Therese Southgate, and Robert W. Mayo, comps. *Manual for Authors and Editors: Editorial Style and Manuscript Preparation.* 7th ed. of Stylebook/Editorial Manual of the American Medical Association. Los Altos, Calif.: Lange Medical Publications, 1981.

Council of Biology Editors, Committee on Graduate Training in Scientific Writing. *Scientific Writing for Graduate Students: A Manual on the Teaching of Scientific Writing,* edited by F. Peter Woodford. New York: Rockefeller University Press, 1968.

Council of Biology Editors Style Manual Committee. *Council of Biology Editors Style Manual: A Guide for Authors, Editors, and Publishers in the Biological Sciences.* 5th ed. Bethesda, Md.: Council of Biology Editors, 1983.

Croll, Theodore P. "Preparation of a Dental Case History Report for Publication." *Journal of the American Dental Association* 102 (1981): 59–61.

Cuca, Janet M. "NIH Grant Applications for Clinical Research: Reasons for Poor Ratings or Disapproval." *Clinical Research* 31 (1983): 453–63.

Day, Robert A. *How to Write and Publish a Scientific Paper.* 2d ed. Philadelphia: ISI Press, 1983.

DeBakey, Lois. "Communication, Biomedical. II. Scientific Publishing." In *Encyclopedia of Bioethics,* edited by Warren T. Reich. 4 vols. New York: Free Press, 1978.

DeBakey, Lois, and Selma DeBakey. "Ethics and Etiquette in Biomedical Communication." *Perspectives in Biology and Medicine* 18 (1975): 522–40.

———. "Communication, Biomedical. I. Media and Medicine." In *Encyclopedia of Bioethics,* edited by Warren T. Reich. 4 vols. New York: Free Press, 1978.

———. "The Case Report. I. Guidelines for Preparation." *International Journal of Cardiology* 4 (1983): 357–64.

DerSimonian, Rebecca, L. Joseph Charette, Buckman McPeek, and Frederick Mosteller. "Reporting on Methods in Clinical Trials." *New England Journal of Medicine* 306 (1982): 1332–37.

Dirckx, John H. *Dx and Rx: A Physician's Guide to Medical Writing.* San Bernardino, Calif.: G. K. Hall, 1977.

Editorial. "The Case Report." *New England Journal of Medicine* 277 (1967): 827.

Flegel, Kenneth, and Robert Oseasohn. "Adverse Effects of Diagnostic Tests: A Study of the Quality of Reporting." *Archives of Internal Medicine* 142 (1982): 883–87.

Grunder, T. M. "On the Readability of Surgical Consent Forms." *New England Journal of Medicine* 302 (1980): 900–902.

"Guidelines for Reporting Clinical Trials." *Journal of the American Dental Association* 87 (1973): 557.

Hampton, J. R. "Presentation and Analysis of the Results of Clinical Trials in Cardiovascular Disease." *British Medical Journal* 282 (1981): 1371–73.

Huth, Edward J. *How to Write and Publish Papers in the Medical Sciences.* Philadelphia: ISI Press, 1982.

———. *Medical Style and Format: An International Manual for Authors, Editors, and Publishers.* Philadelphia: ISI Press, 1987a.

———. "Needed: Review Articles with More Scientific Rigor." Editorial. *Annals of Internal Medicine* 106 (1987b): 470–71.

"Improving Reports of Adverse Drug Reactions." *British Medical Journal* 289 (1984): 898.

Ingelfinger, Franz J. "Peer Review in Biomedical Publication." *American Journal of Medicine* 56 (1974): 686–92.

"The Ingelfinger Rule." *Time,* 3 Mar. 1980, p. 74.

International Committee of Medical Journal Editors. "Uniform Requirements for Manuscripts Submitted to Biomedical Journals." *Annals of Internal Medicine* 96 (1982): 766–71. (Also published in *British Medical Journal* 284 [1982]: 1766–70.)

King, Lester S. *Why Not Say It Clearly: A Guide to Scientific Writing.* Boston: Little, Brown, 1978.

Lock, Stephen. *Thorne's Better Medical Writing.* 2d ed. Kent, England: Pitman Medical Publishing, 1977. (Also published by John Wiley and Sons, 1977.)

———. *A Difficult Balance: Editorial Peer Review in Medicine.* London: Nuffield Provincial Hospitals Trust, 1985. (Second Edition, Philadelphia: ISI Press, 1986.)

Manning, Diane. "Writing Readable Health Messages." *Public Health Report* 96 (1981): 464–65.

McBride, Gail. "Now for the Latest News." Editorial. *Journal of the American Medical Association* 245 (1981): 374–75.

McGiffert, Robert C. *Brighter Writing for Dentistry.* Chicago: American Dental Association, 1982.

Meals, Roy A. "Don't Look Back! The Perils of Retrospection." *Medical Dimensions* (Aug.-Sept. 1978): 43–44.

Meinert, Curtis L., Susan Tonascia, and Karen Higgins. "Content of Reports on Clinical Trials: A Critical Review." *Controlled Clinical Trials* 5 (1984): 328–47.

Meiss, Harriet R., and Doris A. Jaeger, comps. *Information to Authors 1980–81: Editorial Guidelines Reproduced from 246 Medical Journals.* Baltimore, Md.: Urban and Schwarzenberg, 1980.

Morgan, Cheryl. Letter. *Lancet* 1 (1985): 644.

Morgan, Peter. *An Insider's Guide for Medical Authors and Editors.* Philadelphia: ISI Press, 1986.

Mulrow, Cynthia D. "The Medical Review Article: State of the Science." *Annals of Internal Medicine* 106 (1987): 485–88.

Murphy, F. Kevin, and H. Bruce Dull. Letter. *Annals of Internal Medicine* 79 (1973): 907.

Murray, Jeffrey C., and Roberta A. Pagon. "Informed Consent for Research Publication of Patient-Related Data." *Clinical Research* 32 (1984): 404–8.

"The News Media and the Question of Prior Publication." Editorial Note. *Annals of Internal Medicine* 91 (1979): 919–20.

Okie, Susan. "Writing for Communication with the Public." In *Written Communication in Family Medicine,* edited by Robert B. Taylor and Katherine A. Munning. New York: Springer-Verlag, 1984, 65–78.

Porcher, Frances H. "Reference Practices of Biomedical Journals: Uniform Requirements Style or Not?" *Council of Biology Editor Views* 9 (1986): 30–39.

Reif-Lehrer, Liane. *Writing a Successful Grant Application.* Boston: Science Books International, 1982.

Relman, Arnold S. "An Open Letter to the News Media." Editorial. *New England Journal of Medicine* 300 (1979): 554–55.

———. "The Ingelfinger Rule." Editorial. *New England Journal of Medicine* 305 (1981): 824–26.

Riley, Harris D., Jr. "Preparing a Case Report." *Southern Medical Journal* 68 (1975): 79–80.

Roland, Charles G. "The Case Report." *Journal of the American Medical Association* 205 (1968): 83–84.

Schiedermayer, David L., and Mark Siegler. "Believing What You Read: Responsibilities of Medical Authors and Editors." *Archives of Internal Medicine* 146 (1986): 2043–44.

Sheen, Anitra P. *Breathing Life into Medical Writing: A Handbook.* St. Louis: C. V. Mosby Co., 1982.

Simon, Richard, and Robert E. Wittes. "Methodologic Guidelines for Reports of Clinical Trials." Editorial. *Cancer Treatment Reports* 69 (1985): 1–3.

Simpson, Ross J., Jr., and Thomas R. Griggs. "Case Reports and Medical Progress." *Perspectives in Biology and Medicine* 28 (1985): 402–6.

Spadaro, Daniel C., Lawrence A. Robinson, and L. Tracy Smith. "Assessing Readability of Patient Information Materials." *American Journal of Hospital Pharmacy* 37 (1980): 215–21.

Staheli, Lynn T. *Speaking and Writing for the Physician.* New York: Raven Press, 1986.

U.S. Department of Health, Education, and Welfare. National Institutes of Health. *A Compilation of Journal Instructions to Authors.* Washington, D.C.: U.S. Government Printing Office, 1979.

U.S. Department of Health, Education, and Welfare. National Institutes of Health. Division of Research Grants. *Helpful Hints on Preparing a Research Grant Application to the National Institutes of Health.* Bethesda, Md.: National Institutes of Health, 1986.

Venulet, J., R. Blattner, J. von Bülow, and G. C. Berneker. "How Good Are Articles on Adverse Drug Reactions?" *British Medical Journal* 284 (1982): 252–54.

Wade, Nicholas. "Medical Journal Draws Lancet on Rival." *Science* 211 (1981): 561.

Zelen, Marvin. "Guidelines for Publishing Papers on Cancer Clinical Trials: Responsibilities of Editors and Authors." *Journal of Clinical Oncology* 1 (1983): 164–69.

Editor

Charles H. Sides is assistant professor of English at Northeastern University, where he directs the undergraduate program in technical communication. He has also served as director of the Engineering Writing Cooperative Program at the Massachusetts Institute of Technology and as associate director of technical communication at Clarkson University. A communications consultant to high-technology and defense industries in the United States and abroad, he has written numerous articles and books about technical communication theory and applications.

Contributors

James C. Addison, Jr., received his bachelor's and master's degrees from Clemson University. He received his Ph.D. from the University of Tennessee. Currently, he is an associate professor of English and the director of the university writing center at Western Carolina University. He has published one book and over a dozen articles.

Ben F. Barton is professor of electrical engineering and computer science at the University of Michigan. Former director of the Cooley Electronics Laboratory there, he has had extensive experience in technical research, teaching, and consulting. His most recent publications in the field of technical communication appear in *The Technical Writing Teacher,* the *Iowa State Journal of Business and Technical Communication,* the *Journal of Technical Writing and Communication,* and *Computers and Security.*

Marthalee S. Barton is lecturer in humanities at the University of Michigan, where her teaching includes courses in the visual display of information as well as literary and rhetorical theory. She was a technical writer for the Bendix Corporation, the Cooley Electronics Laboratory, and the Willow Run Laboratories. Her current research interests and publications are in the areas of rhetorical theory and visual rhetoric.

Nancy E. Brown received a bachelor of science degree in business education from Plymouth State College in New Hampshire and taught in the Business Department at Gardner High School in Massachusetts for nine years. In 1978 she was graduated from Suffolk University with a Master of Science degree in business education. Presently, she teaches part-time at Mount Wachusett Community College in the continuing education division, at Worcester State College in the languages and literature department, and at the University of Lowell. In addition, Ms. Brown writes a quarterly column on letters and memorandums for *Techcomm,* a monthly newsletter.

David M. Craig holds a dual appointment in the technical communications department and the Center for Liberal Studies of Clarkson University. His articles have appeared in such diverse places as the *Dickens Studies Annual, The Centennial Review,* and the *Henry James Review.* Also, he has held a Fulbright senior lectureship in Yugoslavia and has been a member of the Bibliography Committee of the Society for Technical Communication, writing abstracts for the "Recent and Relevant" section of *Technical Communication.* Presently, he is finishing a book on Joseph Heller titled *Tilting at Mortality: Joseph Heller's Fiction.*

Martha Delamater Benz graduated from New Mexico State University with a master's degree in teaching reading and a master's degree in technical and professional communication. For thirteen years, she taught various English and reading courses and managed the English and reading departments at a secondary school. In 1985, she became a technical writer and editor in industry. Presently, she is supervisor of the Test Support and Publication Section at Lockheed Engineering and Management Services Company at the White Sands Test Facility in Las Cruces, New Mexico.

Stephen Doheny-Farina is an assistant professor at Clarkson University, where he teaches technical communication. He has published in the journal *Written Communication* and in the book *Writing in Non-Academic Settings,* and has recently edited and published *Effective Documentation: What We Have Learned from Research.* A special issue of *IEEE Transactions on Professional Communication* devoted to legal and ethical problems in technical communication, edited by Doheny-Farina, was chosen Best Collection of Essays in the 1988 NCTE Awards for Excellence in Technical and Scientific Writing. In addition, Doheny-Farina is an associate editor of the journal *Technical Communication.*

John W. Ferstel, a member of the English faculty at the University of Southwestern Louisiana, teaches literature surveys and advanced writing courses in the undergraduate program. A member of the Society for Technical Communication and the Association of Teachers of Technical Writing, he edits a newsletter for the local National Council of Teachers of English affiliate, in which he is active. In addition to his teaching duties, he is chair of his department's public relations committee and serves as an academic advisor for the department's technical writing concentration.

Barbara Gastel received her bachelor's degree from Yale and her M.D. and M.P.H. degrees from Johns Hopkins. After completing an American Association for the Advancement of Science mass media internship at *Newsweek* and working at the National Institutes of Health, she taught science writing at the Massachusetts Institute of Technology and then spent two years in China as visiting professor of technical communication at the Beijing Medical University. At present she is assistant dean for teaching and teaching evaluation at the University of California, San Francisco School of Medicine. She continues to teach and write about scientific communication. Her publications include *Presenting Science to the Public.*

Brenda Johns is an instructor of technical communication and freshman composition in the English department at the University of Cincinnati.

Mary M. Lay received her Ph.D. from the University of New Mexico in 1975 and has taught at Clarkson University since 1976 where she is now chairperson and associate professor of technical communications. She is president of the Association of Teachers of Technical Writing and served as the association's Modern Language Association liaison from 1984 to 1986. She is the author of *Strategies for Technical Writing* and several articles in *Technical Communication, The Teacher Writing Teacher,* and *Journal of Technical Writing and Communication.* She has taught advertising copywriting and design at Clarkson for seven years.

Raymond N. MacKenzie has served as a consultant to electronics, biotechnological, computer, and legal firms. For six years he was a professor of English at Mankato State University in Minnesota, where he developed and directed undergraduate and graduate programs in technical communication. He has published articles and reviews in various technical and literary journals and books. He is presently a technical writer for Cray Research, Inc.

Roger E. Masse graduated from the University of Wyoming with a master's degree in English and from Rensselaer Polytechnic Institute with a master's degree in technical writing. For seventeen years, he taught technical writing and editing, freshman composition, American Renaissance, and Greek mythology at New Mexico State University. In 1985, he became a technical writer and editor in industry. Currently he is documentation project writer for U.S. Sprint in Dallas, Texas.

Alice E. Moorhead is an assistant professor of English and director of writing across the disciplines at Hamline University in St. Paul, Minnesota. Professor Moorhead, a consultant to architects, construction managers, and engineers, has also conducted several research studies of proposal practices and organizational communication. Currently, she is coauthoring a book on team building for proposal and project teams in the professional service industry.

Avon Jack Murphy has been teaching college writing classes full-time since finishing his Ph.D. in English at the University of Wisconsin–Madison in 1970. Since 1974, his teaching and publications have concentrated on technical writing. He developed Ferris State College's first version of its new technical communication program and directed Northeast Louisiana University's program for four years. He presently directs the technical communications program at the Oregon Institute of Technology. Dr. Murphy's professional activities include freelance technical writing and editing and managing the Society for Technical Communication's Education and Development Committee.

Sherry G. Southard, an associate professor at East Carolina University, teaches a variety of courses in both the undergraduate and graduate technical writing programs. She was formerly at Oklahoma State University, where she directed the technical writing internship program. Her publications include works on internships, editing, instructions, methodology in technical writing, and the rhetoric of scientific/technical literature. In 1984, she won the National Council of Teachers of English Award for Best Article on Methods of Teaching in Technical and Scientific Communication.

Thomas M. Steinfatt received his bachelor's degree in mathematics and statistics, his master's degree in speech, and his Ph.D. in communications, all from Michigan State University. He has published two books and over forty articles and chapters in scholarly books and journals, has created the communication program in the School of Management at Clarkson University, and has served as a consultant in organizational and management development, organizational communication, technical writing, and statistical process control for several large corporations, including General Motors, Niagara Mohawk Power, Rockwell International, and General Electric.

James R. Weber has taught technical communication at the University of Oregon and the University of Washington in Seattle, and is currently a lecturer in technical writing at Washington State University. He holds a bachelor's degree in English and philosophy from St. Olaf College and a Ph.D. from the University of Oregon. In addition to the pedagogy of technical communications, his present research is in the organization of information and the history and philosophy of science. He is currently an editor with Battelle Northwest and lives in Richland, Washington.

Nina D. Ziv is a staff assistant at Merrill Lynch in New York City. Among her duties are writing and editing. She has worked at Bell Communications Research as a technical writer and editor. Before she became a professional writer, she taught freshman composition at New York University and Seton Hall University. She has published several articles on the effect of teacher comments on students' writing and is presently working on a research project on the role of the writer in the workplace.